Bethania Gonzalez

Women

A WORLD REPORT

A New Internationalist Book

Oxford University Press . New York
1985

Oxford University Press
Oxford London New York Toronto
Delhi Bombay Calcutta Madras Karachi
Kuala Lumpur Singapore Hong Kong Tokyo
Nairobi Dar es Salaam Cape Town
Melbourne Auckland

and associated companies in
Beirut Berlin Ibadan Mexico City Nicosia

First published in Great Britain in 1985 by Methuen London Ltd

Library of Congress Cataloguing in Publication Data
Main entry under title:

Women, a world report.

"A New Internationalist book."
1. Women – Social conditions – Cross-cultural studies.
2. Women – Economic conditions – Cross-cultural studies.
3. Feminism – Cross-cultural studies.   4. Women's rights –
Cross-cultural studies.
HQ1154.W82 1985   305.4   85-13573
ISBN 0-19-520490-5

Printing (last digit): 9 8 7 6 5 4 3 2 1
Printed in Great Britain

CONTENTS

Preface

PREFACE

Discrimination against women is a profound and subtle sickness that has lodged itself deep in the subconscious of both men and women as well as in the structure of our societies. This makes it one of the hardest sources of inequality to fight – because it grips women from within and without.

Women's analysis of their situation, and their courage, both to wrestle with their own internalised view of themselves as weak and powerless, and to start standing up for their rights – often against men that they love – has cost them, at best, confusion and heartache; at worst isolation, imprisonment and death. But it has also created a women's movement that has put sexual equality firmly on the world agenda.

The women's movement – in all its forms, with all its differing priorities – has begun to change the accepted values of the whole world. Today women's inferior status is starting to be seen not as something right and natural but as the result of systematic discrimination on the basis of sex. Without this change of values there could never have been a United Nations Decade for Women.

It is tempting to dismiss the Decade for Women as just another international talkshop, another excuse for substituting words for action. Indeed, for the vast majority of women in the world, the years between 1975 and 1985 passed without their knowing – or caring – that the Decade had been dedicated to international concern for their situation. But there have been changes in the last ten years – new laws, new government departments – that have come about directly as a result of pressures on individual governments both from women within their countries, but also from a new current of world opinion arising from Decade activities. Today governments can no longer placidly assume that women are inferior. They must defend their position on a world stage.

This conviction that the Decade for Women has been important is the conviction that lies behind *Women: A World Report*. The book is an attempt to capture the essence of the position of women at the end of the Decade and set it down as a benchmark against which the future can be measured.

Our confidence to begin such a task at all was inspired by other people's confidence in us. For the last fourteen years the New Internationalist Publications Co-operative (NIP) has been producing a monthly magazine – *New Internationalist* – about social issues and world development: the only magazine of its kind that is both enjoyed by its 45,000 readers and respected by international authorities. For the last eight years NIP has also been producing information material for various United Nations agencies (UNICEF, UNEP, UNFPA, WHO) – translating UN-ese into a language that ordinary people can understand, writing articles and creating illustrations, that are sent to newspapers and magazines all over the world. The International Year of the Child, the International Year of the Disabled, the World Assembly on Ageing, and the mid-Decade Conference for Women in Copenhagen, were all brought to the attention of the world's media by material produced by NIP.

Last year we were asked by the United Nation's Department of Public Information to do the same job for the conference marking the end of the Decade for Women. We were also asked to write an official Report on the State of the World's Women 1985, based on a unique set of information gathered especially for the conference. This information, which forms the basis of Part I and some of the content of Part III of the book, is the product of an unprecedented research effort, during the course of which 121 governments filled in questionnaires about the position of women in their countries and all the major UN agencies compiled sectoral reports of independent research to complete the picture. We are very grateful to the UN Branch for the Advancement of Women for allowing us privileged access to this data eight months before the conference.

Our idea that there should be a permanent record of this, the most comprehensive round-up of information on women ever collected, a record that would last long after the hullabaloo of the conference had died down, was shared by Maggie Black of UNICEF, who was the first of a whole series of people to put their energy and support behind this book.

But we wanted the book to be something more than an analytical report. We believe that fact and argument give only a two-dimensional picture, and that insights into individual women's lives are necessary to give that picture true depth. This is why we invited ten women writers to travel to different countries and reflect on how the facts are lived out in the experience of women around the world.

This was to be more than just another piece of international voyeurism – of the rich world ogling at the poor. Our aim was to make it an exchange of insights by inviting women from the poor world to write about women in the rich world at the same time as women writers from the rich world were boarding planes that would take them to their destinations in the poor world. So every subject covered in the essays is tackled twice – once by a Third World woman writing about the rich world, once by a woman from the rich world writing about the developing world.

This international exchange of women writers was both an expensive and ambitious idea and we are very grateful to the Government of Norway, and to UNICEF, UNFPA and UNDP – both for their faith in the project and for the funds that made it all possible. Personal thanks are due to Halle Jørn Hanssen and Grethe Mathismoen of NORAD, Tarzie Vittachi and Tony Hewett of UNICEF, Jyoti Singh and Alex Marshall of UNFPA, and Erskine Childers and Mary Lynn Hanley of UNDP.

The ten writers, whose essays appear in Part II of the book, approached the project with the same enthusiasm and commitment as everyone else associated with it. All agreed, at extremely short notice, to put aside their other work and devote at least a month of their lives to trying to understand and write about women in a country on the other side of the world. Each has brought to the book all the sensitivity and thoroughness of a dedicated feminist artist – and we are very grateful to them. Each is also responsible, in turn, for the opinions expressed in her essay.

Some sacrificed more than a temporary setback to their other work. Marilyn French travelled to India with cracked ribs; Nawal el Saadawi defied a slipped disc to sleep beside the women occupying a London hospital; Jill Tweedie wrote her essay shivering with an unidentified tropical fever. On behalf of the ten contributors, we thank all those women who welcomed them into their homes and confided in them about their lives.

While the ten authors of Part II were coping with the freezing weather of the USSR and Norway and the sticky heat of India and Indonesia, I was trying to make sense of the mountain of documentation amassed for the end of Decade conference and turn it into the 30,000 words that make up Part I. This would not have been possible without Pat Holden of Oxford University's Centre for Cross-Cultural Research on Women. It was she who turned this mass of information into an ordered draft paper on which the first part of the book is based. We are very grateful to her, and to all the other women at the Centre, who helped with comments and advice in the early stages of writing this section.

We are also grateful to Angela Little, Kate Young, Gill Gordon and Alison White of the Institute of Development Studies at Sussex University for their detailed comments, and to the many women in the United Nations – particularly Barbara Politi, Barbara Knudson and Una Ellis of the Branch for the Advancement of Women, and Sue Markham and Enid Burke of the Department of Public Information – who helped shape the direction of Part I.

The statistics in Part III were coaxed on our behalf from the United Nations' computer by the skill and patience of Robert Johnston and Joann Vanek.

The finished product, however, draws from many sources other than the United Nations and I must take full responsibility for the particular way in which fact and argument are combined in Part I.

Throughout its gestation, the book has been constantly attended by Elsbeth Lindner of Methuen – whose energy and tenacity kept our motivation high and made sure we kept to our deadlines – and by Maria del Nevo – who typed every word of Part I, often several times, until we were all satisfied with it.

I have used the pronoun 'we' throughout much of this introduction because, though my name appears on the cover, I consider my contribution to be the product of the New Internationalist Co-operative as a whole. Without the support of my colleagues I would not have had the time, the opportunity, nor the skills to take part in such an undertaking. Five years working at *New Internationalist* has given me the experience and confidence I needed to form the framework for my contribution. And the generosity and hard work of the rest of the group released me from my other responsibilities to enable me to concentrate on the book.

In particular I want to mention Christopher Sheppard. It was he who inspired the enthusiasm that raised the money for the project; he who took on the extraordinary feat of organisation that sent ten women to ten countries and brought them back home safely, all within three months; and he it was who kept up the continuous combination of cajoling and bullying that glued me to my typewriter day after day until the book was finished. For once it is a man whose contribution to another person's work will never be fully recognised.

Debbie Taylor
New Internationalist Co-operative
Oxford 1985

Part One

Women

AN ANALYSIS

by Debbie Taylor

1. THE FAMILY

Division of labour

One third of a million women are in labour as you read this – faces contorted, bodies straining in contractions that will have pushed another 300,000 infants into the world by the time today becomes tomorrow.

Some of those women are lying on clean linen under electric lights, the sharpest edge of their pain blunted by the drugs of white-coated doctors. Others – oblivious to the woodsmoke in their nostrils and the whine of mosquitoes in their ears – are riding raw pain, their bodies buffeted from peak to trough of each contraction, soothed by the voices of mothers, aunts, neighbours, kneeling on the earth floor beside them.

Pregnancy and childbirth: the pain, the power and the privilege that define a woman as different from a man. From two cells, to four, to eight; a tiny pink crescent; the buds of arms and legs; fingers, fingernails, eyelashes: only a woman's body can cherish and cradle and create a new human being. It's a miracle only she has the power to perform.

But the power of childbearing is a blessing laced with bitterness, because in every society in the world it is a power that is turned back against her. And, instead of defining just one difference between men and women, women's ability to bear children is used to define their entire lives. It is used to create and justify a role for women that extends their responsibility for caring for children far beyond the nine months of pregnancy. The labour of childbirth is just the beginning. Though the cord that binds mother to child is severed, the role that binds woman to domestic work and child-rearing holds fast throughout her life.

There can be few generalisations that hold as true throughout the world: unpaid domestic work is everywhere seen as woman's work, woman's responsibility. It is important, vital work. Food must be cooked, infants fed, clothes washed and mended, water and firewood collected. And it all takes time. A woman in a Pakistani village, for example, spends around 63 hours a week on domestic work alone.[1] Even in the rich world, where water comes from taps and cookers heat at the flick of a switch, a housewife works an average of 56 hours a week.[2] And if she has small children that average jumps nearly 40 per cent.[3]

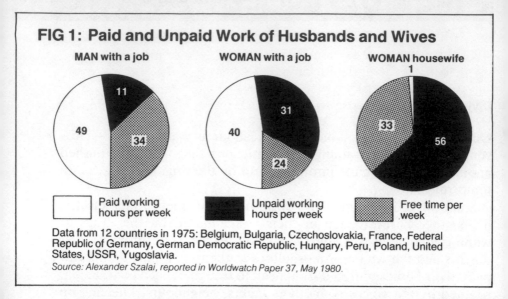

FIG 1: Paid and Unpaid Work of Husbands and Wives

MAN with a job   WOMAN with a job   WOMAN housewife

☐ Paid working hours per week   ■ Unpaid working hours per week   ▨ Free time per week

Data from 12 countries in 1975: Belgium, Bulgaria, Czechoslovakia, France, Federal Republic of Germany, German Democratic Republic, Hungary, Peru, Poland, United States, USSR, Yugoslavia.
Source: Alexander Szalai, reported in Worldwatch Paper 37, May 1980.

But housework is invisible work. Those long hours – totalling 40 billion each year in France alone[4] – go unvalued, unrecognised, unpaid. Yet their contribution to society is enormous. If the services provided free by a housewife in the US in 1979 had to be purchased with wages at market rates, they would cost $14,500 a year.[5] On this kind of calculation it is estimated that unpaid housework done in the industrialised countries contributes between 25 and 40 per cent of gross national product (GNP).[6]

Domestic work is not, however, the only work women do. There are relatively few women anywhere in the world who can claim to be 'just a housewife'. Even in Europe 35 per cent of married women have a job. And of those remaining women without formal employment nearly half are either retired, in full-time education, or looking for work.[7]

But a working woman in Europe can expect little or no help from her husband at home. In Italy 85 per cent of mothers with children and full-time jobs outside the house are married to men who do no domestic work at all.[8] And in Europe as a whole, a working woman has, on average, only two-thirds of the free time her husband has.[9]

In the developing world the picture is the same. There is 'man's work' and there is 'woman's work'. And, because many women do additional work outside the home, whereas few men would dream of doing any additional work inside it, 'woman's work' always ends up simply being 'more work'. In a village in Rwanda, for instance, men tend the banana trees and do most of the paid labour outside the home. Women, on the other hand, do virtually all the domestic work, three-quarters of the other agricultural work, and half of the work with animals. Taken together, women in this village work over three times as much as men.[10] In Java, too, where men do a more equal share of the agricultural work, a survey in one village found that women still worked over 20 per cent longer than men.[11]

Women do not choose to take on extra work in addition to their domestic responsibilities. They have no option. In most parts of the world a woman's labour – in the fields growing food, packing transistors on a production line, typing a never-diminishing pile of letters – is absolutely vital to her family's survival. In fact it is a rare family indeed which can manage on the proceeds of just one person's labour. Eighty-three per cent of women with four children in France have full-time jobs outside the home too. And they are working because they need the money.[12]

The chief injustice lies less in the extra work women must do outside the home than in the assumption that it is their role – and their role alone – to do all the work inside it. This assumption is a triple injustice. It is unjust because it means that women around the world end up working twice as many hours as men.[13] It is unjust because they are not paid for those hours of work. And – the final insult – it is unjust because domestic work is looked down on as not being 'real' work at all – *because* it is unpaid. The circle is finally closed by men's refusal to take on work that is both unvalued and unpaid. Woman's work it is and woman's work it will stay – part of a vicious circle that keeps women trapped on the treadmill of a double day.

But it may not always have been like this. Many social historians believe that domestic work became unvalued and invisible as a result of the development of the cash economy. It seems likely that before people were paid for their labour or their produce, no one type of work was valued more than any other. Work was simply work: for survival. And in parts of the world where cash and wages have not yet penetrated, women and men still tend to do relatively equal amounts of work. But the cash economy only pays certain people for certain types of work, so setting those people and that work above the rest.

There were no wages for woman's domestic work in her own home. Yet it was work that had to be done. And it is this two-edged imperative – the necessity for domestic work to be done, plus men's refusal to do it – that etches women's domestic role so deeply into the structure of society.

Work or children

The trap is sprung. The maze is drawn. And women are caught within it, hedged in by their double burden of work. There are ways out of the maze, of course. And the more obvious of these have already been explored. In Sweden, for instance, working hours have been made more flexible, a buoyant economy and high wages have made job-sharing and part-time work feasible for both men and women, and paternity leave is available for the fathers as well as the mothers of newborn babies. In theory it is as near-perfect a solution as one could devise. Yet the Swedish government reports that, as of 1985, only one in five new fathers has taken advantage of his paternity leave.[14]

In the centrally-planned economies, and in kibbutzim communities in Israel, the emphasis is more on paying wages for domestic work and child-care. But, instead of paying one woman or man for domestic work carried out within their homes, economies of scale have been achieved by removing domestic work from the individual home as much as possible: children are cared for in crèches; meals and laundry facilities are provided at work. But the economies of scale involved in this solution have inherent drawbacks: in the kibbutzim parents and children found they missed the intimacy, warmth and privacy of traditional family life;[15] while in the USSR there is a disturbingly high rate of illness among the 30 per cent of children cared for in overcrowded crèches.[16]

Solutions like these, that depend on the good-will and commitment of men (at home and in government) seem unlikely to succeed. This is because the status quo – with women providing *gratis* the major part of the world's domestic services – suits both husbands and governments very well. They have a ready-made class of labourers providing, for nothing other than board and lodging, a whole spectrum of services that would otherwise have to be purchased in the market place.

The failure of more just, more humane solutions for easing women's double workload has left them with some very difficult decisions to make. They can continue working a double day, with all the hardship that entails. They can struggle to effect some kind of compromise by working part-time or neglecting their domestic responsibilities. Or they can have fewer children.

Many are in an impossible position. If they work a fifteen-hour day they put their own mental and physical health at risk. If they work fewer hours they may not earn enough or grow enough food to support their families. If they do less domestic work they may put the health of their children at risk. Small wonder that, for these and many other reasons, women are beginning to take advantage of the new forms of contraception that are now available in many countries – and are opting for fewer children.

The family-planning boom

Today there are more women using contraception than ever before. An estimated 50 per cent of women in the world who want to stop having children, temporarily or permanently, are able to fulfil that wish.[17]

In some countries the increase in contraceptive use has been dramatic. In Colombia, for example, the percentage of married women using contraception more than doubled in the decade up to 1980, from 21 to 49 per cent – an increase of 2.8 per cent a year. In Jamaica, Malaysia, Thailand the increase has been even greater at between 3.4 and 4.2 per cent a year. Even in industrialised countries, where the numbers of women using contraception are already very high, there is still a steady increase each year. In England and Wales, for instance, the percentage rose from 69 to 77 per cent between 1967 and 1975. And, over the same period, the rate of increase was 0.6 per cent in Hungary and 0.4 per cent in the US.[18]

TABLE 1: Increased Use of Contraception

Country	Period	Average annual change (%)	% currently using contraception
EGYPT	1974-1982	1·0	34
KENYA (rural)	1967-1978	0·2	8
COLOMBIA	1969-1980	2·4	49
JAMAICA	1975-1979	4·2	55
MEXICO	1976-1979	2·8	39
BANGLADESH	1976-1979	1·4	13
PHILIPPINES	1968-1978	2·4	39
THAILAND	1969-1981	3·8	59
UNITED STATES	1965-1976	0·4	68
JAPAN	1971-1981	0·3	56
FINLAND	1971-1977	0·5	80
HUNGARY	1966-1977	0·7	74
UNITED KINGDOM (England & Wales)	1967-1976	1·0	77

Source: Recent Levels and Trends of Contraceptive Use as Assessed in 1983, United Nations, New York, 1984.

At long last it is possible for substantial numbers of women to choose when, whether and how many babies they will bear. And for those women that choice means better health for themselves and their babies. Just as, in a garden, seeds planted too closely together yield small, sickly plants with little resistance to disease, so babies born too soon after one another stand less chance of a healthy life. Studies in Bangladesh, Nepal and Pakistan found that babies born (to the same mother) within one year of each other were nearly three times as likely to die before their first birthdays as babies born more than four years apart.[19]

One-twelfth of the world's babies die in their first year of life.[20] They die from many causes: diarrhoea, tetanus, polio, measles, typhoid, pneumonia, malaria. But these diseases are thirteen times more likely to kill the 22 million tiny underweight babies – born either too soon, or just too small, weighing less than 2,500 grammes.[21]

It is not just the new infant that is threatened either. *Kwashiorkor* – an acute form of malnutrition where the child's body goes into a sort of metabolic shock from being deprived suddenly of protein – is a Ghanaian word meaning 'the child removed from the breast too soon', deposed by the demands of another new arrival.

And, just as seeds sown too closely take all the goodness from the soil that nourishes them, so a woman's body too becomes sapped of its strength: less able to work long hours in field or factory, less able to withstand the cold of a long New York winter or the ills that lurk in the warm mud of a Bangladesh summer. Two-thirds of women in Asia, half of all women in Africa, and a sixth of Latin American women are anaemic.[22] Anaemia has many causes, lack of food being one of the most important, but it is also one symptom of a general physical weakness – a weakness doctors call 'maternal depletion syndrome'. In Bangladesh, where women bear an average of over six children, they call it *shutika*.

Most women understand only too well what incessant childbearing can do to their own and their children's health. And half of all women in the thirty-one countries investigated by the World Fertility Survey have decided they do not want any more children.[23] In the space of just one generation, the average number of children women want has dropped from six to four, and a quarter of married women are now using some kind of contraception.[24]

Availability of contraception

Contraception offers a way out of the punishing cycle of work, pregnancy and breastfeeding; of one child in the womb, one at the breast, another tugging at the hem of her dress as a woman bends to the chores of the day.

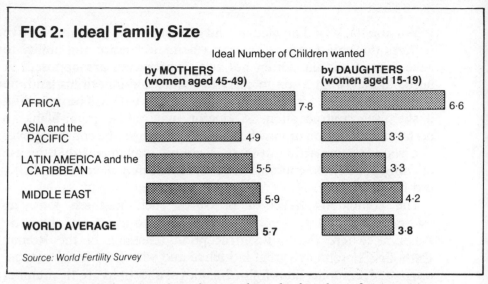

FIG 2: Ideal Family Size

Ideal Number of Children wanted

	by MOTHERS (women aged 45-49)	by DAUGHTERS (women aged 15-19)
AFRICA	7·8	6·6
ASIA and the PACIFIC	4·9	3·3
LATIN AMERICA and the CARIBBEAN	5·5	3·3
MIDDLE EAST	5·9	4·2
WORLD AVERAGE	5·7	3·8

Source: World Fertility Survey

But the family-planning boom has had other far-reaching effects.It has meant that at last – after centuries of exponential expansion – world population growth has begun to slow down. Many countries in the rich world have already achieved zero population growth (where the number of babies born equals the number of people dying) and, at current rates of increasing contraceptive use, the total number of people in the world is due to stabilise at around ten billion in the year 2100, a figure two and a half times greater than the world population today.[25]

These global averages conceal wide regional differences. In Africa, for instance, less than one-tenth of married women are using contraception, they have an average of around seven children each and, in some countries, the trend over the last decade is for women to have more rather than fewer children. The number of children African women say they want has, however, begun to drop. Women aged between fifteen and nineteen years old told World Fertility Survey researchers that they wanted an average of 6.5 children. But this is still twice the number that young women in Asia and Latin America would ideally like to have.[26]

Clearly a woman's ideal family size will be influenced in part by her knowledge of contraception and its availability. World Fertility Survey findings, for instance, reveal that half of women who know about modern methods of contraception live within thirty minutes' travel from a clinic, health post or hospital where this is available. And in ten of the African countries covered by the survey, there were large numbers of women (between 32 and 92 per cent of those questioned) who had never heard of modern methods of contraception at all.[27]

Nor are lack of knowledge and the shortage of contraceptive services the only factors affecting a woman's desire and ability to have fewer children. Often her own preferences are opposed. A husband may want a son to carry his name and inherit his land; he may want to prove his virility or might fear his wife will be unfaithful if she uses contraception. A doctor may refuse point-blank to perform an abortion or may be unwilling to prescribe contraceptives to a young or unmarried woman. A church may decree that the use of contraception is immoral. A government may have an explicitly pro-natalist policy.

The combined effects of pressures such as these force an estimated 120,000 women each day to turn to abortion.[28] In Latin America, where the anti-contraception teachings of the Roman Catholic Church have great influence and where the word 'macho' originated, complications following illegal abortions are the number one killer of women aged between fifteen and thirty-nine.[29] In the Soviet Union, where contraception is not freely available, four out of five pregnancies end in abortion.[30]

The sheer number of abortions (estimated at around 50 million a year) is a poignant testimony to the lengths women will go to stop themselves having another baby.[31] In the rich world the guilt and heartache many women experience – and which cuts deep into their relief – is bad enough. In the poor world, where only one person in two ever sees a trained health worker,[32] a woman who decides to have an abortion is a woman deciding to risk her life. And she knows this only too well, having seen the bloodless faces of other women in the village, or having overheard whispered conversations about a cousin who never came back from hospital.

But, for these women, abortion – heartbreaking and dangerous though it is – often seems the only solution. They calculate the threat to themselves, or to their other children, that a new baby would bring. And they take their decision.

Why women have children

The decision to have or not to have children is forced on women by a world that makes it necessary for them to earn a living, but also dictates that it is their duty to look after their children when they are born. The world cannot claim the right to restrict a woman's choice on whether to have children unless it also takes on to its own shoulders the responsibility to provide for or raise those children.

Not all women want fewer children, however. An ideal family size of four children is a world average that includes women who want no children at all, as well as those who are happy with eight or more. And those children are wanted for a reason.

In rural areas of the poor world children are valuable: not just for their bright-eyed smiles and the joy of watching them learn and grow; but because their labour is needed and their piercing young voices can scare more birds off more ears of corn than they could ever eat. In Latin America, for example, where women bear an average of fewer than five children, the biggest families are found in regions where crops like coffee and peanuts are grown. These crops need individual planting and weeding, and their fruit needs picking one by one – so those extra pairs of young hands can make the difference between a ten- and a fifteen-hour day in the fields.[33] In Mexico 72 per cent of parents say the reason they had children was for 'economic support'.[34]

But help with meeting today's needs is only one reason for having more children. Insurance against tomorrow's needs can be just as great an imperative. In most countries old-age pensions are a mere dream for all but a handful of people with government jobs. And, because so few countries have welfare systems covering all their citizens and so few businesses have pension schemes for their employees, it is estimated that only 23 per cent of men earning wages and 6 per cent of women will be receiving a pension by the year 2000.[35] Statistics like these mean children have an added value. Dependent now on their parents, those children will, in their turn, act as providers for their own dependent mothers and fathers when they grow old.

Children cannot stay children for long in such families. Mothers who bear eight babies and work a full day in the fields have no time to give them all the care they need. These children must grow up quickly and earn their keep.

But many babies born into this situation do not grow up at all. Lack of food, lack of money, lack of time and lack of health care, mean that the countries with the highest birth rates are also those with the highest infant death rates. In the rich world, the average infant mortality rate is 15 per 1,000 live births. In the poorer parts of the developing world, where the birth rate is around two and a half times higher than in the rich world, average infant mortality is 129 per 1,000.[36] With children needed so badly, but with a one in eight chance of each one dying, women must have even more children to ensure that enough survive.

The international community now understands the reasons why some women have five, six, seven or more children even where contraception is available. In 1974 the first World Population

Conference took as its slogan 'Development is the best contraceptive' in recognition of the fact that poverty is one of the main causes of population growth, and that simply providing more contraceptives is only a partial solution.

The failure of the family

It is not only poor rural women who want more children. The double burden of responsibility that forces a woman to weigh up the costs and benefits of work and children and choose between them means that many women – rich and poor – who are using contraception would dearly like a first, or another, baby.

Using contraception may release them from their biological destiny of conceiving and carrying babies. And it is certainly the first step in releasing them from their social destiny of child-care and domestic work, which enables them in turn to extend themselves in other directions – to apply for a job, to attend a meeting, to stay on at school – to stretch a hand into the worlds that men have occupied freely for so long. But the price of that freedom is often the sacrifice of a wanted child.

That women must pay this price, or make this choice at all, demonstrates the failure of the family to serve women's needs in modern society.

In traditional subsistence communities, where labour and harvest are shared, men, women and children are bound together with ties far stronger than love: joined by the firm knots of interdependence. But cash, jobs and wages loosen the knots and create new ones. Wages are tied to wage-earners. Jobs are tied to towns. The ties that bind women to domestic work loosen last of all, so it is men who have tended to take the majority of jobs.

In theory jobs for men and housework for women should sort people neatly into nuclear families. In practice the trend is for men and women to separate, rather than cling to one another cemented together by their complementary roles in the nuclear nest.

Female-headed households

One study of seventy-four developing countries found that around one in five households are *de jure* headed by women; regional totals being 22 per cent in sub-Saharan Africa, 20 per cent in the Caribbean, 16 per cent in the Near East and 15 per cent in Latin America.[37] These estimates are high enough, but the *de facto* figures are thought to be much higher, with perhaps as many as one-third of all households in the world being headed by a woman.[38]

Migration is a major cause of this high number of female-headed households. The population of the world's cities doubled between 1950 and 1980 and will have doubled again by the year 2000, when half of the world's people will live in cities.[39] And most of those people will not be hailing cabs or boarding elevators in the concrete and glass high-rises of the rich world. They will be scrambling into buses and rickshaws, standing in queues at factory gates, spilling into the shanties and townships, the *favelas* and *barrios*, of the poor world.

In many of the poor world's cities – with the possible exception of those in Latin America – men far outnumber women. And this global exodus of men leaves an equal number of women managing alone in the countryside. In some parts of Africa the figures are dramatic, with over 40 per cent of households in Kenya, Botswana, Ghana and Sierra Leone headed by women.[40] In Latin America, too, substantial numbers of households in both urban and rural areas are run by women: a third in Jamaica, for instance, and a fifth in Peru, Honduras, Venezuela and Cuba.[41]

These women are doubly disadvantaged. They are often left without help at crucial times of the year, having to manage the ploughing, the planting and harvesting on their own with as much help as their relatives, children and friends can spare. And their rightful share of their husband's wages is often spent far away in the city, leaving them waiting in vain for a letter to arrive at the village post office. Stranded without help from their husbands, such women are often cut off from government help too – ignored by agricultural projects, overlooked by training schemes.

Nor is migration the only factor prising women and men apart. Divorce rates are rising all over the world, in rich and poor countries alike. Since 1960, for example, the divorce rate has doubled in almost every European country, trebled in the Netherlands, and there has been a more than fivefold increase in the UK.[42] Over one million children in the US see their parents divorced each year[43] and in Barbados the divorce rate rose tenfold between 1948 and 1975.[44] In Bangladesh and Mexico one in every ten women who have been married has been divorced or separated. In Colombia that proportion jumps to one in five, while in Indonesia one in three women who have married has broken up with her husband.[45]

Many of these divorces are due to men leaving their wives. And it is a man's economic power – the money in his wage packet, the salary in his bank account – that levers him away from his wife and children. A man who works forty hours a week for a low wage, for example, may see his wife and children as expensive nuisances. She is forced to ask him for money, he accuses her of nagging, and the pressures catapult them apart. A man with a larger salary tends to leave for different reasons. He can afford to treat his wife as a commodity, discarding the old and used to make way for the new.

But the jobs that lead men to abandon women can cause women to abandon men too, particularly in the rich world. A woman with a professional job, for example, has less need of a man to provide for her children. With an adequate income of her own and the confidence that comes from a good education, she can begin to pick and choose, selecting only the man who offers enough money, prestige or love to make up for the fact that he leaves all the domestic work to her. And many women decide that – all things considered – they may be better off unmarried. Between 1960 and 1970 there was a thirty-fold increase in the numbers of unmarried couples living together in the US,[46] and illegitimate births in Denmark, the US and Sweden trebled between 1960 and 1976.[47]

A similar phenomenon is occurring in some of the poorer urban areas of the developing world – and for similar reasons. Here, however, the likelihood is that neither partner has a job. Here, too, a man who refuses to do domestic work turns out to be more trouble than he is worth, and increasing numbers of women are deciding to do without husbands. In the Dominican Republic and in Panama, for instance, 'non-formal unions' outnumber marriages and in many other Latin American countries they comprise one-fifth of households,[48] while in Barbados dissatisfied wives presented twice as many petitions for divorce as dissatisfied husbands in 1975.[49]

Migration, jobs and wages are strong magnets wrenching marriages apart. But death is the strongest of all. In many countries it is not a living man that abandons a woman, but a dead one.

One in ten women in Bangladesh who have ever been married are widows; one in twenty in Colombia and Mexico.[50] In the rich world women in their sixties outnumber men by four to three. In older age groups the ratio is still more uneven, with twice as many women as men aged over eighty.[51] This unevenness is because of women's longer lifespan, which averages six years more than men's in the rich world and two years longer in the poor world.[52] One third of people living alone in the US are old women,[53] and old women outnumber old men living alone in the UK by four to one.[54]

In some parts of the world an old woman never loses her niche in the family, often acting as mother to her grandchildren while her daughters and daughters-in-law are out working. Eventually, however, many old women need to be cared for themselves. And, as usual, it is women who take on the responsibility. In the industrialised world 70 per cent of the health care for old people is provided by women at home.[55] And, again, it is women who are forced to choose between domestic work, children and employment. In the UK, for example, an estimated 300,000 women remain unmarried and childless so that they can care for their ageing parents.[56]

Depending on the family

Governments who are unable or unwilling to provide services for dependent members of the community – such as children, the disabled, the unemployed, the frail elderly – tend to assume that something called 'the family' will step into the breach and scoop them all up into a warm and all-providing embrace. And it is women – albeit within 'the family' – who are expected to provide these services as part of their domestic role. But basing national plans on this assumption is neither realistic nor just.

The necessity for women to work outside the home, together with the rising rates of divorce, separation, migration and illegitimacy, demonstrate that it is unrealistic. And placing these responsibilities on women's shoulders alone is unjust.

A society that values both the welfare of its children and the autonomy of its women has a responsibility to ensure that women are able to choose the number of children they have and that they have the support they need to provide for and care for those children without prejudicing their desire to fulfil themselves in areas other than child-rearing and domestic work.

Who grows the world's food?

At dawn, when the sun is just a sliver of pink, and acacia trees with grotesque silhouettes scratch at the sky, a round of cocks crowing – one from the seat of a tractor, one from an overturned oil can, one from the thatched roof of the granary – wakens women in the drylands of Africa. As one body they rise, tie their scarves round their heads and their babies on their backs, set sticks to burn under cooking pots, slop food for chickens and pigs, pile porridge in bowls, curse the dog, queue for the standpipe. As the sun rises – a malevolent orange eye – they step onto the track, worn through the bush by generations of work-hardened feet, and make their way to the land for the day.

Dawn in Asia's wet plains sets women stirring too: crawling from their folds of mosquito net, wrapping their saris tight, blowing life into charcoals, coaxing children to eat rice, and calves to eat gruel, driving buffalo to the mist-shrouded paddy fields, then stepping into tepid brown water and bending as they will bend all day.

A church bell ringing and dogs barking nudge Andean women awake. A prayer is whispered, a skirt fastened, water hauled from the well in the village square, goats tethered and milked into an old aluminium bucket, beans heated and tipped onto tin plates. Then, closing a rickety door, they step onto the steep, stony track that winds down from their houses to the fields.

Others are woken by prayer calls from mosque minarets; by donkeys braying under olive trees; by cows lowing, their udders swollen and tender with milk. These women, who live in the world's rural areas, are farmers in everything but name. And their labour produces half of the world's food.[1]

The women, of course, have always known who weeds the sorghum, transplants the rice seedlings, picks the beans and tends the chickens. But it has taken a long time for the rest of the world to discover these facts. In Africa, for example, three-quarters of agricultural work is done by women.[2] They are half of the agricultural labour force in Asia.[3] And even in Latin America and the Middle East (where men tend to deny that their mothers, wives, daughters, do any work outside the home) detailed questioning reveals that women are doing a substantial amount of the farming there too.

FIG 3: Division of Labour in Africa

Percentage of each type of work done by women and men in Africa.

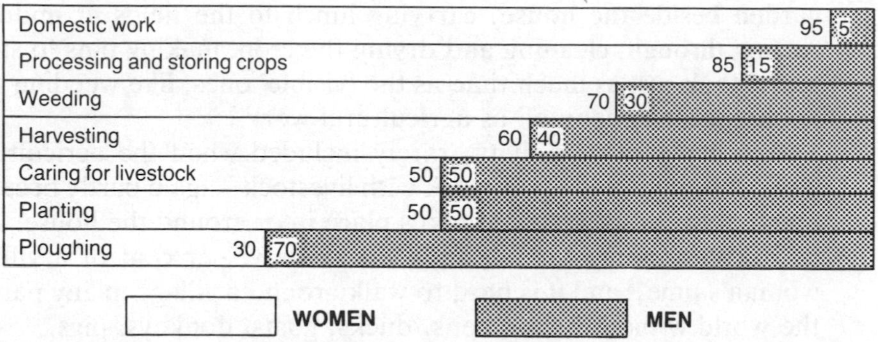

	Women	Men
Domestic work	95	5
Processing and storing crops	85	15
Weeding	70	30
Harvesting	60	40
Caring for livestock	50	50
Planting	50	50
Ploughing	30	70

☐ WOMEN   ▨ MEN

Source: United Nations Handbook on Women in Africa, Economic Commission for Africa, 1975.

Underestimating women's agricultural work

In Peru, for instance, the 1972 census indicated only 2.6 per cent of women working in agriculture. A local survey in one area corrected that figure to 16 per cent. But a carefully worded questionnaire, designed to subvert people's tendency to underestimate or under-report women's work, revealed that smallholding should properly be considered a women's farming system because it occupied women from 86 per cent of households almost to the exclusion of men.[4]

In Egypt too, the 1970 census discovered only 3.6 per cent of women doing agricultural work. But local investigations revealed that, in the south, half of wives plough and level the land, and between 35 and 40 per cent are involved in planting, tilling and harvesting.[5]

But it is not only husbands ashamed of their wives working that means women's farming activity is underestimated. As with their domestic work, much of women's agricultural work tends to be overlooked because it is unpaid. In Malawi and Botswana, for example, over three-quarters of women work unpaid on the land. And there are far more women than men doing unpaid agricultural work in many countries. In Mali and Ghana the ratio is over two to one; in Cameroon it is more than three to one; and in Liberia unpaid women working the land outnumber men by over four to one.[6]

Even when unpaid work is taken into account, however, women's agricultural workload still tends to be underestimated. This is largely because so much of it takes place away from the fields and the pastures. One study in Pakistan, for example, found that women's 'invisible' agricultural activities – like their vegetable garden beside the house, carrying lunch to the fields at midday, sorting through, cleaning and drying the crop, making bins to store it in – took just as much time as the 'visible' ones, like weeding and hoeing, usually counted as agricultural work.[7]

Another area of activity, rarely included when the agricultural work is being totted up, is work with livestock – again partly because much of the work involved takes place in or around the house. Yet in Pakistan caring for livestock takes up 35 per cent of a village woman's time,[8] and it is hard to walk around a village in any part of the world without seeing hens, ducks, goats, donkeys, pigs.

It is not only in developing countries that women's farm work is underestimated. The traditional European 'farmer's wife' – who just bakes bread, churns butter, feeds a few hens, and clears up after her mud-spattered menfolk – may be just a benign myth. Surveys in Turkey and Spain found farmers' wives working up to seventy hours a week out on the farm itself.[9]

Invisible farmers

It was not until four years into the Decade for Women – at the World Conference on Agrarian Reform and Rural Development in 1979 – that the international community began to realise the extent of women's contribution to agriculture. Why has it taken so long? There has not been the same problem in appreciating the value and volume of men's agricultural work – paid *and* unpaid.

The delay has been largely due to people gazing at the world's agriculture through the distorting prisms of men's and women's sex roles. Man, the breadwinner, is assumed, and expected, to be working in the fields. Woman, the wife and mother, has a veil of invisibility drawn around her when she does the same. And, just as she becomes invisible when she does what the world sees as 'man's work', so the other agricultural work she does becomes invisible and classed as domestic work: her vegetable plot becomes a 'kitchen garden'; the baskets she weaves to hold harvested grain is 'craft-work'; her hours of pounding and grinding and husking grain is called 'food-processing'. As a farmer she simply disappears.

Modernisation for men

That women farmers in the developing world have been made

invisible is only too evident from the statistics for agricultural innovations and projects. Information collected from forty-six African countries showed that only 3.4 per cent of trained government workers providing agricultural advice to people in rural areas were women.[10] Other research puts the figure still lower, at just 2.9 per cent.[11] In other parts of the world the situation is the same. In Nepal, for instance, studies show that women provide between 66 and 100 per cent of the labour in many agricultural activities and make 42 per cent of agricultural decisions – eg choosing which seeds to plant, deciding how much and what kind of fertiliser to apply.[12] But a review of government projects in 1983 discovered that, of all the agricultural advisors trained to help villagers, only one was a woman – and she had been trained in 'home economics', not agriculture.[13]

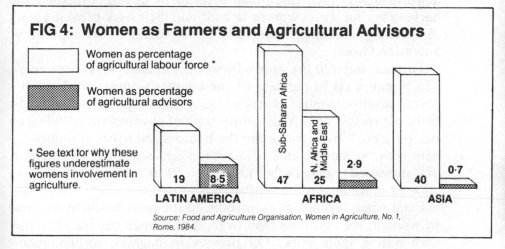

FIG 4: Women as Farmers and Agricultural Advisors

Women as percentage of agricultural labour force *

Women as percentage of agricultural advisors

* See text for why these figures underestimate womens involvement in agriculture.

LATIN AMERICA   19   8·5

AFRICA   Sub-Saharan Africa   47   N. Africa and Middle East   25   2·9

ASIA   40   0·7

Source: Food and Agriculture Organisation, Women in Agriculture, No. 1, Rome, 1984.

This tendency – to help women farmers only with those skills that are associated with their domestic role – has been found in many other countries too. In Ghana, where women grow half the food, around a third of cash crops like cocoa, rice, sugar and cotton, and manage two-fifths of the coffee farms, over 70 per cent of agricultural workers assigned to help women were only trained to teach about nutrition and the preparation and storage of food.[14]

But at least these women were getting some preferential treatment. In other places agricultural workers seem to have inherited the same blind spot as the people who selected and trained them. In western Kenya, for instance, agricultural workers visited men growing cash crops five times more frequently than they visited women growing the same crops. Ten times more female than male farmers in Kenya have never spoken to an agricultural worker at all.[15] And in the Yemen Arab Republic, it was not until village men migrated in huge numbers to look for work in neighbouring rich oil-exporting countries that women in rural areas received training and advice from government workers.[16] In this case the men had to disappear before the women became visible.

As the Food and Agriculture Organisation (FAO) commented glumly: 'Throughout the Decade developing countries revealed rather discouraging information about women's access to agricultural education, training and extension services.'[17]

Tools for change

But it is not only training and advice about agriculture that has been directed more at men. When new technology is introduced it usually helps men with their traditional tasks of ploughing, irrigation and harvesting, but leaves women to continue their back-breaking work of weeding, thinning, transplanting, by hand or with primitive knives and hoes.

The rain-watered rice grown by women in Gambia, for example – which makes up 84 per cent of the country's entire rice harvest – covers twenty-six times as much land as the irrigated rice grown by men, but receives only one twenty-sixth of government spending on rice projects.[18] In Sierra Leone the tractors and tillers introduced to help with swamp rice cultivation made men's working day shorter, but increased women's workload by 50 per cent because they allowed more land to be cultivated.[19]

Even when technology is introduced for tasks traditionally done by women, the machines tend to replace women completely rather than easing their work. Oil presses in Nigeria, tortilla-making machines in Mexico, sago-processing machines in Sarawak, are all owned and operated by men.[20] And in Bangladesh rice mills, employing only men, have been introduced, depriving many local women – who used to be paid to husk rice for better-off families – of one of their main sources of income.[21]

FAO sums up the situation: 'In all regions the introduction of modern agricultural technology is primarily aimed at male tasks and used almost exclusively by men.'[22]

Costs and benefits of development

Agricultural development has advanced at a different pace and in different ways through the various regions of the world. Two major global trends can be distinguished, but these two trends – towards large-scale commercialisation and the growing of cash crops for export – have superimposed themselves on landscapes already eroded and shaped by history. It would be surprising, given the preferential treatment men have received from their ministries of agriculture, if these global trends had benefited men and women equally. But the picture in each major area of the world is slightly different.

Latin America

In Latin America an existing pattern of grossly unequal land ownership – with a few powerful families owning huge farms and a majority of people either without land or working very small plots – has begun to be reshaped by a mixture of incomplete land redistribution and increasing control by multi-national corporations of large tracts of prime agricultural land.

With the exception of a few countries – such as Peru and Nicaragua – where land redistribution programmes have been widely applied, the dominant trend in this region is for the gap between rich and poor to widen as the new commercial farms swallow up smaller plots of land and evict people from their homes on the *latifundia* or family estates.[23]

Here the tradition is to employ men as farm labourers, far outnumbering women in paid agricultural work in this region. In Costa Rica, Guatemala, Honduras, Panama, Chile and Colombia, for example, the ratio is ten to one.[24] Women tend only to be hired when extra hands are needed at harvest time. For the most part they work unpaid on their family's land – where it is increasingly difficult to compete with the produce from the big farms – or migrate to the towns in search of paid employment.

Even the restraining hands of land reform – which have cushioned the impact of these changes on some of Latin America's rural poor – have tended to leave women unguarded. In Chile, for instance, land was only allocated to people who had been in continuous employment on an estate for at least three out of the previous four years. Since most women were only hired at harvest time, most did not qualify for land.[25] In Honduras, too, though a survey showed that one in eight village households were legally headed by women they were only allocated land in the new settlement schemes, or *asentiamentos,* if they had a grown son living with them.[26] Only in Nicaragua has land been given to women as independent individuals, regardless of whether there is a man in the family.[27]

Asia

In Asia – with the exception of China and Vietnam – a general pattern of 'development packages' (including high-yielding varieties of rice and wheat seed, fertilisers, pesticides, irrigation and tractors) has been superimposed on an existing picture of land scarcity and increasing landlessness.

Here the maxim 'to him that hath shall be given' applies only too well and the changes have tended to benefit only those who are relatively well-off – who can afford to experiment with a new type of fertiliser, or who have enough land to risk a few hectares trying out a new seed variety. Those with smaller plots of land, unable to compete with their richer neighbours, fall into debt and are eventually forced to sell up – swelling the ranks of those dependent on wages from working on other people's land. Between a quarter and a half of the rural population in Pakistan, India and Bangladesh are without land – and their numbers are growing.[28]

The result of these changes for Asia's women are mixed. The high-yielding seeds require more work (more weeding, more spraying, more planting and transplanting) and it is women who tend to be employed on the big farms to do these jobs. Though their average earnings are less than men's (with 56 per cent of women in rural Java earning under 3,000 rupiahs a month compared with just 14 per cent of men, for example[29]) these increased job opportunities are some consolation. On the other hand, if the seeds are grown on her own family's land, the chances are that a woman will have to do all that extra work herself – without pay.

Africa

In sub-Saharan Africa a recent and troubled colonial history, poor soil, low population density and traditional or communal rights to land, have been overlaid by a general move towards replacing subsistence crops like yam and sorghum with export crops like cotton and coffee.

Here, as in all regions, it is men who have been encouraged and helped to grow the new crops – despite the fact that in Africa, more than any other part of the world, it is women who do most of the agricultural work, and despite the fact that large numbers of men have migrated to the cities in search of work, leaving many households run entirely by women.

Unlike most other parts of the world, traditional land rights in parts of Africa have guaranteed women's independent access to land. But these rights have tended to be undermined – first by colonial land policies, and then by development projects, which have allocated land ownership to men. In Burkina Faso, for instance, until the sweeping reforms initiated by the new government in the last year, all new tenancies (for both food and cash crops) were given to men, despite women's tradition of growing all the family's subsistence food.[30] And in Kenya a woman now only has access to land if she has a husband or son alive.[31]

Land, loans and the law

The sweeping changes in agriculture in recent years have – with the exception of just a few countries – worsened the situation for the poorest and least powerful of the world's people. In a world that harvests enough each year (1,798 million tons in 1983–84, for instance[32]) to feed its population adequately twice over, an estimated 450 million people – one in ten – are malnourished.[33]

People go hungry when food is available for two simple reasons: because it is not their food in the first place, having been grown on land they do not own, and because they do not earn enough money to buy it. So increasing landlessness without an adequate income is a potent cause of hunger. An estimated 600 million people in the rural areas of the poor world have no land.[34]

In many parts of the world it is new laws and competition with big commercial farms that have caused many millions of men to lose their land and, therefore, the ability to benefit directly from the fruits of their labour. But women regularly lose their land rights under some of the oldest laws in history: the laws of marriage and inheritance. Laws passed before the Decade give women the right to own land in most countries but, in the vast majority of cases, the laws of marriage and inheritance are superimposed on the new laws and steal those rights back again. So complete is this disinheritance of women, that it has been estimated that they own less than one hundredth of the world's property.[35]

Under Islamic law, for example (which operates in much of North Africa, the Middle East and parts of Asia), daughters inherit only half of what a son inherits and a widow gets just one-eighth of her husband's estate if she has children, one quarter if she is childless. In Peru, Bolivia and Brazil too, married women are restricted in their ability to administer property without their husband's consent. And it has already been explained how land reform has tended to exclude women. Even when several Honduran women formed their own farmers' group and applied – as a group – to the authorities for land, their request was denied.[36]

In Asia almost all women are landless because of inheritance and divorce laws which prevent women gaining access to a man's land. Even where women can inherit – under the customary laws of the Hindu Mitakshara, Parsee and Christian sects in India, for example, or under Sawlawi law in Sri Lanka – they receive smaller shares than male heirs. And in the Philippines, laws prevent a woman acquiring land at all without her husband's consent.

Even in Africa, that one region where women have had traditional rights to land on a large scale, the customary laws still tend to discriminate against women. In Sierra Leone, for instance, where an estimated 40 per cent of rural households are without an adult man, chiefs tend to allocate women a plot of communal land that is only a third or half the size of plots allocated to men.[37] And, in one part of Ghana, a study of 1,696 women farmers found that 59 per cent had had to forfeit their land because they had lost their husbands – through death, divorce or migration.[38]

Without land, property or a substantial regular income (collateral in banking terms) it is almost impossible for women (or men for that matter) to get loans. Only 5 per cent of the money lent by African commercial banks goes into agriculture at all, and almost all of that goes to men.[39] Even women with land find it difficult to get credit. This is partly due to the expenses involved for banks administering the small loans most women want. In Sierra Leone, for example, the majority of rural women cultivate cash crops of some kind. But only half are able to make a profit because they cannot borrow the small amount of money they need to invest in, say, fertiliser, for their crop.[40] Similar problems occur in Zambia.[41] While in Ghana, even those women with large farms found it hard to get credit from the bank. The banks simply refused to trust the women, allowing only 7 per cent to take out loans, compared to 27 per cent of men.[42]

With the banks' doors slammed shut in their faces, women are forced to turn to relatives or money-lenders, the latter charging exorbitant interest rates – around 50 per cent a year in Ghana,[43] for instance, and up to 240 per cent in Nicaragua.[44] Wary of being caught up in an unending spiral of debt, most women continue to farm without modern agricultural aids.

The FAO puts it like this: 'In the Third World agricultural productivity cannot be substantially increased, nor can rural poverty be alleviated, unless women's access to key productive resources and services is substantially improved. The consequences of patriarchy for agricultural productivity are very expensive. Developing countries cannot bear their heavy cost'.[45]

Famine in Africa

The heaviest of the costs to which FAO is referring is famine. It is now becoming clear that the acute food shortages in Africa, while dramatically and tragically exacerbated by drought and war, may be due in large part to the way women have been systematically excluded from access to land and from control of modern agriculture in that region.

The processes are subtle but are beginning to prove devastating. And the devastation is greatest in Africa because this is the region where women do a greater proportion of agricultural work (between 60 and 80 per cent[46]) than in any other continent. In Africa the pressures that bear down on rural women all over the world are magnified and mount up, one upon another, to force Africa's women onto their knees, taking Africa's food production down with them.

Even in 1980 – before the current drought blew its scorching winds across the continent, searing crops to dust – Africa was only 86 per cent self-sufficient in food.[47]

Part of the problem is the sheer amount of work African women are expected to do. In Malawi, for example, women do twice as much work as men on the staple maize crop and an equal amount in the cotton fields, *plus* their domestic chores at home.[48] A survey in Burkina Faso found families lost weight during the rainy season – not because there was no food available, but because their long days in the fields left women too exhausted to cook.[49] And in Zambia, Ghana, Botswana and Gambia, studies found that the amount that was harvested depended, not on what the land could yield, but on the amount of work women could fit into the daylight hours.[50]

In Ghana, too, when cocoa prices plummeted and large numbers of men migrated to the city, leaving women to shoulder all the agricultural work alone, many women decided to replace the traditional yam crop with less nutritous cassava because it takes so much less time to cultivate.[51] And it was in Ghana that acute malnutrition – called by its Ghanaian name of *kwashiorkor* – was first identified, having been brought to doctors' attention by its appearance in huge numbers of small children being fed cassava as a weaning food.

Migration of men not only leaves women with too much work to handle alone, but in Botswana – where tradition forbids women to handle cattle – they are forced to pay male neighbours to plough their fields for them and may find themselves at the end of a long queue so that their land is not ready when the first of the fickle rains arrive.[52]

Another reason for declining food production in Africa is the introduction of cash crops – to men. In the Ivory Coast a shortage of food staples resulted when the government encouraged men to grow cash crops, because some of the best land (where women had previously been growing food) was claimed by their husbands for the new cash crop and because wives had to spend so much of their time working on their husbands' fields.[53] Malawi's groundnut harvest – grown chiefly by women – was down too, and for the same reasons, after a World Bank project encouraged men to expand staple maize production for export.[54]

And the failure of plans for Gambia to become self-sufficient in rice by 1980 led to an *increase* of nearly 300 per cent in rice imports between 1966 and 1979, because, although Gambian women grow 84 per cent of the country's rice, the agricultural advice and investment was given to men alone.[55]

The combined results of factors like these is a reduction in *per capita* food production in Africa over the last two decades. As FAO points out: 'Despite the well-documented, crucial role that women play in food production in this region, agricultural modernisation efforts have excluded them, leading to negative consequences for food production and the perpetuation of rural poverty.' [56]

Passive resistance

Women have not submitted lightly to their loss of land and livelihood. Some are objecting in the only way they can. They dare not actually go on strike: married women risk divorce and loss of their access to land if they defy their husbands, and mothers are prevented from withdrawing their labour completely through fear for the welfare of their children. But they are refusing to co-operate.

When government pricing policies sent men's maize profits soaring in Zambia and led to more land being put under maize, women kept working doggedly in their own groundnut fields and refused to turn them over to the more lucrative maize: because they – and not their husbands – kept the money from sales of groundnuts.[57]

A similar situation is seen in northern Cameroon, where women without husbands (who can therefore keep the income from selling the rice they grow) are found to work far harder than wives, who have to see the reward for their work go straight into their husbands' back pockets.[58] In Tanzania, too, when new hybrid maize seeds, plus fertiliser and pesticides, were given to men, their wives – who do most of the work in the fields – tended to neglect the new crop because it increased their workload while the profits went only to their husbands.[59] The exact opposite happened in Zimbabwe, however, and yields rose dramatically when the same hybrid maize package was introduced, because the new seeds were given to women.[60]

Investing in women

It is a tragedy that women are forced into conflicts like these, because the evidence points to the fact that, given the same kind of help, encouragement and incentives as men, women are actually better farmers. On reflection, this should come as no surprise: they have the experience; they work much closer to the soil than men; they see the crop through every stage of its development, as opposed to just swooping in at ploughing and harvest time as men are prone to do; they see more directly – in the skin of their children, in the grain in the cooking pot – the results of their labour on the land.

In Kenya, for instance, where 38 per cent of the farms are run by women, those women manage to harvest the same amount per hectare as men, despite men's greater access to loans, advice, fertilisers, hybrid seeds, insecticide. And when women were given the same level of help, they were found to be more efficent than men and produced bigger harvests.[61]

Zambian women were equally successful when they were taught to grow onions as a cash crop between rows of their usual subsistence crops. So much did they earn, in fact, that the men demanded to be given the same assistance – and then tried to insist that the women tend their onions too. In this case the women refused.[62] But women have not always been able to hold on to their advantages. In Nigeria, for instance, when the price of women's rice crop rocketed in the 1970s, men began to take over the paddy fields and claim the income for themselves.[63]

The key, says FAO, is to ensure that women can acquire and hold on to independent access to land and loans – independent, that is, of men. All-women co-operative farms and rural credit schemes appear to be the most promising way forward. And these have been tried with some success in countries such as Vietnam, Bangladesh and India.[64] But, laments FAO, 'Policy-makers and international experts have persistently resisted the idea of all-women's co-operatives'[65] – even in West Africa where such co-operatives are traditional. And country-wide agricultural projects aimed specifically at women have not yet been implemented in any country, forcing FAO to conclude that: 'It is virtually impossible to identify any country in which national strategies have generally benefited women's role in agriculture', adding that, 'No successes at the national level can be reported at this time.' [66]

Yet when women are able to profit directly from their work in the fields, they are not the only ones to benefit. Studies in Burkina Faso, Bangladesh, Nepal, the Philippines and Swaziland have indicated that, when women do have time or money to spare, they use it to improve the health and well-being of their children.[67, 68, 69, 70, 71]

Expansion and recession

Though three-fifths of the world's people live their lives by the rhythm of the seasons – bending and straightening as the earth breathes in and out, submitting to the sun, praying for the rain, ploughing and sowing and waiting and weeding and reaping and ploughing again – the rest are ruled by different rhythms.

In the industrialised world the day begins when the machines are switched on. Sometimes that day stretches right through the night: hospitals and airports hum, efficient and subdued under flickering neon lights; the steel furnace roars, never sleeping, belching white flame, vomiting red liquid iron; the mine shaft elevator cranks up to the surface, spewing coal-blackened bodies into the showers, gulping down a new bellyful of miners for the next shift.

Clocks, bells, switches jolt these workers awake. Buses, trains, trucks, traffic jams, ferry them to office and factory.

Two-fifths of the workforce of the world – nearly one billion people – are hitched to the machine that runs modern society. It is a machine whose iron hands reach into every country of the world, extended on the arms of modern transport. Some countries have been barely touched, with just a few factories and an airport to link them with the global machine. In others the iron embrace is complete, with most people thinking of work in terms of wages and weekends, shifts and promotions. In North America, for example, 96 per cent of men with jobs and 98 per cent of women were working in services or industry in 1980,[1] whereas in the poorer parts of Africa the majority of the population still works in agriculture and only 24 per cent of men and 13 per cent of women in the labour force were then working in the modern sectors.[2] Even these totals – the lowest of all the regions of the world – are on the increase as these countries begin to embark on their own industrial revolutions.

Today we are witnessing the expansion throughout the world of a process that has its roots in the wealth accumulated by early traders and the investment of that wealth in the first factories, making textiles in India, nails in England, wheels in France. A few people had worked for wages before this period – as cooks, scribes, milkmaids, stable-boys. But the vast majority either worked on the land as serfs or subsistence farmers or ran their own small family businesses – as potters, builders, millers, bakers. With the advent of industry, however, the world became increasingly divided into employers and employees; the former amassing and reinvesting wealth, the latter earning and spending their wages on goods and services.

Cities began to expand as people flooded in from the countryside for the new jobs, and, increasingly, life in the countryside began to be dictated by the needs and the wealth of the city.

In its early phases industry expanded in a fragmented, piecemeal way. More recently, however, the increasing size of some multi-national corporations and the increasing power and wealth of some industrialised countries have brought the process of expansion more and more under their control.

Today these industrial giants stalk the earth freely from country to country, checked only by cartels and tariff barriers, maximising profits by searching out wider markets, cheaper raw materials, cheaper labour. And in their wake they tow whole retinues of service industries – laundries, restaurants, clinics, accountancy firms, secretarial agencies – paid for by taxes and wages.

Fuelled by cheap raw materials and cheap energy from the developing world, the expansion of industry and services reached a peak in the 1950s and 1960s, piling up wealth in the industrialised world and spilling over into the cities of the developing countries. Wage employment increased rapidly – in rich and poor countries – until, in the 1970s, the dramatic rise in the price of oil, and the subsequent recession in the world economy, swerved industry off its headlong course of expansion and brought it skidding to a halt.

The last decade has been a time of retrenchment, with industry cutting back in the rich world and pushing forward harder into developing countries to take advantage of low wages and low taxes, fewer trade unions and labour laws, new plants and markets.

Jobs for women

In modern industrial society jobs have always tended to be created on the assumption that workers have no domestic responsibilities. They are expected to be available at places and times to suit the employer. This is the main reason why women, though half of the world's population, are only a third of the world's official income-earning labour force.[3] And this proportion has changed only slightly in recent years. In 1950, for instance, women were 31 per cent of the income-earning labour force, compared with a total of 35 per cent today.[4]

FIG 5: Women in the Labour Force in 1985 (estimate)

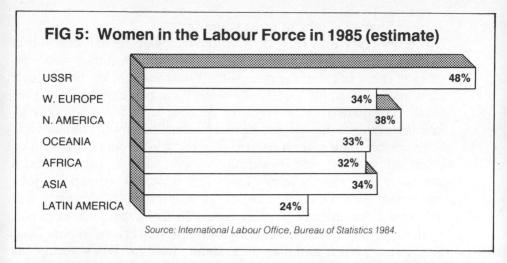

USSR	48%
W. EUROPE	34%
N. AMERICA	38%
OCEANIA	33%
AFRICA	32%
ASIA	34%
LATIN AMERICA	24%

Source: International Labour Office, Bureau of Statistics 1984.

Though the proportion of women with jobs has stayed relatively constant over the last thirty-five years, the actual numbers have swelled considerably. Over the last decade, for example, 100 million more women came into the labour force (a rate of 10 million a year) and there are now an estimated 676 million women in the world in wage employment.[5] This increase in the numbers of women employed is part of the general employment boom that accompanied the expansion of industry and services and boosted the labour force as a whole by 38 per cent between 1960 and 1980.[6]

The increase has not been even across all sectors, however. Though one in three of the world's paid jobs go to women, they are only one quarter of those employed in industry – in rich and poor world alike.[7] Their share of industrial jobs is growing, however, increasing from 24 to 28 per cent between 1960 and 1980 – largely as a result of the rapid expansion of industrial employment in parts of Asia.[8] In fact the number of women employed in industry increased by 104 per cent in that period, compared to a mere 70 per cent increase for men.[9]

It is in the service sector that women take the largest share of jobs. In the developing world the proportion is 27 per cent,[10] but in the rich world half of all service jobs are done by women.[11]

One reason why women, rather than men, tend to be employed in the service sector is that men tend to be occupied in the strenuous jobs of heavy industry: digging coal, lifting ingots of pig-iron, laying bricks. Another reason is the old one of sex role stereotypes: jobs in the services (as secretaries, cleaners, filing clerks, canteen workers) dovetail so neatly with women's traditional domestic roles of supporting and cleaning up after men that they have quickly become seen as 'women's' jobs in most countries.

But whatever jobs they do – as tea-ladies or egg-packers – it is clear that the majority of women take jobs because they need the money: either because the money their husbands earn is not enough to support the whole family, because their husbands do not give them a fair share of their wages, or because (in an increasingly large number of cases) they do not have a husband to support them at all.

There are other reasons, of course, why women work. For educated women with rewarding careers, a job can be more satisfying than childbearing. Even less educated women, in jobs where the work is hard and tedious, find a job has advantages over and above the income it gives them. In Colombia, for example, women grading fruit and tending hothouse flowers for export liked the fixed hours and were grateful not to be working as housemaids.[12] In Chile, while mothers chafed under the double burden of factory and domestic work, younger women liked the escape the factory represented from the dirt and weather to which farmwork exposed them. They liked meeting people and being able to buy clothes for themselves.[13]

Wage differentials

Some good news of the Decade is the increase in the number of countries – from twenty-eight in 1978 to ninety in 1983[14] – who have equal pay legislation on their statute books, making it illegal to give men and women different wages for the same work. Though this has been soured slightly by the minority of countries who have actually reversed their equal pay laws during the Decade, it is still a major advance.

At last it is possible to detect a slight narrowing in the wage gap between men and women. One study of twenty-four countries around the world found that in 1975 a woman working in manufacturing industry earned an average of only 70 cents for every dollar earned by a man doing the same or similar work. In 1982 she earned 73 cents for every dollar in his wage packet.[15] It must be said that part of this improvement is due to the increased demand for women workers. But much must be attributed to the new laws enacted during the Decade.

These averages do, of course, conceal very great regional differences. Women in Japan and the Republic of Korea, for instance, take home less than half the wages earned by men,[16] while women in Denmark, Norway, Sweden, El Salvador, Burma and Sri Lanka fare best, with average earnings under 20 per cent lower than men's.[17]

The averages also fail to take into account the millions of women – working as tailors at home, as seasonal agricultural labourers, as maids – who tend to be excluded by both equal pay legislation and official wage statistics. In Peru, Nigeria and Bangladesh, for example, agricultural workers are excluded from equal pay laws.[18] In the Philippines it is people working at home or in small businesses who are excluded.[19] Yet there is evidence that it is in these sorts of occupation that wage differentials between men and women may be the greatest. In the urban areas of Java, for instance, the proportion of women earning less than 3,000 rupiahs a month is ten times the proportion of men.[20]

So, though the earnings gap between men and women working in industry, as deduced from government statistics, appears to stand at around 25 per cent and to be closing, this difference is likely to be dwarfed by the real gap between the contents of the average man's and woman's pay packets.

In some cases a minimum pay law may have better success than an equal pay law in equalising earnings – because it automatically elevates the wages of all workers earning less than a certain amount, and women nearly always predominate in these low-paid occupations. Indeed, in Portugal, the earnings gap more than halved (with women's average wages rising from just 52 per cent of men's in 1973 to 71 per cent in 1980) following the introduction of minimum pay legislation.[21]

But, though tinkering with wage laws can do – and has done – a great deal to reduce the inequality between women's and men's earnings, it can do nothing to affect the more fundamental inequality underlying the fact that, despite the new laws, women continue to earn less than men doing similar work. In the end it is women's social role – the role that compels them to carry the burden of domestic work alone – that is lodged at the heart of the problem.

Unequal hours

Because of their responsibilities in the home, most women are simply not able to put in the same number of hours at their jobs as men. In Sri Lanka, for instance, women work an average of ten and a half hours less per week than men in manufacturing industries.[22] In other countries, too (in Egypt, Singapore, Australia, Japan, the UK, for example) the difference is somewhere between four and five hours.[23] In fact, overall, women employed in the rich world do an average of three hours less paid work per week than men – but over seventeen hours *more* unpaid domestic work than men.[24] In

France, for instance, women do a total of 12,700 million hours of paid work a year – half of the hours put in by men. But they more than make up for it with the 40,000 million hours of unpaid housework they do, which is four times the amount done by men.[25]

Women's domestic responsibility cuts into their ability, and inclination, to do shiftwork and overtime. It also means they are more likely to try for part-time work when it is available. Both factors result in a shorter paid working week than men have. In the UK, for instance, 41 per cent of women with jobs are working part-time, compared with just 2 per cent of men.[26]

Another factor that helps push women's wages below men's is time-based pay rises. Because women are often forced to, or choose to, interrupt their working lives to have children, they tend to fall behind men taken on at the same time. Even when paid maternity leave is available (and an International Labour Office (ILO) analysis of 127 countries found that, for those categories of jobs for which maternity leave was available, an average of between twelve and fourteen weeks was offered,[27] with some centrally planned economies, such as Poland and the USSR offering up to three years' leave[28]) women who want to stay away longer often forfeit their wages while they are absent. For some women the setback can be more drastic. Many lose their jobs altogether when they leave to have a baby and find themselves having to begin again at the bottom of the pay ladder when they go back to work.

Fringe penalties

A third reason why women earn less – again related to their domestic roles – is because they are usually not entitled to the tax and fringe benefits available to men. In Zambia, for instance, women are taxed at a higher rate on the assumption that men will meet most of the family's expenses.[29] Bonuses are usually assessed as a percentage of total earnings, which mean men's bonuses tend to be bigger. Training is less likely to be given to woman employees because employers judge that it is wasted on people who 'will just leave to have babies'. And, when housing allowances are paid, they are usually added to the salary of the 'household head' – almost invariably assumed to be the man.

The penalties continue even beyond women's official working life. Because they work fewer hours, have earned less money, and usually have an earlier age of retirement, women's pensions – when these are available at all – end up being lower too. In the Federal Republic of Germany, for instance, retired women receive, on average, only half of the full pension.[30]

Unequal work

These factors do not add up to the whole story, however. The most important reason why women earn less than men is not because women do fewer hours and get fewer benefits. It is because women tend to do *different* work to men. Equal pay for equal work is a fine guiding principle. But, as ILO points out, 'there is no equal work'.[31] And, once again, women's domestic role is at the heart of the problem. Not only does the quantity of housework restrict the quantity of paid work a woman is able to do, but the quality of housework has come to define the quality of paid work they are offered.

The social role that dictates that women should cook, clean, make and mend clothes and care for children *inside* the home stays with women when they work outside it, impelling them towards particular occupations consistent with the role of domestic nurturer. Domestic work is the work women have always been forced to do and it now tends to be seen – in societies as different as Egypt, Canada and the Soviet Union – as the sort of work for which women are best suited.

Two-thirds of European women who are out at work have jobs in the service sector,[32] where they comprise 45 per cent of the workforce.[33] In Latin America, too, and the Caribbean, women far outnumber men employed in services – by a ratio of over four to one in the majority of countries in the regions.[34] In industry, on the other hand, the situation is reversed, with men outnumbering women by around three to one in most countries.[35]

Even in the centrally planned economies, where there has been more of an effort to encourage women to take jobs usually considered to be 'men's work', 45 per cent of women are working in service jobs.[36] In the USSR, for example, 82 per cent of people holding health, physical education and social security posts are women, and they have 74 per cent of the jobs in public education.[37] In all, 66 per cent of Soviet women work in the services, and that percentage is rising.[38]

In industry, too, women's traditional domestic role influences their employment opportunities. Though women are only one quarter of the industrial workforce in rich and poor world alike,[39] they often take double that proportion of jobs in the textile industry. In Barbados 54 per cent of textile workers are women; in Tunisia the proportion is 49 per cent; and Puerto Rico and El Salvador are not far behind, with women making up 46 and 42 per cent of the textile workforce respectively.[40]

These traditional stereotypes have been just as hard to shift in China. The traditional bandages that bound, stunted and deformed Chinese women's feet have been removed. But the stereotypes that bind women to their domestic role still restrict their choices. In the countryside well over 90 per cent of cotton and silk-weaving is done by women. But they are only 40 per cent of those working in brick factories and farm machinery workshops, and less than 20 per cent of those working the coal mines.[41]

If 'women's work' was as well-paid as 'men's work' there would be less cause for concern. But the majority of occupations in which women predominate (as cleaners, waitresses, nurses, food and textile workers) are badly paid. Just as society undervalues the unpaid domestic work women do in the home, so those same skills - dexterity, sympathy, patience – are undervalued when applied to work outside in the world of employment. And, because this is how the world sees them, the majority of women find it difficult to conceive of a different future for themselves. In Portugal, for example, when teenage school-leavers were given a selection of thirty occupations to choose from, 85 per cent of the girls chose one of a set of just five 'women's' jobs.[42]

Bosses and secretaries

Taken together, the pressures that lead women to work unequal hours and to choose unequal work make it very unlikely that many will rise to top administration or managerial positions. Such jobs require both a confidence and a freedom to work long hours that few women possess. And, in every country in the world, this is borne out by the statistics. In Indonesia and Bangladesh, for

TABLE 2: Type of Occupation

	BOSSES		SECRETARIES	
	Women	Men	Women	Men
GERMANY (Fed.Rep.)	1·3	4·2	34·0	9·6
HUNGARY	0·1	0·2	16·4	3·5
NORWAY	2·0	6·6	26·0	2·5
UNITED STATES	3·8	10·4	27·9	5·5
JAPAN	0·4	6·4	18·2	9·4
EGYPT	0·8	0·9	25·0	6·5
BAHRAIN	0·4	1·1	46·0	5·8
SINGAPORE	1·2	8·2	14·9	5·7
VENEZUELA	1·6	9·2	16·7	7·6

Percentage of female and male workforce in administrative and managerial (bosses') and clerical (secretaries') jobs.

Source: International Labour Office, Yearbook of Labour Statistics, 1983, Geneva 1984.

instance, less than 1 per cent of managers are women.[43] The figures are slightly higher (at between 3 and 10 per cent) in Egypt, Peru, Japan, Australia and Norway.[44] In the US 15 per cent of managers are women.[45] And in only a small minority of countries – such as Barbados, El Salvador and Hungary – does the proportion rise above 25 per cent.[46]

Instead, talented, hard-working women often find themselves working as secretaries or clerical assistants to their male bosses. While men outnumber women managers and administrators by over three to one in the US, Norway and Australia, for instance, women are over five times as likely to be working as secretaries or clerks than men in those countries.[47]

Unemployment

The Decade of Women has also been the Decade of Recession as countries and corporations reeled from the impact of the oil shock of 1975 and staggered through the tremors that followed. One effect of the increase in oil prices has been for corporations to cut their labour costs wherever possible.

In the poor world unemployment is largely due to an increased number of people opting to seek wage employment. In the rich world unemployment also arises from a reduction in the number of existing jobs. Though it is thought that unemployment in some developing countries is 5 times as high as in the rich world, it is only in the rich world that comprehensive unemployment statistics are regularly collected. In the OECD countries, for example, 4.9 per cent of the male workforce and 6.2 per cent of women were unemployed in 1975. By 1982 those figures had risen to 7.4 per cent and 8.2 per cent respectively.[48]

And unemployment figures for women often underestimate the problem. Research in Europe, for instance, indicates that only 42 per cent of women who have lost their jobs or are looking for work ever register as unemployed.[49] These figures suggest that, when unemployment is high, women are more likely to be out of work than men. In 1982, for instance, women were around one-third of the labour force in the OECD countries, but even the official estimates put the number of unemployed women at 12 million – well over 40 per cent of the 30 million people registered as unemployed.[50]

Women's jobs tend to be threatened more than men's for two major reasons. First, many women are employed in less skilled occupations easily replaced by machines. New technology has been

FIG 6:   Unemployment in the Rich World

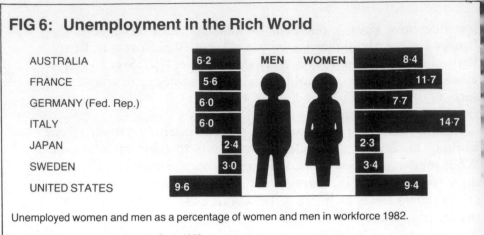

	MEN	WOMEN
AUSTRALIA	6·2	8·4
FRANCE	5·6	11·7
GERMANY (Fed. Rep.)	6·0	7·7
ITALY	6·0	14·7
JAPAN	2·4	2·3
SWEDEN	3·0	3·4
UNITED STATES	9·6	9·4

Unemployed women and men as a percentage of women and men in workforce 1982.

Source: OECD, Economic Outlook, Paris 1983.

introduced in offices, in manufacturing industry, and in the distributive trades. Computers, photocopiers, word-processors, robot arms, automatic sorters stand gleaming and whirring, efficiently doing the work once done by living, breathing women. Technology has replaced less skilled men too, of course. But women are hit hardest.

Another reason why women's jobs are more vulnerable is because they tend to involve temporary or part-time work – often because there is no other work available for them. Women tend to change their jobs more often too, leaving to look after a new baby or to follow a husband transferred to another part of the country. Women are also less likely to be members of, or actively involved in, a trade union and have fewer rights as employees. This makes them less able to organise to protect their jobs.

Some of women's service jobs are less vulnerable than their industrial jobs, however – both because they tend to require more skill (it is not yet possible to replace a nurse or a primary-school teacher by a machine), but also because they are lower paid. Ironically, the very injustices that lead women to accept low wages for their work means that, for the time being, many of them are still cheaper than machines and their jobs are safe.

Free trade zones

In the developing world, too, there are still large numbers of workers who are cheaper than machines. And this is truest of all in the free trade zones (or 'export processing zones') that have sprung up in many developing countries who want to attract industry to their shores.

In the free trade zones governments desperate for foreign investment have created the industrial equivalent of a rose garden for multi-national corporations. Taxes are low, labour is cheap, laws are relaxed, currency controls are waived. Some have even introduced anti-strike laws.

Corporations setting up shop in these new industrial havens have, according to the ILO, shown 'an overwhelming preference for young women' workers.[51] In fact women's employment in free trade zones is the fastest-growing sector of employment in the world at the moment.[52] In Malaysia, for instance, 85 per cent of people working in the Bayan Lepas free trade zone are women aged between eighteen and twenty-four.[53] In Mexico, under-23-year-old women also comprise 85 per cent of the workforce.[54] And in Mauritius young women are 80 per cent of the newly-hired free trade zone workers.[55]

Young women are preferred for a number of reasons. They are willing to accept low wages, often because there is no other work available for them; they are docile, having been raised in societies where a husband or father's word is obeyed without question; they are reputed to be dexterous, because their hands are small, their eyesight keen and they are used to being allocated tedious, painstaking tasks at home; they tend to leave – or are fired – when they have children, so employers are free of the obligation to pay them extra for long service. This high turnover also means that (even in those free trade zones where trade unions are permitted) few women are around long enough, or are committed enough to a future in their factory, to push for better pay and conditions.

The informal sector

The expansion and relocation of industry into the developing world has not only threatened jobs in rich countries, it has also begun to threaten the livelihood of people in the poor world too. Though it may provide much needed – albeit low-paid – employment for some, it undermines the employment of many others at the same time.

The scores of people selling leather sandals, rice cakes, rough cotton skirts and trousers, hand-rolled *bidis*, pink and green sweets, bags of noodles, tortillas, roast bananas, cups of coconut-milk, lime juice, thick brown sorghum beer; the hundreds waiting for hour after dusty hour at the side of a road, their baskets of goods beside them; the thousands dodging in and out of traffic queues, balancing their trays over their heads; the tens of thousands squatting in market-places, hunched over tiny charcoal braziers: the precarious livelihood of these millions of people who work on the margins of official life, who occupy the teeming no-man's-land of the informal sector, is put in the balance by the arrival of the smart new shops and industries. How can they compete with the new goods and services that are suddenly for sale? People now want to buy plastic shoes, straight from the production line. They want cellophane-covered crisps and chocolate, glass-bottled soft drinks, cartons of perfect white filter-tipped cigarettes, ring-pull cans of clear, golden beer.

Between 20 and 70 per cent of the labour force in Third World cities make a living in the informal sector.[56] With an average of over 50 per cent of poor urban populations so engaged, the informal sector occupies approximately one in eight of the world's adult population. Yet ILO admits that there is a 'startling dearth of information' about this huge and vibrant slice of world society.[57]

What evidence there is, however, reveals an important, valuable, but very vulnerable sector, often occupied largely by migrants, unable to make a living on the land, unable to find a formal job in the city. Individually the majority of such people can barely subsist on their earnings. In Jakarta, Lagos and the poor urban areas of Bolivia and Peru, for example, average daily earnings in the informal sector are just 50 cents – half the daily wage of the worst-paid labourers.[58] But the sector itself generates around a third of the wealth of many cities in the developing world.[59]

Despite its considerable contribution to local wealth (estimated at 33 per cent in Asuncion, 30 per cent in Lima, 28 per cent in Ahmadabad and 25 per cent in San Salvador, for instance[60]) the value of the informal sector has never been fully appreciated by governments. They tend to see it more as an inevitable adjunct to unsightly slums and a reservoir of tax evasion and crime. But the sector serves several vital functions: providing a living for its millions of workers and transferring commodities from small-scale producers to consumers.

The evidence also indicates that in some regions the informal sector is overwhelmingly occupied by women. In West Africa, the Caribbean and South Asia, between 70 and 90 per cent of all the farm and fishing produce consumed locally is bought and sold by women.[61] In Ghana, for instance, women do 88 per cent of the trading, and the figure is 54 per cent in Thailand and an enormous 91 per cent in Haiti.[62] Untrained, unskilled, often illiterate, and almost invariably without any capital to set themselves up in a formal business enterprise, such women rely on these informal trading activities as their only chance of earning an independent income.

The only way people in the informal sector can compete with the new mass-produced goods and services is by seeking economies of scale themselves, going 'formal' in other words, and trying to fight the new traders on their own terms. But this means getting loans and advice, learning to handle figures, investing in transport, making contacts, signing contracts, doing deals – all activities women are less well equipped than men to do. And, inevitably, men are beginning to take over the only sector that, in some parts of the world, women can be said to control – joining forces with the new industries in a pincer movement to drive women traders out of business.

4. HEALTH

Birth and Death

The coffin, with its frail, precious contents, is light on the mens' shoulders as they carry it to the mound of fresh mud that marks the open grave. The headstone is old, the earlier inscriptions only just readable: 'Here lies Mary, treasured daughter, taken in her first year. Peter, a much-loved son, died, aged five, laid to rest in this grave. Nicolas, poor baby, born dead, never to open his eyes on this world.' Below these, the latest inscription is freshly etched, its light grey starkly cut into the dark mottled stone: 'Agnes Belinda Johnson, beloved wife of Samuel James Johnson, loving mother of Betty, Paul, Marjorie, Benjamin and John, died in childbirth aged thirty-four. May she rest in peace.'

The scene is Kentucky in the United States; the time is the mid-nineteenth century. But it might be now, anywhere in the poor world today. Over half a million women die in childbirth every year in Africa and Asia.[1] And the world total is probably very much higher. In Latin America, for instance, three out of every thousand mothers in Ecuador and up to twenty out of every thousand in Honduras die before they can look into their new baby's face or hold it in their arms.[2] And in almost all poor countries, according to the World Health Organisation (WHO), complications arising from pregnancy and childbirth are one of the five leading causes of death among women of childbearing age.[3]

Though thousands die, many millions survive and have to live on with the scars of a difficult pregnancy: displaced or weak wombs, cycles of debilitating infection, exhaustion, incontinence and bleeding. An estimated 25 million women a year are seriously ill after having their babies.[4] The worst problems are found in those countries in North Africa and the Middle East that practise the more drastic forms of female circumcision, where the vagina is sewn shut between pregnancies; and in those where abortion is illegal and contraception is not freely available. In Latin America, for example, complications following illegal abortion are the number one killer of women aged between fifteen and thirty-nine.[5]

Much of the danger and suffering surrounding and following childbirth could be avoided if women were examined early in their pregnancies to check for abnormalities, if they were attended at the time of the birth by trained midwives or doctors, if there were emergency health care at hand should something go wrong and if family-planning facilities were available to all women who want them. But the WHO estimates that 51 per cent of births are delivered by untrained traditional birth attendants,[6] and that two-thirds of women in the developing world have no access to a trained health worker.[7]

The dangers are increased by the weak state many women's bodies are in by the time they feel the first pains of labour: thin from lack of food, exhausted from work and the demands of previous pregnancies. Two-thirds of women in Asia, half of African women and a sixth of women in Latin America are anaemic,[8] proportions which increase markedly when they are pregnant, when two out of every three women in the poor world have the haemoglobin-starved blood of anaemia.[9]

These women are suffering from 'nutritional anaemia', caused simply by lack of the right kind of food. In India, for instance, though rich women eat around 2,500 calories a day and put on an average of 12.5 kilogrammes of weight during their pregnancies, poor women eat around 1,400 calories a day and gain only 1.5 kilogrammes during those crucial nine months.[10] And in Gambia one study found rural women in their last three months of pregnancy actually lost weight – an average of 1.4 kilogrammes each.[11]

TABLE 3: Food, Pregnancy and Infant Mortality

	FOOD	ANAEMIA	LOW BIRTH WEIGHT	INFANT MORTALITY
	(Production as % of requirements in 1981)	(% of pregnant women with anaemia)	(% babies born weighing under 2500gm)	(% of babies dying in first year of life 1982)
TANZANIA	83	59	13	10
BANGLADESH	84	66	50	13
ZAMBIA	93	60	14	11
MALI	72	50	13	13
INDIA	86	68	30	9
ZIMBABWE	90	27	15	8
PAKISTAN	106	65	27	12
INDONESIA	110	65	18	10
PERU	98	35	9	8
KENYA	88	48	18	8
PAPUA NEW GUINEA	92	55	25	10
EGYPT	116	75	14	10
COLOMBIA	108	22	10	5
PHILIPPINES	116	47	11	5
THAILAND	105	48	13	5

Source: World Development Report 1984, World Bank.
"Prevalence of Anaemia in Women in Developing Countries", World Health Organisation, Geneva 1979.
"The Incidence of Low Birth Weight: A Critical Review", World Health Organisation Quarterly, Volume 33, 1980.

Little wonder, then, that such women bear tiny, underweight babies. One-sixth of all babies weigh under 2,500 grammes[12] when they are born and 95 per cent of these take their first uncertain breaths in the poor world,[13] where they account for one-third of all infant deaths.[14] Some of these babies never draw breath at all. One study has indicated that only one in two pregnancies in Bangladesh culminates in a live, kicking baby.[15]

Not all women are pregnant at any given time, however. It has been estimated, for example, that only one in six women of childbearing age in the developing world is pregnant, and that proportion drops to one in seventeen in the rich world.[16] Nevertheless there is a tendency in health research to treat all women as though their bodies were little more than vehicles for procreation. This tendency is partly due to the scarcity of health statistics comparing men's and women's rates of illness. It may also be due to the problem the world in general has in seeing women in any role other than their childbearing and child-rearing one.

But the illnesses of the general population affect women too. At least one person in three harbours some species of parasitic worm;[17] one in twenty has bilharzia;[18] and malaria, once thought to be on the decline, has made a massive comeback to grip one person in six in the sweats and shudders of its fevers.[19] Taken together, infectious and parasitic diseases cause around 40 per cent of deaths in the poor world.[20] In the rich world, on the other hand, where hygiene and higher living standards make it harder for the poor world's plagues to survive, only 2 per cent of deaths are from these diseases[21] and half of the population dies of heart disease and one in five dies of cancer.[22]

Sickness in any country is bad enough. But in the poor world – where many families' livelihood is precariously supported only by constant hard work – a sudden acute bout of illness or a strength-sapping chronic disease can be disastrous. People with anaemia in Indonesia, for example, have been found to be 20 per cent less productive than healthy adults[23] and bilharzia's annual impact on the income of its victims has been estimated to total around $650 million.[24]

But not all sickness has a medical cause. Traffic accidents kill 250,000 each year;[25] accidents at work kill 100,000 and maim millions annually;[26] and at least 10,000 die and 500,000 are seriously poisoned every year by careless use of pesticides.[27] Some work hazards are likely to affect women more than men. Byssinosis, for instance, is an incurable lung disease caused by inhaling cotton fibres and thought to afflict one-quarter of India's textile workers, who are predominantly women.[28] Pesticide poisonings, too, may affect women more, since their agricultural work tends to bring them into closer contact with the crops. And in the electronics industry in South-East Asia, 25-year-old workers (almost all women) are called 'grannies' by their younger colleagues because they all have to wear glasses from damaging their eyes peering through microscopes assembling tiny silicon circuits.[29]

In fact, WHO reports that their commitment to the aims of the Decade for Women has led some governments to start sponsoring research and gathering statistics to discover more about women's particular vulnerability to certain diseases. Over a quarter of the seventy-six countries reporting to WHO now monitor all health statistics of men and women separately, and 54 per cent collect mortality and nutrition figures separately.[30] There is now more information available on the health of women than ever before, and some interesting findings are beginning to emerge.

One example is the figures on lung cancer. WHO estimates that smoking causes around one million deaths a year,[31] and tobacco consumption increased at a rate of between 4 and 13 per cent in the rich world and 33 per cent in the poor world between 1970 and 1980.[32] Once a habit indulged in largely by men, the recent increase in women smoking is now threatening, says WHO, to 'chip away at increased life expectancy for women'.[33]

Life expectancy statistics are perhaps the most poignant testimony of women's physical hardship in many countries. In the rich world women live, on average, six years longer than men.[34] The reasons for this are not clear. But it implies that, under appropriate conditions, women's natural lifespan is longer. It follows, then, that those countries where the gap in life expectancy between men and women is narrowest are those where life is especially arduous and dangerous for women and female children.

In some African countries, although life expectancy is very low for both men and women, women still tend to live longer, on average, than men – as one would expect given their naturally longer lifespan. But in parts of Asia (such as India, Pakistan, Bangladesh, Bhutan and Nepal), while life expectancy in general is slightly higher than in the poorest African countries, *women's* life expectancy is as low as, or even lower than, men's.[35]

Again, the exact reasons are unclear. Life expectancy figures are an average that include infant deaths as well as deaths of adults. But discrimination against females is undoubtedly the deep, underlying wound. When rumours of infanticide emerge – as they have done recently from India[36] and China[37] – it is always girl babies that are killed. A Bangladesh survey found more under-five-year-old girls than boys were malnourished because they were allocated smaller portions of food, and that infant girls were 21 per cent more likely than boys to die in their first year of life.[38] In Nepal the picture is similar with more malnourished under-five-year-old girls than boys and with women 50 per cent more likely than men to go blind as a result of chronic lack of food.[39] A survey in Botswana, too, found girls more likely than boys to be malnourished.[40] And in Turkey it is reported that rural men are given the lion's share of whatever food is available.[41] Other research shows that, in some countries, when girls fall ill they are less likely to be taken to the health centre than boys.[42] Add these factors to the strains of childbearing and it is not surprising that women's greater life expectancy has been eroded in many parts of the world.

Mental health

Discrimination against women clearly has tangible effects on their bodies. And it may have equally profound, but less tangible, effects on their minds. Statistics from all over the world indicate that women are twice as likely as men to suffer the kind of distress we know as mental illness.

In Bangladesh, for instance, women outnumber men among the mentally ill by two to one.[43] There are twice as many women as men diagnosed schizophrenic in Sweden.[44] In the UK 11 per cent of men and 17 per cent of women are hospitalised at some time in their lives for mental illness, and twice as many women as men take tranquillising drugs.[45] The same is true of the US, where twice as many women as men are hospitalised for depression, twice as many receive electroconvulsive therapy, and twice as many are on tranquillising drugs.[46]

Whether these figures are a real reflection of human psychological suffering or a result of a greater tendency for psychiatrists and doctors – usually men – to diagnose a distressed woman as being crazy is unclear. But, whichever way these statistics are interpreted, they reveal a particularly heavy burden of mental anguish carried by women. And many countries, such as Canada, are becoming increasingly concerned at the overprescribing of tranquillising drugs to women.[47]

Primary health care

The Decade for Women saw the launching of what WHO calls 'the most optimistic statement of purpose ever made by the world community'.[48] In September 1978, 134 nations met at Alma Ata in the USSR and pledged their support for a world-wide effort to bring 'health for all by the year 2000'. Primary health care was to be the key to the success of this effort. The member nations agreed that some of the world's worst health problems could be tackled not by training more doctors and equipping more hospitals, but by simple preventive methods and a selection of basic drugs.

The principles were simple enough. If 80 per cent of all illness in the world is caused by the lack of clean drinking water and sanitation, then improving water and sanitation would have to become a priority. With malnutrition affecting one in four people and making them more vulnerable to disease, basic nutrition would also have to be part of the package. On the medical front, a simple vaccination could prevent some of the commonest infectious diseases. And, where drugs were not enough, an army of primary health-care workers – trained in the principles of prevention as well as cure – could help motivate people to change their habits and make their communities safer places in which to live.[49]

The commitment to primary health care has important and far-reaching implications for the health of less-advantaged people generally and for women in particular. It plays a spotlight on the causes of disease and it picks out women, centre-stage, as bearing the brunt of responsibility for their families' health.

Suddenly the eyes of health planners have begun to turn towards women: as cooks and feeders of children: as fetchers of water and firewood; as custodians of cleanliness and hygiene; as teachers of healthy habits; as people who bear babies, who breast-feed and wean them; who care for the sick, the disabled and the old – in other words as a vital resource on whom the world's health depends and whose own health, therefore, needs preserving above all.

'Women are the vast untapped resource for development,' declared WHO in 1980. 'The anchor of our strategies for health development should relate to all-round improvement in the status of women and children who form the majority of any population.'[50]

Forty-eight out of seventy countries reporting to WHO in 1983 have now formulated a national primary health care policy and a further eight are putting their emphasis on rural areas.[51] The effects of this shift of emphasis from expensive curative hospital medicine for the few to less costly preventive measures for the many – some for all instead of all for some – have been dramatic.

Nutrition

The United Nations Children's Fund (UNICEF) estimates that 200 million under-fives are malnourished, 10 million of these so severely that they risk death.[52] Other statistics show that a bottle-fed infant is up to five times more likely to die – of malnutrition, infection or both – than a baby fed on breast milk.[53] And a survey in the Philippines found that 60 per cent of mothers with malnourished children had no idea there was anything wrong with them because their chronic lack of food was making the children stunted rather than making them thin.[54] Facts like these demonstrate the potential of helping women feed their children better.

Fifty countries have now begun nutrition programmes, and twenty-five of these have developed them especially for women.[55] In the Ivory Coast, for example, research has been conducted into locally-grown food to develop a nutritious diet that the poorest family can afford.[56] In the Virgin Islands pregnant women and malnourished children are provided with margarine, wheat-flour and dried milk powder to supplement their diets.[57] And the importance of extra food like this has been demonstrated in Guatemala, where one project giving supplementary food to pregnant women reduced the incidence of low birth weight among babies by 75 per cent.[58] In fact eleven governments report that they now have food subsidy programmes to keep the price of staples within reach of the poor.[59]

Water and sanitation

The Decade for Women saw the launch of another major worldwide initiative: the International Drinking Water Supply and Sanitation Decade in November 1980. The aims of the Decade are to install enough pit latrines and standpipes in rural areas and individual taps and sewerage systems in cities to give everyone access to clean water and safe disposal of waste by 1990. It is a daunting task. WHO estimates that, in the developing world (excluding China), 25 per cent of people in cities and 71 per cent of those in the countryside are without safe water to drink and 47 per cent of town-dwellers and 87 per cent of people in rural areas have no adequate sanitation.[60]

The consequences of being without these basic amenities are ill health for all and great hardship for women, who often have to walk long distances to fetch water. A person needs around 5 litres of water a day for cooking and drinking, and a further 25 to 45 litres to stay clean and healthy.[61] But the most a woman can carry in comfort

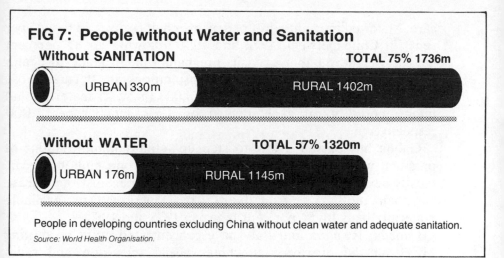

FIG 7: People without Water and Sanitation

Without SANITATION — TOTAL 75% 1736m

URBAN 330m — RURAL 1402m

Without WATER — TOTAL 57% 1320m

URBAN 176m — RURAL 1145m

People in developing countries excluding China without clean water and adequate sanitation.
Source: World Health Organisation.

is 15 litres. Even if she lives near a standpipe, that means about fifteen journeys a day with a full bucket.

But some women live so far from the nearest water source that they only have time to make one journey a day. In Burkina Faso, for example, some women leave at dusk to walk to the water hole, sleep there over night, and return at dawn to escape the harsh rays of the sun. Small wonder that an estimated 8 million children die each year of diseases that might have been prevented by sufficient clean water from a nearby tap.[62]

Now some twenty-six countries are making a special effort to look into women's particular needs in their attempts to meet the targets of the Water Decade.[63]

Maternal and child health

A major advance for women, arising from the new emphasis on primary health care in many countries, is the increasing attention paid to providing better care for pregnant mothers and their babies. Maternal and child health (or MCH, as this aspect of primary health care is called) involves pre-natal check-ups, immunisation and advice on child-care, breastfeeding and weaning foods. Forty-two governments reported that they have expanded their MCH activities during the Decade, with Senegal actually restructuring its entire Ministry of Health to incorporate this new commitment.[64]

Proponents of MCH in the US have estimated that 2.7 million dollars spent on pre-natal services would save between 10 and 12 million dollars currently spent keeping premature, low birth-weight babies alive in intensive care units.[65] And governments as different as Portugal and Chile have seen the benefits of investing in pre-natal care. Maternal mortality dropped by over half (from 1.63 to 0.65 per cent) in Chile between 1972 and 1981 following an 81 per cent increase in the number of visits pregnant women made to health workers.[66] And when pre-natal consultations in Portugal rose eightfold (from 19,000 in 1975 to 150,000 in 1982) maternal and infant mortality rates plummeted by 12.9 and 12 per 1,000 respectively.[67]

Gabon has passed a law to step up tetanus immunisations of pregnant women.[8] Tetanus kills an estimated one million a year, mostly newborn babies who can be immunised against the disease via their mothers.[69] And Ivory Coast increased its available maternity beds by 54 per cent between 1975 and 1980.[70]

Canada, Rwanda and Italy have concentrated more on putting MCH on the airways, launching special television and radio campaigns on subjects like contraception, pregnancy and sexually transmitted diseases. A follow-up study in Italy discovered that 73 per cent of women questioned remembered something from the campaign in that country.[71]

There has also been more attention paid to screening whole populations of women to pick up diseases in their early stages. Nine countries have introduced such screening procedures, including the USSR, which has established a twice-yearly medical check-up for women at their workplace.[72] And in China deaths from cervical cancer dropped from 111 to 8 per 10,000 following the introduction of screening.[73]

Women as health workers

It is not only as recipients of health care that women have benefited in recent years. As providers, too, their traditional contribution is at last beginning to be recognised. As part of their normal domestic role women everywhere do, as WHO acknowledges, provide more health care than all the world's health services put together.[74] And, in the majority of societies with no regular access to modern medical facilities, it is women who often emerge as especially committed and skilled to become the village healer or midwife – the *dai* in India, the *hilot* in the Philippines, the *panbolan* in Thailand. Sierra Leone's 13,600 traditional midwives, for example, deliver 70 per cent of births; and 80 per cent of births in Honduras are delivered by such women.[75]

In the past these women have found themselves in opposition to, and excluded from, modern medical advances, looked down on as dangerous and ignorant quacks by the (largely male) medical profession. In the not-so-distant past, they were even burnt in Europe as witches. With the advent of primary health care, however, such women's skills have at last begun to be appreciated and, instead of being fought against or ignored, these women are now being trained all over the world in the principles of primary health care. In 1972 only 37 per cent of developing countries reporting to WHO had launched training programmes. By 1982, 82 per cent had done so.[76]

India had trained a quarter of a million *dais* by 1981. Nicaragua has been training them at a rate of 900 a year.[77] By 1978 Ethiopia had trained 45 per cent of traditional midwives; in Ghana and Sri Lanka the totals were 25 and 95 per cent respectively by 1976.[78] By 1976 Thailand had trained 26 per cent, Indonesia 15 per cent and Ghana 25 per cent. And the numbers are growing all the time.[79]

Costing less than 2 per cent of the money it takes to train a doctor, the logic is clear. The benefits are clear too. In one part of India, for instance, deaths for neo-natal tetanus were reduced from 90 to 10 per 100,000 in the three years following the launch of the *dai* training programme there.[80]

But indigenous *dais* and *hilots* are not the only women in the front line of providing primary health care. Women often comprise the majority of the new village health workers too – barefoot doctors, as they have come to be known. And, as the majority of primary school teachers, women teach about health in schools as well. And overwhelmingly it is women who are nurses – often the first step in the referral chain linking village health worker to hospital. In fact nurses outnumber doctors in developing countries by roughly ten to one[81] and are much more likely to be stationed in rural areas.

Resistance from doctors

But here their involvement stops. In the higher ranks of the health services – among the doctors, the health ministry officials, the hospital administrators – where the high pay and the power reside, women are grossly under-represented. Yet this is where the policy decisions get taken, and where the money is distributed from – and that money tends to stay just where it is. Three-quarters of the world's health problems could be solved by primary health care. But three-quarters of developing countries' health budgets are spent on doctors and hospitals.[82] In Ghana, for instance, hospitals serving just 10 per cent of the population gobble up 90 per cent of the country's health budget.[83] In Latin America 200,000 new doctors will don their white coats and pick up their stethoscopes in the next five years, many more than are needed, while the real requirement is for one million primary health care workers in the villages.[84] In Bangladesh there are plans for a new cancer research institute in Dacca, while 76 million people are without any health care at all.

As a primary health care proponent in Bangladesh commented to WHO: 'There is a limited appreciation of the role of primary health care in the higher curative echelons.'[85] From India the comment was more outspoken: 'Doctors' inability to understand the importance of prevention, and hence their lack of interest in the various health programmes, is, to a very large extent, responsible for the inadequacy of the rural services.'[86]

Yet WHO estimates that an extra $50 billion annually until the year 2000 would bring primary health care to all – that's just two-thirds of what the world spends each year on cigarettes.[87] Dr Mahler, Director-General of WHO, sums up the situation succinctly: 'In theory you can do primary health care in spite of doctors. In reality, if they decide to fight primary health care, I think, on the whole, they will win.'[88]

5. SEX

In the beginning

India is the birthplace of the *Kama Sutra*, that erotic love manual with sex positions described in detail and intercourse prescribed as lengthy. It is the place where temple carvings portray humans and animals indulging in every kind of sexual act. India is also the place where hardly a day passes without a young bride being burned alive because her in-laws are not satisfied with the dowry she brought to her marriage.

Greece is where, in ancient times, the love goddess Venus cast her spells on the human race from towering Mount Olympus. It is also where a young woman's virginity must be preserved until marriage and where shame and censure rain down on an unmarried mother.

In the United Kingdom every city boasts its strip clubs, every news-stand its rack of 'girlie' magazines, every chemist its discreet stock of contraceptives. Here is where a lesbian mother must fight in the courts for the right to raise her own child.

Sex is a tangled web, snarled and knotted with the threads of religion, economics and history, interwoven with the bonds of love and marriage. To understand the place of sex in society today means trying to untangle that web, to examine each thread separately.

Beginning where all threads begin takes the search for understanding back into the depths of prehistory. Here the only traces of evidence are fossilised bones and the remains of rough stone tools. There are no writings or inscriptions to tell us whether men and women were married, whether incest or homosexuality were forbidden, whether virginity was prized or dowries paid. So piecing together the fragments of our prehistoric sexual past is more a question of framing a feasible hypothesis than of poring over ancient remains. And logic may be a better tool for the task than an archaeologist's pick and shovel.

Prehistoric sex

Logic suggests that studying our closest biological relatives (other primates, like monkeys and chimpanzees) may yield some clues to the nature of sex between the first human beings. Primates – like early humans – have a complex social life, but no organised economy and no ceremonies of birth, marriage or death. They grow nothing, harvest nothing, own nothing, sell nothing. They are the nearest example available of what pre-cultural humanity might have been like.

Recent studies of primates indicate that previous interpretations of primate societies – in which adult males are portrayed as dominant over a submissive harem of females – have wrongly projected the prevailing sexual inequality between *human* males and females on to our primate relatives. On the contrary, female apes and monkeys have now been discovered to occupy the central position in their societies, supported, in a complex matriarchy of mothers, aunts, grandmothers and sisters, by their alliances with their male and female offspring.[1]

In fact adult males tend to be relegated to the periphery of this close-knit group of females and infants, their relative isolation being more an indication of their exclusion from the group rather than their dominance over it. And it is females who are the initiators of sex, not males. Far from being the sexual despots portrayed by primatologists of the past, recent research reveals that males must wait patiently until females have weaned their latest infant and are eager to have sex again. What is more, a female may initiate intercourse with a variety of males while she is in oestrus, thus dispelling once and for all the myth of the passive primate harem, exclusive sexual property of a single promiscuous dominant male.

Great caution is needed when generalising from animal studies to humans, because such generalisations have often been used to create a genetically and biologically determined view of human beings which – ignoring human subtlety and complexity and, more importantly, humans' highly developed control over the biological side of their nature – justifies every ugly sort of racism, sexism and classism in society.

Bearing this in mind, it is possible to venture a hypothesis about what sex might have been like for the early human woman in a pre-patriarchal epoch. Since sex would have been initiated by her, with a man (or woman) of her choice who had no ultimate economic or physical power over her, and since sex was not yet understood to be linked with pregnancy and childbirth, it seems reasonable to suppose that sex would probably not have occurred at all were it not a pleasurable experience *for women*.

If these conjectures, backed by evidence from contemporary primate societies, are correct, it would appear that woman's power in early human societies would have resided largely in her alliance with her children, an alliance which, by sheer weight of numbers, countered man's greater physical strength. Extending this logic, it seems clear that a man's main hope of increasing his power would have been to undermine this close network of women and children and, by dividing, rule them.

Marriage

The discovery of man's role in procreation gave him the lever he needed to wrest woman's power away from her. And marriage is the weight he has used to lean on that lever and force a rift in the alliance between woman and her children. On the surface marriage appears to be the way in which men ally themselves with women. But a closer analysis reveals that marriage is also the means by which a man cements an alliance with, and gains power over, a woman's children.

Two vital rules allow the institution of marriage to sever the link between woman and her children and create a new link between those children and man. These two rules – common to marriage in every country of the world – are fidelity and inheritance. A woman's fidelity is the only way a man can ensure that the children she bears are the result of intercourse with him. That it is *woman's* fidelity rather than man's that is crucial is demonstrated by the many ways in which a married woman must signal that she is attached to her husband: the red tikka on her forehead, the ring on her finger, the changing of her name to his. The children of the marriage bear the man's name too in the vast majority of countries, as a tangible way for them to recognise their link with their father.

The alliance is finally sealed by inheritance. In previous sections of this Report, governments summing up progress towards equality between men and women during the Decade have admitted that the laws of marriage and inheritance are usually superimposed on laws allowing women equal access to land and income, tending to pass control of whatever wealth a woman manages to amass into the hands of her husband.[2] He can then use that wealth to purchase the loyalty of his children (his male children in particular), prising them away from their infant closeness to their mother.

The marriage contract secures for a man control of the wealth accrued through the labour of his wife and children and of wealth amassed previously via inheritance. And the terms of the contract are made clear by the various economic exchanges that take place between a husband and wife's respective families at the time of the marriage. In both cases it is the children as well as the wife who are bartered and the man who profits most from the exchanges.

The economic underpinnings of marriage and its function – historically as well as in the present, in many countries – to give men control over children are illustrated by the large numbers of women who are divorced by their husbands for failing to bear any children at all or for bearing only girls. Another, more dramatic, illustration is found in India, where in-laws dissatisfied with their side of the marriage – the dowry – pour petrol over the new wife and burn her to death.[3]

Religion and morality

When man's role in procreation was realised, and his control of it enshrined in the marriage contract, woman's previous role in religious ceremonies began gradually to be destroyed too. Today's major religions are controlled almost exclusively by men.

Christianity and Islam – the two biggest world religions, which together inform the spiritual and moral lives of half of the world's people[4] – both have a ruling male deity (God the Father and Allah), male prophets (Jesus the Son, John the Baptist, Mohammed) and male priests. Women are denied a place in the priesthood and often excluded from the mosque. In the other two major religions – Hinduism and Buddhism, to which another quarter of the world's people adhere[5] – there is not a single mighty masculine ruling deity. But women are still denied a place in the priesthood and may even have to be reincarnated as men before being considered fit to achieve ultimate spiritual fulfilment.

The way all the great world religions interlock so neatly with men's control over women and children is echoed again and again in religious practices all over the world: the veiling of Christian nuns and widows and the veiling of Islamic women in the *chador*; the denial of sexual pleasure and the substitution of sexual shame; the establishment of marriage as a moral institution. Some religions even try to undermine woman's power over childbirth, insisting (as in Christianity, for instance) on baptism as a symbolic 'rebirth in God the Father', or (in Hinduism and Islam) on a ritual cleansing of the 'polluting' results of menstruation and childbirth.

Virginity, circumcision and shame

Religion and marriage together combine to remove woman's power to decide when, whether and with whom she will have sex, and what form that sex will take. In many countries a woman is expected to remain a virgin before marriage, and after marriage she is expected to have sex only with her husband. Only by these means can a man ensure that a woman's children belong to him alone.

Female circumcision is the most extreme way of ensuring virginity and fidelity. But there are many others – guilt, honour, shame, for instance – all of which have the backing of male-controlled religion to ensure that women adhere to the terms of the marriage contract.

There are two major types of female circumcision. Its milder form – *sunna* – practised in twenty countries, mostly in East, West and Central Africa,[6] is 'excision', where all or part of the clitoris, and sometimes the internal vaginal lips, are removed. In the second, more radical, type of operation – 'Phaoronic circumcision' – all of the external genitalia are removed and the outer vaginal lips sewn shut ('infibulation'), leaving just a tiny opening through which urine and menstrual blood can pass. In Mali, Sudan and Somalia the majority of women are infibulated.[7] In fact at least 74 million woman and girl-children are circumcised in Africa alone – and that total does not include Chad, Niger, Togo, Benin, Tanzania, Zaire, the Arab Peninsular, or the Muslim countries of Asia, where substantial numbers of women are circumcised.[8]

Though it has become closely associated with the Islamic religion, and spread to Malaysia and Indonesia along with the expansion of Islam into Asia, female circumcision dates back over 2,000 years, to before the birth of Islam.[9] And in many Muslim countries (Pakistan, Iran, and Saudi Arabia, for instance) the practice is almost unknown. In fact, female circumcision has occurred at some time in every continent of the world, sometimes quite independently of its link with Islam.[10]

As recently as the 1930s, for example, female circumcision has been recorded in India, Australia, Mexico, Peru and Brazil.[11] In Russia, one Christian sect quoted St Matthew's gospel as their justification for the practice: 'There be eunuchs that are have made themselves eunuchs for the kingdom of heaven's sake.'[12] In late nineteenth-century Europe too, and up to 1937 in the US, circumcision was regularly used by doctors to 'treat' nymphomania and masturbation and prevent hysteria.[13] In the words of one proponent: 'The patient becomes tractable, orderly, industrious and cleanly'[14] – the perfect wife and mother.

The aim of the operation (and of that part of religious morality that tends to uphold it and other less drastic restrictions of woman's sexual pleasure) is to ensure that sex, for women at least, is linked with procreation, not enjoyment. If women enjoyed sex they might be tempted to have intercourse outside the marriage contract, thereby undermining a husband's control over her children. The

Roman Catholic Church's refusal to permit birth control appears to be grounded in precisely this fundamental aim and demonstrates again how male-controlled religion upholds a man's control over his wife. The Pope's declaration on the subject, *Humanae Vitae*, requires 'that each and every marriage act must remain open to the transmission of life'.[15]

The power to say 'no'

Insisting on virginity and fidelity prevents women from saying 'yes' to sex with anyone other than her husband. But there are many additional pressures that prevent her from saying 'no' to him too.

Arranged marriages, for example, are usually contracted between a young teenager and an older man. In many countries the majority of women are married while still in their teens. In the Indian subcontinent and in Africa, for instance, 58 and 50 per cent of women respectively are married before their twentieth birthdays.[16] In fact all over the world the custom is for women to marry men who are older – and therefore more experienced, usually more educated and more dominant – than themselves.

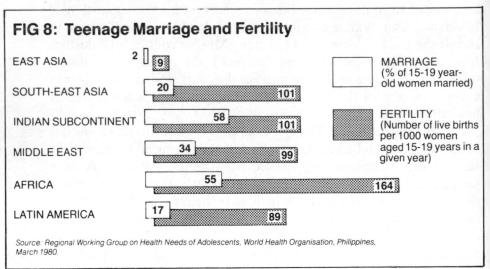

FIG 8: Teenage Marriage and Fertility

	MARRIAGE (% of 15-19 year-old women married)	FERTILITY (Number of live births per 1000 women aged 15-19 years in a given year)
EAST ASIA	2	9
SOUTH-EAST ASIA	20	101
INDIAN SUBCONTINENT	58	101
MIDDLE EAST	34	99
AFRICA	55	164
LATIN AMERICA	17	89

Source: Regional Working Group on Health Needs of Adolescents, World Health Organisation, Philippines, March 1980.

Another factor that undermines a wife's ability to refuse to have sex with her husband is the 'patrilocal' custom of many countries, where a wife leaves her own family and moves in with her husband's family. Cut off from all sources of support, the new wife becomes the most inferior person in her new home – until she bears a son.

Even in countries where a married woman is able to choose her husband and lives alone with him away from her in-laws, the laws of marriage make it almost impossible for a wife to prosecute her husband for rape. But it is not only married women who are unable to refuse their husbands. Unmarried women, too, often find themselves unable to refuse a *potential* husband. Caught in the trap between the fear that a man will not be interested in her if she does *not* offer sex, and the fear that he will lose interest if she does (thereby relinquishing her bargaining card of virginity), many young teenagers take the risk and have sex before they feel they are ready.

The physical consequences of a young woman's restricted ability to say 'no' to sex are well-documented. In a world where only three-fifths of under-fifteen-year-olds and half of fifteen- to nineteen-year-olds have access to sex education or contraception,[17] only an estimated one in three teenagers who are having regular sex are using contraception.[18] The result is pregnancy: often unwanted and, particularly among lower age groups, positively dangerous.

Adolescent pregnancy is associated with anaemia, retarded foetal growth, premature labour, underweight babies and complicated births.[19] In the Dominican Republic, for instance, teenage mothers are nearly three times as likely to die in childbirth as mothers aged between twenty and twenty-four.[20] In Japan, too, teenage mothers are over twice as likely to die in labour as their older sisters.[21] There are dangers for the baby as well. Babies born to teenage mothers are around 50 per cent more likely to die in their first year of life in Bangladesh, Indonesia and Mexico than those born to older mothers.[22]

But not all young mothers go through with their pregnancies. In the US, for instance, where two-thirds of teenage pregnancies are

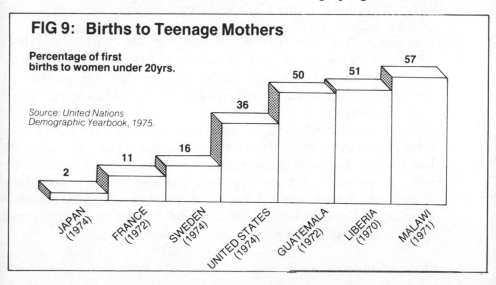

FIG 9: Births to Teenage Mothers

Percentage of first
births to women under 20yrs.

Source: United Nations
Demographic Yearbook, 1975.

2	11	16	36	50	51	57
JAPAN (1974)	FRANCE (1972)	SWEDEN (1974)	UNITED STATES (1974)	GUATEMALA (1972)	LIBERIA (1970)	MALAWI (1971)

unintended,[23] one-third of all abortions are to teenage mothers.[24] In Sweden, too, 63 per cent of pregnancies among fifteen- to seventeen-year-olds and 37 per cent of those among eighteen- to nineteen-year-olds end in abortion.[25] And there is evidence that teenage abortions are more hazardous than those performed on older women because teenagers tend to put off going to their doctors for longer. In England and Wales, for example, more than one in four pregnant teenagers wanting an abortion did not visit their doctor until after three months of pregnancy, when the risks to health are much greater.[26]

Related to women's inability to refuse to have sex entirely is their lack of control over the *type* of sex they have. Obviously it is sex with penetration and ejaculation that leads to pregnancy and abortion. A woman using contraception can usually avoid these consequences (leaving aside the health hazards of many forms of contraception), but other consequences of this type of sexual practice are often unavoidable for the woman who feels unable to refuse to have sex with her partner.

Twenty different kinds of venereal disease have now been identified.[27] For men the consequences of such infections tend to be (with the exception of syphilis) relatively fleeting – pain and embarrassment at worst. But for women the consequences can blight their whole lives. Between 12 and 20 per cent of untreated cases of gonorrhea and a similar proportion of chlamydia infections cause a condition called 'pelvic inflammatory disease',[28] which in turn increases by tenfold the chances of an ectopic pregnancy [39] and, in a substantial number of cases, can cause infertility.[30] An estimated one in ten couples in the US in 1976 were found to be involuntarily infertile largely because of pelvic inflammatory disease – and the figures are similar in the UK. In fact the WHO estimates that, worldwide, as many as one in twenty couples are involuntarily infertile.[31] Another serious, sometimes fatal, consequence of penetrative sex is cervical cancer – a disease almost unknown among celibate women.

These tangible physical consequences of a woman's inability to refuse a particular form of sex and to have that refusal respected are bad enough. But even if a woman escapes these, she must still cope with the mental consequences – fear, shame, guilt, self-loathing – that her acquiescence brings and which arise from society's demand that she bears the entire moral burden of woman's *and* man's sexual behaviour on her shoulders alone.

Pleasure and orgasm

It would be surprising, given these restrictions on a woman's freedom to initiate or refuse sex, or to control the type of sexual activity she and her partner engage in, if sex were a joyous and pleasurable experience for women. And, sadly, the figures for the sexual pleasure of *uncircumcised* women in the rich world may be lower than figures for circumcised women in the Arab world.

Kinsey's landmark research on North American women in 1953, for instance, indicated that only between 70 and 77 per cent of women have ever experienced orgasm at all – either by masturbation or during intercourse.[32] In contrast, a major study of 4,024 Sudanese women found that 88 per cent of women who had the *sunna* type of circumcision operation, where the clitoris is removed, had experienced orgasm.[33] In a smaller study of 651 Egyptian women the figures were lower (with only 41 per cent of circumcised women experiencing orgasm)[34] but reports of that research did not differentiate between the type of circumcision operation the women had, so may have included women who had been infibulated too. The Sudan research discovered that only 20 per cent of infibulated women had ever experienced orgasm, and the majority had not even heard that such a thing was possible.

It is tempting to dismiss Kinsey's 1953 figures as having little relevance to today's post-sexual-revolutionary society. But a recent study in Denmark in 1981 (the country where the sexual revolution is reputed to have originated) reveals that only 47 per cent of Danish women have ever masturbated to orgasm at all.[35]

Not surprisingly, half the women questioned in research conducted in Somalia, where the majority of women are circumcised, said they disliked intercourse, while half the men said they had no idea whether their wives enjoyed it or not.[36] And this disregard for women's sexual pleasure is echoed in reports from all over the world. 'The man wants sex and the children come,' complain women in Sri Lanka.[37] 'Sex is for the men to enjoy,' agree women in Bangladesh. 'We ourselves do not get much pleasure from it.' And their men admit: 'A man is like thirst and a woman like a river. Whenever a man is thirsty he has to go to the river to quench his thirst. For us sex is a matter of only five minutes. We go wha-amm and it's finished.'[38]

In the UK, too, the same echoes bounce back from the caves of intimacy. A recent study of 10,000 women found that 36 per cent 'rarely' or 'never' experienced orgasm during intercourse and most admitted faking it to please their husbands.[39] Even more revealing, perhaps, is Kinsey's additional finding that unmarried men masturbate twice as often as married men, whereas marriage makes no difference at all to the frequency of women taking their solitary pleasure.[40]

The physical sensations of normal, male-controlled, penetrative sexual intercourse (which give a man the perfect moist sensual environment for his penis, while a woman's clitoris must snatch at what pleasure it can from crude, dry, pelvic bumping and grinding) are a major reason why so many women get so little pleasure from sex. But another is the ambivalence they carry with them into the bedroom. Kinsey found, for example, that religious beliefs had little or no effect on a man's sexual pleasure, but could slice as powerfully as the circumcision knife into a woman's enjoyment, undermining with guilt and shame any pleasure she might otherwise experience.[41]

Prostitution

When women get so little pleasure from it, sex becomes simply a service which, along with the work involved in childrearing, married women are expected to provide free. Seeking pleasure in sex might be shameful to many women. But actually demanding payment for these services is even more shameful. Yet prostitution is not, in itself, any more degrading than any other work. Neither is the related occupation of surrogate motherhood. What the prostitute and the surrogate mother have in common – the characteristic that actually defines their shame – is the fact that they are not the sexual property of just one man. They are offering an independent service to any man who wishes to avail himself of it. At the cost of social censure, they receive an income for services that their married sisters are providing free.

A group of militant French prostitutes have argued that what is shameful about their occupation is not its moral status, but the fact that it is almost invariably the occupation of poor women.[42] This is true in Paris; and in the UK, where the Yorkshire Ripper's prostitute victims were all poor working-class women;[43] and in Thailand where 1 per cent of the entire population gets some income from prostitution, and where 96 per cent of Bangkok's prostitutes come from the north and the north-east, the two poorest parts of the country;[44] and in India, where interviews with some of Calcutta's 10,000 prostitutes reveal that it is an occupation of last-resort for women unable to get any other job.[45]

The close link between paid and unpaid prostitution is made very clear by the new sex-tourism packages offered by some holiday agencies in West Germany, Holland, Japan, Singapore and Hong Kong, agencies which double as marriage bureaux. For an all-in price a man can buy a holiday in Thailand and a beautiful young Thai wife. An estimated 2,000 Thai women travel to Bonn as wives each year and, by the same time the following year, 1,000 of these have ended up working as prostitutes in the Bonn red-light district.[46]

Romance and love

A large number of women are prostitutes. But a much larger number continue to provide sexual and domestic services free of charge to their husbands. Sheer social and economic powerlessness are major pressures forcing women to accept the terms of the marriage contract. But romance and love disguise these unequal terms with flowers and lace.

The lovelorn young girl is induced to believe that, through marriage, she will live happily ever after; the frustrated wife is induced to overlook the reality of her subservience to her husband – by the bouquets, candle-light and pent-up passion of a powerful and pervasive romance industry.

The most famous international publishers of romantic fiction are UK-based Mills and Boon, with 1,500 titles on their list, each of which sells between 80,000 and 100,000 copies apiece.[47] They have been translated into Spanish, French, Dutch, German and even Tagalog and Bahasa Indonesian. In Malaysia fifteen Mills and Boon titles are published each month, around eight of which climb straight into the country's best-seller list.[48] And the plots are always the same. As Barbara Cartland (perhaps the world's leading romantic fiction writer and author of 300 novels) says herself: 'All my heroines are good, pure and very, very womanly, tender and sweet. All my heroes are sporting and very, very dominating, but honourable, because that is what a woman wants.'[49]

In most countries – with the possible exception of the UK – the typical television soap opera is modelled on those produced in that Mecca of soap, the US. And the plots underlying the soap bubbles could have been written by Ms Cartland herself, with the feminine woman netting the masculine hunk while the dominant, sexually voracious woman finds her prey eluding her every time. And, just as written romance is oozing, sticky and sweet, into the poor world, so the rich world's appetite for film romance is catching on too. An estimated 71 per cent of television programmes in the developing countries are imports from the rich world, and US-produced soap operas are by far the hottest properties.[50]

Women's magazines and advertising add the finishing touches, entangling the tender allure of romantic love inextricably with the athletic exotica of penetrative sex and the mundane demands of a woman's domestic duties. As Christian Dior explains, with disarming candour: 'Properly manipulated, housewives can be given the sense of identity, creativity, the self-realisation – even the sexual joy – they lack, by buying things.'[51]

Rape and incest

Romance and love are offered to women in exchange for wifely services. But vital to the package – and perhaps the element that makes it so appealing – is the image of women as weak, fragile flowers being plucked and protected by powerful men. The implicit bargain between him and her is: 'If you will love me and only me forever, I will protect you from harm and hunger and make you happy.'

Unfortunately, many men fail to honour their side of this bargain. And this is why romance is really nothing more than the acceptable face of pornography, in the sense that, just like its uglier *doppelganger*, it justifies and enhances men's power over women. Because, far from protecting women from harm, marriage often makes women *more* vulnerable to male violence – from their husbands.

One quarter of violent crime in the US, for instance, is wife assault.[52] And these are just the cases that are reported. Many more women keep quiet out of loyalty or fear, backed by the knowledge that the authorities are usually unwilling to intervene in 'domestic disputes'. As a result, secret refuges for wives fleeing from violent husbands can be found in countries as different as Norway, India, Thailand and the UK.

But bruises, black eyes and broken ribs are not the only injuries husbands inflict – often without punishment – on their wives. One UK study found one in seven wives had been raped by their husbands.[53] Unfortunately the marriage contract so legitimises a man's sexual demands that it is only recently that the offence has been considered a crime at all.

Nevertheless rape in marriage is now illegal in some countries: in the Soviet Union (since 1960), Czechoslovakia (since 1950), Poland (since 1932), Denmark (since 1960,) Sweden (since 1965), Scotland (since 1982) and Canada (since 1983), for instance.[54] But what evidence there is implies that it is notoriously difficult to prove in court. In Australia, for example, a husband can only be convicted if he commits some violence to his wife in addition to the rape.[55] And it was not until 1979 that a woman won a rape prosecution against her husband in the US.[56]

But it is not only wives who are raped. Daughters, too, also fall victim to the sexual violence of the man in the house. Research in countries as far apart as Australia, the US, Egypt, Israel and India indicate that as many as one in four families is incestuous. And, in the vast majority of cases – between 80 and 90 per cent – it is girls being sexually used by their male relatives, usually their fathers.[57]

In Cairo, for instance, a 1973 study found between 33 and 45 per cent of families contained daughters who had been raped, molested or 'interfered with' by a relative or close family friend.[58] Kinsey's study in the US found incest in 24 per cent of families,[59] and the figures are similar in Australia and the UK.[60] Two-thirds of Israeli victims were less than ten years old,[61] one in sixteen of victims in an Indian survey were aged between six months and six years,[62] and a quarter of US victims were aged under five.[63] Extending these figures to the rest of the world implies that as many as 100 million young girls may be being raped by adult men – usually their fathers – often day after day, week after week, year in, year out.

Part of the shock that attaches to facts like these comes from the betrayal of trust, the abuse of power, that they imply. The young Muslim girl must wear the *chador* outside the house to protect her from the lustful eyes of a stranger. Young Christian girls are warned against accepting sweets from a man they don't know. And women all over the world are fearful of walking the streets late at night for fear of a rapist lurking in the shadows.

But the real dangers can often lie *inside* the house. Just as wives and daughters are abused by the men to whom they are closest, so rapes outside the family circle are overwhelmingly committed by men who are known to the victim. A study of 1,236 London women, for instance, discovered that one in six had been raped, one in five had fought off an attempted rape, and that half of the assaults had occurred either in the house of the woman herself or in that of her assailant.[64]

Pornography

It has been said that 'if rape is practice, pornography is theory'. And indeed the content of most pornography bears out this assertion. Pornography is the mirror image of romance. In romance a man is strong and protective, a woman is soft and pure. In pornography a man is strong and rampant, a woman is soft and impure. Romance therefore gives women a sense of security; pornography gives men a sense of virility. The end result: a woman full of trust and a man full of lust.

The pornography industry generates an estimated seven billion dollars every year – more than the giant film and music industries put together.[65] Pornographic films outnumber other films by three to one and gross around $365 million a year in the US alone.[66] That's a million dollars a day. And the pornographic magazine market is even more lucrative. In the US, for instance, a total of 165 different magazines are bought by an estimated 18 million men each month, generating approximately half a billion dollars a year.[67]

But it is not only men who are influenced by this megatrade in sweat and saliva, leather and lingerie. So powerful is pornography, and so smoothly does it blend in with the advertising of products for men, that many women find their own sexual fantasies and self-images distorted too. Romantic fiction is seldom sexually explicit, tending to fade out in a tantalising row of dots when two lovers touch lips for the first time. This leaves the sexual stage vacant, and pornographic images are free to take a starring role. The two leading actors on this stage are the sadist, played by man, and the masochist, played by woman. She enjoys rough sex (though she may complain at the time), relishes a bit of pain, likes it quick, prefers penetration, is crazy for all the things he likes best.

If, as feminist theorist Shulamith Firestone argues, eroticism can be defined as the sensual pleasure that arises out of intimacy, closeness and trust,[68] then pornography – in focusing on distance and strangeness, on appearance and performance – is profoundly anti-erotic. And it cheats both men and women of the chance of exploring their own free sexual expression.

The sexual revolution

Contraception, in breaking the link between sex and babies – backed by the growing pornography, romance and advertising industries – has brought about a sexual revolution in the rich world that is beginning to spread to the developing countries too. In the US, for instance, only 27 per cent of teenagers had had sex in 1971. But by 1976 that total had risen to 35 per cent.[69] In Japan too, the numbers of sixteen- to twenty-one-year-olds who had sex increased by 15 per cent for boys and 7 per cent for girls between 1960 and 1974.[70]

In fact the WHO has identified three sets of social phenomena –

sexual-moral syndromes – in different countries of the world, each associated with a particular phase of socio-economic development and industrialisation. The first is the traditional subsistence society, where women marry very young, bear many children, where sex outside marriage is rare, and where many women take recourse to unsafe abortion as a form of family planning. The second is the modern industrial society, where marriage is late, sex before marriage is rife, women have very few children, contraception and abortion are common. The third pattern is the society in rapid transition between the traditional and the modern, a pattern found in many of the urban areas of the developing world.[71]

The modern sex industry trio – pornography, advertising and romance – all express a dualism that women are supposed to embody, but which is impossible for them to bridge: as the whore and the madonna. In traditional societies the split is real and women must simply choose between the two roles, to be part of the class of wives or the class of prostitutes. But in modern societies, in the throes of the sexual revolution, where sex is increasingly linked with pleasure rather than babies, it is women who have to cope with the ensuing moral confusion.

Men are free simply to take advantage of the new free sex. But women find that sex is now a service they must provide outside *and* inside marriage, at the same time as trying to ensure that they do not prejudice their bargaining position in the marriage contract. Men's continuing social, moral and economic power means that the sexual revolution has not necessarily been good for women. They have lost the bargaining currency of virginity, without the compensation of more sexual enjoyment. While there may be a few more orgasms and a bit less shame around, this is often at the cost of women defining their sexual feelings in male terms, in the service of male sexuality.

The body beautiful

Having lost virginity as a counter in the sexual power game, women have had to find another means of attracting and keeping a man. And beauty is the new currency of the sexual revolution. Preservation of beauty – always a major preoccupation of women in modern society – has now become almost an obsession and has been substituted for the preservation of virginity in the competition to catch a prize male.

The beautiful woman is slim, young, not-pregnant. She is all-smooth, all-gleaming, shorn of 'excess' body hair, with a flawlessness difficult for the majority of women – swollen with pregnancy, harrassed at the stove, exhausted on the assembly line – to maintain. Maintaining such beauty eats up so much time and money – on clothes, make-up, hairdressers, saunas, health food, sunbeds – that most women can only preserve their appearances at the expense of their fulfilment as independent individuals.

The costs are high even for conventionally beautiful women. But they are higher still for the many millions more whom modern society considers ugly: the disabled, the fat, the skinny, the pregnant, the old.

Sex for women is so intimately linked with beauty in today's industrial world that many people consider it unthinkable, or even disgusting, for 'ugly' women to have sex. In one study, for instance, 39 per cent of doctors questioned believed it was not possible for any woman over the age of fifty to have unfulfilled sexual needs.[72] Yet research has shown that 47 per cent of 60- to 71-year-old couples have 'regular, frequent' sex and that 4 per cent of 70- to 79-year-olds have intercourse every three days.[73]

A second sexual revolution

For all these reasons – the way sex is linked with male control of women, with reproductive rights, with women's own sense of beauty and self-worth, with women's sexual enjoyment, with violence against women – feminists in the rich world have concerned themselves closely with sex issues. Often this has confused and angered male political activists. Shortly after the Russian Revolution, for instance, Clara Zetkin reported to Lenin that, in the discussion groups she had organised for working-class women, the subject kept turning to sex. Lenin was horrified and instructed her to guide the discussions towards more 'central' proletarian themes.[74]

She obeyed. But Lenin, despite his power, was not able to stem the tide of talk completely. The sexual revolution has forced sex out of its dark corner of shame and given people permission to peer at it. And, while most men have been content merely to ogle, women are beginning to dissect it, analyse it and reform it to suit their own needs.

Some women are turning to each other, deciding to explore lesbian sex – either in response to a deeply felt physical and mental attraction towards women, or as a political decision to experience their personal and erotic natures independently of men. Others, secure in the new forms of contraception and the new job opportunities that have opened up for women in some countries, are starting to refuse to force their bodies into the fantasy-forms of male-defined sex, are questioning their attraction to the stereotyped masculine man, are searching instead for that rare man who is willing to forsake the divisive power of pornographic sex for the confusing, frightening, vulnerable intimacy of eroticism.

6. EDUCATION

The enrolment boom

Eighty young voices – a tangle of trebles and falsettos – sing Japan's national anthem. Eighty small uniformed bodies stand to attention in eight neat rows, smallest at the front, tallest at the back, eyes watching the red and white flag their teacher hoists up the flagpole. With the air already shimmering with heat, they march, row by row, to their classrooms to begin the day's lessons.

Other voices – more hesitant, less tuneful – droning a six-times table, come through the open door of a Botswana schoolhouse. Not a breath of wind moves the papers lying on the teacher's desk, and the corrugated iron roof is a magnet, sucking down the sun's heat, concentrating it into the gloomy room, glueing skimpy tunics to the children's backs, making them fidget restlessly on the rough wooden benches.

In Thailand the schoolroom is raised from the ground on teak stilts – to catch the wind that rustles the bougainvillea flowers and sets the chimes tinkling as they hang in the big open windows. At the foot of the steps is a jumble of small sandals – one pair for each voice that reads haltingly in turn from the schoolbook.

In the UK, with the indoor shoes off and outdoor shoes on, muffled in hats, coats and scarves, children's voices rise to an excited crescendo as, satchels snatched up in wool-gloved hands, they run from school gates to sweet-shop to bus-stop and home to baked beans, television and homework.

Today there are more children at school than ever before as an education avalanche gains momentum, sweeping away illiteracy and ignorance in villages and cities through the world. This year 82 per cent of boys and 71 per cent of girls of primary school age are in school,[1] the beneficiaries of a global enrolment effort that peaked in the 1960s and 1970s and reduced the proportion of people unable to read and write to just 29 per cent by 1980.[2] Spending on education skyrocketed during this period, increasing sevenfold in the developing world (from 8 to 55 billion dollars between 1965 and 1978) and more than fourfold in the rich world (from 88 to 419 billion dollars over the same time).[3]

Though primary schooling has expanded the most in absolute terms, there have been equivalent relative increases in secondary school enrolment and in the percentage of young adults going on to colleges and universities. Approximately half of secondary school-age children in the world are in school this year, and around one in six 18- to 23-year-olds are in further education.[4]

The education gap

The increases have been most dramatic among those who were the most disadvantaged – children in poor countries. In Africa, for example, where illiteracy rates are the highest in the world, 82 per cent of women and 58 per cent of men were illiterate in 1970. But in just ten years those totals had been reduced to 73 and 48 per cent respectively.[5] In Asia, too, where 53 per cent of women and 35 per cent of men were illiterate in 1970, those rates had dropped to 47 and 30 per cent by 1980.[6] In fact, the United Nations Educational, Scientific and Cultural Organisation (UNESCO), predicts that, if current trends continue, literacy will continue to win the race against population growth and only one in three women and one in five men will be unable to read and write by 1990.[7]

Nevertheless, this still leaves many more women illiterate than men. This literacy gap persists in every region of the world and is widest, ironically, in Europe, where one of the largest overall proportions of people can read and write. Here, though illiterate people are only an estimated two per cent of the population, illiterate women outnumber illiterate men by two to one.[8]

The literacy gap is paralleled by an education gap at every level of the education system. In 1985 there are seven girls for every eight boys in primary education; around five girls for every six boys in

TABLE 4: School Enrolment over the Decade

	1975		1985	
	GIRLS	**BOYS**	**GIRLS**	**BOYS**
PRIMARY SCHOOL				
Rich World	92·9	92·6	93·1	92·9
Poor World	54·1	70·6	65·1	78·4
World Average	64·0	76·3	71·2	81·6
SECONDARY SCHOOL				
Rich World	83·6	80·5	89·9	87·3
Poor World	28·5	41·5	37·1	48·1
World Average	45·0	53·3	49·8	57·5
FURTHER EDUCATION				
Rich World	28·0	32·8	31·9	34·7
Poor World	6·2	12·4	9·8	16·1
World Average	13·6	19·3	16·0	21·3

Percentage of age group enrolled in appropriate level of education.

Source: "Tendances et projections des effectifs scolares par degré d'enseignement et par âge, 1960-2000 (évaluées en 1982)" UNESCO, 1984.

secondary school; and about four women for every five men at college or university.[9]

These are world totals, however. In the rich world, where many countries have compulsory education, enrolment rates are very high (around 93 per cent in primary school and 88 per cent in secondary school[10]) and there are almost equal numbers of boys and girls in school. It is in the developing countries that some very large differences emerge. In Nepal and Pakistan, for instance, there are more than twice as many boys as girls in school.[11] And this difference is even more striking in the Yemen Arab Republic, where over five times as many boys as girls are in school.[12]

Closing the gap

The good news of the Decade is that the education gap is closing at last. Though boys still outnumber girls at school, girls are edging forward slightly faster in the race towards literacy. In some countries the improvement has been quite dramatic. In Zaire, for example, the gap between the number of boys and girls in primary school has diminished – from 25 per cent to just 8 per cent over the last decade – in parallel with an increase of around 18 per cent in the overall numbers of children in school at that level.[13] In India the proportion of boys in primary school hardly changed at all, compared with a 12 per cent increase in the proportion of girls sitting behind a primary-school desk.[14] The education gap has been halved in Bolivia and Peru over the Decade,[15] while in Sudan and Iraq massive education gaps of around 50 per cent at primary level at the beginning of the Decade had been cut to less than 15 per cent by 1985.[16]

And, as these children work their way up the education ladder – from pencil to biro, from addition to calculus, from ABC to literature – so that gap at secondary school level is beginning to close too. In the developing countries girls made up only 37 per cent of the secondary school population in 1975. By 1985 their share of secondary places had jumped to 41 per cent.[17]

Favouring sons

The gap remains, however, in all countries without compulsory education. And it is proving a stubborn gap to close. Even in the rich world, where the numbers of girls and boys are more or less equal at the largely compulsory primary and secondary levels, and where girls even outnumber boys at secondary school (with 90 per cent enrolment compared to 87 per cent for boys[18]) as soon as the compulsion is lifted (no country yet has compulsory tertiary education) boys outnumber girls. In the poor world the imbalance is much greater, with only three girls for every five boys in further education in 1985.[19]

To understand why parents continue to favour their sons over their daughters when it comes to choosing whom to educate means seeing education as an investment. And it is an investment of time as well as money for many parents. Many governments, in the developing world especially, make a charge for school fees, insist that pupils wear a uniform, and ask parents to bear the cost of their children's books and paper. Add the cost of transport to and from school every day, and school can seem like an expensive luxury to a poor family.

Their choice of whether to send a child to school is influenced by two major concerns: the amount of work the child could be doing now to help support the family while she or he is still of school age; and the chance of the education investment paying off in the future – in the shape of a good, well-paid job that will help the family when the child leaves school.

Children at work

In much of the rich world, child labour is outlawed and children tend to be a drain on the economic well-being of the family. But in many countries the work which even quite a young child can do is often a major reason for having that child in the first place.

In Rwanda, for instance, where enrolment in secondary school is generally very low, and where boys outnumbered girls at that level by around three to two in 1975, one study found that mothers with daughters are relieved of approximately 40 per cent of their domestic work, leaving them free to spend more time in the fields.[20] And, in Burkina Faso, where a little girl starts her chores at home and on the land at an average age of seven, but where her brother is free of all work responsibility until four years later,[21] boys out-numbered girls at primary school by around two to one in 1981.[22]

Little girls have more responsibilities than their brothers largely because mothers are more overburdened than fathers and because, in most cultures, it is more fitting for a daughter to help her mother than a son. Already, then, these young girls are learning different lessons: they are learning to balance their domestic role with their schooling and are being set on a conveyor of compromise that will restrict their choices at every stage of their lives.

Some girls miss out on schooling altogether, spending their days scrabbling weeds from around corn stalks or selling bananas at the side of the road. Others find they tend to spend less time at school than their brothers – because it is they who are kept at home when their younger brothers and sisters are sick or when an extra pair of hands is needed at harvest time. Many more are forced to skimp their studying because their hours of pounding grain for supper, or fetching firewood, eat away at the time they would otherwise spend doing homework.

Jobs for girls

Parents may be willing to sacrifice their daughters' help in the present if they feel that the future benefits will make that sacrifice worthwhile. But, in many countries, two important factors again tip the balance in favour of sons.

Firstly, in some cultures a girl is only economically valuable to her family while she is unmarried. As soon as she marries, whatever she earns will be added to the total earnings of her husband's family. In some countries this economic loss to her own family is well acknowledged and a 'bride-price' is paid by the husband's family by way of compensation.

But perhaps more important than this is the fact that – even in parts of Asia where female employment is rising faster than anywhere else in the world – a son is more likely to get a job than a daughter. And, even if she does strike it lucky, the odds make it overwhelmingly likely that her job will be less well paid than her brother's – for all the reasons already explained in the section on industrialisation.

Sex or school

Economic reasons are not the only ones that prevent girls going to school or continuing their education for as long as boys. Moral reasons can be equally powerful.

In strictly Muslim countries, for example, where men and women tend to move in completely different worlds, where better-off families keep their wives and daughters secluded or covered in the *chador* whenever they venture out of the house, and where premarital sex is considered an utter outrage for women, many parents keep their daughters away from co-educational schools as soon as puberty approaches, and attendance at secondary schools tends to be very low.

In Ethiopia and Morocco, for instance, there are nearly twice as many boys as girls in secondary school, while in the Yemen Arab Republic and Pakistan boys outnumber girls by well over three to one.[23]

In such countries pubescent girls are prevented from associating with boys altogether. In other countries it is the actual consequences of that association that cause girls to leave school. Pregnancy – wanted or unwanted, legitimate or illegitimate – is another major reason why girls are less likely than boys to complete their education. In every country these costs of adolescent sexuality are borne by girls alone.

Lessons in inequality

Though girls tend, on average, to get fewer years of education than boys, the United Nations Educational, Scientific and Cultural Organisation stresses that it is the quality rather than the quantity of girls' education that prevents them from advancing in the world of work, keeping them confined in badly paid occupational ghettos.[24]

From their earliest years in school girls tend to be channelled towards subjects that are likely to be of more use to them in the kitchen and the living-room than in the outside world. They learn art, literature, domestic science and dressmaking while the boys are struggling with knotty mathematics problems, spending hours in the physics and chemistry labs, or covered with sawdust in the woodwork department.

By the time teenagers are ready to go on to more specialist training, the worst of the damage is already done. Boys are already comfortably rolling along the tracks of science and technology, tracks that will take them onwards and upwards towards power and prosperity. Girls, on the other hand, are rolling along different tracks altogether: tracks that take them inexorably towards factory and filing cabinet, to frying-pan and fireside.

Two-thirds of girls at Danish technical colleges in 1982, for example, were being trained in just three subjects: the clothing trade, textile design and the hotel industry.[25] And, thousands of miles away in Ghana, the picture is exactly the same. Here, as in Denmark, girls take around 20 per cent of the technical college places. And here too the vast majority of girls are studying just three subjects: dressmaking, embroidery and catering.[26]

Not all countries have such a poor record for training girls, however. Venezuela, for example, doubled the percentage of vocational training places allocated to women in just five years:

from 26 per cent in 1976 to 52 per cent in 1981.[27] In Czechoslovakia, too, there has been an even greater increase in technical school places for women: from just 13 per cent in 1975 to 31 per cent in 1980.[28] In fact the centrally planned economies have been making more sustained efforts and have had greater success than any other region in encouraging girls to specialise in traditional 'male' subjects. In the German Democratic Republic, for instance, there are actually more women than men training in mathematics and science.[29]

In other countries, however, narrow specialisation in schools means that some colleges become *de facto* sex-segregated. In Dar es Salaam technical college in Tanzania, for example, there are only twenty women students and the government has decided to relax its entrance requirements to encourage more women to go into further education.[30] In Kenya, too, it was not until 1978 that any girls were enrolled in any of the country's technical colleges.[31]

With so few girls getting any vocational training at all, and with the majority tending to be concentrated in so few subjects, there is more competition for whatever jobs are available. Less skilled and less well-paid in the first place, such jobs become even more badly paid as the large numbers of applicants force the wage level down. In the Federal Republic of Germany, for instance, only 25 per cent of apprenticeship jobs are reserved specifically for women, while twice that number are reserved for men.[32]

Underachievers

The fierceness of the competition most children face is very discouraging. And in the developing world – where there are few secondary schools, even fewer universities, and an undersupply of jobs – the odds some children face must be heartbreaking. In Mexico each year the 1968 Olympic Stadium is packed with 75,000 young hopefuls writing the university entrance examination.[33] And in Sri Lanka, one firm offering seven jobs to youngsters with at least six 'O' level passes was deluged with 11,000 letters applying for the jobs.[34] In the rich world too, when unemployment rates are high it is young school-leavers in most countries who must face those years in the dole queue.[35]

It is difficult for any child to stay motivated when their chances of success are so slim. But a girl's motivation is undermined much more thoroughly than a boy's. True, he has to cope with this shortage of opportunities for success. But she has the additional disadvantage of being born into a world that does not even expect her to succeed, a world that perhaps does not really want her to succeed, a world that has been systematically schooling her for failure.

In her first books, where Janet helps Mother with the cooking while John is taken on a tour of Father's office; in advertisements, where women coo over the whiteness of a sheet they have just washed; on television, where wives and mistresses battle for the true love of a dashing young doctor; girls are taught what their role in life is to be. And, rather than helping them fight these stereotypes, teachers and school curricula simply add their bricks to the walls which – like blinkers – restrict a girl's vision of a different future, keeping her walking down the narrow corridors that lead to wifehood and motherhood.

Studies in the rich world, for example, have demonstrated that teachers behave very differently towards boys and girls in the classroom. Girls are rewarded for being quiet, docile and neat in their work; boys are rewarded for getting the right answer.[36] The creative, intelligent, lively girl, who fidgets and laughs and is always putting up her hand for attention, is seen as 'naughty'. A boy acting in the same way is simply 'bright'.

The sheer quantity of attention boys and girls get from their teachers is different too. One study found boys in a mixed classroom getting over twice as much attention as girls. And even when the teachers were told the results of the research and made a conscious effort to act more fairly, the girls still got only 40 per cent of their time.[37]

Some research, also in the rich world, has discovered girls in single-sex schools do much better than those in mixed schools, and it has been suggested that co-education – far from being the great leveller of the sexes – may in fact be bad for girls.[38] This is because, while co-education ensures that equal amounts are spent on girls' and boys' schooling and corrects previous imbalances in the quality of teachers in boys' and girls' schools, it tends to exaggerate the social differences between the sexes. Girls in a classroom with boys are more likely to behave as girls are conventionally expected to, and to be rewarded for behaving in this way; they are more likely to choose, or be pressurised to choose, 'female' subjects to study; and teachers tend to see them as females rather than as individuals with individual talents and aspirations.

Sadly, the people they turn to for guidance at school are part of the problem. Though large numbers of the world's teachers are women, it is only at primary level (where 52 per cent of teachers are women) that they outnumber men.[39] Among the more specialised, numerically fewer, secondary school teachers men outnumber women by nearly two to one.[40] Not only are women outnumbered at this more advanced level, they also tend to be teachers of arts subjects: the very subjects that girls are encouraged to study.

And, as one might expect, in the upper echelons of education (among head-teachers, school administrators and governors, and in ministries of education) where curricula are designed, budgets allocated and decisions taken, UNESCO reports that women are even less well represented.[41]

The media

The messages from teachers and school-books blend in smoothly with the messages from parents and the media until only one clear, ringing imperative can be heard: the imperative of the domestic role. The media are, historically, relatively recent educators of the global family, but they are very powerful instructors and many governments are becoming concerned at their power. Unlike schools and teachers, advertisements, feature films and television are – with the exception of those in the centrally planned economies – not under direct government control.

During the Decade many countries have begun research into the portrayal of women in the media. And, in almost every country, these studies have unveiled a media portrait of women as housebound and decorative – a sort of sexy washing-machine.

Mexico, for instance, reported that woman is portrayed as either the 'soul of the home' or as 'sex object'. In Turkey she is 'mother, wife, sex symbol'. Ivory Coast women are renowned for their 'charm, beauty, frivolity, fragility'. And in the Netherlands she is 'mother and housekeeper'.[42]

The weft of the media, woven through the warp of history, education, employment, make up the fabric of woman's domestic role, the mantle of her inequality. And, as with all other spheres of society, the media are overwhelmingly controlled by men. In Italy, for instance, 53 out of 100 male journalists recruited in 1967 had become chief editors by 1982. But not one of the 100 women journalists recruited at the same time had risen any further than editor.[43] And in Yugoslavia women journalists are concentrated three times as heavily in the less prestigious 'feature' pages dealing with culture, fashion and the home.[44]

The Decade has seen some progress, however. Thirty-eight out of 62 countries reporting to UNESCO said that they could detect an increasing tendency to portray women in professional roles.[45] And in the centrally planned economies these changes are reported to date back to the adoption of their current political stance which guarantees women's right to work. Cuba, for example, reports that: 'Since the 1959 revolution the image has undergone a total change. The image now presented is that of the worker, an involved participant in all branches of Cuban daily activity.'[46]

There are signs of positive discrimination in some countries too. Sweden has a feminist radio station, 'Radio Ellen', which 1 per cent of the population tune into daily.[47] And, bowing to trade union pressure, the media in Norway must now appoint a woman in preference to a man when the two are equally qualified for the job.[48] Similar, though less radical, actions are also reported from Czechoslovakia, Denmark, Indonesia, Mexico, the Netherlands and Switzerland.[49]

Education and liberation

Though education – in schools, in society, in the media – does tend to steer women on a course that sets them down firmly in the home and in badly paid jobs, it also teaches them the rules of navigation. And those rules, an understanding of the world's language and symbols, give women a power they have never had before. True, they learn to read about cookery and poetry – but they do learn to read. True, they learn to count stitches and to measure out flour and currants – but they do learn to count. And these basic skills give women, at last, a framework for reflection. As Paulo Friere, the revolutionary Brazilian educationalist, declared: 'I can read. Therefore I can control the world.'

And there is powerful evidence that education is one of the most potent ingredients, in a general mix of advantages, for changing women's lives. In fact the World Fertility Survey discovered that women's ability to read and write was more closely related to their fertility, their use of contraception and their children's health than even their income.[50]

Women with more than seven years of education in countries as different as Kenya, Bangladesh, Portugal and Mexico were found to be four times as likely to use contraception than those without schooling.[51] And women with secondary education in Syria have an average of four children, compared with an average of nine for women who had never been to school.[52] Similar dramatic differences were found in Sudan, Colombia and many other countries, where seven or more years of schooling reduced the

TABLE 5: Education, Contraception and Infant Mortality								
	CONTRACEPTION (% of married women using efficient contraception)				INFANT MORTALITY (% of babies dying in first year of life)			
YEARS OF EDUCATION	0	1-3	4-6	7+	0	1-3	4-6	7+
KENYA	2	3	5	11	10	9	8	7
EGYPT	16	24	30	48	15	14	13	8
INDONESIA	20	26	28	32	10	11	8	6
BANGLADESH	4	6	7	20	14	13	11	12
PORTUGAL	13	21	36	51	6	4	4	3
COLOMBIA	14	24	38	46	9	8	5	4
MEXICO	8	17	29	46	9	8	7	5

Source: World Fertility Survey.

average fertility rate by more than half.[53]

Part of this decrease is due simply to the amount of time women spend in education. If pregnancy means she must drop out of school, then a young woman is more likely to postpone childbearing until after her examinations. And, when she does leave school and manages to get a job, once again she will want to make the most of this opportunity and may delay her first baby for even longer.

More articulate and confident than her uneducated sisters, she has a better chance of winning an argument with her husband or in-laws about having children too, and will be less intimidated by the white-coated health worker at the family-planning clinic. And, once her child is born, she will be more able to decide for herself which set of conflicting advice about child-care she should follow. In Egypt, Indonesia, Colombia and Portugal, for instance, babies born to mothers with over seven years of education are twice as likely to survive their first year of life as those born to uneducated women.[54]

These findings should not be used as an excuse to substitute education for justice, however. Education is just one factor in a complex of interacting and interlocking cogs and wheels that help a woman take more power over her life. If it can act so dramatically on her freedom of choice within her role as wife and mother, then the potential of an unstereotyped education system to launch a woman finally into the world of men must be great indeed.

7. POLITICS

Equality

The scales of world equality are out of balance. The side marked 'woman' is weighed down with responsibility, while the side marked 'man' rides high with power.

Tilting first under rules that say women must do all domestic work, the scales are tipped further by men's greater opportunities to earn wages. Advantage builds on advantage until today they are tilted so steeply that almost all of the world's wealth is on man's side, while most of the world's work is on woman's.

The United Nations Decade for Women is an effort to right the scales, a first step in redistributing the wealth and the work, the power and the responsibility more fairly between man and woman.

Since the birth of the United Nations after World War Two, equality between men and women has been a fundamental tenet of the UN Charter. In 1945 the Charter affirmed its 'faith in fundamental human rights in the dignity and worth of the human person, and in the equal rights of men and women'. Two years later, a UN Commission on the Status of Women was established. Nearly three decades later concern for the plight of the world's women and their continuing inequality led to the declaration of 1975 as International Women's Year, marked by a World Conference in Mexico City, attended by delegates from 133 countries.

The Conference adopted a plan of action and established two bodies, supported by voluntary contributions, to take a more direct role in improving the position of the world's women. One of these (the International Research and Training Institute for the Advancement of Women) concentrates on gathering and disseminating information, and the other (the Voluntary Fund for the UN Decade for Women) finances innovative projects for poor women around the world.

That same year the UN General Assembly declared the ten years between 1976 and 1985 to be the UN World Decade for Women, its themes – equality, development, peace. And, five years later, in 1980, a second conference was held in Copenhagen to maintain the momentum of the Decade and to report on progress made so far in improving the position of women. This time 1,326 delegates from 145 countries attended to hear the preliminary results of research conducted during the Decade.[1]

They heard that: 'Women suffer dual oppression of sex and class within and outside the family. The effects are strikingly apparent in the present world profile of women. While women represent 50 per cent of the world population, they perform nearly two-thirds of all working hours, receive only one-tenth of the world income and own less than 1 per cent of world property.'[2]

The extent of the injustice was acknowledged, and the veil of invisibility that hangs over women's contribution to the world's well-being was drawn back at last. Woman's work became visible: her bearing and raising children, her sole responsibility for domestic work, her provision of most of the world's health care, her growing of half the world's food – all of this done for no wages – plus over a third of the world's paid labour too.

This, then, was the situation in the first half of the Decade. At the end of the period there are some signs that governments have begun to take their debt to their nations' women to heart. Ninety per cent of countries now have official government bodies dedicated to the advancement of women, and 50 per cent of these have been established since the beginning of the Decade.[3] While some of these bodies are minor departments, peripheral to the pinnacles of power, and most have been allocated insufficient resources, thirty-seven countries report that their women's bureaux act as 'lead agencies' and twenty describe them as 'major advisers' to central government policies.[4]

There is also evidence that the influence of these advocates for the advancement of women are having a significant effect on those policies. Sixty-six out of ninety-two countries have now incorporated specific programmes and provisions for women in their National Development Plans, and the majority of these – sixty-two countries – have made these changes since the launch of the Decade.[5]

The majority of countries have also instituted constitutional and legal equality between women and men, and there are only a few nations (Bahrain, Kuwait, Oman, Qatar, Saudi Arabia, the United Arab Emirates) in which women are not eligible either to vote or to stand for election.[6] Fifty-eight governments have backed up their equality legislation with an effort to ensure that women are aware of their rights, and forty-five countries – thirty in the developing world – offer free legal advice to help women fight for those rights.[7]

Inequalities remain, however, because the new laws are implemented so slowly, because they are often overridden by custom, and because old laws have yet to be repealed. In Benin, Gabon, Ivory Coast, Montserrat and Zaire, for instance, a married woman is not allowed to move house without her husband's permission. And there are twelve countries in which a woman must also seek his approval if she wishes to take a job.[8] True, thirty-one countries report that they are gradually dismantling discriminatory legislation, but thirty have admitted that they have not yet made a start.[9]

It is a vicious circle. Change is unlikely to come quickly while men take the majority of the decisions. Women will not be free to participate in that decision-making until those changes have taken place. There are some encouraging signs, however, that women are beginning to rise into the higher echelons of power in some countries and to take their rightful place beside men.

In Western Europe, for example, two-thirds of people questioned by a series of EEC surveys said they believed it was time to break down the strict stereotypes of women's and men's social roles.[10] And, between 1975 and 1983, there has been a significant change in attitudes towards women's places in politics. Asked whether they thought politics should be left to men, 41 per cent disagreed in 1975. Eight years later 71 per cent disagreed.[11]

These changes in grass-roots attitudes are only slowly being reflected in real political power. Though women form between 20 and 30 per cent of elected members of parliament in Denmark, Sweden and Finland,[12] in the majority of European countries women take only between 5 and 11 per cent of the seats of government.[13] In Japan too, though women make up 20 to 40 per cent of political parties' rank-and-file members, they are practically non-existent among the party leadership.[14] A better picture is seen in Norway, where 40 to 55 per cent of party members are women, and between 21 and 47 per cent of the governing bodies.[15]

The centrally planned economies generally have longer histories of constitutional equality for women. But change has come only slowly there as well. In Poland, for instance, women's participation in government increased by 21 per cent in the four years between 1976 and 1980, but they still made up only 25 per cent of those in national public office.[16] In the USSR, too, though 27 per cent of women are members of the Communist Party, only 8 of the 320-member Central Committee are women, and the Council of Ministers and the powerful Politburo have no women members at all.[17] China admits to a similar, though less extreme, pyramid of power. 'The situation of our women cadres resembles the shape of a pagoda: the higher the level, the fewer the women.' The shape has begun to change, however, with the percentage of women in the National Congress nearly doubling from 12 to 21 per cent between 1954 and 1978.[18]

Elsewhere, however, throughout the developing world, the United Nations has found 'no consistent increase over the Decade' in women's participation in politics.[19] Costa Rica and Venezuela are typical, with women taking less than 6 per cent of places in government.[20] Only 15 out of 200 members of parliament elected in Tanzania in 1980 were women[21] and only 1 of Kenya's 159 MPs elected in 1983.[22] In Malaysia, too, out of 154 MPs there are just 7 women.[23]

Development

There are many reasons for the delay in women mounting the stairway of power. One important reason is the length of the stairway itself. It takes time to climb from tier to tier, and many women have only recently gained the confidence and education that allow them to take the first steps.

But perhaps the most important factor impeding women's progress to power is their domestic role. If women have to do all the cooking and cleaning when they get home from work, they have much less time than men to take part in political activity. In the USSR, for instance, women have an average of only 19 hours a week free time compared to men's 31 hours.[24] In fact, taking an average of twelve countries in the rich world, women with jobs outside the home have just 24 hours' free time – only two-thirds of the leisure hours of a working man.[25] The difference in some developing countries is even more extreme: in Ivory Coast and Burkina Faso, for instance, men have three times as much free time as women.[26,27]

The same domestic role that renders women invisible to development planners, that prevents them from advancing in the world of work, that keeps them working twice as hard as men, also prevents them taking the very political initiatives that are needed to alter their situation. Inequality of political power is just the tip of an iceberg of inequality that freezes women's opportunities for advancement in every sphere of life.

As the UN documents prepared for the World Conference on the Decade for Women point out: 'The overriding obstacle identified by virtually all governments, irrespective of economic or regional groupings, is the deeply rooted traditional value system and attitudes which subordinate women and establish stereotyped sex divisions of roles in society.'[28]

Governments may have identified the obstacle, but many are reluctant to 'redress the prevailing disadvantaged situation and properly respond to women's natural function of childbearing' and bring about 'the sharing of social, economic and political responsibilities, including family responsibilities'. The reason the majority of governments give for this reluctance is economic recession.[29]

In the rich world recession is the main excuse given for failing to provide the social services that would help relieve women of some of their burden of domestic work. In the poor world governments maintain that recession makes it necessary for them to concentrate first and foremost on general development policies, and prevents them treating women's inequality as top priority.

In both hemispheres of the globe the reply from men in government is that women must wait until things improve. Women's problems cannot be dealt with until the current crisis is passed, until recession eases a certain amount and until development advances to a certain stage.

The trouble is that women cannot wait. Because both development and recession are riding rough-shod over them.

In the rich world it is women whose jobs tend to be more vulnerable when there is high unemployment. It is they who are expected to pick up the pieces when hospitals, nursery schools, day-care centres, old people's homes, are closed. In the poor world it is women whose rights to land are eroded, whose work in the fields is ignored, whose income from trading is threatened.

Poor countries are right to be suspicious when the rich world wags a reproving finger and tells them they should treat their women better. They are right to point out that the rich world cannot criticise them for inequality within their countries while the gap between rich and poor nations yawns so obscenely wide. But perhaps they are wrong to think that equality is divisible, to believe that it can be applied selectively to one section of society but not to another.

The need for a New International Economic Order is painfully clear. The richest fifth of the world's population live in countries with an average *per capita* Gross National Product of $9.470 (forty-five times higher than the poorest fifth of the world's people) and an average infant mortality rate of just seventeen per thousand – one-seventh of the infant mortality rate of the poorest fifth of the world.[30]

But inequality within nations can be just as dramatic as inequality between them. In Brazil, Panama and Peru, for instance, the richest fifth of the population get over 60 per cent of the country's income, while the poorest fifth must share just 2 per cent.[31] And it is not only developing countries who favour the rich. In the USA and Canada,

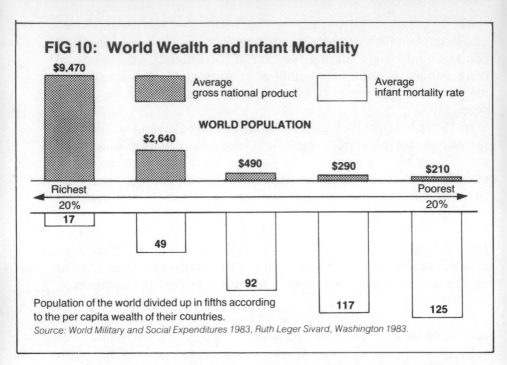

FIG 10: World Wealth and Infant Mortality

Average gross national product

Average infant mortality rate

WORLD POPULATION

$9,470

$2,640

$490

$290

$210

Richest 20%

Poorest 20%

17

49

92

117

125

Population of the world divided up in fifths according to the per capita wealth of their countries.

Source: World Military and Social Expenditures 1983, Ruth Leger Sivard, Washington 1983.

for example, the richest fifth of the population get over 40 per cent of the income, while the poorest fifth must make do with just 5 per cent between them.[32]

An idealist can hope that a New International Economic Order would correct the balance within as well as between countries. But a realist will share the doubts of the late Martin Luther King, writing from Birmingham City Jail in Alabama in 1963: 'History is the long tragic story of the fact that privileged groups seldom give up their privileges voluntarily.'[33]

Equality and justice are qualities of whole societies, of the whole world. And that is as true of men and women as it is of rich and poor. As black civil rights activist Frannie Lou Hamer wrote: 'the freedom of the white woman is shackled in chains to mine and she is not free until I am free.'[34]

Women have fought beside men in wars and revolutions. They have worked, twice as hard as men, in helping to create their nations' wealth. But, time after time, they have had their reward snatched away from them and been ushered, again and again, back into the kitchen with their children. Women – the poorest of the poor, the hungriest of the hungry, the most overworked, the most disadvantaged, the most disinherited – are tired of waiting for men to decide when the time is right. The time *is* right – *now*.

Peace

It seems clear that few men are likely to give up their power, nor are they likely to take on more of the responsibilities that have always fallen to women, simply for equality's sake. The extra work they would have to do unpaid, and the cut in salary and status they would have to suffer, are not changes many men would willingly embrace. But if men will not welcome those changes for the sake of equality and justice alone, perhaps they will countenance them for the sake of their own self-preservation.

The penalties for inequality between women and men are very severe. And they are not borne by women alone. They are borne by the whole world.

Power, tempered by the wisdom and restraint of responsibility, is the foundation of a just society. But with too little responsibility, power turns to tyranny. And with too little power, responsibility becomes exploitation. Yet in every country in the world power and responsibility have become unbalanced and unhitched, distributed unequally between men and women. The previous sections of this Report have demonstrated the penalties of women's too-great burden of responsibility and their too-small slice of power: they are hardship, sickness, hunger, even famine. But the penalties of man's disproportionate share of the world's power (without the intimate day-to-day knowledge of the effects of that power, or the responsibility for ensuring that the basic needs of the household are met) are just as great.

Of course not all men are tyrants or despots and not all women are martyrs to duty and hard work. But *masculine* and *feminine* social roles have tilted the majority of men and women in those directions to some degree. And a tour of world statistics demonstrates the dangers of masculine power unleashed from feminine responsibility.

Since 1945 there have been 105 wars causing around 16 million deaths – almost all in the developing world.[35] And male soldiers were not the only victims; 9 million civilians were killed[36] and a further 8.3 million people had become refugees from the war zones by 1983.[37] Today the world has stockpiled an estimated 50,000 nuclear warheads that together pack a punch five thousand times greater than all the firepower used in World War Two and enough to destroy half a million Hiroshimas.[38] And this mountain of death is still growing, consuming around 666 billion dollars a year, and will have doubled in size by 1990.[39]

But the costs are not only measured in dollars. Every minute (in which the world spends 1.3 million dollars on arms) thirty children die from a combination of malnutrition and disease.[40] A single nuclear submarine costs as much as the entire education budgets of twenty-three developing countries containing between them 160 million schoolchildren.[41] Though the vast majority of arms spending is accounted for by the US and the USSR, developing countries are also spending large amounts of their scarce wealth on arms. It has been estimated, for instance, that the massive foreign debt of developing countries to the banks, financial institutions and governments of the rich world is only one-twentieth of the value of their arms imports.[42]

TABLE 6: Education and Military Spending		
	EDUCATION (Spending as % of Gross National Product)	**MILITARY** (Spending as % of Gross National Product)
RICH WORLD		
SWEDEN	9·6	3·4
NORWAY	7·9	3·3
UNITED STATES	6·4	5·2
AUSTRALIA	5·8	2·4
JAPAN	5·8	0·9
FRANCE	5·2	3·9
USSR	5·1	10·7
POOR WORLD		
GUYANA	9·9	3·3
CUBA	8·6	5·6
SAUDI ARABIA	6·4	22·4
JORDAN	6·2	14·1
KENYA	6·1	5·0
SYRIA	5·8	20·1
MALAYSIA	5·6	4·0

Source: UNESCO Statistical Yearbook, 1981.

These, then, are the priorities of a world where power is concentrated in masculine hands. As historian R.H. Tawney has pointed out: 'Militarism is a characteristic, not of an army, but of a society.'[43] And surveys of the world's military governments have shown what a commitment to militarism means: it means twice the spending on arms compared with civilian governments; it means three times the violence against, and torture of, civilians; it means six times the number of coups.[44]

If it is men who predominate among the drivers of the war machine, it should not be surprising to find women among the most passionate of those working for peace.

Nine months after the beginning of World War One, while their menfolk were busy with threat and counter-threat, toting the colours of manhood and war, over 1,000 women from twelve countries met together in The Hague, in the Netherlands, and founded the Women's International League for Peace and Freedom – the first international peace movement.

That was seventy years ago. Today women are still working for peace and trying to act as a countervailing force to the snarling stand-off of the Cold War. In 1977 Betty Williams and Mairead Corrigan were awarded the Nobel Peace Prize for their efforts towards peace in Northern Ireland. In 1978 women in all Nordic countries marched in protest against the neutron bomb and 3,000 demonstrated in Stockholm and Gothenberg. In June that same year, hundreds of women victims of Hiroshima and Nagasaki gathered with other women from all over the world in the US, joining many thousands of American women demonstrating their support for the UN's first Special Session on Disarmament in New York. The following year the Soviet Women's Committee held a special conference in Moscow on 'a peaceful and secure future for all our children'. In July 1980 70,000 women in the Federal Republic of Germany and half a million Scandinavian women signed petitions demanding an end to the nuclear arms race. The following year 5,000 gathered at a women's peace rally in Tokyo and the women's peace camp at the Greenham Common US Cruise missile base in the UK was set up. In December 1982 30,000 women formed a human chain around the base, and in April 1983 a sister base was set up in Comiso, Sicily. In July that same year thousands of women set off to march from Berlin to Geneva, where peace talks between the US and the USSR were taking place. In November Australian women set up another peace camp in Pine Gap to protest at the siting of a US military base on Aboriginal land. And the following year three more peace camps were set up in Ireland, Denmark and Sweden.[45]

These women are doing more than simply protesting about war. They are not so naive as to think that removing the nuclear arsenals would automatically bring about a peaceful world. As the women at Greenham Common put it: 'Peace isn't just about removing a few pieces of war furniture, or bringing about an international ceasefire. It is about the condition of our lives. Peace is the absence of greed and domination by a few over the rest of us.'[46] And women protesting at the Pentagon in the US echo that sentiment: 'There can be no peace while one race dominates another, one people, one nation, one sex, despises another.'[47]

The world, where masculine power is severed from feminine responsibility, is a world shot through and through with the wounds of structural violence. And war is only the bloodiest of those wounds, the most visible manifestation of a quieter violence that the powerful perpetrate against the powerless.

To put it more simply: all the arms in the world don't offer the security of one embrace.

1. FAMILY

1 Dixon, R.B., *Rural Women at Work* (Baltimore: John Hopkins, University Press, 1978).

2 Szalai, A., 'The Situation of Women in the Light of Contemporary Time-Budget Research'. UN World Conference for International Women's Year, Mexico City, 1975.

3 Oakley, A., *The Sociology of Housework* (Martin Robertson, 1974).

4 Adret, 'Travailler deux heures par jour', in Goldschmidt-Clermont, L., *Unpaid work in the Household*, ILO, Geneva 1982.

5 Gauger, W.H and Walker, K.E., 'The Dollar Value of Household Work', in Goldschmidt-Clermont, op.cit.

6 'Review and Appraisal: Employment', presented to the World Conference to Review and Appraise the Achievements of the United Nations Decade for Women: Equality, Development and Peace (Nairobi, Kenya, July 1985) A/CONF.116/5.

7 'Women in Statistics', Supplement No. 10 to 'Women of Europe',Commission of the European Communities, 1981.

8 ibid.

9 Szalai, A., op. cit.

10 Ubanobenshi, O., 'La Participation de la Femme Rwandaise a l'effort de production'. Institut des Sciences Agronomiques du Rwanda. Unpublished thesis, June 1977. Reported in 'Rural Women's Participation in Development', UNDP Evaluation Study No. 3, New York, June 1980.

11 White, B., 'Population, Involution and Employment in Rural Java', *Development and Change*, 1976, Vol. 7, pp. 267-290.

12 'Women in Statistics', op. cit.

13 'Report of the World Conference of the United Nations Decade for Women', Copenhagen 1980, A/CONF.94/35.

14 'Review and Appraisal: Health', presented to the World Conference to Review and Appraise the Achievements of the United Nations Decade for Women: Equality, Development and Peace (Nairobi, Kenya, July 1985) A/CONF.116/5.

15 Pollard, N., 'The Kibbutz – an Ideal Society?' *The Ecologist*, Vol. 12, No. 3, 1982.

16 McAuley, A., *Women's Work and Wages in the Soviet Union* (George Allen and Unwin, UK, 1981).

17 'World Fertility Survey: major findings and implications', World Fertility Survey, 1984.

18 *Recent Levels and Trends of Contraceptive Use as Assessed in 1983* (United Nations, New York, 1984).

19 'World Fertility Survey', op.cit.

20 'Progress in Primary Health Care: A Situation Report', WHO, Geneva,1983.

21 Ghosh, 1978, reported in 'State of the World's Children report', 1980, UNICEF.

22 Royston, E., 'Morbidity of Women: The Prevalence of Nutritional Anaemias in Developing Countries', WHO Division of Family Health, Geneva, 1978.

23 'World Fertility Survey', op.cit.

24 ibid.

25 'State of the World's Population Report', 1984, UNFPA.

26 'World Fertility Survey', op.cit.

27 ibid.

28 'State of the World's Population Report', 1980, UNFPA.

29 Veil, B., 'Latin America's Abortion Epidemic', IPPF *Medical Bulletin,* Vol. 16, No. 4.

30 McAuley, A., op.cit.

31 Tietz, C., *Induced Abortion* (Population Council, New York, 1979).

32 'Progress in Primary Health Care: A Situation Report', WHO, Geneva 1983.

33 'World Survey: Women in Agriculture', presented to the World Conference to Review and Appraise the Achievements of the United Nations Decade for Women: Equality, Development and Peace (Nairobi, July 1985) A/CONF.116/4.

34 'State of the World's Population Report', 1983, UNFPA (information pack).

35 United Nations World Assembly on Aging, Vienna 1982 (information pack).

36 *World Development Report 1984,* World Bank (Oxford University Press).

37 Buvinic, M. and Youssef, N., 'Woman-Headed Households: The Ignored Factor in Development Planning', USAID/WID, Washington DC, 1978.

38 Newland, K., 'Women, Men and the Division of Labor', Worldwatch Paper 37, Worldwatch Institute, Washington DC, May 1980.

39 'State of the World's Population Report', 1980, UNFPA.

40 'Women of the World: Sub-Saharan Africa', US Bureau of the Census and US Office of Women in Development, 1984.

41 'Women of the World: Latin America and the Caribbean', US Bureau of the Census and US Office of Women in Development, 1984.

42 'Women in Statistics', op.cit.

43 Anderson, M., *Sociology of the Family* (Penguin Books, 1980).

44 Massiah, J., 'Women as Heads of Households in the Caribbean: Family Structure and Feminine Status', in *Women in a World Perspective*, UNESCO.

45 'World Fertility Survey', op.cit.

46 Glick, P.C., 'Living Arrangements of Children and Young Adults', *Comparative Family Studies*, 1976, Vol. 7.

47 'World Fertility Survey', op.cit.

48 ibid.

49 Massiah, J., op.cit.

50 'World Fertility Survey', op.cit.

51 United Nations World Assembly on Aging, Vienna 1982, op.cit.

52 ibid.

53 ibid.

54 ibid.

55 ibid.

56 ibid.

2. AGRICULTURE

1 Aronoff, J. and Crano, W.D., 'A Re-examination of the Cross-Cultural Principles of Task Segregation and Sex Role Differentiation in the Family', *American Sociological Review*, Vol. 40, 1975.

2 'The Data Base for Discussion of the Interrelations Between the Integration of Women in Development, their Situation, and Population Factors in Africa', UN Economic Commission for Africa, 1974.

3 'World Survey: Women in Agriculture', op.cit.

4 ibid.

5 ibid.

6 'Women of the World: Sub-Saharan Africa', op.cit.

7 Dixon, R., op.cit.

8 ibid.

9 'Women in Statistics', op.cit.

10 'World Survey: Women in Agriculture', op.cit.

11 'Women in Agricultural Production', *Women in Agriculture* No. 1, FAO, Rome, 1984.

12 'World Survey: Women in Agriculture', op.cit.

13 ibid.

14 ibid.

15 ibid.

16 ibid.

17 ibid. It is not usual for the FAO to be so outspoken. The section of the Conference documentation submitted on behalf of FAO was written by a woman.

18 ibid.

19 ibid.

20 Ward, B., 'Women and Technology in Developing Countries' in *Impact of Science on Society*, Vol. 20, No. 1, 1970.

21 'World Survey: Women in Agriculture', op.cit.

22 'Women of the World: Latin America and the Caribbean', op.cit.

23 'World Survey: Women in Agriculture', op.cit.

24 'Women in the World: Latin America and the Caribbean', op.cit.

25 'World Survey: Women in Agriculture', op.cit.

26 ibid.

27 ibid.

28 BBC 'Global Report' documentary, 1983.

29 Daroesman, R., 'Optimum Participation of Women in Economic and Social Development', ILO, Jakarta, 1978.

30 'World Survey: Women in Agriculture', op.cit.

31 ibid.

32 'Food Outlook', FAO, Rome, 1984.

33 BBC 'Global Report' documentary, 1983.

34 ibid.

35 'Report of the World Conference of the United Nations Decade for Women', op.cit.

36 'World Survey: Women in Agriculture', op.cit.

37 ibid.

38 ibid.

39 ibid.

40 ibid.

41 ibid.

42 ibid.

43 'The Role of Women in the Solution of the Food Crisis in Africa' (Implementation of the Lagos Plan of Action), Arusha, Tanzania, October 1984.

44 ibid

45 'World Survey: Women in Agriculture', op.cit.

46 ibid.

47 'The Role of Women in the Solution of the Food Crisis in Africa', op.cit.

48 'World Survey: Women in Agriculture', op.cit.

49 Mitchnik, 'The Role of Women in Rural Zaire and Upper Volta', ILO.

50 Moore, M., Institute of Development Studies Discussion Report No. 43, Sussex, UK, 1974.

51 'Women in Food Production and Food Security', Government Consultation on the Role of Women in Food Production and Food Security, Harare, Zimbabwe, FAO, July 1984.

52 'The Role of Women in the Solution of the Food Crisis in Africa', op.cit.

53 'World Survey: Women in Agriculture', op.cit.

54 ibid.

55 ibid.

56 ibid.

57 ibid.

58 ibid.

59 'Women in Food Production and Food Security', op.cit.

60 ibid.

61 'World Survey: Women in Agriculture', op.cit.

62 Tinker, I. and Bo Bramsen, M., 'Women and World Development', Overseas Development Council, 1976.

63 'World Survey: Women in Agriculture', op.cit.

64 ibid.

65 ibid.

66 ibid.

67 ibid.

68 ibid .

69 Baeza, X.A., 'El diptico campesina – asalariada agricola' in Leon, M. (ed.) *Las Trabajadoras del agro,* Asociacion Colombiana para el estudio de la poblacion, Bogota, Colombia, 1982.

70 Buvinic, M. and Youssef, N., op.cit.

71 Staudt, K., 'Agricultural Productivity Gaps: A Case Study of Male Preference in Government Policy Implementation', USAID/WID, Washington DC, 1978.

3. INDUSTRIALISATION

1 ILO Bureau of Statistics.

2 ibid.

3 ibid.

4 ILO Labour Force Estimates and Projections 1950-2000, Geneva 1977, Vol. V.

5 ibid.

6 'World Survey: Women in Industrial Development', presented to the World Conference to Review and Appraise the Achievements of the United Nations Decade for Women: Equality, Development and Peace (Nairobi, July 1985) A/CONF.116/4.

7 ILO Bureau of Statistics.

8 ibid.

9 'World Survey: Women in Industrial Development', op.cit.

10 ILO Bureau of Statistics.

11 ibid.

12 'Rural Women in Latin America: A Social Factor in the Past Decade (1975-1984)' Economic Commission for Latin America and the Caribbean.

13 ibid.

14 'Review and Appraisal: Employment', presented to the World Conference to Review and Appraise the Achievements of the United Nations Decade for Women: Equality, Development and Peace (Nairobi, July 1985) A/CONF.116/5.

15 ibid.

16 ILO *Yearbook of Labour Statistics –* various editions.

17 ibid.

18 'Review and Appraisal: Employment', op.cit.

19 ibid.

20 Daroesman, R., op.cit.

21 'Review and Appraisal: Employment', op.cit.

22 ILO *Yearbook of Labour Statistics –* various editions.

23 ibid.

24 Szalai, A., op.cit.

25 Adret., op.cit.

26 Barrett, M. and McIntosh, S. *The Anti-Social Family* (Verso, 1982).

27 'Review and Appraisal: Employment', op.cit.

28 ibid.

29 UN Economic Commission for Africa, Arusha, Tanzania, 1984, E/ECA/REIWD/OAU/4.

30 UN World Assembly on Aging, Vienna 1982 (information pack).

31 'Review and Appraisal: Science and Technology', presented to the World Conference to Review and Appraise the Achievements of the United Nations Decade for Women: Equality, Development and Peace (Nairobi, July 1985) A/CONF.116/5

32 'World Survey: Women in Industrial Development', op.cit.

33 ILO Bureau of Statistics

34 'Women of the World: Latin America and the Caribbean', op.cit.

35 ibid.

36 ILO Bureau of Statistics.

37 'Review and Appraisal: Employment', op.cit.

38 'World Survey: Women in Industrial Development', op.cit.

39 ibid.

40 ibid.

41 Croll, E., 'Equal Opportunities for Women', *China Reconstructs,* March 1982.

42 'Review and Appraisal: Employment', op.cit.

43 ILO *Yearbook of Labour Statistics 1983,* Geneva 1984.

44 ibid.

45 ibid.

46 ibid.

47 ibid.

48 'Employment Outlook', OECD, Paris, 1983.

49 'Women in Statistics', op.cit.

50 'Review and Appraisal: Employment', op.cit.

51 'World Survey: Industrial Development', op.cit.

52 ibid.

53 ibid.

54 ibid.

55 ibid.

56 Sethuraman, S.V., 'The Urban Informal Sector in Developing Countries', reported in 'World Survey: Women in Trade', presented to the World Conference to Review and Appraise the Achievements of the United Nations Decade for Women: Equality, Development and Peace (Nairobi, July 1985) A/CONF.116/4

57 'Review and Appraisal: Monetary Factors, Service and Trade', presented to the World Conference to Review and Appraise the Achievements of the United Nations Decade for Women: Equality, Development and Peace (Nairobi, July 1985) A/CONF.116/5.

58 'World Survey: Women in Trade', op.cit.

59 ibid.

60 ibid.

61 ibid.

62 ibid.

4. HEALTH

1 'Review and Appraisal: Health', op.cit.

2 Mangay-Maglacas, A. and Pizurki, H., 'The Traditional Birth Attendant in Seven Countries', WHO Public Health Papers, No. 75, Geneva, 1981.

3 'Progress in Primary Health Care Development'. op.cit.

4 ibid.

5 Veil, B., op.cit.

6 'Review and Appraisal: Health', op.cit.

7 'Progress in Primary Health Care Development', op.cit.

8 Royston, E., op.cit.

9 'Review and Appraisal: Health', op.cit.

10 'State of the World's Children Report', 1982-3, UNICEF.

11 Chambers, R., Longhurst, L. and Pacey, A., *Seasonal Dimensions to Rural Poverty* (Frances Pinter Ltd., 1981).

12 'State of the World's Children Report', 1979 UNICEF.

13 ibid.

14 'State of the World's Children Report', 1982-3, UNICEF.

15 US Department of Health, Education and Welfare, 'Syncrises: The Dynamics of Health', Washington DC, 1976.

16 Royston, E., op.cit.

17 'Progress in Primary Health Care Development', op.cit.

18 ibid.

19 ibid.

20 ibid.

21 'Health Sector Policy Paper', World Bank, February 1980.

22 O'Neill, P.D., *Health Crisis 2000* (WHO, Geneva, 1982).

23 'State of the World's Children Report', 1982-3 UNICEF.

24 'Water and Sanitation for All?' Earthscan Briefing Document No. 22, November 1980

25 'Road Traffic Accidents', WHO Technical Report Series.

26 'Workers at Risk', WHO Technical Report Series.

27 Weir, D. and Schapiro, M.,*Circle of Poison Pesticides and People in a Hungry World* (Institute for Food and Development Policy USA, 1981).

28 Kinnersley, P.,*The Hazards of Work: How to Fight them* (Pluto Press,1974).

29 'Women Working Worldwide: The International Division of Labour in the Electronics, Clothing and Textile Industries report of a War on Want Conference in London, 1983.

30 'Review and Appraisal: Health', op.cit.

31 'Cancer is a Third World Problem too', WHO information pack, Geneva, 1984.

32 Muller, M., 'Tobacco and the Third World: Tomorrow's Epidemic?', War on Want, 1978.

33 'Review and Appraisal: Health', op.cit.

34 UN World Assembly on Aging, op.cit.

35 World's Women Data Sheet of the Population Reference Bureau, Inc.,Washington DC, 1980.

36 *World Paper,* November 1982.

37 *Washington Post,* January 1985.

38 'Review and Appraisal: Health', op.cit.

39 Earthscan Bulletin, October 1984.

40 Clement-Jones, D.J., 'Finding, Measuring, Relieving Malnutrition in Botswana', Government of Botswana, 1980.

41 'Review and Appraisal: Health', op.cit.

42 ibid.

43 WHO Health Statistics Annual.

44 ibid.

45 Ingleby, D., *Critical Psychiatry* (Penguin Books, 1981).

46 Schrag, P., *Mind Control* (Marion Boyars Publishers, 1978).

47 'Review and Appraisal: Health', op.cit.

48 'Progress in Primary Health Care Development', op.cit.

49 ibid.

50 'Review and Appraisal: Health', op.cit.

51 'Progress in Primary Health Care Development', op.cit.

52 'State of the World's Children Report', 1979, UNICEF.

53 'State of the World's Children Report', 1982-3, UNICEF.

54 ibid.

55 'Review and Appraisal: Health', op.cit.

56 ibid.

57 ibid.

58 'State of the World's Children Report', 1982-3, UNICEF.

59 'Review and Appraisal: Health', op.cit.

60 ibid.

61 'Water and Sanitation for All?', op.cit.

62 ibid.

63 'Review and Appraisal: Health', op.cit.

64 ibid.

65 'State of the World's Children Report', 1981-2, UNICEF.

66 'Review and Appraisal: Health', op.cit.

67 ibid.

68 ibid.

69 'Progress in Primary Health Care Development', op.cit.

70 'Review and Appraisal: Health', op.cit.

71 ibid.

72 ibid.

73 ibid.

74 ibid.

75 Mangay-Maglacas, A. and Pizurki, H., op.cit.

76 'Progress in Primary Health Care Development', op.cit.

77 ibid.

78 ibid.

79 ibid.

80 Mangay-Maglacas, A. and Pizurki, H., op.cit.

81 'Progress in Primary Health Care Development', op.cit.

82 Morley, D., Rodhe J. and Williams G., *Practising Health for All* (Oxford University Press, 1983).

83 'Progress in Primary Health Care Development', op.cit.

84 ibid.

85 ibid.

86 ibid.

87 ibid.

88 ibid.

5. SEX

1 Small, M.F., *Female Primates: Studies by Women Primatologists*(Alan R. Liss Inc., 1984).

2 'World Survey: Women in Agriculture', op.cit.

3 'Sexuality', *Women's International Bulletin,* No. 25, ISIS, Baltimore, USA, 1982.

4 *Encyclopaedia Britannica.*

5 ibid.

6 Hosken, F.P., 'Female Sexual Mutilations: The Facts and Proposals for Action', *Women's International Network News,* 1980.

7 ibid.

8 Abdalla, R.H.D., op.cit. *Sisters in Affliction: Circumcision and Infibulation of Women in Africa* (Zed Press, London, 1982).

9 ibid.

10 ibid.

11 ibid.

12 ibid.

13 ibid.

14 ibid.

15 Dominion, J., '*Humanae Vitae* Revisited', *The Tablet,* 27 October 1984.

16 WHO 'Study Group on Youth', op.cit.

17 ibid.

18 ibid.

19 ibid.

20 ibid.

21 ibid.

22 ibid.

23 ibid.

24 ibid.

25 ibid.

26 ibid.

27 ibid.

28 ibid.

29 ibid.

30 ibid.

31 'The Epidemiology of Infertility', report of a WHO Study Group, WHO, Geneva, 1975.

32 Kinsey, A.C., Pomeroy, W.B., Martin, C.E. and Gebhard, P.H., *Sexual Behaviour in the Human Female* (W.B. Saunders, Philadelphia, 1953).

33 Shandall, A.A. 'Circumcision and Infibulation of Females', Faculty of Medicine, University of Khartoum, reported in Abdalla, R.H.D.,op.cit.

34 Karim, M. and Ammar, R., 'Female Circumcision and Sexual Desire', Ain Shamis University Hospital, Cairo, 1965, reported in Abdalla, R.H.D., op.cit.

35 Garde K. and Lunde, I. 'Female Sexual Behaviour: A Study of a Random Sample of 40-year-old Women', *Maturita,* Vol. 2, Denmark, 1980).

36 Abdalla, R.H.D., op.cit.

37 Huston, P., *Message from the Village* (Praeger, in co-operation with the Overseas Development Council, 1979).

38 Arens, J. and Van Beurden, J., *Jhagrapur: Poor Peasants and Women in a Village in Bangladesh* (published by the authors, Amsterdam, 1978).

39 Chester, R. and Walker, C. 'Sexual Experience and Attitudes of British Women', in Chester, R. and Peel, J. (Eds), *Changing Patterns of Sexual Behaviour,* (Academic Press, London, 1979).

40 Gebhard, P.H. and Johnson, A.B., *The Kinsey Data* (Saunders, Philadelphia, 1979).

41 Kinsey, A.C. et al, op.cit.

42 'Sexuality', *Women's International Bulletin,* No. 25, op.cit.

43 Hollway, W., 'The Ripper and Male Sexuality', *Feminist Review*, No. 9.

44 Thitsa, K., 'Providence and Prostitution: Image and Reality for Women in Buddhist Thailand', CHANGE International Reports, UK, September 1980.

45 'Sexuality', *Women's International Bulletin,* No. 25, op.cit.

46 Thitsa, K., op.cit.

47 Consumers' Association of Penang, *Abuse of Women in the Media*(Penang, Malaysia, 1982).

48 ibid.

49 'Paperback Romance', *SHE,* September 1981.

50 Harrisson, P., *Inside the Third World* (Penguin Books, 1980).

51 Friedan, B., *The Feminine Mystique* (Penguin Books, 1963).

52 Barrett, M. and McIntosh, S., op.cit.

53 Hall, R., James, S. and Kertesz, J., *The Rapist who Pays the Rent* (Falling Wall Press, Bristol, 1981).

54 ibid.

55 ibid.

56 ibid.

57 Kempe, R.S. and Kempe, C.H., *Child Abuse* (Harvard University Press, Massachusetts, 1978).

58 El Saadawi, N., *The Hidden Face of Eve* (Zed Press, London, 1980).

59 Kinsey, A.C. et al, op.cit.

60 Ward, E., 'Father-Daughter Rape' (Women's Press, London, 1984).

61 Franklin, A.F. (Ed.), *Second International Congress on Child Abuse and Neglect, London, 12–15 September 1978, Abstracts,* (Pergamon Press, Oxford, 1978).

62 ibid.

63 ibid.

64 Hall, R.E., *Ask Any Woman* (Falling Wall Press, Bristol, 1985).

65 Consumers' Association of Penang, *Abuse of Women in the Media.*

66 ibid.

67 ibid.

68 Firestone, S., *The Dialectic of Sex* (Bantam New York, 1972).

69 WHO Study Group on Youth, op.cit.

70 ibid.

71 ibid.

72 'Sexuality', *Women's International Bulletin* No. 25, op.cit.

73 Comfort, A., *A Good Age* (Mitchell Beazley 1976).

74 Ehrenreich, B., 'What is This Thing called Sex?' *The Nation,* Canada,24 September, 1984.

6. EDUCATION

1 'Tendences et projections des effectifs scolaires par degré d'enseignement et par age, 1960-2000 (évaluées en 1982)', UNESCO, 1984.

2 'Literacy Targets in an International Development Strategy', UNESCO, 1980.

3 UNESCO *Statistical Yearbook,* 1981.

4 'Tendences et projections', op.cit.

5 'Analyse comparative de la solarisation et de l'analphabetisme feminins et masculins', UNESCO, 1980.

6 ibid.

7 ibid.

8 ibid.

9 'Tendences et projections', op.cit.

10 ibid.

11 ibid.

12 ibid.

13 ibid.

14 ibid.

15 ibid.

16 ibid.

17 ibid.

18 ibid.

19 ibid.

20 'World Survey: Women in Agriculture', op.cit.

21 ibid.

22 World Development Report, 1984, op.cit.

23 'Tendences et projections', op.cit.

24 'Review and Appraisal: Education', presented to the World Conference to Review and Appraise the Achievements of the United Nations Decade for Women: Equality, Development and Peace (Nairobi, July 1985) A/CONF.116/5

25 'World Survey: Industrial Development', op.cit.

26 ibid.

27 'World Survey: Industrial Development', op.cit.

28 ibid.

29 'Employment of Women in the German Democratic Republic', Vienna Seminar on the Economic Role of Women in Europe, ECE/SEM.6/R.S.

30 'Review and Appraisal: Education', op.cit.

31 ibid.

32 'Employment of Women in the German Democratic Republic', op.cit.

33 Little, A.W. and Dore, R.P., resource booklet for the film *The Diploma Disease,* Institute of Development Studies, Discussion Paper No. 179, Sussex, UK, 1979.

34 Deraniyagala, C., Dore, R.P. and Little, A.W., 'Qualifications and Employment in Sri Lanka', Institute of Development Studies, Research Reports: Education Report No. 2, Sussex, UK, 1978.

35 WHO Study Group on Youth, 1984, op.cit.

36 Spender, D. *Invisible Women* (Writers and Readers, 1983).

37 ibid.

38 'Review and Appraisal: Education', op.cit.

39 UNESCO *Statistical Yearbook*, 1983.

40 ibid.

41 'Review and Appraisal: Education', op.cit.

42 'Review and Appraisal: Communication and Media', presented to the World Conference to Review and Appraise the Achievements of the United Nations Decade for Women: Equality, Development and Peace (Nairobi, July 1985) A/CONF.116/5

43 ibid.

44 ibid.

45 ibid.

46 ibid.

47 ibid.

48 ibid.

49 ibid.

50 'World Fertility Survey', op.cit.

51 ibid.

52 ibid.

53 ibid.

54 ibid.

7. POLITICS

1 *Looking to the Future: Equal Partnership between Women and Men in the 21st Century* (Humphrey Institute of Public Affairs, University of Minnesota).

2 ibid.

3 'Review and Appraisal: Part I – General Development', presented to the World Conference to Review and Appraise the Achievements of the United Nations Decade for Women: Equality, Development and Peace (Nairobi, July 1985) A/CONF.116/5.

4 ibid.

5 ibid.

6 'Women: United Nations Work for Women', Branch for the Advancement of Women, Vienna, 1984.

7 'Review and Appraisal: Part I', op.cit.

8 ibid.

9 ibid.

10 'Women and Men of Europe in 1983', Supplement No. 16 to Women of Europe, Commission of the Economic Communities, Brussels, 1984.

11 ibid.

12 'Review and Appraisal: Part I', op.cit.

13 ibid.

14 ibid.

15 ibid.

16 ibid.

17 McAuley, A., op.cit.

18 Croll, E., *Chinese Women since Mao* (Zed Press, UK, 1983).

19 'Review and Appraisal: Part I', op.cit.

20 ibid.

21 ibid.

22 ibid.

23 ibid.

24 McAuley, A., op.cit.

25 'Women in Statistics', op.cit.

26 'World Survey: Women in Agriculture', op.cit.

27 ibid.

28 'Review and Appraisal: Part I', op.cit.

29 ibid.

30 'World Bank Development Report', 1984, op.cit.

31 ibid.

32 ibid.

33 King, M.L., *Why We Can't Wait,* 1957.

34 'The Movement', *Pictorial History of American Civil Rights Movement.*

35 Leger Sivard, R., 'World Military and Social Expenditures 1983: an Annual Report on World Priorities', Washington, 1983.

36 ibid.

37 ibid.

38 ibid.

39 ibid.

40 ibid.

41 ibid.

42 ibid.

43 Tawney, R.H., *Equality* (George Allen and Unwin, UK, 1931).

44 Leger Sivard, R., op.cit.

45 Many thanks to Danielle Grunberg of the Women's Peace Alliance, UK, for compiling this information from various sources.

46 Harford, B. and Hopkins, S., *Greenham Common: Women at the Wire* (Women's Press, 1984).

47 'Why We're Here' – Statement from Women's Pentagon Action in Jones, L., *Keeping the Peace* (Women's Press, 1983).

Part Two

Women

TO WOMEN

FAMILY

Development has led to a move away from subsistence farming and towards wage employment almost everywhere in the world. This shift has severed the complex bonds of interdependence between men and women and parents and children and led to changes in family structures around the world.

From Norway, Toril Brekke travels to the dusty scrubland of rural Kenya, where so many men have gone to the cities in search of jobs that over one-third of households are run by women, where fewer than seven per cent of married women are using contraception, where women bear an average of eight children each, and where those children are needed to help in the fields and to care for their parents when they grow old.

From India, Anita Desai travels to Norway in the depths of winter, to frozen farms and fishing ports, to ice-bound cities. Here two-thirds of women are out of work and half of all marriages end in divorce. Two-thirds of married women are using contraception and each bears an average of only two children apiece. In Norway the bonds between family members have loosened to such an extent that wives enter into legal contracts with husbands to ensure that their children are provided for, and parents draw up similar contracts with their children as insurance for their old age.

Anita Desai

The Norwegian woman? I knew her.

Her name was Nora. She lived in a doll's house, lit up for Christmas, filled with gifts and good things to eat – surrounded by children, a husband and friends. She was Nora who, when she discovered the extent to which her husband despised and distrusted her, asked him 'What do you consider is my most sacred duty?' and on being asked, 'Isn't it your duty to your husband and children?' replied, 'I have another duty, just as sacred. My duty to myself.'

She was Hedda Gabler who dressed in a sumptuous gown, lived in a splendid house and had the ability to wrap every man round her little finger but chose to put a pistol to her head instead.

She was the fair young woman in Edvard Munch's painting who stands dressed in white beside a river and gazes into the distance, as well as the dark woman in scarlet who stands under a tree and looks triumphantly at the pale and frightened man between them.

She was Cora Sandel's heroine Alberta who ran up the stairs to the top of her house from where, through a small window, she could see the sun for precisely three minutes in the long northern night before it vanished again and 'suddenly lifted her hands to the light to test the warmth . . . then blushed as if she had done wrong'. She was the timid Alberta who went skiing with her companion, 'that other invisible bold girl . . . and when they crossed the open space just outside the town . . . they glided together and became one person. After that nothing was impossible. After that, imperfections no longer existed . . . she was as free and light as a bird. She was the bold girl who had no need to hide her face, her hands or her thoughts, who was not afraid of people and did what she wanted. . . .' She was the Alberta who gazed at a print of Rembrandt's Polish Rider and wondered, 'What was he riding from, what was he riding to? The four edges of the picture seemed to enclose the wide world itself. He rode through it, released from all that had been, moving untrammelled towards all that might be. An aura of freedom and loneliness surrounded him, making me hot and cold, making the heart beat faster.'

I knew her, I felt, although I had never met her. Now I was going to find her. I looked out of the plane's window and watched the West Asian desert landscape of rose and dun darken into the blue mountains of Yugoslavia and Bulgaria, sprinkled with snow which turned, as we flew northwards, into billows and mantles and sheets

of snow that swallowed up forests, hills and towns and in turn were
swallowed by the night.

In all that darkness, Norway appeared like some sprawling
drifting sea creature – long loops and chains of pale lights that
glimmered as they dangled from the centres where the lights
clustered together and glowed as if Norway were a phosphorescent
octopus, some creature from the depths floating in the black North
Sea.

At first sight, the barren island of Frøya seemed too inhospitable
to house any life, any spirit at all, or to foster any aspirations beyond
the will to survive. The only vegetation was the lichen clinging to the
rocks; the few trees that had been planted were stunted by the gale
that whipped the island unremittingly. In the depths of winter, with
the temperature 30 degrees below zero, there was naturally no sign
of agriculture, but from the distance between the houses (all of wood
and the spare pioneer school of architecture) and the occasional
red-painted barn, it was clear that in the summer the small patches
of soil between the rocks did yield some crops. In places turf had
been cut and stacked; it was still considered good fuel even if oil and
electricity were plentiful. Everywhere the sea made its presence felt –
its salt, its spray and its roar. The rest of Norway's 4 million people
might have turned away from the sea and the forests, those
traditional sources of income and employment, to newer one
(32 per cent are employed in the social and personal services now; 17
per cent in the wholesale and retail trade and restaurants; 9 per cent
in transport, storage and communication, 8 per cent in construction
and 20 per cent in the production of oil, fuel, machinery and
manufactured goods), but on Frøya it was the sea and its yield that
had the most overpowering presence.

On the west coast, where the wind blows so hard that the gulls
cannot perch and are tossed about above the waves like spray, there
is the largest fish-processing factory on the island. It employs 120
people all through the year and in summer takes on another 40 to 50
employees, chiefly women (always chosen for part-time work
everywhere in the world, but there is no other resemblance to, say
an Indian factory where the number would be on a different scale
altogether: one with 120 workers would certainly not be considered
'large'). The few men who worked here were either driving around
lorries and vans, pushing trolleys or carrying packing cases. The
women were all involved in the actual processing of fish.

Standing in slushy water that swilled about on the floors, wearing
gumboots and rubber gloves and plastic aprons, they worked the

machines that sorted the fish – cod, salmon and herring – into various sizes (big, bigger and biggest) or those that cut the fish into fillets. At long tables they stripped the fillets of skin and bones (a single bone left in a herring could lead to the cancellation of a valuable order). Some worked the machine that pressed air out of the plastic bags into which the fish were packed, or slipped the packets into cardboard containers. If they looked out of the windows they would see the sea tossing upon the rocks, and gulls flapping like bits of laundry against the grey clouds, but they did not look. Their red, wet hands moved unceasingly, mechanically. To stand in that position for eight hours a day, only the hands kept occupied, must surely strain their backs unendurably. The supervisor – young, male, cheerful and lively, who had clearly never stood cutting fish in an assembly line himself – told me that they had once tried seating the women at work but found the seated position gave them worse backache and they preferred to stand. The 'heavier work' – like driving lorries and vans – was all done by men, he assured me, clearly implying that the women's labour was comparatively light. The women did not contradict him. They smiled to themselves and went on with their work. They were mostly middle-aged or elderly women, with grey hair. The younger women would probably not be content to work at anything so tedious and repetitive, and would look for easier or more lucrative jobs on the mainland if the island offered none. It was the older generation who accepted the fact that the island had few jobs to offer and that whatever was available must be seized and held on to, and found nothing demeaning in cutting, cleaning and packing that everyday comestible, fish.

At the end of the eight hours of work which fetched them 1200 to 1700 kroner a week, they would go home to their wooden houses on the barren rocks, to make dinner and wash and care for their families. They had always worked. They looked surprised when I asked if the factory had a crèche where younger women could leave their babies (as the largest factory of an area in India would have) and told me that children were looked after by their families; it had not occurred to them that this could be done by an organisation. There were no day-care centres on the island as there were on the mainland, not because they were not needed but because the women had not demanded them. Yes, there was a trade union, they told me, and they were members, but it was clear that none of them played any role in it. I was to remember this passive participation later when I was told how difficult it was to involve women in any political activity; this was still considered, for one reason or another, a male preserve. What about pensions, I asked – would the factory pay them pensions when they retired?

Now they knew me for the total foreigner that I was, and smiled as at an idiot: everyone knew that pensions are paid by the state, not the employer, and everyone, male or female, employed or unemployed, is entitled to one on reaching the age of retirement. At the end of a working life, spent at home or in the factory, there was the pension. With this safe knowledge, they went on cutting and cleaning the fish to be exported to Japan (white salmon, the finest), to France (fresh, marked 'superior') and the USA (frozen, not marked 'superior'). They would continue like this till they retired and collected their pensions, and then would stay home to bring up the grandchildren. As for their daughters – it seemed unlikely they would also spend their lives in a fish factory.

Arvid Witzøe's much smaller factory at Flatvalsundet, an even more bleak and unpopulated stretch of coastline where the grey waves towered up and crashed on to the streaming rocks, presented a variation on the theme: it represented New Enterprise. Witzøe had left the island as a boy, fetched up in the electronics industry in Oslo, done well and lived life at high pressure. Then one day he was knocked down in the street and returned to Frøya with a broken hip and ribs. He decided to remain on the island and find his way back into its isolated quiet and peace. To do so, he had to create work for himself and bought a small fishnet factory that was for sale. That was two years ago; he had had a hard year struggling to set it up and now was beginning to see success ahead.

It was still a small enterprise to look at – a wooden barn-like structure, battered by the sea. Downstairs in the basement he stocked his materials and ran a small shop that catered to fishermen, fitting them out with steel-tipped boots, orange plastic raincoats and hats, and all the tools of their trade. Upstairs in the great, empty, echoing room his employees sat working nylon rope into nets.

Of the eight employees, six were women. 'They are much better at the work,' Witzøe said and, seeing their hands deftly work the crewel through the thick ropes and tie knots, one could see why: the work bore a close resemblance to embroidery. These nets are used in the new industry of 'aqua-fishing', in which boats are not employed. The nets are set up like pens (or cages) in fjords and inlets of the sea, and salmon fingerlings – 250 grammes each in weight – are introduced into them. There they live for two years till they grow to weigh two or three kilos each, and then they are lifted out. The nets have to be extremely strong to withstand storms and attacks from predators such as minks, as well as closely woven enough to prevent the hovering gulls from filching any fish. The advantages of this form of fishing are so obvious that it is growing in popularity and Witzøe can look forward to rapid expansion.

He took on six girls to train them for this specialised work; the person who is doing the training is an elderly, grizzled seaman. He is explaining the work to the girls, who are at various stages of their training – one is already quick and deft, another slow and hesitant. A young girl with one artificial hand is unrolling lengths of net and attaching them to ropes from end to end of the barn. They earn 1600 kroner a week, work eight hours a day and bring their own coffee and sandwiches. They came into the small office room to sit on long benches at a wooden table, roll cigarettes, smoke and tell me about themselves – modestly little. Apart from the girl with the artificial hand, they were all housewives with children at home – the smaller ones left with grandmothers or neighbours, the older ones at school or helping out at home. The factory was obviously too small to justify either a canteen or a crèche. In any case, they preferred to bring their own meals so that their pay would not be lowered. No, they had no union yet and the pension would of course come from the state. Five minutes for a cup of coffee and a cigarette, and then they were back at their nets.

What would a woman on Frøya do if she could not or did not want to be employed by one of its new industries?

Randi and Marit had each bought one half of a wooden house at the western end of the island, near a petrol pump and the docks. Randi had set up a clothes shop for the young in the half called 'Mix and Match'; it stocked the smartest of jeans and some carefully selected cotton ready-mades. Randi herself is blonde and smart, dressed completely in red with bright red nail-polish to match, and a manner that is contrastingly soft-spoken and gentle. She is married to a schoolteacher and has a two-year-old son. She had worked in a bank till she decided to launch a business of her own; her husband helped her with the accounts and book-keeping as well as the housework and the care of their child. She had taken a bank loan to start the business; the first year had been hard, the second better, and now she had made in two months what she had in the previous two years – young people were flocking to her shop for the smart denims and cottons instead of taking the ferry to Trondheim to do their shopping.

Marit, on the other side of the building, runs a shop called 'Kitoe' which stocks clothes for small children and, in one corner, cosmetics for women. She is appropriately older and more matronly, a large and jolly woman in a jumper. Her husband is a fisherman, away at sea for months at a time, and she needed to do something that would give her company. She and a friend took a bank loan to start the shop that provides it. They run the establishment with housewifely care and pride.

In order to learn why women almost invariably chose conventional careers and so rarely ventured into what is traditionally considered as being best left to men, I had to visit a school and see how such choices are made.

I had already been given the telling statistics from 1982 (statistics which include study of the subjects both at a general and specialist level in high school): 98 per cent of students in the domestic science department are girls, 86 per cent in handicrafts and the art section and 99 per cent in health and social work departments; but only 10 per cent in the marine and fishery department and 15 per cent in manual and industrial departments. The trend continues through college and the university – only 16 per cent of the students at the institutes of technology are girls, 15 per cent in the colleges of engineering; but 87 per cent in the colleges of health education, 74 per cent in the colleges of education and 71 per cent in the colleges of social work. Whereas languages attract 65 per cent girls and psychology 63 per cent, economics only attracts 24 per cent and mathematics 27 per cent. What is more, although 52 per cent of those who completed their primary school education were girls, only 49 per cent of those who completed their high-school education were girls, and although 58 per cent of those who received lower degrees (less than two years' duration) at the college level were girls, they formed 38 per cent at the medium level (two to five years) and only 24 per cent at the third level (more than five years), while at the highest level (researchers) the girls formed 12 per cent. Clearly an education prepares girls for marriage and housework more readily than for the professions. This is receiving attention from the Ministry of Education, which is trying to reverse the trend by giving teachers a special course in the equal status of women, bringing out books in which such a status is accorded to women, and making computer science compulsory in schools up to a certain level. However, the effect is still minimal. Nor is a parallel stress being laid on education for boys in the fields of domestic and social work – in fact, this is entirely missing and appears to be the most obvious shortcoming of the system.

Frøya's high school is not imposing on the outside – a low, shed-like building like all the others – but inside there is what appears to a visitor from India an Aladdin's cave of educational equipment. No one, neither the fair and youthful principal nor the teachers, most of them equally youthful, can fathom the depth of my amazement, envy and wonder: not even the best or richest school in India could offer their students so much choice, so many opportunities or the latest and finest equipment.

In the arts department the students are working on illustrations for a book they have read, *The Ice Palace*, and using pencil, charcoal, oils and etching materials. In another section there are buckets of clay, plaster casts and live models for the sculpture class. Upstairs, in the weaving section, exciting designs are being worked out on the looms. There is a buzz of activity as they prepare for an annual exhibition to be held in the town. The teacher, a gipsy-like woman with red cheeks and a flowing scarf of rainbow stripes, blows around from one student to another, proud of their achievements and encouraging them to do more. Six of the students are girls, only one a boy. It must take courage on his part to break into what is clearly regarded as a 'girlish' activity.

Not a single boy has dared venture into the domestic science department. Here, in a large laboratory-like hall – metallic and white and spotless – are eight girls in white caps and aprons, taking down notes dictated by a woman teacher. The health department next door is empty, but one only has to take a look at the equipment to see that this would not attract any boys either – little cradles with baby-sized dolls, cupboards of baby clothes, laundry machines, vacuum cleaners and explicit charts to do with 'sexual hygiene' and 'mental hygiene' (a picture showing a young man returning home from work with a bouquet of roses and a young woman opening the door to him with a welcoming smile).

After such strong traditionalism, the industrial workshop downstairs presents something unexpected. Predictably, the larger number of students working at the machines and handling tools are boys, but amongst them are three girls who have chosen the course for different reasons. Elli, with a blonde fringe and little rings in her ears, was working away with a spanner and said she wanted to grow up to be a driver of heavy vehicles; slim, dark and shy Anita held a saw and said she wanted to make furniture and run her own furniture business, while Gudrun had taken the course simply because she enjoyed it and had no plans for the future at all. The boys continued to work at their machines as I talked to the girls, whom they seemed to take seriously and not as a joke; the girls said they were never teased and, in fact, thought it more fun to study with boys than with girls. If girls can cross the barrier with such ease, why can't boys?

The marine biology department upstairs, lined with microscopes and specimens floating in spirit, could boast of only one girl amongst all the boy students and, likewise, there was only one girl on the boat in the nearby harbour where students are trained for a career in fishing. On the outside it looked no more impressive than a kitchen pot tossing on the glassy waves, but inside it was magnificently equipped. Up on the bridge the students were learning to use electronic equipment that scans the ocean bed for shoals of fish, making fishing a very different occupation from what it was for their fathers, although it still means much hard work and rough weather up in the North Sea.

How was it that, offered such choices and given absolute freedom to choose (the equal status of men and women being the law of the land), girls and boys still overwhelmingly made the traditional choices? Clearly, these traditions are instilled into them at a much earlier stage – in primary schools where it is assumed that boys' skills at mathematics, science and technology deserve encouragement and attention and that there is no point in wasting time on helping girls with such 'different' subjects since they will in any case grow up to be housewives. (One mother showed me statistics to prove that the same discrimination is carried out amongst handicapped children, far more being done for the male handicapped than for the female handicapped both by parents and schools.) These traditions are also instilled in day-care centres where boys are given cars and building blocks to play with and girls are given dolls and kitchen equipment, and – probably most effectively of all – at home, where children more often than not follow the examples set by their parents.

I met one woman on Frøya who made it seem possible to bring new ideas across the sea from the mainland and participate in public, political life as men do.

Unni Essnes's appearance was no different from any other young teacher at the primary school – a large, plump, fair woman in jeans, ill at ease with the English language and shy, but she is one of the two women on the island who last year started the Women For Peace movement on Frøya. Was she a member of any other women's group? No. Had she been a political activist as a student? No. Did she see the local movement for peace linking up with similar ones elsewhere in the country or across the sea on the continent? No, nothing of the sort, the very idea made her smile. She was neither a feminist nor an activist, had no political ambitions whatsoever but simply wanted to protest against nuclear armaments which she thought of as a threat to life. Last year, on 9 August, she had collected all the school children, taken them down to the seashore, set out in a boat and scattered flowers on the waves in memory of the dead of Hiroshima. Then they had marched to the town hall and presented a petition to the mayor; she and her friend had organised the march and written out the petition. This year she planned to organise a concert and invite musicians to play and sing for the peace movement. It was hard to see this shy young woman arranging a public event on such a scale but she spoke of it in a quiet, matter-of-fact way that convinced me she would do what she said she would.

On the mainland, in the rich agricultural district of Trondelag, there was less of a sense of an isolated community. If there were any boundaries between farmland and town, they were obliterated by the snow. The clustered wooden houses of the town of Verdal thinned out and turned into wooden farmhouses separated from each other by a frozen lake, a stand of blue firs or a snowy field. The only building of stone was the small chapel with its steeple of grey slate and gravestones like pebbles scattered on a wintry slope.

Up here in the north the sun made only a brief appearance, giving the deep snow a pale rose glow although no warmth. The Volls' farmhouse stood like a fortress against the cold, magnificently large and double-storeyed, surrounded by great red barns and protected by a huge tree like an etching or a woodcut, holding up empty nests in its bare branches and a frozen bird bath at its foot.

Indoors all was luxuriously warm, the iron stove thrumming with heat from the burning logs, and scented with the good smells of freshly baked bread. Elisabet Voll, large and round and rosy as an apple in her woollen slacks and jacket, poured out hot coffee and, over buttered rolls and bowls of bilberry and cloudberry jam, told me that the Voll family had bought the house several generations ago from a German immigrant who had built it and owned large tracts of land in the valley which he had sold in order to emigrate to the USA; his descendants often came in the summer to look at 'the old country'. They had bought fifty acres to begin with and now owned ninety, on which they grew wheat and potatoes. When their cows multiplied to such a number that another barn was required, they sold them and took to rearing worms instead. She did the book-keeping and accounting and sat by the telephone all morning to take orders for worms from sports shops all over the valley. Oh, she helped in the fields too, in spring and in the harvest, and cut the grass in the orchard herself. Her husband helped her in the house whenever he was free, scrubbing and washing the floors for her because of her bad back.

This sharing of work and responsibility was something that had been learnt and acquired over the years: farmers had always had an association and would bring their wives to its meetings but in the thirties the farmers' wives formed an association of their own. They met to have coffee and cake together and also to run courses in weaving and embroidery. The men, who brought them to the meeting in horse carriages, would sit in the next room, drinking coffee and doing handiwork as well – leathercraft or woodwork. At present Mrs Voll is president of the association and it has become a much more political organisation. One of the first things the women fought for was for the farmers' wives to share the income with their husbands – after all, they shared the work. They insisted on having joint accounts at the bank, or accounts of their own. This had given them a new sense of independence as well as responsibility, self-respect and status. Their next demand had been for a pension for farmers' wives from the government since they did just as much work on the farm. This had given them equal status with the men and their relationship was now of equals.

Other family relationships had been sorted out differently. Mrs Voll's old mother lived in a room on the upper floor. Their eldest son helped them on the farm. When he married he moved into a smaller house on the land, and in a few years' time they intended handing over the farm to him and changing houses as well. Mrs Voll was looking forward to having a smaller place to look after. In the old days it had been the custom – which has not died out, I learnt – for a contract to be drawn up between parents and children at this stage: the son would have to stipulate, in writing, how many rooms he would allow his parents to keep as long as they lived, and the exact amount of fuel with which he would supply them, as well as milk, eggs, etc. . . . Sometimes the parents got such a good deal that they would be able to sell some of the milk, eggs or wood and earn a small income. I was shocked to the core – in India, what would people have *thought* (and, more importantly, *said*) of parents so mercenary or children so lacking in a sense of duty as to be required to make a legal assurance of looking after them in their old age!

Mrs Voll laughed and went on to tell me of some of the changes in this rural society. Her daughter worked as a kindergarten teacher and it was unusual now for a farmer's wife to stay on a farm and have no other occupation. Now that roads and cars made transport easy, most women from the farms worked in town at least on a part-time basis. Quite often the farmers did too, since all the new

farm machinery gave them so much time to spare. Earlier it had
been difficult for women to participate in social events in town, or
even to take their children to school parties and dances, but now
parents spent most of their time driving their children from one
activity to another. Loneliness? Isolation? They didn't exist, smiled
Mrs Voll, switching on the television set in order to watch the finals
of the winter sports in Austria. Mr Voll came in from the fields,
muddy from digging ditches, to have a cup of coffee and see Norway
win.

The Friedlands' farm was smaller, and closer to the town, and
these two factors made a certain difference. At one time the valley
had been emptying out, with all the young people drifting away in
search of employment, but ten years ago a gigantic factory was built
in Verdal to make oil-rigs for the North Sea. People were once again
drawn to the town for work, the population had risen, and had now
stabilised. Verdal had grown and spread and small farms, like the
Friedlands', were threatened by property-dealers as well as by large
farms that continued to expand because the government's policies
were slanted in their favour. They received grants and subsidies for
which small farms were not eligible. Expansion was impossible: if
farms were producing milk, for instance, they were paid a good
price for the first eighty litres, less for the next forty and still less for
the next so many litres. The Friedlands had been driven to selling
their cows and had taken to rearing pigs instead – more profitable
and less work, requiring nothing but cleaning and feeding. They
belonged to the Small Farmers' Association which had fought many
bitter fights with the rich and powerful Farmers' Association, and
found it hard to keep their small farm on the income it brought in.
Ryder had a job as a primary school teacher and Kjersti worked
four days a week in the computer section of the oil-rig factory,
having recently taken a two-month course in data-processing. If this
were so, why did they keep on the farm?

At this they looked at each other and laughed – tall, curly-haired,
blonde Kjersti and dark-haired Ryder – and said they could not
consider another life, tradition meant too much to them. Kjersti was
born on a farm, ten kilometres away; they had met each other on
Saturday nights at country dances, and this farm had belonged to his
parents. In his old age, his father had sold all the livestock and
equipment; Ryder had had to re-stock the farm to make it viable
again. The old house had grown too small for them now they had
two children, and he had built the new one for half a million kroner.
To buy all the machinery he needed, he would need to borrow
another million kroner, a debt he could not contemplate, and so he

did without, preferring to find himself a job in town. His mother still lived in the old house at the back, and he had drawn up a 'contract' with her whereby she was entitled to live in it till she died and also receive some fuel. Kjersti found her a great help in minding the children when she was away at work since there were no day-care centres in Verdal or a crèche at the factory. Like Mrs Voll, Kjersti looked incredulous when asked if she was ever lonely. She had never known the sensation. Even when the children were babies, she had visited her friends on nearby farms for coffee and cake and taken them along with her. They never went to restaurants or cafés in town, that was 'not done'; instead they had parties at home or went to dances at the weekend.

Curiously, it is as one draws closer to the towns that one comes across the first signs of loneliness and boredom.

Seeing a sudden splatter of electric light on a snowy slope below the black fringe of the forest, I imagined it must be one of those country dances which seemed such popular meeting places in the area, but was told no, it was a bingo hall that attracted chiefly women – and amongst them a large number of older women. They could be seen in its glaringly lit, deafeningly loud and sadly comfortless hall gambling with an almost fervent air – desperate for a change of luck, or else simply for life, noise, lights and company. The winters are very dark after all, and very long – anyone without a family or a comfortable home would hardly have the courage or the strength to stand up to one. And there are people without.

In this fertile valley where there were no slums and no tower apartment blocks and people lived comfortably in large houses, one did not expect to find an old people's home, yet there was a suspiciously large one – a long, low, double-storeyed building with a corridor running through it in which nurses in white bustled up and down, giving it the chilling atmosphere of a hospital.

'My daughter tried to take care of me at home,' said Fru Selmer, a sprightly lady with springing grey hair and alert eyes, whose only visible handicap was her inability to walk alone; she had to push a small table on wheels in front of her. 'She used to pay a social worker 600 kroner a month to come and take care of me by day, but she used to worry about me if she had to leave me at night. She felt I couldn't be left alone, so I came here, with my husband,' a retired schoolteacher like her. He had recently fallen ill and been moved to another old people's home reserved for the very sick. She had visited him a few times but now that it had grown so cold – 27 degrees below zero – he had begged her not to come. She had been asked if she wished to move to a single room (she must have wondered if they meant permanently) but found it so small that it could only hold a bed and not even a table and decided to stay on in the double room, sharing it with a woman who had lost her memory. 'She can't even remember where the dining-room is – I have to show her every time,' laughed Fru Selmer, whose memory was excellent – she asked me probing questions about the political situation in India. One wondered what companionship a woman with her mind could find in this forlorn and restricted society.

Fru Petersson seemed to fit in more comfortably. Wearing an embroidered kerchief on her head and an embroidered apron over her green skirt, she talked of the handiwork they did here and the tablemats she had made and sold for 700 kroner at the annual Christmas sale. 'We had a Christmas party too,' she said. 'The worst Christmas of my life,' winced Fru Selmer. Other entertainment was provided by occasional visitors – school children who came to sing carols, or social workers who came to give talks.

The chief source of entertainment was of course the television set. In the next room a circle of aged people sat on the green and yellow sofa, watching a programme on winter sports. An elderly gentleman with a vacant expression propped himself up by placing his hands on his knees and watched the skiiers expertly fly and leap and twist on the snow-speckled screen. Occasionally someone would get up and wander towards the dining-room, which stood empty except for eight tables – each with eight chairs around it and a lace doily and a potted poinsettia on top. On the walls were oil paintings of ships at sea and sheep in meadows.

To an Indian visitor it seemed that here the old had at once a great deal more and a great deal less than they would have in India, where they would never be given up by their families but would have to continue to share whatever hardships and troubles and suffering and pleasure the family went through till their bodies could no longer bear it.

'The trouble is,' said the two old ladies, 'there are not enough staff. At night there is only one nurse to look after us all on two floors. If we ring a bell, it can be a long time before she comes – some of the people here need attention all the time.'

Unexpectedly, the little town also had a centre for battered women. In fact, in the last year it had handled thirty cases from the surrounding villages and farms, a surprisingly large number for such an unpopulated valley. It was only a small wooden house in a quiet suburb of snowy yards and leafless trees, with the usual lace curtains and candlesticks in the windows. Indoors, there was no sign of violence or calamity – the drawing-room table had the standard lace tablecloth and poinsettia in a pot, the kitchen refrigerator contained milk and eggs.

The centre was founded four years ago and run by 150 volunteers who took turns at spending a night in the place. The only full-time worker was a young girl, in casual T-shirt and slacks, who had started as a part-time volunteer and applied for the full-time job when it was advertised; now she worked five days a week. The centre received a subsidy from the social welfare department and had become widely known, although it was not advertised and its address was kept secret. The telephone number was public and well advertised. The police sent them cases of maltreated women or children brought to their attention; earlier they had not known what to do with the victim. Some came on their own – recently a woman of forty-five came from a distant village, married for twenty years and tired of it all. Some of them brought their children (the two rooms upstairs had cots in them, heaped with flowered quilts), like one woman who arrived with her children, all of them barefoot and in shorts: they had fled when the husband started drinking and threatening them during a holiday weekend. Most of the women had been married for years; none of them came after a single quarrel, but all had endured a great deal before they took the drastic step of leaving home. They could stay at the centre for a month or two till something else was arranged for them, and the centre helped by taking them to a doctor for medical aid, a lawyer for legal aid, and the employment bureau for a job. A majority of the women went back to their husbands after a while in the hope of making a new start, but frequently returned – the dream of the ideal home and blissful marriage once again destroyed. The decisive factor in making them leave was usually the maltreatment of children, who were often raped (although none could bring themselves to use the word 'incest'). 'We feel there are many cases of incest, although that is not what they are called,' said Marit, the social worker. She showed me pictures the children had painted for her and that she had pinned to the wall – they showed cheerful homes with chimney-pots, bright curtains and flower-pots.

The telephone rang continually for her attention. Sometimes it was a violent husband abusing her and demanding his wife back, but fortunately none of them had discovered the address. That is unlike India, where such centres have often been the scene for drama and even police action. Marit was surprised to hear this, imagining that Indian families always lived in perfect harmony. Of course they do not – only the state does not acknowledge this as it does in Norway.

Predictably, the sounds of disharmony, of dissatisfaction and the demand for change grow as one moves closer to the urban centres, their streets and high-rise buildings, industries and unemployment.

In the pleasant southern port city of Frederikstad, there was just a murmur. Siri, Mette and Niru had met for supper in one of those bright Scandinavian homes where the furniture is of stripped pine, the textiles cheerfully coloured, potted plants are flowering and candles are lit. There were rolls and cheeses on the table, and Niru had brought a cake that was served with mounds of whipped cream. All remarked on the pleasure of coming out of their own homes to this little party – an admission that released sudden revelations.

Niru, who had left her four-month-old baby at home with her husband in order to come, spoke of the despair she had gone through during the grey, rainy November days and how each had seemed like an endless pile of washing to be done. 'What is a girl like me doing here?' she had asked herself. 'I like people, I like going out. I am going crazy sitting indoors with two babies and all this washing to do.' This was rather more than the complaint of a bored housewife: she was a trained radiologist who had worked in a hospital in Oslo before coming here and having babies. Now it would be time before she could go back to work – if indeed she were lucky enough to find another job. People naturally preferred to employ men, who did not go on maternity leave (this could be up to one year); by law a father could take two months' paternity leave but few had the courage to face their colleagues' ridicule by doing so. It was considered to be in the nature of things that Niru should give up her job and stay home with the children while her husband worked. He, a neurologist, helped her all he could, had been brought up by his mother to do housework and cook and clean, but was at work in the hospital all day and came home late.

Blonde Mette in grey silk looked wise with her spectacles. She had two small adopted sons from Indonesia but confessed, 'I couldn't give up my work. When they were babies, I stayed home with them but realised that was not enough for me. I need the company of adults. I need adult talk, I need intelligent work.' Unable to find a place in a day-centre – which are so few as to be almost as exclusive as British public schools – she left them with a 'day-mother' in order to teach in a primary school. The 'day-mother' tradition is an old one in Norway – a woman who takes in small children and looks after them while their mothers are at work. It is not always satisfactory – the 'day-mother' may not have adequate space at home or live near a playground, or else might take in too many children. Mette, for instance, had sent her sons to one on condition they would be the only ones in the house, then discovered that the woman had taken on more children. But until vacancies could be found in the day-care centre, it was the only system that made it possible for a mother to go out to work – and clearly this was essential for Mette if she was to remain an individual and not merely an amenity for others in her family.

Siri, who also had two adopted children, from the Philippines (with the birth rate steadily falling in Norway so that there are now just 1.7 children per family, and no children for adoption any more since social welfare has made it possible for an unmarried mother to bring up her children herself, many childless couples in Norway have adopted children from Africa or the Far East), claimed she was perfectly content to stay home as long as her children were small and needed her. 'I don't mind, I'm perfectly happy, I have so much to do,' she said. Then Mette mentioned that there was a vacancy in the school where she taught and if Siri applied there was a good chance she would be accepted. Instantly Siri's hands began to shake, she leant across the table, her eyes flashing in the candlelight, and cried, 'Yes, yes, of course I'll apply – I'll write tomorrow. Oh, do you think I really might get the job? Oh, who will look after the children? What will I do with them?' It was clear that housekeeping and babysitting had little attraction compared to that of a job, a salary, and respected, fulfilling work.

The day-centre is the answer for mothers of pre-school children. Open from seven am to five pm, they cater for children from seven months to seven years (after which another problem begins as primary schools at the junior level keep children for as little as two or three hours on some days, making it essential to have hobby centres or homework centres to keep them occupied during the rest of the day). A day-care centre usually receives funds from the government as well as the local county council, but some enterprising parents have started them in their own homes when their children could not get places anywhere. The one I saw in Frederikstad received 27 per cent of its funds from the local council and charged 900 kroner per child. In Oslo it could cost from 1000 to 1200 kroner per child (as much as the pay of a factory worker and therefore definitely not for the lower rung of workers). There is such a huge demand for places in them – in 1983 835,000 Norwegian women (56.3 per cent of the female population) were out at work, putting in an average of 29 working hours a week – that it is said to be almost impossible to place a child in one. Preference is given to children with special problems (eg, handicapped children, children of divorced parents, or adopted children), so that parents are almost tempted to invent handicaps when there are none. Only 24 per cent of children under seven are at present in day-care centres – a tiny percentage compared to the rest of Scandinavia and some other Western countries like West Germany.

I had only to visit one to find out why a place was such a coveted privilege. Although the one I saw in Frederikstad looked like a plain wooden shed in the snow-filled yard, when I stepped inside I found every kind of comfort and facility one could want for one's child. There were only forty-eight in it, divided into groups of eight, each looked after by three women. Another employee worked in the kitchen where one meal a day was prepared – usually milk and bread. Each section had a bathroom with low wash-basins, small toilets and a row of toothbrushes as if for a family of dwarves. There was a rest room with bunk beds and mattresses on the floor (some children came for only a few hours a day, others stayed all day) and a playroom as full of toys as a toyshop, and tables for painting and clay-modelling and paper-cutting.

A young woman was telling one group a story about a rabbit, illustrated by a big cuddly rabbit puppet on her hand. Some older children – mostly boys with an excited, tomboyish girl or two – had made streets of wooden blocks and were playing with cars. In the kitchen a teacher was making waffles, as there was to be a party for parents a little later. What with the toys, the fun, the food, one might have thought there was a Christmas party on.

The principal, a young woman with short dark hair and spectacles, admitted rather shamefacedly that it was really too much, the children were quite spoilt. It was not necessary for children to have so much; she herself, as a child, had played with sticks and stones, had had one doll and no other toys and been perfectly happy. If children were given so much, they ceased to be happy about possessions or acquisitions, and took everything for granted.

Parents were coming in from the grey dusk outside to pick up their infants, hugging and kissing them. One could see they were not worrying about such surplus and affluence – they were trying to make it up to their children for having left them there, perhaps slightly guilty about not shouldering what they had been brought up to think of as their responsibilities.

In Frederikstad's Old Town, where the seventeenth-century buildings are of stone and timber painted pale blue or yellow, the artists have taken over the old barns and sheds and transformed them into studios. Here people seemed to know how to manage things better: life, work and the family were not divided into separate and watertight compartments but, on the contrary, linked and allowed to merge into each other to form a harmonious whole.

Tulla and her husband had bought an old rectory that was about to be demolished in the country and reconstructed it in the Old Town. They had let out the upper floor to a young couple with a baby so that they could help each other with the baby-sitting (they have two themselves) and the children could toddle into each other's apartment for company. She housed her kiln and clay in the barn next door while her husband had his print-making equipment in the loft upstairs. She made bowls and dishes in warm, rich earth colours; his prints were black and white, precise and meticulous. She made me tea and he took the little boy Nikolaus to play in the loft. There was an acceptance of all the aspects of living, no avoidance and no rejection.

In the feminist activist Bibi Boriesson's house out in the woods beyond Frederikstad, three generations lived in the easy familiarity of an Eastern family. Her mother-in-law, Norway's great poet Inger Hagerup, lay in bed under a floral quilt, trying to read by lamplight and keep her mind off the pain that wracked her frail, aged body. Her son (a playwright) returned from Oslo, where he had attended a rehearsal of a play to be shown on television, made himself supper and went in to give her her medicine. Bibi's mother Eva, a potter who has her studio next to the kitchen, fed the baby its porridge while Bibi talked of her student days and her first taste of politics, in 1972, during the protest against the American presence in Vietnam, her work for equal rights and equal pay, her growing interest in the Third World and her wish to combine her work for women in the West and the East. Her little daughter played with a Siamese cat. There seemed to be no walls in the house between its inhabitants, and it had the relaxed air of an Eastern extended family.

Perhaps it is in a big city that one really comes face to face with loneliness. Perhaps it has to do with walking in dark, icy streets and looking in through lighted windows (Norwegian homes are brilliantly lit, highly coloured and overheated to defy the bleakness of the steely winters) at the candles, the flowers and the family life inside, when one is outside in the darkness, alone. Norway has a family culture and anyone who does not have one must feel at a loss, unprotected. Most suicides are said to take place at Christmas – that celebration of The Family – and again in spring, when those who are excluded from its enchanting rites feel the most abandoned.

Toril stands at the window of her large house below Oslo's famous ski jump, the Holmenkollen, and watches the sun set behind the bare willows and poplars. She has a cigarette between her fingers and smokes almost without a break. 'No, I don't think a woman should live alone,' she says. 'I think marriages should last, that children should live with their parents. I think it is terrible when a marriage breaks up.' She had married at twenty-one, had three sons and was divorced at thirty-one. As a novelist, it was a struggle to live and she had moved back into her childhood home with her mother, a painter, who was also divorced. Toril lived upstairs with her sons, and her mother downstairs; the children ran up for their meals and came down to practise the piano in their grandmother's studio.

She joined us at the window and watched the fire of the sun turn to ashes, leaving the yard shadowy and forlorn. 'This used to be a friendly neighbourhood when we first lived here,' she said. 'Then there were many children – they would play together. Now there seem to be no children, only old people, and no one talks to each other any more.'

There are now so many single parents in Norway (in 1978 one marriage in four had ended in divorce, in 1983 more than one-third broke up and, as fewer women were marrying, single adults made up 40.7 per cent of the population) that Britta, who had worked for years in the National Bureau of Social Welfare, left to set up a bureau to help them. She had an office in a block of flats that seemed chiefly to house dentists and doctors; she had had to have extra locks and bolts fitted on the door to keep out the burglars who were always trying to break in in search of drugs. Inside, it looked cheerful and friendly with a pine table, benches with cushions and the ubiquitous potted plants. She received financial aid from the Consumers' Society, the Bureau of Social Welfare and the Oslo County Council. It costs 75 kroner a year to join her organisation and subscribe to the magazine she brings out, giving single parents valuable information about available aid. She has 1500 subscribers, but there are 100,000 single parents in Norway. She gives them advice on how to draw social security or council funds for as long as their children are under ten or they themselves are unemployed. In Norway one can draw dole for eighty weeks, consecutively or within two calendar years. Usually this amounts to 2 per 1,000 of expected income (excluding child benefit). For a woman who is not well qualified or trained, this is not a large sum. Once a parent finds a job, or a child goes beyond Class III in school, the welfare ceases. Exceptions are made for parents who are studying, since there is currently a drive to persuade mothers to go back to studies given up when they married, and to qualify for better jobs (special aid is available to them). Social welfare started in 1969 and reached its peak in the seventies, at the height of Norway's industrialisation and prosperity, but has declined in the eighties with recession, unemployment and a conservative government in power. Britta worried about the future of social welfare, since the biggest problem of single parents is of course economic.

There are many other problems related to a life of pressure, tension and (frequently) guilt. She found herself having to arrange psychiatric and medical aid as often as economic aid and estimated that one in three people in Norway need psychiatric help – a fact which she attributed to living in high-rise apartment blocks, loneliness and the strains of facing life alone.

Another area that has not received enough official attention, the dark young Indian girl Nita told me, was that of immigrant women. She and the elderly, matronly Mrs Chawla had founded the Foreign Women's Association with the aim of filling this gap – foreign women being the weakest and most exploited of urban society. Some had been fetched from their countries to marry immigrants and were bewildered by the strange land; or else had been married to men brought from their countries for the purpose, and had found them incompatible. Broken marriages were common, the divorce rate high, and physical battering as well as nervous breakdowns frequent. Others, highly qualified in their own countries, could not hope to get any but menial jobs in shops and factories here; need made them accept such jobs and condemn themselves to second-class lives. Their children, although materially better off then they might be at home, were exposed to jeers and maltreatment in school with no means of retaliation – the police seldom being willing to interfere or provide protection. Nazism was growing, as evidenced by graffiti in working-class areas and the violent attacks on immigrants. Nita said despondently, 'This is a growing trend all over Europe and I see no hope for the future. We ought to join hands to fight it – the only thing that matters in the world is having power. But the immigrants here are divided into groups and Iranians won't have anything to do with Iraqis, or Pakistanis with Bangladeshis. They live in their own ghettoes and grow lonelier and more isolated all the time. The Norwegians think of immigrants as the dark people, living strange lives, performing strange rituals, and making no effort to participate in Norwegian life or speak the Norwegian language. How can they, when no Norwegian ever invites them to their home or speaks to them?'

The Equal Status Council is the official body to establish and safeguard the equal status of women. It was founded in 1972 and reorganised in 1979 when the Norwegian Act Relating to Equal Status was passed. This Act is enforced by both the Ombud for Equal Status Between Men and Women and the Appeals Board. (Norway invented the office of the Ombudsman, then changed the name to Ombud.)

The Ombud's office, the top floor of the post office building in central Oslo, does not look in the least official. Tea and cakes were laid out on a long, low table that did not resemble a board-room table anywhere else. The walls were hung with prints. One poster showed a dainty little moustached man asleep in bed while his enormous naked wife struggled to dress herself beside it – a reversal of the stereotypical scene. 'Do you think that sexist?' laughed the Ombud and her assistant; they didn't. They were very proud, too, of the poster designed for 1975, the International Year of the Woman, its design based on the Norwegian sculptor Vigelund's figures of three women twined about with a creeper, representing growth and fecundity, attractively rendered in the green and blue shades of nature in summertime. On a side table stood an enormous arrangement of dried flowers given them by 'the Ministry' – huge sunflower heads, that symbol of the women's movement, as well as prickly thistles which made the two women laugh again. Their own offices were bright with photographs, prints, potted plants and lamps, displaying the Norwegian woman's genius for domesticity.

Eva Kolstad, the Ombud – a middle-aged, grey-haired woman in a grey wool skirt and bright red jacket – has a dry but pleasant manner, friendly and relaxed, and laughs easily. 'If I were a younger woman, I would have had a much harder time, and would not have been taken seriously. My age is a help in this job.' Her assistant, round-faced and matronly, with short hair and spectacles, talks with great vivacity and speed. They combined personal anecdotes with official reports easily and humorously. Eva Kolstad told me she belonged to a generation in which it was not common for girls to be educated beyond the primary school, but her father had wanted her to have further education and, after his death, her mother had seen to it that she had it. Although she went to work, she attended business school in the evenings to study accountancy. She had led an active career in politics as well, and been Norway's delegate to the UN Commission on the Status of Women for seven years. She is married and her husband is proud of her achievements; he is also quite pleased that she should earn more than him.

This does not in the least prevent her from understanding the problems other women have in struggling to achieve that status. As an Ombud, she receives complaints regarding discrimination against women in every area, but chiefly in the field of employment. Norway was the first country to outlaw such discrimination from advertisements for jobs, and sexism has been successfully removed from these advertisements although a constant vigil has to be maintained to see it does not reappear. Charges of discrimination by potential employees were looked into, even if they were made after the appointment of a man in place of a woman had already been made; these were regarded as test cases that would help women in the future. Employers still preferred to employ men as women were expected to take maternity leave and sick leave for their children (which men were not) and they could explain this away by saying that women were seldom as well qualified as men since they tended to study arts or social sciences instead of taking vocational training, and married too young to go to university for higher degrees. The Council was trying to remove all traces of the traditional role of women from educational material – books, toys, pictures and equipment – and has insisted on teachers taking special courses on equal status. There was also a drive on to make it compulsory for girls to study computer science so they would not be excluded from the latest field of employment as from earlier ones, and all kinds of financial aid were being made available to mothers who wished to go back to their studies. Women employees also needed protection because they were often part-time workers who did not have the same recourse to funds and aid as full-time male workers, and it was felt that far more aid was needed to set up day-care centres and emergency centres for battered women – two areas in which Norway inexplicably lags behind the rest of Scandinavia and much of Western Europe.

The Council found it more difficult to protect the rights of domestic workers – women who worked twice as long as men at housework (even if they had jobs outside the home they put in an average of 4.2 hours a day in contrast to 2.5 hours by men in 1980–81). Boys would have to be persuaded to take up domestic science. The situation was better in the country than in the cities, I was informed, because countrymen are accustomed to working with their hands, and academics, teachers and professors are the best of all, being more willing to take paternity leave and play an active role in the upbringing of their children. Eva Kolstad thought it was harmful to talk, as Alva Myrdal had once, of 'The Dual Role of Women' and not emphasise that men were required to play a dual role as well.

Then there were the divorced women's rights to be protected, alimony to be obtained from reluctant fathers, and contracts to be drawn up between couples who preferred not to marry so that the woman could be certain of aid from the father if she had children.

Such talk of 'contracts' sounded strangely offical to Indian ears – curiously cold and practical instead of emotional and human as one would expect in such matters. I wondered what kind of human relationship could call for official intervention.

Pornography. When social relationships break down, requiring such intervention between men and women, boys and girls, what is the result?

Women have tended to think of pornography as something existing between the covers of lurid magazines or behind dirty curtains in a sleazy part of town. It took a recent television programme to open the eyes of Norway's population to the extent and grossness of the phenomenon.

'I saw a group of men slice off a women's breast and cut it into pieces and eat it,' said fifteen-year-old Katerina with a shudder, wrapping her arms about her vulnerable child's body. 'So now I am going to Tai Kun Du classes – I don't want that to happen to me.'

Her mother, who had watched the programme with her, told of a woman's body fed into a giant mincing-machine so that it emerged in strings of bleeding sausage meat.

Nightmares? The overheated imagination of the rabid? These were clips from video films that are on sale all over Scandinavia; they had been put together for the television programme in order to bring the full horror of pornography to the attention of the nation and force the authorities to ban the import and distribution of pornographic video films from the USA. Did it? When it was shown to a selected body of officials they had to leave the room in order to go outside and vomit, but they would not bring out a ban. Why? It would violate the freedom of expression, they said. Yet when a magazine appeared with a nude male for a centrespread, it was whisked off the stalls in a matter of hours: 'freedom of expression' could not go so far as to turn a man into a figure of fun.

'Freedom of expression', then, permits American psychopaths to kidnap children of fourteen years or less, cage them or lock them up, rape and assault them, then murder them in ever more gruesome ways before the eyes of a camera and a film crew that packages these films for video and distributes them all over the world. Such 'snuff' films are the latest rage in video. Men and boys pay money to see them and learn that sex and violence are one, that rape and murder are pleasure, that the humiliation and torture of the weak is power. Officials watch with helplessness – or complicity?

Such are the successes and failures of an officialdom created by a state that has taken on itself the duties and responsibilities, doubts and pleasures that are still the lot of the family and the individual in less organised parts of the world.

But the state has not done away with the individual. It cannot.

It was not always easy to find an individual on the icy streets of Oslo, devastated by winter and emptied out by the wash of night and dark. I had to go into the candlelit, whitewashed basement of 'Alexandros', a Greek restaurant, in search of one.

Elisabet had discarded her winter coverings in the hall that was fast becoming choked with damp fur and wet boots, and was sitting – dressed in a black skirt and a white blouse with wide, summery sleeves – with a cigarette and a glass of retsina before her, listening to the music of the bouzouki. She was very fair and her eyes behind her large spectacles were of such a pale grey as to seem almost colourless. It was the story she told me that had all the colour – vivid and fresh and startling.

She came from a small village in the north where she lived on a farm. It was ruled by her tyrannical mother, a woman of powerfully orthodox beliefs who instilled in Elisabet a lifelong aversion to organised religion. She went to the local primary school but did not do well; she felt the teachers were against her and were not interested in helping an intelligent but awkward girl, preferring to give their attention to the boys in the class whose education had to be taken more seriously. She left by marrying a young man with a weak and gentle nature and going with him to Oslo where he found work as a postal clerk. They lived in an abominably inadequate and unhygienic flat; of her four children, one died in infancy. This death brought in the social workers who helped the young couple to move to a healthier locality. Seeing Elisabet's situation and sensing her true potential they encouraged her and helped her to resume her studies. In high school she came first in mathematics and was known as a brilliant scholar. This had given her so much confidence that she divorced her husband and moved to a small flat nearby. She was working as a shopgirl by day and studying computer science by night. When she was qualified, she was certain she would get a job in a field that seemed to her exciting and promising.

And her husband? Elisabet smiled. He had always enjoyed housework more than she did; now he had given up his job to stay home and look after the children. His colleagues thought him a martyr and the neighbours (particularly the old ladies) thought him a hero and brought him cakes and sympathy. Old women and wives in the neighbourhood abused her as she went by. She smiled again. 'I have a strong will, I can stand it.' The social workers were helping her, and she had one supporter at home. Who?

She burst out laughing. 'My mother-in-law!'

Still laughing, we went out into the street – once more buried under our pelts, layer upon layer of sober grey and black. She turned and went up the road to her tram stop, walking between the lines that showed black on the white snow. I watched her till she turned the corner and vanished.

Then I realised who she was: she was Ibsen's Nora, giving back her wedding ring to her husband and walking out into the night because she had 'my duty to myself'; she was Cora Sandel's Alberta, who had also left a family to go away alone: 'She walked alone, certain of only one thing. She had finished groping in a fog for warmth and security. The mist had risen now, there was clear visibility and it was cold. No arms around her any more, not even those of a child: naked life, as far ahead as she could see, struggle and an impartial view. She would go under or become so bitterly strong that nothing could hurt her any more. She felt something of the power of the complete solitary.'

Anita Desai is the daughter of a Bengali father and a German mother. She was educated in Delhi, and now lives in Bombay. She has written several books for children, and a volume of short stories entitled *Games at Twilight*. Her novel *Fire on the Mountain* won the 1978 National Academy of Letters Award, while *Clear Light of Day*, written in 1980, was nominated for the Booker McConnell Prize, as was *In Custody* in 1984. Anita Desai is married and has four children.

Toril Brekke

It was the Quaker who suggested we should go and see Rose's new house. As soon as they'd finished work in the weaving-shop, we left; the long-legged Quaker with a camera hanging from his shoulder on a strap, Rose, Rachel and myself.

The track is narrow and we walk in single file, the sun scorching our backs, while the Quaker talks enthusiastically about his fellow believers back home who had sent him a sum of money that they wanted him to donate to charity. This coincided with the birth of Rose's last child. He had visited her and, after noticing how dilapidated the old house was, he had given her the money to build a new one. He had even helped her to buy the furnishings and had driven to Kisumu to buy corrugated tin for the roof.

Rose walks ahead in silence. Even Rachel, who is usually chatty and cheerful, walks without saying a word. I have a presentiment that something is not as it should be.

The nearer we approach Rose's place, the slower she walks, and even the sound of one of her children crying doesn't make her walk faster. The Quaker is describing how corrupt the headmaster is at the school where he teaches and he continuously almost stumbles over Rose. The headmaster has embezzled a whole year's money and has bought a small bus, a matatu, which he drives people around in, earning money and letting the school go to blazes.

We have arrived. We have greeted the other women in the courtyard and Rose's horde of children, eight of them between the ages of one month and fourteen years. They're standing in a frightened bunch, just behind the white man with the camera. A few yards in front of us, alone in the dry grass, is Rose. She is barefoot, dressed in a long blue skirt and a short white vest that I know has a long tear down the back. Her arms hang loosely at her sides, her fists clench and unclench, she stares at us, looks through us or past us with a look I can't fathom: rejecting? desperate?

There she stands, erect and serious. On either side of her, wooden stakes are stuck into the ground – twenty crooked stakes that mark the square outline of a planned house, a skeleton with half of a roof covered in tin. Rose stands in the shadow under the roof, alone, in front of the Quaker, her children, the other women, Rachel and me. The white man takes his picture. His cheerful mood from the trip along the track has disappeared, he gives Rose a resigned look, he says he will not return until the house is finished.

He says it won't be long before he returns anyway, and then he'll take back the corrugated tin if nothing has been done. Then he makes a bad attempt at smiling, as if to soften the toughness of his words.

Rose is silent. She walks out of the shadow, turns her back on the monster of tin and stakes, turns her back on us all and walks slowly towards the old house, a round, wind-warped mudhut with a straw roof.

'You don't understand,' says Rachel.

We're back on the track, the Quaker, Rachel and I.

'But it must be possible to finish the house?' he asks.

'Building houses is a man's job,' says Rachel.

Then her husband should build the house when he returns from the city.

'But he refuses. He says, when others start the house, then they can finish it.'

'Does he want his wife to live in a house that will fall apart in the next rainy season?'

'You don't understand. . . .'

Reality is a dusty, red track. Sisal plants. Brambles. Rachel disappears into the bushes and returns with a pile of firewood on her head.

People must be happy in this country, I've thought, under the brilliantly coloured crowns of the jacaranda and flamboya; happy, I've thought, with the taste of passion-fruit, pineapple juice and refreshing coconut milk on my palate.

But ahead of me on the track walks Rachel, black and shining in the heat, in a red blouse and a yellow kanga round her waist, the firewood on her head and a profile that tells me she is wondering how she can get these white people to grasp the meaning of the picture that is now preserved on the film in the man's camera: the picture of Rose under the tin roof.

I've been living with Rachel's family for four days. A large courtyard surrounded by mudhuts and houses. Two of the oldest houses belong to the parents-in-law: he has only had one wife, now she lies dying in her hut. Her husband walks about in blue overalls and a brown cap, spending his mornings working on his shamba. His food is made by one of his daughters-in-law. The old couple have had four children. The three daughters have been married off and live in other places; the son, John, is a teacher in the city where he has a small apartment which he shares with his third wife, who is young and still childless. But John comes at least once a week and sleeps with one of his other two wives, Rachel and Eleonorah. Eleonorah is his first wife; she is also a teacher at a nearby primary school. She's the one with the best residence in the yard – a square house with three rooms and a cemented floor. The roof is of tin and not straw, and she has a gas cooker and a battery-operated television. I am borrowing one of her rooms. Rachel, on the other hand, still lives in her round mudhuts. She has two, one kitchen-hut and one sleeping-hut.

I am sitting in the kitchen-hut watching Rachel prepare dinner. She is boiling spinach in a pot over an open fire. The little room is filled with smoke that stings the eyes, some hens flap around our feet, and a couple of young goats. I want to talk about Rose.

I think it's about men and women. About old traditions. I tell of a book I have read, where it said that when African men marry they have to build a house for their wife. Perhaps Rose's husband is offended because other people are concerning themselves about something that is his responsibility?

Rachel sits on a stool, her legs wide, making ugali, a kind of maize-porridge. She nods.

'The wife of the husband shall live in her husband's house,' she says.

I think of Rose's husband. About the wretched huts his wives live in. He has three wives and they all live as badly as each other, huts full of cracks and blackened ceilings, almost falling apart. The small patch of earth he owns is not enough to feed such a large family. I think of his children, ragged and badly dressed, all of them home during the day because there is no money for school uniforms and books. I think about Rose's husband who's been in Nairobi for almost a year looking for a job and recently came home wearing the same clothes, his pockets just as empty as when he set out. (Where had he lived in Nairobi? In Mathare Valley, where 150,000 people are packed together in plank and cardboard shelters. I've been there, I've met Ann, a seventeen-year-old prostitute, and her mother who supports herself by selling bad liquor.)

Rose's husband who comes home and finds the weird skeleton of a house in the yard. His own yard. Which other men had the right to build on his ground?

Is this what it's all about?

Rachel nods again. This is what it's all about. Among other things.

Her two-year-old son runs into the hut with tear-stained cheeks; the puppy has bitten his naked toes. But not too hard, for his toes show no damage, and a couple of minutes later the incident is forgotten.

'Why didn't the Quaker understand all this?' I continue.

'He did it out of kindness,' says Rachel. 'He's kind. I was with him when he went to congratulate Rose with her latest child. I remember his face when he entered the hut and saw how bad the walls and roof were. He didn't want Rose to live like that. And he was angry with her husband who let his wife live like that and had never sent either a letter or money after he left. . . .'

1700 charitable shillings. Twelve pieces of tin and twenty thin, wooden stakes. The start of a house that would be six times as big as Rose's old hut. Six times as big as the huts of her co-wives. This is what it's all about. And to use 1700 shillings for corrugated tin when a pair of trousers for one of the youngsters costs 30 and there is no money for trousers. Or school uniforms. Or blankets to have over them at night in the rainy season. Or a cockerel or a piece of fish to have at least once every two weeks. . . .

'You're beginning to understand,' says Rachel.

I sit in the doorway of my room and read *Viva*, the Kenyan magazine for women. The lay-out is first class and the headings could easily have been printed in an American, French or Norwegian women's magazine.

'Your guide to the premenstrual syndrome', 'The male menopause', 'Faithful husbands: do they exist?'.

Before me in the courtyard, large, pale, shackled cows and small, spotted goats graze. A hen prepares herself for laying beneath a washing basin propped against the wall beside me. John comes home from town. He walks past Rachel's huts without even glancing inside, turns the corner and makes for Eleonorah's door. I think 'gas cooker' and wonder if she has bought anything good to eat from the market on the way home from school.

I continue to read the article about the faithful husbands. A strange article, seen from my point of view in the doorway, because it's about faithfulness in a monogamous marriage. I have met African men, of course, who have chosen a life with one wife as a matter of principle. Like George in Nairobi. I was shown their wedding photographs. George and Ruth on the church steps; him in his black suit and her in a white wedding dress, the wedding cake – a tall marzipan cake with a tiny couple on top. It was all so homely that I didn't reflect on what I had experienced until later.

Christianity *contra* African traditions. And: how many Africans can afford black suits and lace dresses? And marzipan cakes?

Rachel comes swinging across the courtyard, her skirt flapping about her and a flowered scarf around her head.

'What are you doing?'

'I'm reading about why African men aren't faithful.'

She stops in front of me, gives me a questioning look.

I hand her the magazine. She looks at the illustrations of the article: a man creeping home late at night with his shoes in his hand. A classical European cartoon.

'What does it say?' asks Rachel.

'Mainly a lot of rubbish,' I say.

It's about man's search for his dream-woman, one he perhaps knew in his youth, but never got. Maybe he marries a woman who resembles her, then he becomes disappointed and continues to search for his dream-woman after he's married. It's about how the sexual needs of men are greater than those of women. About personal hygiene; how men who have dirty wives go to other women.

I look at Rachel and for some unknown reason I feel ashamed for bringing the magazine with me here, a Kenyan women's magazine that has no relation to the Kenyan woman standing before me; a magazine from another world – my world more than hers. And it strikes me how far we have to go; for Rachel, for the élite women in Nairobi, for myself and my fellow sisters at home; how far to freedom and equality.

'Do you frown on African polygamy?' Rachel asks.

I shake my head.

'It's not like that where you live?'

'It's illegal to marry more than one woman at a time,' I say. 'But a lot of men have mistresses for short or long spells. Quite a few women have lovers.'

'And that's okay?'

'No, far from it. It creates complications. Jealousy, divorce. . . .'

The first time I saw polygamy was in Muranga, in the heart of Kikuyu country. The Kikuyu are Kenya's largest tribe. Jomo Kenyatta was a Kikuyu.

Ruth and George took me there, to her parents. We drove from the capital early one morning, through dry, flat countryside, through Thika, with its enormous American-owned pineapple plantation, through colourful villages; a main street with pastel-coloured façades; a pink butcher's shop, a bright yellow milk-bar, a small apple-green house with 'Hotel' painted over the door.

We are nearing Mount Kenya and the landscape is becoming lush and fertile, full of small ridges and hills, cultivated fields, lively streams that glitter in the sun.

When we arrive, Ruth's mother and brothers are in the tea fields. Fast-moving hands pluck the fresh, light-green shoots and throw handful after handful into the baskets they carry on their backs. There is a great contrast between the town-dwellers and the tea-pickers. Mother Mable, barefoot and sweating, her sons in rough working clothes with woolly hats to protect them from the sun, the husband wandering with his scythe on his shoulder (after pruning the coffee bushes), wearing black working trousers with light-grey patches on the knees and crotch. And Ruth and George; him in his neatly pressed summer suit and suede shoes and her in a beautiful, sky-blue summer dress.

The joy of reunion, smiles, shaking hands.

At the other end of the field a lone woman walks. When we go to eat lunch I ask George if the woman should also join us. He laughs and replies in a low voice: No, not at all. She is the tea-picker's first wife and lives completely alone. Once, the two women and their children shared the work in the fields, but they quarrelled so much the husband divided the field in two. Two elderly women with each their half field. Two elderly women who rarely talk to each other.

Later I meet Esther in Kibera.

'How is your relationship between your husband's first wife and yourself?' I ask.

'We're the best of friends,' laughs Esther. 'When my parents no longer could afford to send me to school, I asked my friend if she could convince her husband to marry me too, and he did. . . .'

I remember a television programme I saw in Norway, where an African woman defended polygamy. I quote her words for Rachel: 'In the West you try to hide all forms of unfaithfulness; in Africa we're not so hypocritical – a husband's women know about the other women because everything is open.'

It's getting dark; we sit inside and light a lamp.

A lizard dashes across the wall; I hope it eats the huge bee that disturbed me earlier in the day and flew up into the rafters.

'Maybe it's wrong, when we Africans believe that everything is better among the whites,' says Rachel slowly, 'but . . .'

We're drinking tea and somebody knocks on the door. It's John and Eleonorah. Mr and Mrs Joshwa, him in a dark suit with comfortable shoes, her in a lovely red dress but barefoot. Will he greet Rachel, whom he hasn't seen for four days? Will they react to Rachel sitting here? Am I alone in thinking that Rachel is destroying the illusion of the Joshwa couple on an evening visit to a European woman?

I fetch a plate of biscuits and a bowl of bananas and pour tea for everyone.

John is jovial, in the best of moods, he talks a lot – mainly to me. His wives are silent. He talks about Kenya, the country's economy, foreign aid, the contrast between the towns and rural areas. What do I think of Nairobi?

'A featureless city that could be almost anywhere.'

'What about Kisumu?'

Kisumu. 'Little Bombay', on the banks of Lake Victoria. Dominated by Indian commerce, Indian restaurants, shops, factories . . . . I like Kisumu, but wonder what Africans think about Indian domination.

'They came here in 1904 to build a railway,' John explains.

He talks about the English who simply transported labour from the one colony to the next, ships full of railway-workers with one-way tickets. I'm fascinated by the picture before me, a picture of the chatty, learned John, with a wife at each side. I try to understand what it's like to be him. What it's like to be Eleonorah, Rachel . . .

'What about Mombasa?' John asks.

'Ah. Mombasa, a pearl among cities . . .'

I forget my personal views. I am in Mombasa – by Fort Jesus – where the street vendors have their stalls along the pavements – in the ancient Arab quarter. John has also been there and we exchange streets, buildings, pictures with shared enthusiasm, until I become silent and let him continue alone. As I stop I find myself on a roof overlooking the old harbour. Beneath me, a gang of youths lie in the grass and smoke marijuana. Beyond them is the entrance to the enclosed stairway, where the Arabs once forced African slaves down to their ships.

Centuries of humiliation. Who had they become when their country was freed? Who are they now? When I ask Rachel about old songs and dances she shakes her head. Nairobi is full of breakdance. I find it strange that when women talk about themselves, they use the term 'the African woman' not 'the Luo woman' or 'the Kenyan woman'. I think about the incidental borders between the countries that the Europeans once drew up.

John talks about the long train journey between Kisumu and Mombasa. The railways that bind the country together . . .

Rachel sits in the shadows, outside the cone of light from the lamp. Silent. Rachel who grew up just a few miles away. Rachel who came here on foot, owning nothing, to live with a man who had paid her bridal fees. What does Rachel know about taking a train, about Nairobi and Mombasa . . .

John says thank you for the tea and rises to leave. I shake their hands and bid them goodnight. I show them out, and stand in the darkness, listening to the sounds in the trees and the grass. Above me a quarter-moon lies white in the night sky.

I prepare for bed and can hear Eleonorah moving about in her own room. I wonder: if Rachel had a choice, I'm sure she would choose a gas cooker before her husband's nightly advances. I wonder: how much does she earn weaving? How long must she save to be able to afford her own cooker?

It was the Quaker who helped them to start weaving. Fifteen women who sit together for a few hours each morning and weave belts. Pretty patterns in red, yellow, blue, green. They have their own house which has a terrace. The house is built with funds that the Quaker obtained through a foreign-aid organisation. It lies on a piece of ground belonging to John's family, just outside the courtyard where Rachel and Eleonorah live.

The women wander in around ten o'clock, by which time they have already spent hours working on their shambas, made tea for their families, have washed up and got the oldest children off to school.

Each income is based on how much they produce themselves. Some work fast, some slowly. Some have to leave their work at the looms for a while, to go home and prepare food for their children coming home in the school lunch-break. Others have fellow-wives or mothers-in-law who relieve them of some of the household chores.

The Quaker keeps a large ledger in which he registers how many belts each of the women makes. Once a month he goes to Nairobi with the finished products. Then returns with the money.

'What do you spend the money on?' I ask Judith, one of the women in the group.

She's thirty-two years old and has given birth to nine children. She became pregnant at school and married the child's father, who was already married.

'A lot of things . . . food, clothes, school uniforms,' she answers.

I ask how many of her children attend school.

'Four.'

Nine minus four, I reckon, and ask who looks after the five others, when she is here.

'No, there are only three at home now. My first child was still-born. The second died of smallpox a couple of weeks after it was born.'

'Why have you had so many?' I ask.

'Do you think I wanted them all? I'm sick as a dog every time I'm pregnant, sick the whole nine months. And when the child arrives – I've no milk for it.'

'But doesn't your husband understand that you shouldn't be pregnant so often when it makes you so ill?'

'Having a lot of children is a sign of wealth for a man.'

'But think how ill it makes you.'

'He doesn't know that I'm ill.'

'But he must notice it.'

Judith sits and ponders. Then she says, 'You see, the African woman never complains. At least not to her husband. A woman who complains is a bad woman. A sick woman is also a bad woman.'

She tells me about her friend who aborted three times, in the middle of each pregnancy. After that her husband sent her away.

'And who do you think wants her now?'

Mary is another one of the women in the group. She also became pregnant whilst still at school. I ask if she married the father of the child.

Mary laughs and shakes her head. The father was her teacher.

'Why did you go to bed with him?'

Mary laughs again. Don't I know what men are like? When a teacher wants one of his female pupils, what else can they do except submit? Anyway, he'd allowed her to continue at the school after her family could no longer afford to pay the fees.

'What did he do when you became pregnant?' I ask.

'He threw me out of the school.'

'Wouldn't he accept the responsibility?'

'He said there was no proof that he was the father. "Haven't you other sponsors?" he asked.'

'Had you?'

Mary gives no direct answer.

'Isn't it the same where you come from?' she asks instead. 'That a lot of girls are dependent on sugar daddies to pay their way at school?'

Sugar daddies. I remember a pink bus that drove in front of us when I came from Muranga with George and Ruth. The bus windows were filled with gaudy decorations and on the rear window was written 'Sugar Daddy'. I asked the others what sort of strange vehicle it was and was met with a giggling silence. Finally George explained: it was a trip organised by rich, old men who paid young girls to join them.

'No,' I explain. 'No Norwegian girl is dependent on a sugar daddy to pay her way at school. There are women who sell themselves. But for other reasons.'

Mary nods, apparently satisfied with my answer.

She is quite beautiful, sitting there in the light of early evening, large brown eyes, full-mouthed, high cheek bones. Her hair is plaited in an intricate pattern with woollen threads that intermingle with the black hair. I know it takes five or six hours to arrange it like that, but the hair-style lasts for months.

'What did your parents say when you became pregnant?' I ask.

'Nothing. What could they say? They couldn't afford the school fees and knew the money had to come from somewhere. . . .'

Mary had married another man. He was already married and didn't mind the child having another father.

'Did you love him?'

She laughs.

'Love him? Maybe not in the beginning. I grew to love him after a while. But I don't any more....'

Mary is twenty-four years old. She has had three children with this man.

'Why don't you love him any more?'

'He's not good to me. He drinks too much. Drinks up all our money. What I earn weaving. When I try to talk to him about it he's nasty to me.'

'What do you mean, nasty?'

'Do white men never beat their women?'

'Of course.'

'I'll tell Florenz that.'

'Why?'

'Because Florenz dreams of marrying a mzungu, a white man. White men are much kinder than African men, or so Florenz thinks. . . . What do you do when your men beat you?'

I tell her about the shelters for battered and raped women. But I also explain that this is something new and that many people consider violence in the family to be a private matter, and that women were ashamed to admit it and often tried to hide it.

'They feel ashamed? The African woman never feels ashamed,' says Mary. But she has no place to go for help. She tells about the time she went to her mother-in-law for help. But her mother-in-law didn't believe her and told the husband. This time she was beaten even worse, for telling tales.

What goes on in a woman's hut concerns only herself and her husband. No man allows his wife to tell others what goes on between them . . . the only thing you can do is to move from home. And that's the same as divorce . . . and a divorced woman is a bad woman.

Mary lives alone with her children. Her husband has lived far away for over a year.

'Has he found a job?'

'I don't know.'

'Does he send you money?'

'No – the only thing he's sent since he left is a letter saying that he's coming home in April . . . but I hope he stays there. That he finds a job and sends money home. He can come home once a year, then maybe we could avoid quarrelling, just that one time . . . .'

I lie on my tummy on the bed where Eleonorah's daughters usually sleep, and glance through my notes in the light of an oil lamp that belongs to the Quaker. I think of Judith and Mary, I think of how it must be to go through nine pregnancies and nine births in fourteen or fifteen years. I remember my own three – the spewing, the pelvic pains, tiny feet that kicked against the bladder and ribs; sleep interrupted by continual trips to the lavatory; but what if the lavatory is a hole in the ground, a latrine fifteen yards from the house? What if the house is a small mudhut and the bed is a single mattress that you share with children already born, five, six, seven children and you with your huge belly on a single mattress. . . . What about when the hut is wind-warped and full of cracks that you fruitlessly try to fill with straw mats and bits of rag, like Rose's, and the world outside is full of puff-adders and green mambas. . . .

These are my thoughts when somebody knocks on the door.

'Karibu,' I answer.

'Karibu,' Rachel repeats ironically as she glides inside. 'How could you know who was knocking – do you wish anyone welcome when you're lying in bed?'

I rise with the blanket around my shoulders and place the lamp on the table.

'You forgot it again,' says Rachel. 'That's why I'm here.'

The shutters. I've forgotten the shutters again.

This is the second time she comes to warn me; the last time
excused myself by saying that I was used to curtains and no
shutters, and that there is mosquito-netting between the window
frames and at least no mosquito can get inside; and that the netting
is dark and dense so it's difficult to see what's happening inside, and
anyway, who on earth would be sneaking about on the ground that
Rachel's family owned at this time of the evening? I was just about
to extinguish the light anyway. . . .

Rachel goes round closing the shutters.

'Why is it so important?' I inquire, convinced that there is
reason why she shrinks from telling me.

'What have you learned today?' asks Rachel.

'That African women don't complain or gossip. And that they're
good at keeping secrets.'

'Secrets?'

'Like why it's important to close the shutters at night.'

Rachel laughs.

'You whites are different to us,' she says. 'There's a lot about
Africa you'll never understand. . . .'

'Such as?'

Rachel hesitates. She has the same look as she had at the
market-place when I asked her if it would be okay if I took a picture
of the witch-doctor who sat on a blanket and sold strange medicines.
I tempt her to open up for me by telling her about the Laplanders
or Sami people as they should be called, home in Norway. 'Yes, in
Norway we have two tribes, and the Sami are one of them – and
they can do all sorts of things; like reading the future in the palm of
your hand and brewing strange, herbal concoctions, and if I'm not
mistaken one of my ancestors was a Sami and he could stop the flow
from a bad wound, just by concentrating on it; and they can also cast
spells.'

'How?'

'Cast spells on people.'

'With the evil eye?' Rachel asks.

'That too. And with the aid of thought.'

'Bewitched people with the evil eye. That's what it's like here.
Women who are suddenly bewitched, who run around naked during
the night, round and round, often in a group. And if you look into
their eyes, you go mad.'

So that's why it's necessary to put up the shutters and lock the
door.

Rachel shudders, glancing uneasily at the darker corners.

I say, 'If I had given birth to nine children in fourteen years and worn myself out trying to feed and clothe them, I'm sure I would have needed a few nightly runs too. . . .'

Rachel stares at me, at first offended, then she starts to laugh.

'It's nothing to laugh about,' she laughs.

'No,' I laugh.

I lock the door after she leaves. Then I go to bed and turn off the light. Through the shutters I can hear the music from the crickets. Then I sleep.

I awake after a few hours. Has it started to rain? No – it's drums. And voices, some distance away, rising and fading. Is it the night witches? I'm in utter darkness and can't see a hand in front of me. Barefoot I creep over to the door, open it and peer out. The black African summer night is torn by a blue-white light some distance away. The wet grass before me is momentarily illuminated, the trees beyond, the shamba behind the trees. Then everything is black again, until a new flash of light splits the sky. It looks as if it's coming from the same place as the drums and voices. Are they fireworks? What are they drumming and making such a din about? Am I right in believing that the sound is coming closer and closer? A cat strokes along my leg, startling me. The dogs in front of Eleonorah's door start barking. Other dogs answer them. Then the dogs are silent again. I think: What if I had been a white settler's wife a hundred years ago, here in the village in the middle of darkest Africa surrounded by night; dark night illuminated by a blue-white light, dark night filled by the sound of drums that come closer and closer. . . .

I go back inside again, lock the door and pull the blanket over me. I'm no settler's wife. Anyway, I've read somewhere that African lightning is not necessarily followed by thunder and squalls of rain. And the drums are certainly not getting any closer. I calm myself with the thought that most probably somebody over there must have died.

The next time I awaken it's four o'clock. Eleonorah's cockerel is crowing coarsely.

The morning is soft and mild. The large, fair cows with their heavy horns are grazing between the houses; two speckled cockerels chase each other around the courtyard; the little puppy jumps up and licks Rachel's son in the face. He howls with joy-filled fear. Eleonorah has gone to school. Rachel invites me to morning tea; half a cup of tea, and half a cup of milk and sugar.

The weaving-group are to have a meeting today. They will discuss how they will manage after the Quaker has left. He's leaving in a couple of months.

'We've no business sense,' says Rachel.

'You've been to school,' I say. 'You can do simple arithmetic.'

'Yes. But still.'

'What do you mean?'

'No Luo understands business.'

'Nonsense,' I object.

'It's not nonsense. The Kikuyu can do it. The Indians can do it We can't. Quite a few have tried. They've received goods from a Indian in Kisumu. The goods should be sold within a month, the you return and settle up and fetch more goods. But when it comes t paying the Indian there's no money to pay him with. Because there' always something you lack: salt, sugar, flour . . . and so you tak from the money that has been put aside for the month. The Kikuy can do it. The Indians can do it. We can't.'

'The Luo in Kibuyuni can do it,' I say.

Kibuyuni. Down by the coast, in the Kwale area, not far from Mombasa. I tell Rachel about the women's group in Kibuyun where Digo, Kamba, Taita, Duruma, Kikuyu and Luo have unite to improve the conditions in the village. I tell about how the her and goats are cared for, about money in the bank.

'When the bank account belongs to the whole group, nobody ca take out money for their own personal use,' I say.

And I explain how the money eventually becomes a small shop, maize-mill and a clinic.

Rachel nods thoughtfully. Her look is filled with bank accoun and clinics. She has told me about her trip to Kisumu, when sh gave birth to her last child. On the way there she had been driven i the matatu. The day after the birth she had to leave the hospita and with the child on her back, had to walk the long road hom again.

In Kibuyuni the women have a clinic just around the corner. The built it themselves and when the building was completed, th authorities financed the equipment and the position for a doctor an a nurse.

I remember the pride of the women in the small village, pride c having achieved something, pride of having mastered the triba differences, the religious differences.

Kenya is full of such groups of women. They start with grou saving, sparingly. Part of what they earn on the sales of fruit an vegetables goes into the common account. The sale of eggs. Sma tea-kiosks. Toasted corn-cobs. Occasionally they tackle bigge projects, like the digging of a well. Traditionally it's the women ob to fetch water, and for many of them hours are daily spent wandering to and fro under the hot sun with their heavy burdens – on their heads, as is the custom of the Luo, or on their backs, held by a thong around the forehead, as is the custom of the Kikuyu.

'It would be wonderful with a clinic,' says Rachel.

The time is soon ten and Judith and Rose wander into the courtyard. Rachel fetches the key to the weaving-shop and follows them to unlock the door. A few minutes later, Sophie comes. She sits on the ground beside me and leans against the wall of Rachel's kitchen-hut.

Sophie is twenty-eight years old, the mother of five, her belly large with number six. She alone has the responsibility for her children; her husband, like many others, has moved to the city in search of work.

I look at her worn face and think of the women's group in Kibuyuni, that holds monthly meetings for new parents and discusses family-planning and dishes out free contraceptives. The authorities are indecisive on this matter. For a period they'll encourage smaller families and prevention, then comes a period when it is hardly mentioned. At the moment the newspapers are full of the recent death of Minister Oloitipitip, who had thirteen wives and eighty children!

Man's pride, woman's burden. In the West we discuss the stronger *contra* the weaker sex. Here it is the women who do all the carrying; water, firewood. I remember Mother Mable in Muranga. Mother Mable in the enormous tea-field. When her sons were not at school they helped her pick tea, but each evening, when the basket was tightly packed with tea, it was Mable who had to carry it. Sixty-year-old Mable, with up to eighty pounds on her back, had to carry it the two or three kilometres to the delivering point.

When asked why the men can't do the carrying, Rachel told me that the mothers of the men would laugh at them. They would scorn the men and call them women.

I look at Sophie, who sits in the grass before me, and ask if she has anybody to help her, now that she is heavy with child. She shakes her head.

'No co-wives?'

'No. We were two once. But the other upped and left a year ago. She took three of the kids with her, leaving two behind for me to take care of.'

'What about your mother-in-law?'

'She won't help me. She's envious because I earn money weaving.

She comes every week to borrow money. Sometimes I have som
and can give her what she wants. But usually I have none. We'
paid once a month. And there's always so much to buy. . . . Wher
don't have the money to give her, she says bad things about me, sa
that I'm mean.'

Sophie wipes her brow. She's sweating. A different kind of swe
that has nothing to do with the sun. Is she ill? Is the child on its wa
I ask her and she replies with a grimace. Sophie looks at me – a
appraising look.

'My husband was home recently,' she says.

I don't get it. What has the recent visit of her husband to do wi
her sitting here, sweating and in pain? Sophie will say no more
laboriously she climbs to her feet and waddles across to the two wl
sit weaving on the terrace.

A picture of the courtyard encircled by huts and houses. Tl
drainpipe that carries the water off Eleonorah's roof and down in
a large tub in the rainy season.

The jacaranda bushes with their violet flowers. The sedate cow
The wizened old man in the brown cap in the background. Tw
women in the foreground.

Sophie and Rachel. The one big with child and sway-backed, tl
other easy and lithe. She gesticulates, she strokes her friend's arr
they return together, and together they disappear into Rachel
sleeping-hut. They emerge a few minutes later; Sophie is clutching
small bundle in her fist. They're speaking a language I dor
understand and Rachel holds one of Sophie's hands in both of her
She releases her and Sophie leaves. Out between the huts belongir
to the others she goes, slowly down the dry, red road.

So many stories.

Rachel stands before me washing clothes. Trousers and shirt
underpants and vests that belong to the Quaker. She takes F
washing to earn a little extra. I offer to help, but she thanks me ar
refuses. It is her job.

She works fast, with snappy movements. Her voice is low ar
angry.

Men in the bars. African men of all ages, side by side on tl
barstools; and at small tables packed with bottles and glasses. Me
digging deep in their pockets for a few shillings, money that chang
hands, money for beer and hard liquor. Loud-mouthed men. Me
with hungry looks, indifferent looks, nonchalant looks at the fe

women who share the bar, women who have moved from their men, women who have been chased away – prostitutes.

Men on their way home in the dark. Men stumbling into their huts to their wives; stumbling over sleeping children, throwing themselves on the woman they own to have what they desire. Does she refuse his body? Dare she say no?

'That's the way it is,' says Rachel. 'Remember us talking about circumcision the other day? The Luo have never practised it. You know that. But what difference does it make when it's all a question of fear? The fear of being pregnant again. The fear of being sick. The men do as they like. They go to anyone they fancy. A man can have two, three, four wives, but he can still go to other women if he wants. We live in the man's hut. The hut belongs to him. We belong to him. When my sister became a widow, her husband's brothers emptied the hut completely. As their brother was dead they claimed that everything belonged to them. . . . You ask me about love? Look at Sophie; she was one of the cleverest at school. She wanted to study – be somebody. She was in love with a boy she studied with, they had agreed to get married when he had completed his studies. He'd even paid a small advance on her bridal fee. But whilst she was at school another man came to her parents without her knowledge and paid the whole bridal fee. When she came home on holiday she was told to go to him. Then she was told that she was married – to a man she didn't know, a man she didn't want. And he forced her to stay with him for days, until he was sure he'd made her pregnant. . . . Now he's lived in the city and worked in a restaurant for a couple of years. He's been to see her twice during this period. The first time he made her pregnant again. The second time he made her ill. . . .

Rachel rinses the Quaker's clothes and hangs them out to dry over some bushes. I wonder if African women cry?

Sophie, Judith, Mary, Rose, Rachel. I'm leaving them there but I'll never forget them. I'm leaving them just a few hours before they have their group meeting. On the way to Kisumu I imagine the meeting, and whilst sitting at the edge of the pool at the Sunset Hotel, waiting for the train, I imagine the questions and answers. What difference does it make if the Quaker leaves? They'll go on weaving belts, they'll expand their production to small kofias and vests, and the girls themselves will take the train to Nairobi and make deals with Undogo and the other shops. Later they'll send their goods by post, monthly, and when the money arrives it'll go straight into their newly opened account.

On the night train I dream of them on the terrace, bent over the colourful wool. Deft hands working. The pride in knowing that they manage it, that everything's working out fine. . . .

I dream that Sophie is well again, that Rachel has a new gas cooker. I dream of Rose's children on the way to school, in new uniforms, with books under their arms.

But Rose's house, that'll never be finished.

Toril Brekke was born and grew up in Oslo. She began a degree in music and political science, but abandoned this to take on a variety of jobs, ranging from selling hamburgers and working in a bread factory, to writing as cultural correspondent for a Marxist paper, *The Class Struggle*, and typesetting for the Norwegian *Evening Post* for four years. She started writing stories and poems at school and in 1976 published her first novel, *Jenny was Fired*. She has written two novels for children, and her most recent book, *The Film on Chatella* (1983), is set in a Lebanese refugee camp. Her main concern as a writer is with social problems. Toril Brekke has three sons and continues to live in Oslo.

WORK

Everywhere in the world, tradition dictates that domestic work is women's work. This tradition means that, because most women do additional work outside the home, whereas few men would consider doing additional work inside it, 'women's work' usually ends up simply being 'more work', and the majority of women find themselves working a double day.

From Iran, Manny Shirazi travels to the Soviet Union, to the windswept streets of Azerbaijan on the banks of the Caspian Sea. Here she is reunited with a part of her family she has not seen since she was a small child, and discovers what Soviet-style socialism means for her long-lost female relatives. Here, though women are half of the workforce, most are still employed in 'women's' jobs as secretaries, nurses and teachers. And, though meals are served in the work canteens, most men prefer their food cooked at home by their wives after a long day at work.

From the United States, Marilyn French travels to India, to villages in Gujerat and to the cities of Delhi and Ahmedabad. Here middle-class women with jobs manage their extra workload by hiring servants, but poor women must do household chores as well as a full day on a building site. Here women are so subject to men that a professional woman's chance of promotion depends on the influence of her husband, and a poor woman's wages go straight into her husband's pocket.

Manny Shirazi

My image of Moscow will always be of a city drawn in snow, slow and sleepy, like Muscovite women, overburdened and under pressure. But Moscow must have sunny days too even though I missed them.

Bacu, capital of Azerbaijan, saw its first snow with my arrival. In my aunt's sitting-room, the only picture on the mantlepiece was of me in a snow-white wedding dress, taken twenty years ago. The picture had not aged. We sat round – my aunt, her three daughters and her two sons, with their husbands, wives and children. The room was packed with excitement. I had come to visit my aunt, aged seventy-five, who had come here from Iran with her mother and her brothers in search of work in the 1920s and had got married and could not then return home. Her youngest daughter, Rafi, lifted up the picture and showed it to me and everybody else, saying, 'You are so beautiful in this picture. I want to eat you,' and then kissing it. I did not know whether to be embarrassed or pleased. I looked at the picture closely. In it I looked more naive than pretty, all done up beyond recognition, and did not look particularly happy either. I remember the day I walked around the city trying to hire a wedding dress. We couldn't afford to buy one but the custom was to have one, so we hired the all-lace and chiffon one for the photograph. I wonder how many other women must have had their picture taken in that hired white wedding dress.

My aunt looked Russian through and through, small and square, very pale and tired. I couldn't believe, as I sat in that small sitting-room, that the dream of my family had finally come true through me. My grandmother never stopped talking about her lost daughter, our aunt who was left behind in a stranger's land, whom we should have rescued. At dinners, in conversation with guests, in continuous monologue with herself, she never stopped asking why she was not coming back, why she was delaying it for so long, how she could live alone in an unknown city. My father had made a few plans, so had my uncle, to go and visit her and find out the reasons, but nothing materialised. The hopes and ideas about her return were a daily part of the family routine.

Since the border between Iran and the USSR closed in 1938 – the same year in which Azerbaijani script was Russianised – there has been very little contact between the Iranian and Russian Azerbaijanis. This sad story is typical of most of the Asian part of the USSR, which was only conquered about a hundred years ago, leaving many people with relations and friends on either side of the border whom they have lost for life. So many people live in the dream of reunion and the joy of the last visit. But how did the conquest of the emperors affect women? I wanted to ask my aunt.

'We are glad that you are here, we want you to have a good visit. As you see, we have everything we need. We work, we have our own good place to live in, we have a car. We do not have any problems, any shortcomings, and we all want you to enjoy what we have and share it with us.' Rafi said this on behalf of everybody else too, and the form of the speech surprised me. Why did she want to reassure me?

I took out the pictures of my family, some of them recently sent to me especially for this trip. Each took one and asked me who this was. 'This is my father, this is my mother, this is my brother's wife, and this is my sister.' My aunt kissed my father's photo and held it to her heart. The pictures of my extended family were being handed around by my aunt's extended family.

'No, the women are not all alike,' I explained at length. 'They all have to wear the veil under Khomeini, but they are very different. My sister is a teacher, she likes make-up and dressing well, but my brother's wife is a housewife, has four kids and she doesn't use make-up because my brother doesn't allow it. However she has such striking beauty that the make-up would spoil it anyway. You can't distinguish between them because they have to cover themselves under the veil, and photographing women is frowned upon anyway. Uniformity is the characteristic feature designed for women by the Islamic Government, and the veil is a means by which to conceal women and make of them an unknown mass. It is much easier to manipulate and control a mass of characterless people.'

It felt so cosy and comfortable to be able to talk in the same language, to communicate with them, understand them and be understood, to have so much in common. Then the conversation turned to me and my possible family. As usual, the first question was, 'Are you married?' The second was, 'Have you any children?' The third, 'Where is he?' The fourth, 'Why isn't he or your children with you?' And the last one was, 'What do you do?' In fact, this being Moscow, there was a small exception in that the first question was, 'Coming from London, why aren't you white?' I looked Indian. So the second question was whether I was married. The last question I had hoped to be asked was on the situation of women in Iran and what I thought about it, but this was never asked.

My aunt's three daughters are aged forty-five, forty and thirty-three. The eldest, Marziyeh, is a scientist, the middle one, Aliyeh a dentist and Rafi is a saleswoman. Her two sons were younger, and one worked as a cook and the other one in a factory. Each of the daughters has only two children. I was pleased about this and could not hide my surprise. Iranian Azerbaijanis like large families and I knew that the official Soviet policy was to encourage more children. I asked them about this, and their unanimous answer was that, like the Soviet women, they found children too expensive and also didn't have the time for it. Somehow I felt that the Soviet official birth policy was to control and cut down the population of the Turkish and Persian speaking areas.

I told them about my sisters and brothers, and how each had three or four unwanted children because they are prohibited from using contraceptives, and abortions are illegal. All expressed dismay at Khomeini's Iran, and how he had put the clock back, but they didn't ask any questions. I was surprised that they did not want to know more, to know what women are doing in Iran, how they are resisting and how they are surviving. Instead Marziyeh said, 'They have been liberated by the Russians: it is because of our Big Brothers that they throw the veil away.' I remembered a conversation with some French men who worked on the offshore and oil drilling in the Caspian Sea and thought, 'you have been liberating them in real terms.'

Later on, in a quiet corner in the kitchen, Aliyeh questions me nervously:

A – Was it you who phoned us?

M – Yes, I rang you from Moscow.

A – Really? I couldn't believe it was you. You spoke Azerbaijani so well.

M – It was me. Why couldn't you believe? After all, I am half Azerbaijani. I have been saying for a year that I wanted to come and visit my aunt and her family.

A – We weren't certain.

M – Why not?

A – If I knew I would have sent you a visa myself, so that you didn't need to stay in a hotel.

M – It is all right.

A – Are you alone or with a group?

M – I am with a group, but I am free to visit you as much as I want.

A – Ah, good. I wasn't sure if it was possible.

M – Did you receive my letter and my telegram?

A – Yes.

M – Why didn't you answer them, then? Why didn't you write back? I wanted to know what you wanted, what kind of present to bring.

A – I wasn't sure what to ask for, or how. Have they asked you if

you are coming to visit us?
M – I put your address on my form.
A – Why?
M – Because it asked, I could not conceal it. I thought it would be better.
A – So they have got our address.

Worry and suspicion, fear and sadness clouded her face for a second, but soon she brushed it aside and changed the subject. At a quiet moment when Rafi and I were alone she wanted me to tell her about my visit to Moscow and Leningrad. She had never been there and she thought of going there one day.

R – What was your impression of Moscow?
M – First, I was very excited – the city is full of interesting places, beautiful buildings and of course it's the seat of the world's first workers' revolution. It's also the only capital city in Europe where Christ and his disciples are black, and there are so many beautiful religious paintings. Mind you, this doesn't mean there is no racism in Russia – far from it, despite the existence of 128 nationalities, racism is rampant, and openly too. In their Folk Museum they have historical pictures of the lifestyle of the eskimos in Northern Siberia and some Asian tribes, and the captions say that these people led degrading and primitive lives before the Red Army liberated them.
R – What about Leningrad?
M – I liked Leningrad better, but it must be more interesting in summer. I also saw the girls' school which became the headquarters of the first Soviet Revolutionary government – it's symbolic, isn't it?
R – I guess so. Did you meet nice people?
M – I met a lot of cold people, physically and spiritually cold, especially the women. They looked so worn out – I only saw a few who could smile. Of course you meet women everywhere; nearly all the hotel workers are women, street cleaners, café and restaurant workers.

I met two Tartar women that I liked very much. They were both training to be teachers, one an English teacher and the other a German teacher. They were not happy that they could not meet up with English- and German-speaking people more frequently to practise their languages. I felt that they spoke out-dated English. We went out, ate together and saw a film afterwards and talked for a long time. They thought that the main problem in England was hippies, punks and drug addicts.
R – Is this true?
M – England has hippies, punks, and drug addicts as well as miners, feminists and black women. Nobody asked me about these

people, not even the members of the Communist Party that I met. I found them the hardest to digest. It seemed they were in a strait-jacket, and their views on working-class women were very rigid and mechanical. They said that in some factories women workers can order their evening meals in the morning, hand in their laundry and shoe repairs if they have any, and all will be ready for them to collect before going home. Sauna is in fashion now, some factories have got them and women relax there during their tea breaks. What they said was fine, but what they didn't say worried me. Most of the working women in Moscow and Leningrad are not factory workers – what is the state doing to ease their lives?

The editors of *Soviet Women* denied that patriarchy and racism existed in the USSR; one of them said, 'We just make inoffensive jokes about them.' However, they were right in saying that they didn't think having one or two women in the Politburo (the highest governing body in the Soviet Union, all male at present) would bring about many changes for women. It would be tokenistic. I agreed with them – if women at the top, at the level of policy-making, could change anything, there would have to be more than the token few.

R – There are many women in the Communist Party.

M – Yes, but there are very few women on the Central Committee. In Lenin's time there were two, and now, seventy years later, only six womem have reached this position – it is very slow. In a few months the United Nations will hold a conference in Nairobi on the end of the Decade for Women and will discuss what women have gained in this decade 1975–85. Soviet women said they were the initiators of the Decade, but even without it the progress of women in the USSR wouldn't have been affected.

R – What is that? I didn't know there was a United Nations Decade for Women.

M – Don't worry, not many people know. Women are preoccupied with the reality of their life and work, and working women in Moscow and Leningrad, too, are more concerned about how they can improve their lives. They were, for instance, dissatisfied with the quality of communal services provided for them, which they say is too poor. Even the rich women want better communal services. I met a woman scientific designer and a woman architect, who were both concerned with the problems that their adolescent children had – how to occupy themselves and what career to choose. One woman's son didn't know whether to be a doctor or a musician; they had so many doctors in their family that he didn't think he should be one. They wanted better youth organisations, and career advice services.

R – Some people have problems. Did you meet any woman that you liked and got on well with?

Me – Oh yes, besides the Tartar women, I met two Jewish women in Leningrad and a Russian acupuncturist in Moscow. They were very warm, affectionate and they liked me. They spoke English, they took me out, translated everything for me and we spent hours talking together. One of them told me this horrible proverb: what do Soviet women want? They want all the consumer goods and to lose weight.' I said that a Russian man must have made it up.

One of the Jewish women was very beautiful and energetic at the age of forty. She wasn't married and didn't want to be and I was surprised that neither of them wanted to emigrate to Israel. Instead, they wanted to travel in Europe. They both worked in a travel agency, liked their jobs and travelled extensively in the USSR and Eastern European countries. As single women they felt under moral pressure to marry, raise children and live with a man, but they still preferred the troubles of living with their brother's family and their parents to losing their freedom (single women are not entitled to accommodation of their own).

I really felt for the woman doctor. She was training to become an acupuncturist, she had two children aged four and five and a husband who worked in Leningrad. So she had to travel there regularly to see him as he couldn't take time off. I looked at her pale and shattered face, as if she hadn't slept for months, and asked her how she could take it. She said, 'What is the choice?' But a second later she corrected herself. 'I don't regret it, I wouldn't have chosen anything else.'

R – What is the main difference between women in England and women here?

Me – You know, one day I asked myself, are women in Moscow more socialist than women in London are capitalist? I thought about it a lot, and they are not. I feel the main difference is that women in England fear where their bread is going to come from and women here have bread to eat with fear.

Rafi had taken a few days off work to take me around the town. She was proud. 'You see, we are allowed to do this. I have a precious guest so I can take time off to show you around.' She took me to her work place, a large government department store. She said that all her co-workers wanted to see me. She had spoken about me so much that they were all excited to see me. We went to the fabric department. It was lunchtime, so she took me behind the counter where six women were sitting around a table and eating their lunch. I was greeted, shook hands with them and was invited to sit down with them. Tea was ordered and their dish of meat and potato looked appetising. It was a warm and friendly atmosphere. But I froze when the first question was whether I was married, when another woman asked if I had any children, when another one asked where they were. Why is the first question always about husband and children? Why? I asked them all. 'Because that is the most important thing in life,' one woman said.

M – So I was also told by an editor of *Soviet Women*. But I am more important than my husband or my child.

1st woman – No. If you are not married, you are very lonely and miserable.

2nd woman – Children are assets. When you are old they will be by your side.

3rd woman – Love is good, sex and the rest. Without a man a woman is loveless and sexless.

M – But a lot of headache also goes with all that.

4th woman – Yes, true, but it is the law of nature – man, woman, and children. What can you do about it?

5th woman – Family is necessary for woman, for her future.

I didn't sit quietly, I disagreed and showed my astonishment. But lunchtime was not long enough in which to discuss this sacred issue. Before I said goodbye I asked them why all the sales assistants were women. Where were the men? 'I don't know, perhaps in the factories,' one woman commented. So women work in the service industries, selling, cleaning, cooking, in order that men can become skilled industrial workers? 'No,' one woman said, 'there are many women industrial workers too. We like our jobs. We have been doing them for years, and we don't like to interfere in other things, in politics.' It was a cold, commanding answer and all the women agreed.

Rafi held my hand and pulled me away. 'Let's go. You ask too much.'

During my stay I was constantly offered food – delicious fruits, expensive meat dishes, lots of tea and jam in clear cut-crystal glasses, Azerbaijani-style. After one big kebab meal Aliyeh, Marziyeh, Rafi and my aunt asked me why I didn't put on any make-up. 'Are there cosmetics in England? Are they very expensive?' they asked. I said there was plenty of it, that a lot of women used it too, that I used to use it but that nowadays I did not have much time. Marziyeh said that it didn't take much time. 'Look at your beautiful picture.' The hired wedding dress caught my eye. 'Why don't you do your hair nicely?' Rafi asked.

'It is all right,' I said.

Marziyeh gave me the hair brush, pins and my toilet bag. Aliyeh asked and before I knew where I was the three sisters were gathered around me, one doing my hair, another one my face and one standing by preparing the cosmetics. I didn't say anything, just sat back and relaxed. My aunt was watching and she was bemused.

After some time, among laughter and jokes, and through some discussion on the suitable colour of the eye-shadow to match the colour of my eyes and which rouge to go with the lipstick, in which my consultation was not required, my toilette was finished. I was given a mirror. 'Don't you look beautiful?' they exclaimed joyfully. Yes, I was transformed, my face had not seen so much colour before. I looked glamorous.

A – See, it doesn't take much time.

M – It did, and there were three of you. But why bother?

Ma – It makes one feel good.

M – Not always. I use make-up sometimes, but as it is very rare I sometimes forget about it and suddenly rub my eyes and make all the colours mix up on my face.

A – You have all kinds of cosmetics, nice clothes, elegant shoes why don't you take advantage of it?

M – It makes me angry that women put so much of their time into thinking about make-up, clothes and their appearance, and usually for men. I saw dolly birds in Moscow and Leningrad too, and my God, I was surprised.

Marziyeh agrees quietly, so I take the opportunity to make the point that yesterday, when we were walking around the town, Aliyeh was complaining about her high-heeled boots, that her ears were cold, that she was getting a headache, because her fashionable boots and hat were very impractical. When I asked her why she didn't wear flat boots, a hat to cover her ears, she said it was bad, what would the people say. But why put up with so much discomfort?

'But you have all those nice cheap clothes and make-up. We don't. You have had enough, we haven't. We have to pay through the nose for a pair of nice fashionable boots. You don't appreciate what you have got,' Aliyeh told me.

'You are just like my sister, who rings me from thousands of miles away in Iran and what does she want – a so-and-so lipstick, so-and-so perfume. And she wishes to come to London and camp in Oxford Street. Last time we spoke I got angry and said that she didn't want to see me. She only wants me for London fashion,' I told Aliyeh.

'Don't you say that, don't you blame your sister or us. We have not had the choice, the opportunity to choose. Don't blame us.' Her definite words made me think hard. Fashion here was a radical, anti-establishment statement.

Marziyeh invited me to a traditional Azerbaijani lunch at her apartment. It was a Sunday and they came to collect me in their car as they lived outside the city. There was plenty of time, they told me, and offered to show me around the town. It looked like any Iranian or Turkish town, crowded with loitering men, a sky-scraper contrasting with the old architecture. Most of the monuments in the city square were decorated with images of men – either well-known figures of poets and writers, or macho soldiers symbolising the heroic past and a heroic future that should be. But I also saw two women's statues, one of them a woman poet and the other one celebrating the taking of the veil. Of course, I did not hesitate to finish a roll of film.

When we reached Marziyeh's home, I saw that Aliyeh and Rafi were busy in the kitchen. I had guessed that this was happening and I had told Marziyeh, but she only laughed. It is the women's tradition, she said, all to be a collective host. They had made triangular pastries, probably the night before, which were scattered on plates on all the surfaces in the sitting-room. I realised the hard work this had entailed, but it was done lovingly.

The table was set with many local fruit jams and a black halva unseen in the West. Tea was brought in the usual cut glasses called stekan, and they put spoons of jam in their tea instead of sugar. I preferred to eat the jams, zogal and gojeh. Both were delicious, with a delicate sweet and sour taste, but zogal was denser and richer. My aunt proudly told me she had made them last summer. The black halva was made of sunflower seeds and it tasted unique. So I ate and ate and thought of my poor trousers which would need to be replaced with a much larger size.

Marziyeh's husband was a quiet man, like a lot of other quiet husbands I had met. He had been drinking tea with me and my aunt when she developed a sudden attack of rheumatism and had to be helped to lie down on the bed. I asked him if men helped at home. He said yes, embarrassed that the women were in the kitchen preparing the food. This set him going. He cleared the table, prepared the tea and even asked his young son to help, which surprised me because I had seen the boys sit and order their sisters to serve them with tea and food. My aunt came to his defence and said that her son-in-laws did work at home, but mostly when their wives were on holiday.

I went to the kitchen and asked Marziyeh if I could help her. She said no, that I didn't know the first thing about it. I stood by her and watched her preparing the tomatoes, and pickles.

'What do you do as a scientist?' I asked.

'I do research, sometimes in a laboratory at my workplace and sometimes outside in the fields.'

'What kind of research do you do?' I wanted to know.

'Well, the usual research in a laboratory, nothing sophisticated or unusual.' She was short and vague.

'Don't you want to talk to me about your work?' I asked further. She said something else and the conversation was changed.

Lunch was served late – boiled triangular pastries with fried minced meat mixed with tomato sauce that was made separately and which we mixed together, adding sour cream on top. It not only looked beautiful but tasted delicious too. There was a small hitch – opening the special Bacu champagne took much longer than we thought because of the fear of the splash. After lunch, tea was served, and after tea we had all eaten so much that we could not move.

Marziyeh asked me if there were robots in England, to clear the table after eating and wash the dishes and put them away. Aliyeh said she also needed one to carry auntie up and down to their fifth-floor apartment. I said I also needed one to carry me and my bicycle up and down to my fifth-floor council flat, and that theirs were much cleaner and had no dog shit to step in. We all laughed.

Soon Marziyeh vanished and it took me some time to realise that she was cooking in the kitchen. I went in and stood by her. It was too small a kitchen to fit us all in, and the dirty dishes that were piled up all around. I tried to start washing the dishes and she stopped me, saying that there was no water in the taps till the evening. Strange, I thought.

'What are you cooking now?' I asked.

'His lunch for tomorrow.' I began to protest, but realised that I was only a guest and that I shouldn't push my luck. Instead I said, 'I have come to see you and you have not been out of this kitchen. Doesn't your husband have a canteen in his factory?'

'Yes, but he prefers homemade food,' Marziyeh said calmly.

I said, 'Women are cheaper than robots and they last longer.' She smiled.

Afternoon tea was served in a tired and subdued way, while I sat next to my auntie and rubbed her small feet. She didn't look well. Kemal, Marziyeh's husband, pointed to Stalin's picture on the 1985 calendar and asked me if I liked him. I thought, do I have to answer this question? 'No, but I asked many people in Georgia, women too who like him. They thought without him the fascist would have invaded their country.' He put the picture back, and started a long speech on the heroic deeds of Stalin, how he won the war for them, what a great leader he was, had I heard the story about his son's capture at the hands of the Nazis, and how he wouldn't bargain with them, not even for his son. 'But he has been accused of cruelty and wrong conduct, which was committed in his name by his associates and the government officials.'

'I thought the people won the war,' I said timidly.

'People need leaders,' he stated.

It was very difficult to see my aunt alone. We were always surrounded by noisy children and watchful adults. Most of the daily conversation was about food, children and daily chores. Also, two languages were spoken at home – Azerbaijani with me, Russian with the children and among themselves (when I was not supposed to know something).

Aliyeh had a bad headache for a few days. I asked her what she had done about it. She said nothing had helped. When asked what the doctors had said, she threw up her shoulders and said, 'Doctors, doctors, they know nothing.' The words were not yet finished when I heard Rafi's scream in Russian which shut Aliyeh up immediately. I realised that she was not allowed to complain, that women were watching each other.

Once again Marziyeh asked me what I thought about nuclear war and what the USA was doing. This was mainly because this year is the fortieth year after the end of the Second World War, so there was lots of publicity about the war and how it affected the USSR, how another one should be avoided and so on. I told her that in my opinion war was a man's game that had nothing to do with women. We did not have the power to create one or to stop one, we were only being used. She said that it affected women too, how could we avoid it? I said I knew that but I didn't want to take part in a military competition between the USA and the USSR.

Her husband suddenly jumped in and said, 'Now stop talking politics.'

'Why not?' I asked.

'No, we must not interfere in such matters.'

Sometimes, I just enjoyed sitting next to my aunt, holding her hands, watching television with her or rubbing her rheumatic feet.

We are the silenced women and I did not know how not to be. But
every now and then I wanted to know what had happened to her.
How did she decide to remain behind, a lone woman, when her
mother, her brothers and sisters left for a journey of no return.
What had she been thinking of during those long silenced years?
What was in her memory, what image, which emotions?
M – Do you remember your mother?
A – Only her face, very faintly.
M – Which year did your younger brother leave?
A – Around 1937 or 1938.
M – But your elder brother had returned before that.
A – Yes, because he only came here to learn a skill, and he learned
driving, got his licence and then left.
M – Do you remember my father?
A – He was a boy this size [showing with her hand about one
metre] when I said goodbye to him, amid tears, at the Caspian Sea
port.
M – Did you ever want to return?
A – Yes, my child. (And she sighed deeply.)
M – Why didn't you, then?
A – We weren't allowed. I was given permission to leave but not my
husband, and they divided the children between us. I couldn't leave
two of my children behind, how . . .
     The sudden scream of Rafi shut her up again.
     I got very angry. 'Why don't you let her speak? I have come here,
three thousand miles to see you and speak with you. Why are you
shutting up yourself and everybody else too? Why? Am I the
enemy? I am sick and tired of talking about make-up, dresses and
the bloody American dollar. Why can't we talk about something
else? My aunt was telling me about her life. Why can't Aliyeh
complain about the doctor? What is so bloody sacred about your
doctors? I always complain about everything. Why not? Why am I
the enemy?' I left in a temper. Once again, when I found a moment
to be alone with my aunt, I asked her about her feelings and her
decision to remain in Bacu. She just said, 'My girl, I can't remember
anything. My memory has faded.' What does erase women's
memories, I ask myself.
     Noran is the young daughter of Rafi. We liked each other
instantaneously. Some days she stayed away from school in order to
be with me. One day we went out for a long walk and decided to see
an Azerbaijani movie. We walked around the town and checked all
the cinemas, but there was no Azerbaijani film, so we decided to see
a Russian one and she agreed to translate for me. We searched

again but all the films were from India, Turkey, Spain and France. None were Russian.

The same thing happened in Moscow and Leningrad. The only films I saw were about wars, and very sexist they were too. I also saw *The Invisible Man* in the Russian version, in a cinema with an audience of two thousand, and what nicely filmed rubbish it was.

Noran and I decided that we were out of luck, so we went to a café for tea and a chat. She is tall with short curly hair, a strikingly beautiful face, black eyes, dark bushy eyebrows and a permanent smile on her face. She wore trousers, very uncommon for young girls and women, also a Russian fur hat, and she behaved very tomboyishly.

M – Why don't you go to school?

N – I want to be with you.

M – But you miss your lessons.

N – I won't miss much. They are so boring.

M – Don't you like any of them?

N – Only algebra.

M – What else do you do?

N – Geography, history (boring), biology, (so so). . . .

M – Only do algebra then, if you don't like any other subject.

N – But we can't.

M – What do you want to be when you grow up?

N – A doctor.

M – Well, you have to like biology.

N – I don't know.

M – Tell me, will you wear trousers when you grow up?

N – No.

M – But why not?

N – People will look at me. I will be the only woman in trousers. It would be shameful.

M – Do you want to get married?

N – Yes.

M – But why?

N – Everyone does it.

M – I will be sad if you don't wear trousers and get married. Already I am sad that you don't speak Azerbaijani well, and I think you will forget it at the rate that you speak Russian.

N – It is not only me. Everybody speaks Russian.

We left arm-in-arm for a walk by the sea. It was windy and cold. The Caspian Sea, the largest lake in the world, has a long coast. We walked between the sea and the rows of pines. The cold wind blew on our faces and silenced us.

I had been told to see the Lenin Museum. A group of women guards were talking together and giggled when they saw us, two lonely figures in the long, empty corridors. I was angry that statues, pictures and museums to Lenin were erected in every city. Why? Most of the historical documents about Lenin and his family were in Russian. Even the documents about Azerbaijani revolutionaries were in Russian, except three early socialist papers. Surely they must have had more papers, posters, historical documents in Azerbaijani script? I got angry and told Aliyeh that they should not have allowed their script to be changed. She said, what could she do? 'We are a small people, what can we do?'

'But you were not small, you made the revolution.'

Colleagues of Aliyeh took me to a carpet museum, where there was a small exhibition of Azerbaijani carpets, most of which were from Iran. Having seen so many fantastic Persian carpets, this museum was beginning to bore me, when I heard two men and a woman speaking Farsi (Persian). I was surprised. I asked them if they were Iranians and they said yes and we started talking.

1st man – Do you like this museum?

M – No.

1st man – How much of Bacu have you seen?

M – Some, not everything.

1st man – You must see Lenin's Museum.

M – I have, it was boring, and most of the exhibits were in Russian. Do know when the programme of the Russianisation of Azerbaijan began? When did they change their script?

1st man – The changing of the script to Russian is good. For example, there are four 'O's' in Azerbaijani that you can't write in their original Arabic script.

M – I spoke to a woman Tartar member of the Communist Party in Moscow who said that their language didn't have a script; thanks to Russians, they have now got a written language. I wonder what other justification is used. How come you are here?

1st man – You know the situation in Iran, what Khomeini's supporters are doing. We just had enough and decided to cross the border.

M – Were you allowed to stay?

1st man – Yes, no problem. We are given jobs, houses, everything. . . . What do you think of Azerbaijan and the USSR?

M – I'm disappointed.

1st man – Why?

M – I don't see that the people, especially the people of Azerbaijan, have gained much, and this is a land with rich natural resources. Russians are holding the best jobs and positions. Why? They don't even speak Azerbaijani.

We left the museum and they offered to take us to the monument of the twenty-six revolutionaries. The second Iranian man told us that these twenty-six men were the first Azerbaijani Communist Party organisers, and during the Western invasion of the Soviet Union in 1919 the British kidnapped them and took them out of the country and mass-executed them. There was an ever-burning fire at the monument, and it was customary for the married couples to put a bunch of flowers on it. There was also a relief of four men on the wall. I looked at them, amazed. They did not have Azerbaijani features.

'But these men don't look Azerbaijani, they look Russian,' I exclaimed.

'But that is symbolic, a sign of international socialism,' the second man, Ahmed, said.

'Right,' I said. 'If it is a sign of international socialism, then there should be Azerbaijani features and statues in Moscow and Leningrad too, but there are not. Why should the Azerbaijanis give away their resources, culture and language to the Russians?'

A – You must not judge like this. You must see the workers, the factories where they work. It is the workers' country and they have the best job opportunities, job security and living conditions.

M – Good, but not all the population is made up of industrial workers. The majority of women workers work in service industries: in shops, hotels, cleaning. Even when women get professional jobs such as becoming a dentist, for instance, like my cousin, they have the inferior positions. All the women dentists do filling and dental hygiene while the men make artificial teeth and do dental surgery. Such deliberate segregation is reactionary. What do you do?

A – We both work in factories; we were appprenticed.

M – You see, job segregation right through. What has socialism changed for women? Even the primacy of family, marriage, having children – pre-Engels ideology hasn't been challenged in the slightest.

A – Women have jobs, get money for children, the cost of their weddings is state paid. They have free nurseries, homes, free health and free education.

M – So what? Should we congratulate the proletariat government for its supreme effort to give its citizens council flats, a holy family and free aspirins for life, after sixty-five years of socialism?

A – But sixty-five years is nothing in the life of a nation. It is merely a generation.

M – I disagree. If sixty-five years is enough to send a rocket to the moon, it should be enough to have brought the moon down to the people.

A – You can't judge a country and its achievements in two weeks. You need more time and more study of people's lives.

M – I am neither a sociologist, nor a PhD student. I am a socialist, and I have been brought up in a socialist family whose ideas came from here. I feel cheated. What I have seen has disappointed me.

A – What have the Azerbaijanis in Iran got?

M – I think it would be an insult to compare Khomeini's or the Shah's Iran with the Soviet socialist system. But I have been thinking about it, you know, and I know a lot of Azerbaijanis in Iran and I have spoken to them. They have imagination, they have souls, which are absent here. Yes, religion is the opium of the people in Iran, but sadly too socialism has become the opium of the people.

A – You are very negative and you are wrong.

M – My family has suffered for their socialist belief and I hate to see that it was for nothing.

I spent most of my time discussing politics with the two men and when we came to the end of our conversation I felt sorry that I had not spoken to the woman, Sheerin (although she was talking to my friends), so I gave her my number and asked her to give me a ring soon.

Aliyeh and her husband wanted to treat me to a meal in a restaurant. I knew it would be very expensive – usually a month's wages for a meal for five or six people. I would have really preferred to be with them at home, but they insisted, and also both sisters were dressed up and were looking forward to a night out. So we went to a huge first-class hotel with an elegant restaurant, on top of a hill overlooking the Caspian Sea. We sat down and ordered numerous dishes – kebab, barbecued chicken, caviar, and of course pink champagne. The men started drinking quickly. I showed my anger that their son, a boy of thirteen, was offered champagne – especially when the girls and women were not drinking.

Each man took up his glass and with each drink delivered a long speech to me – that I was their precious guest, that they were pleased to receive me, and that they would look after me and share their food and drink with me, take me out and show me places and spend as much money as I wanted on me, that they wished good health for me and my family and hoped my desires would come true. This I found very oppressive, a show of men's generosity and their ability to occupy the available time, conversing to us and having us

vaiting by them, especially when women didn't drink and didn't talk
much. So I thought that at the first opportunity I would dance with
my cousins.

The band started playing modern Russian and Azerbaijani
discomusic, and a series of cabaret dancers (exactly the way one sees
in pictures in London) came on, wearing nothing much, and with
things hanging from their tits and briefs. Of course most of the
audience were men, who had gone out for a good night drinking
with their mates, and the dancers danced in their direction and
made sure that they had all the pleasure of their eyes. There was one
small exception when a couple did a judo dance and she threw him
on the floor and symbolically killed him.

I got very angry about it all. I have heard that there are such
places in the other socialist Eastern European countries, as well as
in Cuba, but seeing it was something different. And all the fuss they
make about not taking pornographic material into the USSR – what
hypocrisy.

When the cabaret dancers (there was only one man among them)
stopped, then it was the time for the audience to dance. Azerbaijani
dances are usually group dances, and it is common to see men
dancing together or in a group, but one hardly ever sees women
dancing together in a group to Azerbaijani music. I asked my
cousins to dance with me, but they refused and said I should dance
with their husbands and that women dancing together was shameful.
I insisted and used the power of being a precious guest, so Aliyeh
agreed and we started dancing the tango together. As we were the
only women among the pack of couples, all eyes turned to us, and
soon two men approached us, offering to dance with us, as if
menless women needed to be rescued. We confidently refused and
danced on. We went on dancing together, me and Marziyeh, me and
Rafi, till the end of the evening. It was a pleasure to be holding their
big, warm bodies and to be so close to them physically if not
spiritually. We also encouraged other women to join us in a group
dance. We enjoyed it very much but the other husbands were not
pleased. I was glad that I had gone. I had enjoyed myself.

The last drink was toasted by Rafi's husband, who invited me to
return and assured me again that they have a good life, have no
problems, they own a car and they don't involve themselves in
politics. I had to ask again, 'But why not?'

– Why should we?

– Aren't you interested in your government and what it does?
Don't you want changes in your life?

– Yes and no. If it is too much hassle it is better to leave it alone.

M – But isn't it worth it?
K – No, the best is to keep to yourself.

One day Sheerin rang and said that she wanted to see me. She had
problem, she wanted help. We agreed to meet the day after. I didn
know how I could be of help to her. Did she want me to carry
forbidden message? Did she need money? Did she have a friend i
trouble, a lover, and how could I help her? I worried, not knowin
what it was.

We met and walked by the sea towards the tea house on the por
Drinking tea, we could see the sea and a large ship in the port. Sh
pointed to it and said, 'These ships go to Iran from here.' The othe
side of the water was Iran.

She said that she was a teacher and she looked like one, tall an
dark and confident-looking. 'After the Iranian revolution teache
became a religious instrument in the hands of the centr
government, the educational authorities and even the local guar
[Pasdar] who interfered in teachers' work. As it was important tha
the young children should be indoctrinated in Islamic teaching an
nothing else, so we were pressurised every minute from all th
different and sometimes contradictory layers of the hierarchy. Lif
became very hard. At home the family was worried and und
pressure and they took most of that out on their daughters an
wives. For women teachers, life at home became unbearabl
because of the pressures of husband, brothers, and the men in th
street and at work in all the different authorities. I lived in a sma
town in Azerbaijan, and life in a small town is usually invaded an
harassed anyway, but the fundamentalists' demands and control ha
made life a hell for women. So when I heard that my brother wa
planning to escape after spending a year in gaol for allege
subversive teaching, I begged him to take me. First he wouldn't ris
it, but later on he agreed. This was the only way for me, as I ha
noticed the ever-growing mental depression, nervous breakdow
and suicide among women. I didn't want it to end like that for me.
didn't want to die or ruin my life for Khomeini. I wanted to surviv
but it seems surviving is as difficult as living under Khomeini.'

'Yes, I understand, I know exactly what you mean, and it can t
worse too,' I agreed with her. 'But what is your problem now?'

'I am coming to that. Since I have been here it has been fin
Compared with Iran it feels like heaven, especially for women, but
have talked to lots of Iranians and I realise that a lot of people can
here for one reason or another, very few intended to stay for life, b
now they are stuck. This is my worry. I don't want to be stuck her

don't want to die here.'

I sighed. 'Do you know the state of other Iranian political refugees or refugees from other countries, in Turkey, in Pakistan and even in France and England?'

'No, such news doesn't come here.'

I told her that they are in a miserable state, under constant threat of repatriation. In France they sometimes shoot the Arabs, in England there are now fascist immigration laws.

'Your ease of entry accords to the whiteness of your skin and the weight of the money you bring in. So how can I help you?' I asked desperately. 'Tell me what is your position here?'

She continued, 'I have political refugee status, which means I can only move around freely in Azerbaijan. I can get Russian nationality. But it means I won't be able to return to Iran ever, and I do not want that. I have got a job which is okay and am given a place to live, free from the usual harassments that women suffer in Iran. But this fear is hurting me, the fear of being boarded in, being stranded between two systems with no choice. 'How are women's lives in England?'

'Well, I am in a better state now. Thanks to the GLC's grant, I have a good job. But it will finish soon, so my next opportunity will be unemployment. Some features of women's lives in Britain, like unemployment, pornography, street violence against women and wife-battering, are worse than the situation of women here. But for me racism is a major issue. Besides institutionalised racism practised in laws and regulations that, for instance, won't allow my family to come to England and visit me, the racism and xenophobia of the women's movement, of the feminists you work with, of the women you live with and your close friends with whom you share a common political objective, is the most hurtful aspect of life in Britain today.'

'We don't know about these aspects of women's lives in England.'

'Yes, I know, because the system here is also based on racism, racism of the Russian minority against the other minorities and the Turkish people's majority. But how can I help you?'

'First you can just be a contact. I am trying to make contact with lots of other people outside this country and this is a great help in itself. Secondly, could you find out about Geneva's regulation for rights of political refugees and conditions of seeking asylum?'

I agreed to do this and gave her my address. 'But how could I send you anything?' I asked.

'We have to think of a way. I have been told that I can leave the Soviet Union whenever I want to. I would be given three months' notice and could go, but would not be able to return.'

'It is like a dead-end alley, wherever you turn, but I will do m
best.'

The sea behind the glass window of the café was stormy. It was
bad winter this year. I was deeply troubled by the two regimes eithe
side of the Caspian Sea, and the fear they were implanting in peopl
like us.

The goodbye scene with my aunt and my cousins was tearful an
painful. Years of anticipation of a visit had ended, and sadly. Whe
would I see them again? How much longer would my aunt live? Sh
told me to send her love to my father and tell him that she was bitte
that none of them made the visit over to see her, nor invited her t
go over there. But then I had made the visit and I was only
woman, and worth many men like them. 'I will die and take th
hope of seeing them to the grave with me.'

Years to wait for a ten-day visit and it just ends so quickly, befor
you have the time to memorise the taste of the homemade bread

Rafi and her husband and her children came to see me off. Th
train was full of men as usual, and I had insisted that I wanted to b
in a women-only compartment. But, no, in the Soviet Union wome
are so equal with men that there is no such difference. Therefor
one woman could be put in a sleeping couchette with three men c
three women. I got very angry and insisted. The guard agreed, wit
Rafi's husband's persuasion and bribery, to make it a women-on
couchette. Rafi's husband was very gallant and tried to console m
that I should not be afraid. I had to emphasise that I was not afrai
of men, I was sick of them. They are everywhere, in the restaurant
in the streets; the place is full of men, now even in my sleepir
quarters. I wanted comfort. The couchette was too hot and I wante
to take off my clothes and be free there for the few hours that I wa
asleep.

Two women joined me at first, and another woman later. Soc
we ordered some tea, locked the door and took off all our clothe
Couchettes and hotel rooms are either too hot or too cold, no happ
medium. I started the conversation which began at eleven at nigl
and ended at four in the morning. The two friends were called Aza
and Houri. Azar worked as a designer of fabric in a large texti
factory. Houri worked as an organiser of the train schedules. Th
woman who joined later was Georgian, called Tamara (the name
a very powerful and strong Georgian queen in the twelfth century
She was a mathematics student in her last year at Bacu Universit
Houri was thin, looked tired and fed up, something common

Russian women, not just Azerbaijanis. Neither of them were married, they said they were not in a hurry. Azar was younger, smaller and dynamic. She spoke about her factory which employed 3,000 workers, nearly all of them women, except for the men who repaired the machinery.

First I asked them what they felt when they had to sleep in the same couchette with men. They said that they hadn't questioned it. But wasn't it uncomfortable? Didn't it discourage women from travelling at night, especially Azerbaijani women? Yes, they agreed, but was it right to ask for special space for women?

A – Women are equal with men in law and we can't ask for special privileges for women.

M – But that equality in law hasn't changed the reality of women's lives. Look, most of the passengers are men, men are actually given access to travelling and women are barred.

T – But this is our tradition. Women don't like travelling. They prefer to stay at home.

M – No, I thought the socialist government fought against such anti-women tradition and liberated women from such bondages.

A – But you know how Moslem families feel and how they restrict women.

M – Yes, but Soviet government has changed a lot of reactionary Islamic regulation and has curtailed men's power over women. For instance, masses of Moslem women work, they have only a couple of children, don't go to mosque and watch television instead. So why does the Soviet government bring about some changes but keep some of the reactionary feudalist structures like marriage? Why? What do you think, Houri?

She had a vacant look. She had been listening, and nodding her head in disagreement or agreement and not saying much.

H – I am listening to what you are saying. I am thinking about it. I think you are right, but . . .

T – What is wrong with marriage? I want to get married, but want to travel first. Perhaps English husbands are better. Do they like black people like us?

M – Sometimes as exotics they worship you, other times it is a stab in the back or death by accidental fire. But men are all the same everywhere. The thing that is wrong with marriage is that it is the single most oppressive institution for women, and socialist marriages are the best examples. Every film and play that I have seen since I came here has either been about the elevation of the family and marriage, or patriotism and soldiers. . . .

A – How are Iranian men? Have they really all gone anti-women?

M – Yes, I am afraid so. The most sexist and regressive men in the world. Who could think that after so much struggle against the Shah, they would bring such a fundamentalist and medieval government into power and support it for so long without a squeak of protest? Why haven't the Iranian workers, whose living conditions have become at least three times worse since the Shah, gone on strike against Khomeini? And the Iranian intellectuals – men, writers and artists – are worse. You just need to read their writing and see their work to realise how sexist and anti-women they are.

A – Yes, it is bad in Iran for women. But men are like this all over the world, and women actually like to get married and have babies.

M – I don't believe that. If women had other options, they could choose. Marriage and family in the USSR is forced on women.

T – But what do you do, when you need love, somebody to cuddle and kiss with, to share your bed with, to warm the house up for you and to wait for you to come home?

M – Yes, I know what you mean. I need that. We all need that, but we don't have to be tied to one man, or have children for the state. There are other forms of love. (I thought, what about loving women for a change, or what about masturbation?)

A – Are you Moslem?

M – I was born into it. What is your religion, Tamara?

T – Mine is Father Lenin.

M – Tell me about it, because I am losing interest in him and I want you to convince me.

T – He was a great revolutionary and what we have got we owe to him.

M – And not to yourselves?

T – Yes, but if you read his books you realise how profound he was and how mapped out our social achievements today.

M – Was it because he cared for the people or because he wanted people to care for him? After all, his statues and museums are all over the country.

T – No. You are so extreme, but I like debating with you. You have such a subversive outlook.

M – I have to have. Look at Iran's revolution. We tried to change our lives for the better and made them worse. Your revolution improved women's situation but it is stuck in 1920; even the intellects of the communist women have stagnated.

T – Give us time.

M – Well, when I interviewed Soviet women, I asked them when would Lenin's cooks govern. They also said give us time. Is it only

time that women need?
A – No, not only time. . . .

We talked on, about fashion, what kind of furniture we liked when we had our own place, hair-styles and why we should pluck our eyebrows, and we also exchanged recipes. We practically fell asleep as we were mumbling something or other, just like in a dream. I was in a deep sleep when the loud noise of two men walking in and crashing open the door woke me up. I half opened an eye. One was a large soldier and the other an official-looking older man. They must have replaced Azar and Houri who were getting off before me. The short, sweet night of freedom had gone and so had the room of our own. I opened my eyes and tried to get dressed. The couchette looked invaded and I was sorry that the women had gone, and when I looked at the men I regretted it more. Tamara was up too. She was getting dressed to go. Perhaps she will find an English husband, and continue to believe in her Father Lenin. She won't need to hire her wedding dress, the state will pay for it. And perhaps I should have kept reading my Lenin books rather than going to see their outcome.

Epilogue – memory of an early conversation with Rafi.
R – What do you write?
M – Different things.
R – Are there a lot of negative writings about the USSR in England?
M – Sometimes.
R – Will you write negative things about us?
M – Negative things as well as positive.
R – But why?
M – Because nothing is perfect and I like writing. Also it is my job.
R – But why are you critical of the USSR?
M – Because I am not happy about women's lives in Azerbaijan and Russia and I am disappointed with what I have seen.
R – Do you criticise the British government too?
M – Yes, all the time. I am a lucky foreigner who can.
R – What can you gain by it?
M – Nothing much, really, when you think of it seriously. We are small people who are allowed to shout.
R – So why do it then?
M – I don't know. I guess for hope's sake.

Manny Shirazi was born into what she describes as 'an Iranian working-class family'. She wrote her first feminist short story at the age of twelve, and worked in Iran as a teacher for five years. She is a photographer, and mounted an exhibition of photographs of women of Iran at the Women's Art Alliance in 1979. Her written work includes poetry and prose, and she writes in both English and Farsi (Persian). Her most recent novel, *Javady Alley*, was published in 1984. Manny Shirazi is a full-time member of the UK-based feminist collective that produces *Spare Rib* magazine.

WORK – INDIA

Marilyn French

Lalita blows out smoke in quick nervous puffs and her voice rises over the low conversation of guests sipping cocktails in the formal living-room. 'You feminists from the West keep coming here with your solutions, and they're all wrong for India. You have no conception of our traditions. We have always had goddesses, figures of great beauty and power. They fill our art, our myth, our consciousness. We are not limited to the virginal Mary.'

'I wasn't aware I'd offered any solutions,' I say coolly.

She waves this away. 'Oh, not you. But Western women. And everything you write gets published, where our work does not. And your understanding is flat, simplistic. How can you presume to write about India without understanding Hinduism? It takes a lifetime to comprehend Hinduism, because it's not a church or a dogma, it's an attitude toward life! It sets our puny lives in a cosmic perspective; we know we are fragments interconnected within a larger whole. You know the Hindu gesture of greeting? Palms held together before the face? That is called *namaste*, and it means, 'I bow to the divine in you.' Beautiful, no? Profound. I talk to my laundryman, he's very poor and has many children, but he's beautiful. He says women have children as the trees put forth leaves. Hindus let themselves flow with the tide, they don't try to oppose it. You in the West have no comprehension of such an attitude.'

'The marriage system – 'I begin.

'I was not forced to marry! I chose my husband when I was ready, and against my family's wishes. You did too, Tara, no?' She glances at the slender, elegant woman sitting with us, who nods. 'My husband and I travelled for some years before we had children, and I always worked. You too, Tara.'

'But you're upper-class,' I object. 'You were educated, you weren't forced into marriage with a stranger at fourteen, you had access to birth control. You had a voice in your life.'

'India has had women in high places since the constitution of 1950, long before the United States. There are no hard rules here. There are over thirty different states and territories in India, each with its own customs, many with their own language. Kerala, for instance, is matriarchal. Indian women are the daughters of generations of noble, enduring, strong women. They accept their lives. Every woman in this room has a career.'

This fine house is furnished Western-style, with cushioned

couches and chairs, tables with knick-knacks, and heavy curtains;
sophisticated people of the élite class – mostly Indian with a few
Americans – stand or sit smoking and drinking. A staff of servants in
white jackets pass drinks and hors-d'oeuvres. A bearer bends low to
offer Lalita another shrimp. She waves him away brusquely, with
angry contempt.

'But it has not been without difficulty, Lalita,' Tara says quietly.

'Of course not! Of course not! What life is without difficulties?'
Her full mobile face alters expression with each phrase. 'I
remember when I had just started working, writing for a magazine,
and was assigned to interview a businessman who had made a
fortune in electronics. He kept insisting we do the interview over
drinks, alone. At last I became angry and told him he was impudent
asking me for drinks when my father would not have allowed me
even to speak to someone of his caste! Well, that humbled him! He
apologised and I got my interview *with* photographer. Onc learns to
deal with problems!'

Lalita looks at my face and stands up abruptly and strides away,
her peacock silk sari floating behind her.

'I had many difficulties establishing my career,' says Tara kindly.
She is prominent in the civil service, the bureaucracy that
constitutes the non-political backbone of the Indian government. 'I
knew I wanted a carccr. The civil service was the best place for
women because acceptance is determined only by a competitive
exam. I passed my exam, but could not find a post. There was a job
open in Haryana, my native state, where I should properly have
begun. But it involved police work, and the man in charge said I
would be frightened, I could not be tough enough. I persisted for
months, but he was adamant. Finally, my father intervened – he was
important in the state at that time – and I got the job. And handled
it, although,' she confesses with a wry smile, 'it wasn't very pleasant.

'But I didn't get promoted. Then I married and my husband had
an offer on a newspaper here in Delhi. There was a post open in
Delhi and I applied. But the man in charge of *that* said the job
required travel and how could I, a woman, travel alone around
India? I said I could and would. He said my duty was to my
husband, to stay home dutifully. I hounded him, in vain. Then I
tried manipulation. You know, men accuse women of manipulating
them, but what else can we do? A man with my qualifications would
have had that job instantly. Some friends of mine, important people
in Delhi, were giving a dinner party. I asked them to invite this man.
I knew he was not in their social circle and would be flattered. He
was. And he was awed by the guest list. During the party my

husband managed to fall into conversation with him and convey his complete approval of my career.

'I got the job. That was many years ago and I have been promoted many times since. But I've never forgotten the humiliation of those first appointments. And I think younger women face the same problems. There are no women on the level beneath me, they are all stuck down two or three levels.' She sighs. 'It's strange. India is still feudal, with an overlay of modern industrialism.'

A small man with a tragic face has taken Lalita's chair and leans forward. 'Feudal. Yes. Do you know, here I am, I don't mean to brag, but I have a certain position in society, I've been all over the world. But I come from a village, and my mother has not been out of the house since her marriage. She has never even seen the faces of her sons-in-law, only their photographs. The only men whose faces she can see are mine and my father's. She cannot ever converse with other women except when she goes to squat.

'And now,' his voice rises, 'the government intends to bring sanitary latrines to the villages! They don't care that this will isolate many women entirely, by wiping out their one source of contact with other women.' He sighs and sips his drink.

'How is your mother now?'

'Very depressed. Resentful.'

'Many older women become religious,' Tara says. 'They have nothing else.'

'And your father? Is he sorry?'

'Yes, he is filled with remorse. No one loves him. But he was a terrible man, a tyrant. He beat us children all the time, for nothing, he beat her too. Now he says she can go out, but she says, "Why should I? All my life I begged to go out and you forbade it. Now I'm old, I'm sixty-three, and I don't care any more. I'll stay here until I die." And you know, it still goes on, this male tyranny.

'We have a girl, she works in our house, my wife is very fond of her. She brings her baby with her. She earns more than her husband – he works in a house nearby. But he takes her wages. If she needs anything, he decides whether she should have it and he buys it. The baby is in rags, but he won't buy it clothes. My wife kept telling her to keep her own wages, to refuse him. She said he'd beat her. Well, one day she did it, she held back her wages. And the next day she came in. . . .' He hits his cheek with his hand. 'He beat her brutally. Her face was swollen and purple, her lip was cut, her arms and legs were covered with bruises. . . . My wife told her to leave this man, to stay with the baby in our spare room. But she said the men on the street would abuse her and treat her like a prostitute if she didn' have a husband.' He wipes his hand across his face. 'It's terrible, truly terrible.'

'It is terrible,' Vidya says. 'It breaks your heart, every day. That is why we, who have education, who are aware, who can manage, must help.'

We are sitting on the floor of the flat shared by Vidya and Lakshmi and, tonight, by fifty or so other women. It is a women's party and I feel completely at home – I could be back in graduate school in Cambridge, Massachusetts, except that this is an Indian room, austere and immaculate. There is a cot against a wall, and some wooden chairs, and a handwoven rug. A sliding glass screen door fills one wall and opens to a terrace, on which women are sitting and singing . . . American girls' camp songs!
'Tell me why the roses climb,
Tell me why the ivy climbs. . . .'
All the women are feminists, most in their twenties and thirties. Their children are in the adjoining room, sitting on the floor quietly playing or lying asleep. The women have switched to an Indian devotional song, jazzed up with feminist lyrics. Conversation stops as we listen to the singers. I know the *feel* of this room, it is familiar to me, I remember it from years back. The women are filled with love for each other, with excitement and energy and the faith that they can help other women. It is the feel of beginning.
'How do you all come to know each other?'
Rukmini laughs. 'There aren't that many feminists in Delhi!' She has a pale oval face framed by long shining straight black hair, and she is wearing Western-style pants and shirt: most unusual. All the other women are in saris. 'We all work, we're lawyers, doctors, professors, journalists. Neena,' she nods toward a small intense woman near us, 'sells books for a publisher. We have also started a feminist press of our own!' She smiles with delight. 'And we all belong to women's organisations – Saheli or Karmika, women's crisis centres; Ankur, dedicated to women's education; or the Health Collective, which runs workshops.'
Vidya takes it up. 'We began only a few years ago – four or five. At first we lobbied in an anti-dowry campaign, and gave street plays. You know most women are illiterate, and many are confined in their neighbourhoods, so we take our street plays to them.'
'You work all day at your professions and all night in these organisations?'
'What else?' They laugh. Laughter comes easily here, and lasts.
'And some of you are married and have children and homes to

care for as well.'

They survey the room. 'About half of us are married, a third have children. Some of us have managed to remain single,' Vidya cock her head at Rukmini, who grins, 'and *some* of us are even divorced!'

Lakshmi twists around, overhearing. 'Yes, Vidya and I have both committed this shameful act.' They giggle together like girls.

Sujata lowers herself gracefully and sits in the lotus position. 'You should hear what it is like to be a woman alone in India. You canno find a place to live because landlords will not have you. It does no matter how old you are: a woman is supposed to live only with her parents or her husband.'

'Can't you say your parents are alive and well and living in Bombay?'

They laugh again. 'We do what we have to, never fear.'

Sujata arranges her crimson sari on her shoulder. 'When I wa younger, twenty-two and not earning enough for a flat of my own, lived in missionary hostels or the YWCA. These places restrict you horribly! We had to be in by eight o'clock and if we wanted to go to a movie or have dinner with a friend, we had to have a letter from our local guardian.'

'Local guardian?'

They laugh at my shock.

'Yes, some male who would agree – a relative, or a friend's father. Each time you needed this letter. Besides that, they charged 450 rupees a month for a room and bath shared with three other girls, and they served only breakfast and dinner, so if you were sick you starved all day – not even a cup of tea.'

Rukmini interrupts. 'You know Indian women cannot go to restaurants alone. We are treated as prostitutes if we do. Except maybe, the expensive ones, and we can't afford those.'

'Yes,' Sujata resumes. 'And, of course, no guests in the room, no even women friends. And no hot water. This was a problem in winter.' She turns toward Vidya. 'Did I ever tell you I almost lost my job because I'd have to take afternoons off every few days to run home and wash my hair, so I could dry it while the sun was out?'

'And what about getting a job?' Vidya grimaces. 'Indian men – I think Western men are more direct, aren't they? – Indian men are subtle. They schedule your interview for five-thirty. You have to refuse. I had a 98.5 average in graduate school, but it took me four years to find a permanent job. When I would finally get an interview, they would say my duty was to stay home and care for my husband.'

'Your lord and master,' I put in.

They howl.

'Our god! The man we have been married to in our past seven lives and will be married to in the next seven!' cries Vidya.

Lakshmi lounges indolently against Sujata. 'Yes, Indian men lie there watching television and,' she slightly raises a languid arm, 'order you to fetch them a glass of water.' She pops back up. 'They never raise a finger, although you've worked all day!'

'And if you refuse, your mother-in-law will never let you forget it.'

'Oh, the mothers-in-law,' they shriek, laughing, and begin to exchange mother-in-law stories. I watch them. There is no bitterness in their voices, their faces. They shine.

'Yet you are so happy. You are far happier than most American feminists.'

'It is our work.' Rukmini outlines what they do at the crisis centre. 'We have only three full-time people – I am one of them. The rest work several evenings a week and weekends. We don't really advertise, but so many people come. They have such problems!'

Most Indian women are married young by their families to men they have not met before. Even middle-class women are usually married by the age of eighteen. They then move to their husband's parents' home, where they are, essentially, servants. Their primary duty, a duty so emphatic as to override their children's well-being and certainly their own, is to 'make the marriage work'. This means that a woman must adjust to her husband. Whatever he is or does – if he is cold or cruel, if he is never home, or does not give her money, if he drinks or gambles or has other women, if he beats her – is her lot. She is expected to submit, serve, and produce a son. Even women who can articulate the inhumanity of this code feel its imprint deeply.

Divorce is seen as a terrible shame, although among the poor there is some informal 'divorce' and 're-marriage'. But divorced women are an anomaly like widows, there is no place for them. Unless such women have sons old enough to support them, they may starve, for the husband's family thrusts them out, and their own family may be dead or unwilling to take them back. In recent years, the middle-class has become obsessed with dowry. Because of reformist laws requiring that all children share equally in the parental inheritance, daughters expect something from their families. If the family owns land, it is a small parcel that cannot be broken up and still maintain a family. Because girls leave home on marriage and sons remain, parents want to bequeath land to sons (if there is more than one they usually live jointly, in the same house or the same land). To make up for this, they spend hugely on their daughters' weddings, often going into debt to supply them with gold jewellery and expensive gifts for the in-laws – a watch for the husband, a television set, a refrigerator.

Perhaps because of the impact of television, people have become more commodity-minded. They want things; they want to raise their status. And frequently they torment the young bride to squeeze something more from her father. If she cannot, she is abused unremittingly: the Indians themselves call this *torture*. Some such women commit suicide. In the country, they throw themselves down the well; in the city, they set fire to their saris. They feel rejected in the only marriage they are permitted, and rejected by their own families. They have nowhere to go. They prefer death to wretchedness.

But sometimes, the in-laws conspire to kill the bride. They set fire to her sari and burn her to death. Such events are often enough accidental, so it might not seem suspicious – saris are dangerous over the open flame of wood-burning stoves – except that several hundred thousand young women have died this way in recent years. Only two families have been convicted of murder in that period; and families show no reluctance to marry their daughters into families in which the first wife has died violently. In India, it is easier to murder than divorce her. Afterwards, the son is presented with a new wife complete with new dowry.

There are some formal divorces among educated people, but regardless of cause, fathers have the legal right to custody of all sons over five. Women who are self-supporting and want to divorce their husbands are paralysed because they could not bear to lose their sons.

The crisis centres do what they can for such women, and for others who come seeking jobs, legal advice, a place to live, abortions (legal in India), or who have run away from home because they want to marry a man they themselves have chosen. Most people in India are not aware of the kinds of help available to them and the crisis centres have built up a network of feminist lawyers, doctors, social workers, and counsellors who contribute their time and skill.

The most hopeless cases are those in which a woman's own family will not stand by her. Women suffer not only from rejection by their in-laws, but also from sexual harassment called *eve-teasing* – women who walk alone on the streets, especially young women, are accosted, called obscene names, pinched, molested. There is also considerable rape, although it is concealed. In India, rape is still considered the shame of a woman and her family, and the police are brutally unsympathetic.

Like crisis centres everywhere, Saheli lacks money. So the Saheli women take battered wives and children, or runaways, home to their own houses. They have only one room as a secret haven for frightened women. Their headquarters in Delhi have been broken into by irate family members, they themselves have been physically assaulted by the police, accused of kidnapping, threatened with prison. Yet they continue. I am filled with admiration for these women, but they don't need it. Their joy in their work springs out of their gestures, their smiles, their laughter. If people require a cause greater than themselves for fulfilment, these women have one.

'Oh, yes, middle-class women have problems,' Amrita says, pushing aside one of the piles of papers on her desk. She inches her feet closer to the small electric heater on the floor – although it is over 80 degrees Fahrenheit outdoors. 'They worry about being too much in the sun lest they get too dark and unable to catch a husband. But you should realise that nearly half our people live below the poverty line – and in India that means they do not get enough to eat. Half.'

She lights a cigarette. Official women in India tend to smoke. She is very large, grey-haired, in her sixties, with a tired face. But her speech and gestures express unceasing energy. Amrita directs a non-governmental development agency.

'For years, those of us concerned with social welfare worked for legislation to protect workers – a minimum wage, decent working conditions, latrines, health programmes, pensions. But we were doing this for workers in the 'organised sector', those who worked for goverment and industry. And we forgot that 96 per cent of all women workers are in the 'unorganised sector', and many are not even paid for their work. Now the organised workers have become a kind of élite, and of course exclude women even more strenuously, while the great mass of women . . . .' She throws her hands up in a gesture of despair.

'It was the United Nations' establishment of the Decade of the Woman that suddenly made us conscious of the condition of our women, and in 1975 we began to focus on them. Elaben Bhatt, for instance, who worked in trade unionism in Gujarat, started SEWA, the Self-Employed Women's Association that funds women in their own small businesses. It has been so successful that it has been copied in many other states. Vina Mazumdar, who was a member of the Planning Commission (a powerful group, responsible for developing India's Five-Year Plans) tried for years to get the government to acknowledge the fact that women work. It did so only two years ago.

'Men say, "My wife doesn't work" – it's a matter of pride. And the government accepts their word, ignoring the fact that their wives put in a nineteen-hour day but aren't paid for it. Our first problem was just to identify the poorest women, then get them to tell us what they want and need. We don't want to impose programmes on people: we try to avoid American materialism and Russian tyranny. We choose the hard way, but the only way to create a better society. But we are impeded because we need women leaders, and 75 per cent of Indian women – 90 per cent of poor women – are illiterate.'

'Is it necessary to be literate to be a leader?' I hear the disapproval in my voice.

'You have no idea,' she responds sternly, 'of our problems. We have almost 700 million people spread out over more than a million square miles of land. Eighty per cent of them live in the countryside, in small villages connected only by poorly paved, or unpaved, rocky dirt roads. We speak a host of different languages. If we could at least read a common language, it would be far easier to reach more people at once.

'The Institute for Social Studies – a women's research group – set out in 1975 to try to locate poor women and get them to articulate their problems. They went on foot, they lived in the villages. And they have been successful. But now, where do we begin first? Health? Education? Work? Our resources are limited.

'There are now many government development programmes directed at these women, and even more grass-roots organisations initiated by women themselves, all across the country. Some of these are large, with memberships of 18,000 to 20,000 women, but many are small. And it takes tremendous effort, whether you are reaching thousands or only dozens. Oh, every effort counts and awareness spreads. But such a process takes time, and is even harder because women can't read and write.'

Abashed, I murmur, 'Yes, I see.'

She ignores me. 'You know that India is the only country in the world with fewer women than men – 935 to every 1,000 men; and with higher female mortality in every decade until the age of thirty-five! That is a statistic that overturns nature, which creates males more vulnerable before birth and after it. I'm not sure if there is female infanticide – we are Hindus, after all. Middle-class people nowadays often go for sex tests on a foetus, and abort girls. But ordinary people feed girls less and are slower to get them medical help when they fall ill. Then, they marry off their malnourished girls at twelve or thirteen; the girls begin producing children before their own bodies are fully adult.

'There is a reason why people want sons – the marriage system. Girls go to their husband's house after marriage, they are mere transients in their parents' house. Boys remain, and are expected to provide for the parents' old age. Only a tiny percentage of people has any sort of pension plan. What is puzzling is that this preference for boys is *increasing* even as the system disintegrates. For boys nowadays sometimes abandon their old parents. Yet in 1901, there were 972 females to 1000 males: the ratio has grown steadily wider, although things are changing. Kerala, for instance, was traditionally matrilineal and matrilocal [men live with their wives' families], and women controlled the money. But this is less and less true, largely because of industrial development.'

She stops, seemingly exhausted, then sips her sweet milky tea. It is all she needs: she's off again.

'From the time of the British Raj, fertile lands were shifted to cash crops – coffee, tea, rubber. But cash crops are subject to the market, which rises and falls. When it falls, people are left with produce they cannot eat. It was then that mass starvation began. Technology has accelerated this. The Green Revolution!' She snorts. 'Oh, it produced more food! But it required capital: installation of irrigation, buying expensive seeds, fertiliser, pesticides. Poor farmers could not afford them, could not compete with the better-off, who ran them into penury and then bought up their land. Families that lived for centuries on a bit of land are now day-workers in the fields of others, and the cities are crowded with homeless people. Industry too turns people into day-labourers, and it tends to reinforce male dominance, or impose it where it didn't exist before, like Kerala. Industry hires men. Oh, it *uses* women – and uses is the right word. It gives women menial jobs, pays them less than men for the same work, or exploits women who do piecework at home. Sometimes it hires couples, and then the husband takes the wife's wages.

'This is a serious problem because, you see, Indian men spend 70 per cent of their wages on themselves – on drink, cigarettes, prostitutes, entertainment. They want watches, scooters, motorbikes. Although women earn only about 60 per cent of what men earn, they contribute half of all household expenses, because 90 to 95 per cent of women's wages goes directly to the children, the household – to food, shelter, clothing. In India, the survival of the family is the responsibility of women. It has always been so.'

Sunk in my chair, I am brightened by the arrival of some young women in Amrita's agency, who enter smiling and chattering. They sit and begin to tell me about their work. Amrita turns back to the papers on her heaped desk. The tiredness of her face contrasts with the speed with which she reads and disposes of documents.

I face the others. 'If you can summarise them, tell me: what are women's most severe problems in India?' I expect them to answer – the marriage system, lack of birth control, poverty.

But all four of them cry out at once, 'WATER, FUEL, FODDER!' And then laugh.

So I cannot claim I was not prepared. But nothing can prepare you for the reality. Although I visit only two states and Delhi, I cover miles of land – dry, dusty, reddish, beneath cloudless blue skies. In February, it is 100 degrees in Gujarat; in March, 125 degrees in Rajasthan. I am always thirsty; I long for my air-conditioned car, a cold beer, ice-water. But outside my relatively comfortable perch, I see women everywhere. More men than women are abroad in the cities, on their bicycles, scooters, bullock or camel carts, in cars, buses. Sometimes a woman – or a whole family – sits behind a man on his scooter; women crowd the tiny taxis, the buses. And they walk, often with round wok-shaped pots on their heads, bearing vegetables or bricks, leading children. But in the country, one sees mainly women. They walk in groups divided single file along the road, their saris vivid against the monotonous landscape, bearing four or five brass pots of water, or a basket of fodder on their heads. In one spot the road is being widened, and a dozen people are chopping rock on the roadside. Three of them are women – spectral, gaunt, draped entirely in black. They raise their pick-axes and chop; raise and chop. Thirty feet away, in the rubble behind them, two babies rest unsteadily, sitting silent, expressionless, breathing in heavy black streams of truck exhaust fumes.

I want to speak to these women, but it is not advised. They would fear their husbands, who work beside them, and fear being docked for losing work-time. But I manage to meet other women construction workers, more fortunate ones, who are building a high-rise in the business centre of Delhi. In large projects, contractors are required to pay for a creche for workers' children, and to offer equal pay for equal work.

From a distance, the women make a gorgeous picture: slim, erect, golden-skinned, graceful in red, cerise, orange saris, and carrying on their heads pots of wet cement, they move barefoot in a row up narrow planks through the superstructure, along catwalks to the rising wall. There they dump the wet cement, turn, descend, and get more. They do this for eight hours a day. And while it is true that they receive wages equal to men's who do the same work, only men are promoted to be carpenters or masons, who earn more.

These women earn 12 rupees a day. A rupee is worth 8 cents. To be clearer: the poorest quality of ground wheatflour costs 3 rupees a kilo; a family of five requires a kilo a day. The poorest rice costs 2.40 a kilo; the cheapest vegetables, like potatoes, cost 3 to 4 rupees a day for a family of five. The oil to cook them in is 16 rupees a kilo, and the spices basic to all Indian cooking about 1 to 1.5 rupees a day. Milk with 3 per cent butterfat is 2.8 rupees a kilo; with 6 per cent fat, 5 rupees. Tea is 20 to 40 rupees a kilo; rationed sugar, 4 rupees a kilo; unrationed, 6. Meat, which most Hindus do not eat, costs 22 rupees a kilo. Wages of 12 rupees a day can buy a diet of bread, some vegetables cooked in a little oil and spice, and one cup of tea a day for a family of five. Poor Indians do not use tea leaves, but tea powder which is boiled with sugar and milk.

The women gather uneasily, glancing frequently over their shoulders. They are afraid they will be docked for taking time off. They look young, many of them are beautiful, but up close, their saris are soiled and torn (how could they not be?), their faces are daubed with patches of sand and bits of dried cement, and drawn with exhaustion. We talk, then some of us walk to the creche, a small building with two rooms, in which eight infants (mostly boys) are sleeping on the floor. The older children have been taken to the park.

All of them – Ranbai, Saida, Bimla, Jeerabai, and Nazbai – come from the countryside, from families with little or no land; and were married into similar families. They and their husbands worked in the fields for wages, but could no longer survive that way and came to the city seeking work. Two of them think they are around twenty; one cannot guess her age; and Nazbai believes she is forty and her daughter Jeerabai may be nineteen. She has two sons and two other daughters. Until three years ago, when the rice crop failed, plunging the family into destitution, she lived with her children and husband on a small farm shared jointly by five brothers and their families. She came here with Jeerabai and her son-in-law but next year, she says, they will return to the farm.

Two of the infants have awakened, perhaps at hearing their mother's voice, and toddle over to her. Jeerabai picks up the tiny, crying baby girl and puts her to her breast; the other stands whimpering, and Nazbai reaches for her and holds her against her body, squatting on the floor. Neither woman looks at the children or speaks to them. They simply hold them close.

The women's day begins at seven, when they rise, wash, and sweep out their 'jughees'. They live on the construction site, in makeshift hovels of sticks, tin, plastic, and rag. They prepare breakfast, which is always bread. Indian bread is made in flat or raised pancakes, each cooked separately over a wood fire; to make bread is therefore time-consuming. They send the children to the creche and from eight to twelve, one to five, they work carrying cement. At midday they have tea without milk. If they are sick, or extraordinarily tired, and work only four or six hours, they receive half-wages 6 rupees. In the evening, they tend to the children, prepare dinner, which is bread with some vegetables, do laundry, and serve their husbands.

They think they are not the worst off. They have the creche, for one thing: before, their children played in the sandhills and pools of muddy water mixed with cattle urine. They fell from catwalks. They were often ill. Now they are watched, fed, given milk, even taught something. And the builder discharges men caught womanising, so they believe that when their husbands (in fresh shirts and trousers) go to town at night, it is only to the films. The women themselves rarely go anywhere. And although their husbands eat first and have the hot meals (they spoke of these with envy), they have their own ways of insuring that they too have enough to eat. They giggle and look guiltily at each other when they speak of this.

'How?'

They won't say.

'You mean you have to hide – to use deceit – to save some food for yourselves? Your husbands don't share equally with you? You work as hard as they.'

They are embarrassed, confused. Well, men, you know. You can't question or challenge them or they slap you. And after all, they don't have to walk miles every night for water, as they did in the country, because there is a pump on the site. They only have to walk back and forth three or four times a night.

I gaze out over the huge site: mounds and plains of sandy soil, a few cows, a buffalo, some small pools of water, mud, and the skeleton of a building. And a settlement of jughees spreading far out into the wire-fenced enclosure. In the far distance, the outline of a mosque is lavender against the sky. I ask them what is their greatest pleasure in life.

They all agree about this. 'The time we can lie down and rest.'

On the outskirts of Delhi is a rural area called Khanjawla. It is highly populated and extremely poor, and the government has established a development programme here. I am to visit one village within a 'Block' made up of 2,000 families, about 10,000 people. Block Headquarters is a set of tiny offices furnished with a couple of tables and some wooden chairs. Men sit idle, waiting. They stand when my UNICEF guide and I arrive. We are introduced to the Block Development Manager, a heavy man with a coarse face and a thick fist which he keeps pounding on the table: 'The woman is equal in India!' He keeps reiterating this, although I have not challenged it.

He describes in detail the hierarchical structure of governance within the Block and its connections with other Blocks. He emphasises the democracy of the structure, assuring me that one place is reserved for a woman in each local council of fifteen. A man serves tea. Then everyone straightens or stands, and a slim elegant man enters, the Block Development sub-director, who supervises five Blocks. More tea is offered. My UNICEF guide urges that further explanations be curtailed so that we can go to the village. After considerable discussion, the four of us and six other men pile into vans and drive the few miles to the village.

Along the rural road, groups of men dressed in clean shirts and trousers sit under trees, smoke, chat. When I ask, I am told they are waiting for the bus. I look at my watch. It is eleven forty-five in the morning.

'Why are they waiting for the bus at this hour?'

Shrugs.

The manager leans forward. 'The place we are going, the people are all of the lowest caste. They are Valmiki . . . Scavengers.'

'A sub-caste of the Harijans?' Harijans, Children of God, was Gandhi's name for the Untouchables. They are also called Scheduled Castes.

'Yes,' the manager says and falls silent. Then, tentatively: 'I myself am of low caste. I was not allowed to go to the local school, I had to go to the Christian Mission School. That is where I learned English.'

I turn around to face him. I regret my quick judgment of him. Here is someone who has suffered from the system; perhaps he is more humane than he appears, maybe he just has a rough manner. Responding to my attention, he confides, 'In those days, the Untouchables had to sit on the top of the bus, they weren't allowed inside.'

I turn back and consider. 'But how could they tell? I mean, how can you tell a person's caste by looking at them?'

This arouses lively discussion, surprised laughter; it sounds as if they had never thought about this before. 'You can't,' someone says finally.

'Then how would you know if a Harijan sat downstairs in the bus?'

A general whoop of laughter. 'Their clothes, their dress!'

'So if a Harijan had decent clothes, they could sit downstairs and no one would object?'

Again, laughter. 'Yes, yes, but how would a Harijan get decent clothes?'

Dark skin lowers a woman's value on the marriage market. Harijans are excluded because they are poor. Nothing is different, nowhere. Not even in this country where skin colour is so richly varied, ranging from pale Anglo-Indians, to tawny gold, smoky blueish-brown, to deep chocolate. Caste divisions, historians have surmised, were originally colour divisions. Colour divisions led to caste divisions led to economic divisions. Nothing is different.

We arrive at a dusty compound, and file out of the vans into one of the buildings – a small white-washed room. Inside, a dozen women sit on the floor sewing. They rise as we enter, and chairs are brought for five of us – all that will fit. The rest mill outside. I am placed before a rickety table. The women sit down. The manager snaps his fingers at one of them: '*Chai!*' She gets up and leaves the room.

The sub-director, beside me, begins. 'These women are so poor that they never had needle, thread, or fabric. Here we give them materials and a sewing machine,' he nods to a small machine in the corner, 'and teach them to sew so they can clothe themselves and their families, and earn some money. This is the instructress.'

He nods towards the young woman standing beside us, who has been watching him anxiously for her cue. She does not speak English. One after another, she pulls things from a green metal locker and lays them on the table before me. There are tiny boy's trousers and shirts, men's shirts, embroidered tablecloths, and garish appliquéd pictures of gods and goddesses in traditional postures, intended for framing. I pick up the tiny clothes. They are painstakingly stitched. You can see the effort in them. They are soiled, wrinkled, worked-over like a child's first crocheted potholder. But they are good, they will be good. I say so, I smile. The room relaxes as if there had been a possibility of disapproval. The men nod approvingly at the instructor; she smiles.

The manager says something in Hindi, and slowly, four women stand up. 'These are Harijans,' he announces to me.

The women's faces – they are only girls, really – are utterly expressionless. I smile at them, then lean over and whisper to my UNICEF guide, 'Let's get out of here.'

He nods. There is discussion. 'They are bringing tea,' he apologises to me.

The sub-director turns to me. 'Do you want to ask them questions?' He points to one of the women, orders her to stand. I can't speak. Finally, looking at their emaciated limbs, I ask what they eat. The sub-director is annoyed, he doesn't want such questions. But he raps something out. The woman, who is lovely and has great dignity of carriage, turns her face toward the wall with bowed head.

Tea is brought to us, not to them. It is the kind with sugar and milk. I recall the construction workers, who never had milk.

'Do they get milk to drink?'

'Of course they get milk!' The sub-director is now exasperated. He wants me to get them to say how grateful they are to these men for providing them with a livelihood. He speaks in Hindi and another woman rises silently and slips from the room. She returns with a tall glass of cool buttermilk, and places it before me.

'This is what we drink here,' the sub-director says expansively. 'Buttermilk. It's delicious.'

I hate buttermilk. I don't want to be rude, I have sipped the tea, but the mere sight of buttermilk makes my gorge rise. I hand it to the young woman sitting near my feet, one of the Harijans. She accepts it, staring, but does not lift it to her lips. The manager raps out something peremptory. The young woman stands.

'Thank you!' orders the manager.

'Thank you,' she repeats softly.

'Get me out of here,' I whisper to my UNICEF friend.

He does.

We drive to a settlement of cottages, gleaming white under the midday sun. They are made of mud and mortar with thatched roofs – something like what the British call 'wattle and daub cottages' except these are connected in rows. They are windowless, and their openings face narrow winding alleys of packed sand sprinkled with the ubiquitous cowdung. Silently, a group of women appears. I beg my UNICEF friend to keep the men away, and he promises. A scholarly-looking woman in glasses, carrying a clipboard and pencil, leads us down a twisting alley to Maya's house.

Leaving our shoes at the door (it doesn't help; the cowdung attracts flies, which follow us everywhere, settling on every body – though no one but me is bothered by this), we enter an immaculate white room. Against one wall stands a cot made of criss-cross wooden strips. Maya, an erect woman in her mid-thirties, handsome, pulls a small cot out from under the large one, and from somewhere else chairs are brought for the scholarly-looking woman – the interpreter and village organiser – and me. There is nothing else in the room. The women file in, smiling or wary. There are too many for the cots, so Maya pushes them back and goes to a small room that is connected to this one – her kitchen – and fetches some burlap bags torn into single pieces. She lays these carefully on the floor, and the women settle down on them.

I ask them how they spend their day. They are surprised. Why should anyone be interested in that? It takes a while, but soon they are into it, chattering, laughing, arguing mildly.

How you spend your day in this village depends on whether you have a buffalo. Maya does; most do not. But all of them get up at four in the morning, bathe and recite their prayers. Maya then goes to the buffalo stall and mucks it out. She milks the animal, gives it food and water. (This milk is sold. These women never have milk, not even when they are pregnant. Nor do their children, once they are weaned.) Then she returns to the house and prepares breakfast, which is chapati – bread made (this is revealed with embarrassment) of bajra, a cheap maize-like grain. The women sit on the floor beside their low stoves when they cook, pulling their saris up between their legs.

They clean the dishes. When water is scarce, as it is in summer, they rub the utensils clean with fine sand. They sweep their houses with straw brooms, send off those children who go to school, and trek out to the fields. Those who have a mother-in-law, as Maya does (a woman my age, but worn out – no scold here, but a woman grateful to be relieved of much work), leave the small children behind. The others take theirs. These women raise wheat. They work in the fields all day for low wages, often no more than 3 rupees. Those with animals collect baskets of fodder before they return to service the animals again: muck out, milk, feed, water. The children have returned from school now, and the women start dinner – bread with some vegetables. They clean up.

After dinner, they fetch water. They feel lucky because two years ago a pump was installed in their village. Before that, they had to walk two kilometres each way, several times a night, carrying *matka* – large clay vessels – filled with water on their heads. Now they have only to make three or four trips to the pump. Each night they collect enough water for the next day's use, and store it in their kitchens. By ten o'clock, the women can rest.

But this is only their daily routine. There are tasks performed regularly but not every day. The women trudge out to the waste lands where scrub trees grow and collect faggots for fuel, carrying them back in baskets on their heads. They make dried cowdung cakes – also used for fuel. They wash clothes under the pump. And some, like Maya, have other jobs. Maya has had two years of school, so every afternoon, for two hours, she returns from the fields to teach those women who can spare the time the alphabet, counting, hygiene, and recognition of the route numbers on buses. These women are sequestered: their husbands do not permit them to leave the settlement. So I wonder why they are learning bus routes. I infer things are changing in this village.

Most of the husbands have only temporary work of the poorest-paid sort. It is the women's work that keeps the family alive. But the women do not see the fruits of their labour, for the men take their wages and spend them. They frequently go out at night, alone. If the women ask where they are going, they are slapped. I ask if their husbands are not kind to them, grateful for all their work. They hoot with laughter. Kind! Their husbands take their money, they don't tell their wives how much they earn, they go out, they get drunk, and when they come home, they beat their wives.

Yet these women's faces are lovely – sweet, even serene. Not one sits huddled over, defeated. As we talk, they are full of life, laughing, cracking jokes. What gives them pleasure? Their children?

The room falls sombre. No. Children are a burden. And nowadays there are bad sons who do not take care of their parents. No. If they laugh and joke, it is because they have long ago accepted that there is no alternative for them.

They are responsible for the survival of their families, but not for their own lives. They have no choice, and therefore no guilt, shame, or grounds for anger. That is what they are telling me. It is hard for me to understand.

'When you pray in the morning, what is your prayer?'

They pray for 'Shanti'.

'Peace?'

This requires considerable discussion, interpretation. Well, yes, peace: but what peace means to them is a little security, a little less anxiety about survival.

'And what do you want more than anything else in your lives?'

About this there is no question: 'Work!'

'Work?!!!'

Yes, work. *Paid* work. Not everyone, they tell me, has a buffalo, like Maya. Not everyone teaches. I realise Maya's house has been chosen for our meeting because she is the most prosperous woman in this place.

The men have been drifting up to the doorway, peering in, wandering away. They are trying to follow instructions, but they are curious about the high spirits, the laughter and hooting of thirty-five women. They feel left out. Finally, we rise and follow them to a room across the street from the settlement, a new room in a courtyard. Here are chairs enough for all the men, the interpreter, and me. The women sit on the bare floor.

Again, the sub-director begins. These women are extremely poor. They have only their wages for work in the fields, not enough to feed their families. There is a shortage of children's exercise books in India. These women cannot afford to buy them, so cannot send their children to school. Soon, in this room, they will be taught to make exercise books and will be able to earn a decent wage. He sounds self-satisfied, and for once I think: why not?

Still, I can't just smile and nod. 'Who will keep their wages?'

'*They* will, of course!'

'No. Ask them. I want you to ask *them*.'

He does. They shout, they clamour: *they* will! They grin at me, chatter to each other. They have determined this. They shoot questions at the sub-director: when will this thing get off the ground? We are impatient, we are eager!

He is a little surprised. They are far from the intimidated women of our earlier visit. Perhaps spending an hour and a half talking about the work they do has heightened their sense of worth. I gaze over at the interpreter, silent in front of the men, and see her expression. She is quietly delighted. Yes, I think, she has been talking to them, making them see. And for this moment, they are full of themselves.

The work-day of the women in Khanjawla is similar to that of most of the women I met. There are local variations, of course; many that I did not see. Among the Rajputs, for instance, men fetch the water because the women are not allowed out of their houses at all. I don't know who fetches fodder and fuel. Some families are so poor they eat their vegetables raw because they cannot afford cooking oil. And some do not have houses or even jughees, but live on the streets.

Devdholera, a village outside Ahmadabad, is being helped by SEWA. It finances the purchase of buffaloes for women who work as dairy farmers and keep their own wages; it also teaches textile skills, and many of the people here, men as well as women, work at carding, spinning, and weaving. I visit a house, the usual mud and mortar, but this one is built like a stage: three walls and a broader platform. There is a short wall dividing the interior space into two rooms; the platform holds a long narrow loom, at which the man of the house sits weaving a carpet. In one of the rooms is the usual low stove, and a few utensils. The other holds an aluminium cot, the kind one uses at the beach, with plastic stripping. This is the man's bed. His wife and children sleep on the ragged pieces of cloth heaped up in a corner.

A cot is set up outside for me to sit on, and I urge other women to join me. They are too shy, but the male schoolteacher later comes and sits beside me. The women sit cross-legged on the ground, close to my feet; some hover behind me, touching the combs that keep my hair in place, fingering the cloth of my running suit. These women work in textiles, but they are not happy, they tell me. Baluben and Amba have been outside the village and seen the fine houses, with windows and doors, and the sturdy utensils that some people possess. Tidi says the men and women both work, but the men do not help with the housework. Baniben is not a textile worker; she organises and oversees child-care centres in twenty villages and is paid by SEWA. She is forty, she says, but looks younger – for a change. Perhaps that is because she is extremely outspoken. She is unhappy because she travels around on foot and earns 600 rupees a month, more than her husband, 'and everywhere I go I am treated with respect, but when I come home at night, my husband treats me like a servant.'

The women rag her amiably. 'Yes, but you make him cook his own dinner!'

'Sometimes I come home very late and he is sitting there doing nothing, sulking because he has no food. I tell him he has hands! I am his fourth wife; I won't take anything from him.'

The women laugh, but laughter does not last long in this village. Lakshmi begins to complain, and the others all join in. She says women are 'mutilated' from birth.

'When they are only a month old, their ears are pierced. . . .'

'Yes, then their noses. Women have to walk around dragging heavy chains all their lives.'

I am surprised: Indian women are always draped with jewellery, but I thought it was a status symbol. Even poor women may wear two or three rings in their noses, several toe rings, and heavy silver ankle bracelets. They *do* look like shackles. Women who lack silver bangles wear plastic. I thought they liked jewellery.

'And,' Lakshmi continues,'men can walk around more.'

'And go to school.'

The men sidle close to where we are sitting, to listen. They smile, they shrug. 'What can you do? She earns as much as I do,' one man smiles.

I turn to the schoolteacher. 'Don't girls go to school?'

Everyone is embarrassed. 'Yes,' he smiles shyly. 'About as many girls as boys. You know, they need decent clothes, shoes . . . well, we don't require shoes. But paper and pencil . . . we cannot supply it. We do supply books in this school, unlike some others. But girls are removed from school as soon as they are able to work around the house. No girl goes beyond this local school.'

His wife teaches in the school with him, and I ask if I can meet her. But she is away, gathering fuel.

Baniben gives me a look. 'We know it is important for our daughters to read and write. That way, when their in-laws torture them and threaten to burn them, they can write us a postcard and let us know.'

The women in Kavita, a village outside Udaipur, are tribals – non-Hindus, outside the caste system entirely, but as 'low' as Harijans. Their tiny one-roomed houses are windowless and dark; their children are the most ragged and dirty I have seen so far. Some of them have diseased patches on their skin. The women work in the fields for wages and raise goats. Several times a week they must walk far over the distant hill to collect faggots for fuel. But Radi shows me her dark room with some pride: she has a smokeless *chulah*, a stove with a stovepipe that rises through the ceiling. The government and UNICEF subsidise the installation of such stoves, because women who sit over the low wood-burning stoves breathing in smoke for hours each day get lung diseases and sometimes go blind.

The tribal women are also grateful for the pump that was installed here some years ago. Unfortunately, the pump tends to go dry in summer. Although there are pumps in nearby villages, they cannot use them because they are a scheduled tribe. Each caste level uses pumps or wells belonging to others of their own caste, or of those below them. Scheduled castes and tribals can use pumps only in villages occupied by similar groups. The closest such group is kilometres away from this village.

These women are extremely thin, and I ask them what they would eat if they could have anything in the world they desired. They receive the question in silence, and the interpreter must urge them. But it seems to be hard for them to imagine such a thing. The answers come slowly.

'Some wheat bread.'

'A dish with rice.'

'Perhaps something sweet.'

These women keep their own wages and shop with their husbands. Still, the husbands have managed to acquire bicycles on which to ride to their part-time or seasonal jobs although a bus passes near here. Through all my questioning, they remind me that there are no alternatives for women: a woman must accept her life. I think: they are not even Hindus.

As I am leaving, Harku, an old woman who stands no higher than my waist, grabs hold of my arm and speaks passionately. 'What about women in America? Do they sit around like us and talk about their lives? Do they have problems?'

'American women have problems at work. They are not treated equally with men. They complain that their husbands do not share responsibility for children and the house.'

The women look at each other with dismay. 'We thought American women have no problems,' Harku mourns.

'And American women worry about whether or not to marry or have children,' I continue.

When this is translated, a great howl goes up. The women walk off laughing; they throw up their arms and hit each other playfully in mock self-congratulation. 'Well, that's *one* problem we don't have!' they cry. 'Here, we are married and have children whether or not we want it!'

It is with relief that I visit a middle-class family. Here there will be no anxiety about survival, no scrawny babies. They own a compound, two buildings facing each other, one long one with many rooms. The end room has been given to a very old woman who is in some way related to the family. Her husband died when she was young, before she had children, and her in-laws expelled her. She has worked since as a field hand, but now that she is seventy-five, she can put in only a few hours a day in the fields. She has somehow acquired a buffalo, and the sale of milk, plus her wages and the charity of her relatives, keeps her alive. I meet her trudging in with a large basket of fodder for her animal.

The two men of the joint family – brothers who married sisters – welcome me graciously to a large bright room with two windows, two cots with thick mattresses, several wooden chairs, and, enshrined on a ledge, a television set. One brother is a teacher, the other has a motorcycle repair shop in town. They have inherited land and sharecrop it. They are a little frightening looking – very thin, with several days' growth of beard, missing teeth, and fierce eyes. But when they smile, sweetness and a kind of innocence shines from their faces. Many rural men have such a look.

Behind the compound is a system of pipes, a bio-gas apparatus that transforms cowdung into methane gas for cooking. I assume that in this household the women do not have to collect fuel, but when I visit the kitchen, the gas stove sits cold in its corner while Bhagawati's teenage daughter sits on the floor preparing *roti* at a wood-burning stove. (*Roti* is one of many names for bread.) This kitchen has many pots, utensils, even some dishes. Bhagawati leads me to the storeroom, where, to her deep satisfaction, I gasp. For piled up there are many bushel bags of wheat and rice; 100 pounds of potatoes in a heap; and great vats of oil, canisters of sugar and rice. There is enough food here to keep the entire family for a year. There is also a huge shiny black motorcycle, and another leaning against an outside wall. There is even a dog, the first I have seen in India.

The schoolteacher, Bhagawati and their four children use the furnished room, this kitchen, and the storeroom; the repairman, Nirmala and his five children occupy the other side of the house, which has a kitchen of its own and a large former barn, with a cot and a heap of sleeping rugs. I do not ask who sleeps on the cot. Between them is a small open room where the women sit. Nirmala spreads out a bright cloth on its bare floor before we sit. A group of women enters shoeless, most carrying babies; the flies settle on us.

But I cannot get these women to talk. I wonder if they are constrained by the presence of a man, another UNICEF friend. But he is so interested and sympathetic that I do not want to ask him to leave. Besides, I'm not sure he's the problem, because Bhagawati so dominates the conversation. She had four years of school, and works with Seva Mandir, an educational organisation dedicated to the poor. She is a feminist, and when I ask if all this feminist awareness has led to any changes in the village, she tells about the new village hall, built by women and men, from which the men later excluded the women. They protested, and now share its use with the men. But the marriage system remains the same, girls are educated less than boys, and men are still served first in this village.

Some women drift away. Unhappy, I try to capture the interest of those who are left by asking about their work, but no one speaks except Bhagawati. She is assured, secure in her status. She is the richest woman in the village. This is her day:

She rises at five; washes; then mucks out the buffalo stalls, milks the animals and gives them food and water. She prepares the milk for the dairy, reserving some to make yoghurt for the family. She brews some tea, all she takes in the morning; then sweeps the house and goes to fetch water. She makes several trips to the pump a quarter of a mile away. Then she prepares breakfast. They eat the same meal morning and night – bread, rice, potato curry and vegetables. The men rise about seven, wash, eat, and go to work. The sisters clean their pots and send the older children to school, then they take the younger ones and walk to the fields.

Nirmala and Bhagawati supervise the work done on their land. They oversee the sharecroppers and help with planting, weeding, reaping, and marketing. At present they are harvesting sugar cane crops: they wash the vegetables, supervise their packing, and direct the man who transports them to market. They work in the fields until two, when they return for tea. It is in this break that I am visiting them, she explains: the other women keep leaving because they are sharecroppers and must return to work. (So: they are in some sense employed by this family. *That's* why they are silent. Nothing is different.) At three, they return to the fields and work until five. Then home again to milk, muck out, feed and water the animals. They prepare dinner for the family, clean up, and sleep.

'What about that shiny new television set? When do you watch it?'

She laughs, a little embarrassed. It *is* new – she's seen a few things. When there is something special on during dinner, she runs back and forth between the living room (where the men sit) and the kitchen. She did watch a programme about women in foreign places starting great organisations and marching in the streets; she would like to travel and see these things for herself. I suspect she is saying what she thinks will please me, and deflecting my attention from the fact that the television set is really for the men, who sit idle once they return from work.

'Do you ever go out?' I ask. 'To a movie? To the city?' Udaipur, two hours' drive from here, is considered one of the most beautiful cities of India.

She smiles stiffly, shakes her head. Another woman speaks sharply and others murmur agreement. 'Yes, even if a man wants to take his wife to a movie, her mother-in-law forbids it.'

'But you and Nirmala have no mother-in-law. Do the men go out?'

She nods uneasily, smiling hard.

Middle-class women are always less honest than poor women.

If Hindu women and tribals are overwhelmed with work, Moslem women – at least, those I met – are miserable because they are without it. Moslems live together, in little enclaves dotted throug Hindu cities, except in places like Hyderabad, where they live i great numbers. I visit only the poor. Several families share a walle compound, its sides lined with attached rooms, one to a family Between these is a dirt yard where a cow wanders searching for a bi of grass. There is a pump, and someone is heating water for a bat in a large pot set on what looks like an oil drum. The flames flar high and dart out dangerously. No one is worried, although ther are many small children stumbling around in the yard.

Kamarbano's room has a window and a small shelf with chin cups on it; Mumtazjahan has had nine deliveries, but has only thre living children; Anjum has a kerosene stove in her dark house These women work – they tend their many children, prepare meals do laundry, and they are permitted to leave the compound to bu vegetables or visit a neighbour. The men have been requested t give us privacy, but they hover, and take turns listening in. On interrupts: 'They can also go to the mosque.'

'I thought Moslems did not allow women to enter mosques.'

'No, but they can go to *sabil*, a room attached to the mosqu where women can learn Urdu and the Koran.'

I look at Shahjahan, who crouches on the cot beside me and lean against the wall of a house, sullen, with cold eyes. 'So you go t *sabil*?'

She glares at me.

'No, no,' the man continues, 'our mosque here has no *sabil*.'

I look out over the small populated courtyard that is thes women's entire world. I look at Shahjahan's young wretched face she thinks she is twenty or twenty-two, but she has a ten-year-ol son and three other children.

'What would you want if you could have anything at all in life?

She spits the words at me. 'Independence. A little shop. To d something in life.' She stares angrily at my notebook. 'Most of a education!' Her face sets in anger. 'And now that I have answere all your questions, what are you going to give me?'

In the St Nizzamundin section of Delhi is a Sufi Centre. Within it close I can meet some Moslem women who live in jughees, squatter in the public part. They are Akhtari, Guljan, Kallo, Najnabegum Meena, and Shahzadi. When Shahzadi utters her name, all th

omen burst into laughter: her name, they explain, means *princess*.
he laughs too, without mirth. 'I am far from a princess, yes?' She,
ke the others, is wearing a tattered filthy sari, and a child holds her
·g, crying. There are many children here, and most of them are
rying. They wear bits of shirt; their legs are coated with the dust of
ιe streets.

They explain that they are supposed to be in purdah, but are too
oor to maintain it. Yet when they go out, they will pull a tattered
ιri end up over their faces, and hold it there somehow, at the same
me juggling the child in their arms, the one toddling alongside.
heir husbands have only part-time or seasonal work, and they must
ork. Although they go out to work, selling vegetables in the square
 washing pots in someone's house, they remain within the Moslem
ιclave. Rukaya sells *sirni* (sweets) and *bidi* (a cheap cigarette)
om the window of her house, but she was financed by the Sufi
entre.

The women take turns standing, walking a crying child and
ocking it, then sitting down again. Tea is served, and Rukaya gives
ers to her two-year-old son, who drinks it down hungrily. I offer
im mine, and he drinks that too. The other children still cry. It
osses my mind that they are hungry. In bad times, during
ιonsoon (when their jughees are blown down) and when there is no
ork, the families have to beg food here or at a nearby pilgrimage
:ntre. But they are ashamed of taking charity and often go without
ιod for two or three days at a time.

The women all want to be sterilised, but fear their husbands. 'You
ave to do it without his knowledge,' Rukaya explains. 'I did it!' she
rags. 'He beat me when I told him, but what more could he do? It
as done!'

They cannot think about anything they want. They want enough
iod, a real house; they cannot think beyond that and they say it is
etter not to. Apart from anxiety about survival, they say they are –
ιd they use the English word – *bored*. A man crossing the
iurtyard stops, stands by a pillar. The gate swings open and
Iadina comes in *smoking*! I have not before seen a poor Indian
oman smoke. She is short and muscular and she swaggers; noisily,
ιe settles herself among the women. She is not like them, she
ιnounces, turning her open face toward me. She can go where she
kes, she has no husband! Her husband deserted her a few years
ζo, taking their oldest child, a son who is now twelve. She is
venty-six; she misses her son, but is consumed with the problem of
ιaintaining her daughters, her old mother, and herself, alone. She
ies piece-work, sewing sequins in floral patterns on strips of thin

satin for bridal crowns. She must buy her materials herself for 9 t
9.5 rupees a crown, and the entrepreneur gives her 12. He the
affixes them to a backing and sells them for 24. 'Exploitation!' sh
cries. 'But what can I do? It is horrible to be a woman in Indi;
Horrible! Women have no status here!'

The man comes forward. 'If you resent it so much, why don't yo
go abroad to live like the foreign women?'

She speaks excitedly, laughing a little. 'I tried! I tried! I eve
managed to get a passport, but my husband destroyed it!' She look
appealingly at me. 'Please, if I can get another passport, will yo
take me with you to America? I can work hard, I will do anythin;
Please?' She is, partly at least, playing the comic. It is her ability t
be funny and her bravado, I think, that have enabled her to surviv
alone here. I look at the other women. They have no expression o
their faces.

Unlike many Third World countries, India is able to feed itself. An
it is mainly women who raise the food that sustains the nation. Y
women are the poorest, the hardest worked, and the least respecte
people. The only thing worse than overwork is no work at al
Women suffer from two problems: poverty and male oppressio
The poverty is shared by the men; and men too are oppressed
treated like servants by their superiors, exploited. But it is doubtf
that adult men are beaten, in the ordinary course of their day
Their (perhaps) unwritten right to abuse stands as a presence eve
when they do not exercise it – and middle-class men as well as po
ones sometimes do. It is a rare woman who would dare to question
much less challenge, her husband, and only the most severe
abused leave them. And no man is confined to house or town.

Beyond these kinds of oppression is a more subtle sor
oppression by indifference. Indian men do not take an equ
responsibility for providing the necessities of life. In India, these a
water, fuel, and fodder, feeding the family, caring for the childre
Elsewhere, they involve concern for the environment and restrai
of the powers of technology. All the women I met – far more than
have described here – used the same phrase: women have n
alternative. Even if they are reborn, they say, they will be wome
They will be women forever. Forever they will carry on their sli
backs the burden of responsibility for the survival of the huma
race.

No poor woman spoke of accepting her place in a cosmic dram;
or of consolation in a deity. No poor woman saw her situation ;
'right', only as inevitable. That some manage to flower in beaut

and dignity and strength despite their lot is a testimony to them, not to any god. I wanted to embrace these women, lift and carry them off to a place where men take equal responsibility for human well-being; where people do respect 'the divine' in each other, whatever their colour or status; where, indeed, there is no such thing as status.

But where?

Marilyn French was born in New York City, and spent her childhood in Long Island. She was educated at Hofstra College and Harvard University, where she received her doctorate, and has taught in a number of American colleges, most recently as Mellon Fellow at Harvard. She has produced works of literary criticism on James Joyce and Shakespeare. In 1977 she wrote her novel *The Women's Room*, and followed this in 1980 with *The Bleeding Heart*. Both are concerned with modern American women. Her latest book, *Beyond Power: Women, Men and Morals*, is an analysis of patriarchy. Marilyn French currently lives in Florida.

EDUCATION

During the Decade for Women the world experienced the continuing tremors that followed the education boom of the 1950s and 1960s. Today there are more children in school than ever before, and the education gap between girls and boys is beginning to close as more and more parents are deciding, or being compelled by their governments, to send their daughters to school.

From Nigeria, Buchi Emecheta travels to the United States, to the campuses and kindergartens of California, to a nation in the grips of an education epidemic. Here there is a greater proportion of youngsters in college than in any other region of the world, and there are as many women as men studying for their degrees. But many of these newly qualified graduates opt for marriage and domesticity rather than ambition and independence when the college doors close behind them.

From the United Kingdom, Jill Tweedie travels to Indonesia, to village houses on stilts, to paddy fields and buffalo, to the country where, within a single generation, the proportion of girls in primary school has more than doubled, where a woman with at least seven years of education is twice as likely to be using contraception and half as likely to see her baby die in its first year of life.

Buchi Emecheta

It can safely be said that America is a country of recent immigrants. This is very unlike England, say, which people have been migrating to and emigrating from for many hundreds of years, whereas America had its highest influx in the nineteenth and twentieth centuries.

Originally the colonisers were adventurers, ambitious men who were not afraid of change and held, as mentioned in the Declaration of Independence, a great love of liberty. This sense of liberty attracted radicals and dreamers alike: radicals who wished to worship their creators in the way they felt right, and whose native countries could no longer contain their outlandish ideas; dreamers who pondered about the perfect society where everyone would have their proper place and where they could live in elegance and ease. Around New England and Pennsylvania, one can still see the exaggerated Englishness of its present inhabitants.

This type of move from one's native land, from one's friends, family and associates, demands a unique mettle. The crossing of the Atlantic in ships, boats and quite recently by air was a dangerous adventure in itself, to say nothing of the suffering of the Negro women who had to survive the middle passage – a journey in which a woman was packed in with her kind like an animal, during which she might give birth, die of suffocation, during which she could cry tears and blood – and on arrival she was denied the freedom which the rest of America claimed to stand for. Hence those who survived such journeys, be it from Europe or Africa, had to be blessed with strong health. The weak were long dead on arrival, or thrown overboard, or simply driven out of their senses. Only the strong, the tenaciously determined, lived to form the backbone of America today.

The immigrants did not all come at once, but in batches. Following founding fathers who came for religious reasons, the Irish came after repeated failure of the potato crop caused widespread famine in their homeland, the Jews came because of persecution, blacks came because they were forced to, Scandinavians came in search of a better life style; then came the Germans – and quite recently the Koreans and Vietnamese. Africans now come as free men and women in search of education and jobs.

As these different waves of people came, so they brought their culture and way of life. This included their special ways of socialising their children into their particular society. But, due to early numerical superiority, the English culture predominated right from the beginning.

Who then is the American woman? For do not all these immigrants bring their wives along? Like her male counterpart, the woman of America comes from all parts of the globe.

She came from England first, to be wife and sweetheart of the early adventurers, miners and colony-builders. She came with her husband in protest against the religious prejudices of Europe. In America she was expected to live in purity, living the life of a good Christian lady whose price is far above the proverbial rubies. She had to be a faultless church woman, stiff with discipline, and at the same time gentle and loving to her husband. In fact, she had to be man's dream of the ideal woman.

When the good white woman was no longer willing to come, she was snatched from the streets of London and shipped as an indentured servant. Then came the woman who for one reason or another had gone against the law. There were murderers, prostitutes, drunkards and even those women accused of witchcraft. All were forced into ships and brought into America in exchange for commutation of a stiff prison sentence in England. They had to work for up to five years before earning their freedom. By the end of that time, they were rough, coarse, loud and in many cases so tired that they no longer cared about living up to any standard. The best they could do was survive. Their fate was slightly better than that of the slaves, however, in that they had freedom at the end of a certain number of years. Many also went on to marry men in identical situations, convicts who had worked their way to freedom.

Even in those early days, there was already a class distinction. There was the lady, the mistress of a large house, whose husband came with some money or who was already a gentleman, and these would need the services of the poor white woman. In fact the situation was identical to that in the mother country at the time. But as soon as the indomitable will-power and strength of the Negro woman was realised, even the white prostitutes could pretend to be ladies.

From the East came the Asians and their wives. For a very long time these people did not have the courage to mix, as they were cut off by language and the low type of jobs that they did, but their women were the same as others, bearing children and working to help their males. Yet they were not expected to be like the alabaster lady who needed the Negro mammy.

However, the greatest single group of women who helped build he backbone of present America were Negroes. The Negro woman came as a slave. She did not wish to come. Though the middle passage decimated her number, she still survived, to boost the image of the white lady, to work in the fields, to bear and raise healthy slaves for her master. She survived as a play object, a creature to rape at will and an object of derision. It is not a surprise that she was sold at a higher price than her male. She had, without knowing it, created a myth about herself – the myth of the indomitable mammy who reigned supreme in her cabin. But now, in he twentieth century, she is still surviving, doing all the low jobs her slave grandmother did, with this difference – that she is no longer a slave, and enjoys a degree of freedom. But she is still in the dregs of American society.

For during the first Reagan administration, were there not over three million American women living below the poverty line and were they not predominantly black women?

So the American woman could say to you, 'My grandfather is Dutch, my grandmother an African slave, my mother of Irish stock – but I am an American.'

Most American women are descended from mothers and fathers who endured and weathered all the rigours of settling in a new country – rigours such as the weather, endless wars with the native Indians, trips to the Wild West. All along, the weak perished and only the fittest women survived.

As the society developed, it became clear that women were needed to work in farming and rapidly expanding industries. Some women were also needed to be hostesses and socialites – play the piano, sing and entertain, and carry on the family line when the man was no more. This latter happened often, as men insisted on the excitement of forever moving west which invariably brought them in contact with the Indians who fought to defend their territory. Moving west also meant experiencing different climates and unknown routes and hostile animals. All these factors claimed many men's lives.

It became evident in the new colonies that the American woman must have some kind of education or instruction to enable her to cope with all these odds. She might have black slaves to help her, but she needed to be taught how to manipulate and get the best out of them. It was almost universally believed at the time that a woman's brain was smaller in capacity and therefore inferior in quality to that of a man. Some of the earliest women to demand greater educational opportunities for their sex did not dispute this

erroneous myth. They therefore did not desire equal opportunit
for women, but merely believed that more knowledge would make
them better mothers and more efficient housewives. Some of them
opposed the women's rights movement when it began to emerge. I
was, in the main, a younger generation of women, their imagination
and determination nourished and their wits sharpened by the
pioneers, who took the lead in advancing the legal and economic
position of their sex.

Despite all this, by 1812 education for the women of America had
made little progress. It was still limited to the well-to-do few, and
confined largely to such pursuits as embroidery, painting, learning
French, singing and playing the harpsichord. The dimension and
extent of the type of education needed by women had been clearly
stated by the French philosopher Rousseau: 'The whole education
of women ought to be relative to men. To please men, to make
themselves loved and treasured by men, to educate men when
young, to care for them when grown, to console them and to make
life sweet and agreeable to them – these are the duties of women at
all times, and what should be taught them from their infancy.'

However, following the opening up of most of the North
West to exploration and settlement, coupled with Western
expansion and industrial development, women were not only
entering the new textile mills but were also in increasing demand as
teachers for a rapidly growing population. The need to equip them
for these new duties was becoming harder to deny. Nonetheless
subjects such as metaphysics or those that would entail women
coming openly in contact with the public, such as law, were still
regarded as unsuitable.

There were two schools of thought even among female leaders of
the time. One wanted a cautious female advancement in education
and among its supporters were Hannah Mather Croker whose little
tract *Observations on the Real Rights of Women*, published in 1818
shows the conflict between the old and the new. She was not quite
sure of the total independence of the female sex: 'Females may
console themselves and feel happy that, by moral distinction of the
sexes, they are called upon to move in a sphere of life remote from
those masculine contentions, although they hold equal rights for
studying every branch of science, even jurisprudence. But it would
be morally wrong and physically imprudent for any woman to
attempt pleading in the bar of justice, as no law can give her the
right of deviating from the strictest rules of ridicule and decorum.'

The second school of thought rejected the creed that woman must
forever occupy an inferior position because of her inherent

frailties, as demonstrated for all time by the fall of Eve. Its supporters maintained that woman should be restored to her original rights and dignity, a position she held at the commencement of the Christian dispensation, although they felt there must still be allowed some moral and physical distinction between the sexes. They did not doubt that there could be as much difference in the intellectual powers of each individual of the female sex as there is among males. But if they all received the same mode of education, their improvement would be fully equal.

In 1828 and 1829, women's education received a considerable impetus from the teachings of Frances Wright. Born in Scotland in 1795, well schooled and the friend of Lafayette and of many freethinkers, Miss Wright helped co-edit a newspaper in New Harmony on the Indiana frontier and later had her own paper, *The Free Enquirer*, in New York. She achieved further notoriety as a pioneering woman lecturer and through her radical philosophy, of which her advocacy of equal education for women was an integral part. She argued that men were themselves degraded by the inferiority they imposed on women, so every relationship to which woman was a party, be it friendship, marriage or parenthood, suffered as long as she was regarded and treated as a lesser human being. 'Until women assume the place in Society which good sense and good feeling alike assign to them, human improvement must advance but feebly. It is in vain that we would circumscribe the power of one half of our race, and that half by far the most important and influential. If they exert it not for good they will for evil; if they advance not knowledge, they will perpetuate ignorance. Let women stand where they may in the scale of improvement, their position decides that of the race.'

So powerful was her stand that later women's advocates were tagged 'Fanny Wrighters' as the worst kind of abuse.

As the electorate slowly broadened state by state, to include all white males over twenty-one, regardless of property qualifications, the demand that education likewise be made available to all became intensified, in order that the voters could be responsible and intelligent. Despite this urgent need, it took the whole of the nineteenth century to achieve a nationwide system of free education for males from primary school through college. For girls whose families could not afford private education, progress was very slow and non-existent in places. While girls were permitted to go to elementary schools, from the earliest days, their admission into secondary and high school took much longer. The opening of free high schools for girls in such cities as Boston and Philadelphia was a veritable milestone which occurred only after the Civil War.

Since convincing taxpayers and civil authorities that women were entitled to the same educational opportunities as men was going to be a long and laborious task, private institutions continued to be the principal recourse of young women seeking broader schooling. But here too a problem existed. The fees were necessarily high and this limited the student body to those with parents who could afford them. The heads of such female seminaries were thus forced to seek outside funding. From her earliest teaching days, Emma Willard had sought to take education out of the realm of the privileged. She started making grants, in the form of loans, which were repaid by her pupils after they had found teaching posts. Though she lent quite a considerable sum to her pupils she knew even then that this method was not a real solution to the problem.

Teaching was the first of the 'professions' open to women but since they had no training and only the most rudimentary schooling, their prestige was low and they could not command salaries like those of men, who were often college or university graduates. But if men and women were expected to be taught in childhood by teachers, was it too much to ask that teachers of either sex should be at least reasonably educated by the State? The Willard Association for the Mutual Improvement of Female Teachers, founded by Mrs Willard in 1837 as a sort of alliance association, was the first organisation to bring this matter to public attention.

The subjects Mrs Willard taught her girls might have appeared to be higher education to her contemporaries, but they could not compare with what was offered to young men at Harvard and other colleges. The first institution which offered women a curriculum remotely comparable to that available to men on the college level was Oberlin, founded in 1833 in the thirty-year-old state of Ohio. It began life as a seminary and gradually gained a near-college status. It was the first such institution to open its doors to all comers, regardless of race, colour or sex. The founders stated among its primary objectives 'the education of the female character, bringing within the reach of the misguided and neglected sex all the infrastructure privileges which hitherto have unreasonably distinguished the leading sex from theirs'. As such it held a special and deserved place in the affections of the early women's rights leaders.

Looking back from our present vantage point, we can see that the single most significant step away from the concept that women needed an improved education only to carry out better their wifely or teaching duties came with the founding of Mount Holyoke College in 1837. Generally regarded now as the oldest women's college in the United States, it was founded by Mary Lyon, who followed Emma Willard's path but went much further. The school, she stated, must have adequate financial endowment; it must in some degree make education available to girls of all economic groups; it must offer a curriculum more advanced than that envisaged even by Mrs Willard; and it must prepare its students for more than homemaking or teaching. Miss Lyon succeeded because hers was a New England in which wider horizons for women were becoming a possibility, for women were already becoming more than homemakers and pedagogues. They were working by the thousand in the red brick mills springing up beside every creek and river. The year Mount Holyoke opened its doors, anti-slavery women were holding their first international convention in New York, and the Grimké sisters were touring Massachusetts speaking publicly against slavery. The storm unleashed by their unladylike behaviour was convulsing the churches and 'respectable' people. There was a ferment abroad which was stirring even obscure women in villages to ideas and efforts undreamed of a few years earlier. To a person of Mary Lyon's gifts and determination, this was clearly the soil and climate that was needed.

As long as the institution of slavery existed, an educated Negro was not only a contradiction in terms but a threat. To educate them was to disprove the promise of racial inferiority on which slavery was founded and also to arm them for the fight for freedom. It was illegal in the Southern states to teach a slave to read, though there were reports of schools run by Negro women in Louisiana, South Carolina and Georgia. They were for the children of free Negro slaves and they were rare.

By 1790 slavery was being abolished state by state in the North, yet black children were barred from going to the ordinary schools. When Sarah Grimké tried to teach her slave maid how to read, she did it behind a locked bedroom door, yet they were discovered and the lessons had to stop. Many abortive attempts followed this, the most notable being that of Prudence Crandall – a Quaker who was determined to educate black girls. Her efforts were memorable because in 1833 Mount Holyoke was still a dream in Mary Lyon's mind. The voices of the first women to speak against slavery in public had not been raised. The first diffident women's anti-slavery societies would not be organised for another year. Yet Prudence Crandall travelled widely (and in a most unladylike fashion) for funds. She carried on her school in a virtual state of siege for eighteen months, but had to give in, as a result of her concern for her pupils' safety.

The women of America, both black and white, have had to fight throughout their history for the type of education they now enjoy in 1985, although progress was made more steadily through the late nineteenth and early twentieth centuries, so that by the middle of the twentieth century schools were available for most white girls and a few blacks. Most of them, however, still stressed subjects that would turn a young girl into a beautiful and cultivated wife and mother, a comfort and a helpful mate to her husband.

Looking back, one would think that, having fought so hard for the privilege of education, the women of America would by now have been far better represented in leadership roles. This is not to deny the fact that there are one or two – Geraldine Ferraro is a case in point – but they are so few, especially when one considers that women make up over 50 per cent of the American population. Clearly, despite the struggle for education, women in America today are still heavily conditioned to give their own skills and ambition a lower priority than those of their husbands. Several women I met seemed to demonstrate this.

For example, I first met Bea a few years ago when I was at Yale. She was one of the graduate students who took care of me. This year in California I saw her again, but I did not recognise that confident smiling student I met only three years ago. This time she was quite plump and had tied a kind of Rastafarian religious scarf round her head. I asked her about the big dreams she had in 1983, the dream of going further, doing her doctorate and rewriting the history of the American woman. Her laughter made me look stupid. 'All those were dreams,' the laughter was saying to me.

'I am married now,' she countered.

'Ah,' I put in stupidly. 'He must be one of your colleagues or you must have been so much in love with one of your lecturers to warrant your throwing your beautiful dreams into the winds.'

'No,' smiled Bea, 'such black men are not many around here. I married the man who repairs the campus television.'

Now, I am not saying that a good man could not be a road-sweeper, but I just thought that after Yale a beautiful, out-going black girl could have done better. It looked as if she was reading my mind, for she added, 'Every good black girl must marry, Buchi. It has always been like that in my family, and I am expecting our first child in a few months.'

Going on to do her doctorate was out of the question at the moment. I wondered if she would ever do it now, even though she had originally taken the trouble to obtain a grant and a university place. Now she had to submit to the norm that every black girl must marry and raise a family.

Is what Bea is saying in 1985 different from what her slave grandmother would have said in her cabin – even when she was freed from slavery? I doubt it. The only difference is that Bea went to Yale, and did all that studying only to qualify herself to marry a television repair man. In other words, all or most of her education had prepared her to be a better mother. Now she has to work in administration because her husband's income is not enough for them both and with the coming child, she will have to work even harder. All these obstacles are driving her further and further away from her goal of a PhD.

Similarly, I met an American couple in Calabar, Nigeria. The wife was a beautiful cook, a very soft woman, who had grown quite large and waddled about in house slippers all day. One got so used to seeing the professor's wife that way that one came to think she had been born with that ridiculous apron she insisted on wearing. I was taken aback when she showed me a photograph of herself as a young woman, taken on her graduation day.

'You didn't go to college!' I cried.

'I went to university and I read French and American History, majoring in French Literature. I speak about four languages, all European, but Jack does not like his wife to work.'

Jack had shut her up several times in our presence, because 'Cathy gets all her information from the house boys.'

'I am very happy,' she said. And I'm afraid I had to agree with her. She looked happy, and she loved what she was doing – keeping a home while her husband, who was her junior at university, is now the professor and dean of a whole faculty.

One could go on and on giving examples of the American women I met from coast to coast. But one thing I noticed was that these women do not feel robbed of their personality.

At Stanford University I met the head of a research department. She was a very quiet, nice Canadian lady. She said, without mincing words, that she would rather have young men in her department. This was because hers was a funded research section of the university. She found that women always left to get married when the going became too long and difficult, whereas men usually stuck it out. The greater the number of students that saw their courses through, the better for the department and for all the lecturers concerned.

I asked her if this stand did not perpetuate the myth that women give up too easily after their master's degree. 'It probably is a myth, but this is what happens here.'

Well, if this is a myth, which is being confirmed by real-life experiences, why *are* we women hesitant in stretching ourselves to our fullest in the fields considered to be important?

During our time, the media have not done much to explode the myth about women and education. And since education has become available for all, girls have not been pushed as hard by their teachers as boys. The white girl pupil is encouraged to play the delicate beautiful lady, an attitude that survives from slave society. But matters are worse for the black girl because her myth is that of the mammy. Her stereotype is fat, with lolling breasts full of milk, a headscarf to cover her ugly crinkly hair, flashing teeth, she is loud, hot, and never angry. She is the full contrast of the white alabaster woman, whose delicacy is enhanced by the existence of the mammy. The mammy would do all the work, would feed the master's all-white babies, bear slaves for the master and would never say no to him. All these myths originated from slavery.

The power of myths and conditioning is not to be trifled with. It is very strong. Many such images given to people through the ages, and then reinforced in literature, still persist with great influence today. Women, despite all their education, would rather go and teach (or at best lecture) or nurse, or work in medicine as paediatricians or gynaecologists. In other words, extending the home work outside.

Many black youngsters would like to shine through sports or through the world of entertainment. The black woman is still regarded as loose, and people will quickly quote you the number of one-parent families among the black community – hence many of us are wary of feminism as it stands.

For in the American situation, how many black men were hanged for raping white women? I haven't the figures but I am sure it would go into hundreds. But no single white man has ever been hanged in America for all the rapes the black woman had committed on her.

How can we forget that?

Do you then blame us for being careful in following the white woman's footsteps? The blood of the black woman has helped so much in building the America of today, but look at her, living in poor areas of Palo Alto in California; look at her shacks in Sacramento, to say nothing of the east – in New York City and its environs, in Illinois.

Can there be an end to these myths and beliefs? Take the case of the white woman. Literature and tradition have cast her as pure, very submissive and charming. She is there on a pedestal, like a goddess. Men who make the rules in most societies, especially in the

West, set their women up as ideals. And when women had been brought up to behave exactly as men wanted them to, they became a laughing stock. The white woman was always so beautiful that she invariably bewitched her lover, when young, but when she became old she could be burned for being a witch. So she must always strive to be young. She could be gay and charming before marriage, but after her marriage she had to keep her gaiety strictly for her husband – a husband who in most cases was free to wander.

Men did not just make fun of these characteristics which they had bestowed on women, they soon started to write about them. Women were then portrayed in literature as bewitching, delicate and full of charm. And even the first early women writers followed this pattern. As shown earlier, those women who had the courage to ask for education for the white women did not do so to make them independent, but to make them good helpers and soulmates to their husbands.

The black woman came from a completely different culture. Women in old Africa were not all that free, but they had strong relevance in their societies until they came in contact with the white woman. The black woman who could hold her head up and speak in the congregation of her people was listened to. Women did have their own ways of changing their societies. Housework was never regarded as a minor job, because in a society where to get fuel and prepare the meal takes all day, it is a crucial job. Hence the major qualification for any girl was her ability to cook, and she must be blessed with good health and energy to bear babies. The black woman had learnt to survive in these environments, and she had become so adapted to them that in areas like the Ibo societies of Nigeria, she could even organise and fight her own wars.

One example is the so-called 'Aba riot' of the late nineteen-twenties. This was a 'riot' that spread from Owerri in Eastern Nigeria through to Calabar (among women who did not even speak the same language) and stretched to include all the towns in the Rivers area, to Onitsha by the river Niger, then across the river to include women from Asaba area. Although the white male chroniclers called it a riot, it was more like a marvel – that women at that time were able to organise themselves when there were no telephones, no letters: only bush tracks and dangerous rivers. The whole area was equivalent to the distance from London in England to Edinburgh in Scotland, the actual war was organised with women from different groups wearing different war gears, and all using their household utensils as weapons.

Interestingly, the black women of that war were praised by their husbands, so much so that they became legendary figures and we, the children born from such women, sing and raise our hands each time their heroic deeds are told. They received admiration, not rebuke, and in desperation the British administrators jailed all the men whose wives took an active part in the war, in a vain attempt to show the world that men were behind it all. They could not acknowledge that women, especially 'black barbaric' women, could ever organise such a thing, at a time when their own women were still wrapped in cottonwool and kept so busy being ladies.

But other black women, whether they lived in the Ibo land or in Pennsylvania, were less lucky. They came in contact with the alabaster, white Christian woman. Like the African male, the white male was intrigued by the woman who can hold her own in reasonable argument and logic – but he would not let his wife do it. So the black woman is taught by her white sister to be ashamed of her outspokenness. She is taught to pretend, to value the nuclear family rather than her community life style.

So it would seem that the black woman, like most women in the world, was not really free, but the little freedom she enjoyed before meeting her white sister was taken away from her in such a way that she became of even lower status than previously. But now many black women are becoming educated in the Western and in their own cultures. They are beginning to ask questions, questions which even the white lady cannot answer.

Black women all over the world should re-unite and re-examine the way history has portrayed us. Now, when we have all this education, why do we hesitate to change all that has been written about us? Going back and not, as Angela Davis once said, 'moving on' is looking up to the white woman to help us. How can she? She is helpless herself. And not only is she helpless, she is afraid of our anger, and even jealous of the little freedom we had.

What is demeaning about looking after the home I live in? One of the greatest pleasures in life is to sleep between nice crisp cotton sheets. What is bad in my preparing them for myself? Our mothers prepared their sleeping places not for their men but for themselves, and if they felt like bringing a man there, then it was so. But what do you learn in the West? You learn that such jobs are low. And of course, the makers of the society give such jobs to women – so what is the result? The most important chores that make us human are regarded as low – although some women, as I said earlier, have the courage to say that they love having and looking after their children, that they love looking after their homes. In short, what I am saying is that our whole value system should be re-examined.

I had my photograph taken once in my 'office' where I do my writing. The photo-journalist was a staunch feminist, and was so angry that my 'office' was my kitchen and that packets of breakfast cereals were in the background. I was letting the women's movement down, by allowing such a photograph to be taken.

But that was where I worked, because it was warmer, and convenient for me to see my family whilst I put my typewriter on one side. I tried in vain to tell her that in my kitchen I felt I was doing more for the peace of the world than the nuclear scientist. In our kitchens we raise all the future Reagans, or the future Jesuses. In our kitchens we wash for them and cook for them, and we send them out to be grown men and women, and from our kitchens they learn to love and to hate.

What greater work is there than that? I do not think it low. A mother with a family is an economist, a nurse, a painter, a diplomat and more. And we women do all that, and we form over half the world population. And yet we take back seats, even in places as rich as California. Men did not put us there. We put ourselves there. How often do you hear a colleague say, 'I am only a housewife'?

There should be more choices for women. Women who wish to be Geraldine Ferraro should be allowed to do so. We need more of her type, we need more Golda Meirs, more Indira Gandhis, and even more Maggie Thatchers. But those who wish to control and influence the future generation by giving birth and nurturing the young should not be looked down upon. It is not a degrading job. If I had my way it would be the highest paid job in the world. We think it is low because society says so. But it's about time we said: 'It is not so; we will train *all* people, men and women, in housework.'

Moreover, women of all races will not come together to examine their differences as long as we go on thinking that we are here to be sex objects. Thank the Lord, one can now have a child without sexual intercourse. So why not spend your hard-earned money to beautify yourself for yourself? Imagine what life would be like if we were not all directly or indirectly brought up with the primary aim of 'snaring' our male. Imagine if all that effort had been put into developing ourselves for ourselves.

We spend our whole lives doing this and that for men to notice, trying to stay young and attractive, so that we are not prepared to accept being fifty, sixty or seventy. A fifty-year-old American woman with grey hair is old; a fifty-year-old American male with grey hair is dignified; a fifty-year-old female Ibo woman with grey hair is in her prime and almost as dignified as a man. So the African woman claims to be older than she is, and the American woman is forever claiming to be young. Western civilisation has prepared her only for her youth, and has told her that she can appeal to men only as a young woman. So she spends her entire life in search of youth and has little time to examine herself, to realise her own worth. The desire to be a sex object is still the greatest chain most women (especially those from the West) have around their ankles.

The media tell us we are just created for sex and for child bearing. But I am saying that we are here for many, many things – for careers, for motherhood (yes, if you so desire) for politics, for a full human existence and not just being somebody's appendage.

As for the relationship between races, a great divide wedges itself between black and white women. We delude ourselves when we say it does not exist. The white woman is bound by the attitudes of her society, the black woman is bound by that of her white sister because she comes from the so-called master race, and then bound again by that of her very own society. As a result, the black woman is doubly bound.

So this is the time for re-definition and the time for re-examination. If history puts women down, what are we doing to raise our image? Are we women re-writing history or are we just sitting around and allowing it to happen again?

I said in a recent article and in the talks I gave in many countries of Europe and the USA in the autumn of 1984, that the Western woman should go back to re-learn how to be a woman, because at the moment she has so undervalued herself that she is groping in the dark. In short, she seems to be losing her way. Her black sister has not completely done so.

So I am glad that the Western woman is now in Africa, and in Nairobi, in the summer of 1985. And I say, on behalf of mother Africa, 'Welkome, dear sista to the Modar lan'. Afrika go treat you well, well. Welkome.'

Buchi Emecheta was born of Ibuza parentage in Lagos, Nigeria. Her childhood and early married life were also spent in Lagos. She studied Sociology at London University, and has been at different times a teacher, a librarian, and a community worker. Her written work to date includes articles for the *New Statesman* and the *TLS*, television plays, poetry, children's books, and many novels, the most recent being *The Rape of Shavi*, in 1983. Buchi Emecheta has five children, and has lived in London since 1962.

Jill Tweedie

It has rained heavily in the morning and the Javanese countryside steams. Green mountains swoop into ravines ribboned, far below, with rusty rivers and thin long waterfalls. The land curves and plunges away to the horizon, frothing with palm and cabbagy banana trees, an almost outrageously scenic big dipper, more opulent, more royal than all the botanical gardens of the West. At the edge of a small town, a rackety gold-rush sort of place, the asphalt road narrows to a pot-holed track that bumps through rice fields set in the mountain bowl to where high stands of palm trees mark the entrance to a village. A gaudily painted frieze of a man, a woman and two children, hand in hand, is splashed across the cement gates. Crudely moulded letters over them spell out DUA ANAK CUPUK.

Twenty-four-year-old Hendra, a plump little pigeon of a woman – everyone here is small to Western eyes – passes these gates every morning on her way to work in the rice fields, scuffling through a cloud of dust in her thongs and sarong and flowered blouse, her eight-month-old baby slung at her hip, her three-year-old daughter left playing at home under the guardianship of her mother. Hendra lives in the village, in a house nestled by the mossy walls of an ancient palace not far from her mother's house where she was brought up. The house is built on a bamboo frame thatched with dry palm fronds and its three rooms, rattan-lined and earth-floored, are shadowy after the bright sunlight and airy. If she had more money, she and her husband, who works as a *becak* driver in the town, would build a cement bungalow with louvred windows – there are already a few in the village – but as things are they must make do with what they've got, which is, though they do not see it, perfectly designed for the climate and picture-postcard pretty. Bamboo beds make up most of the furniture, their horizontal struts providing ideal storage space: one holds the family's clothes and linen; two more in the long open-fronted hut outside where Hendra cooks, squatting at the clay oven, stuffing its hollowed-out front with kindling, are piled with blackened pots and utensils, dishes, two sacks of rice and a row of drying corncobs. On the other three beds, inside, she and her husband and daughter sit in the evenings and, when night falls, stretch out and sleep. The bamboo poles that divide the rooms are hooked to carry spirit lamps, and grey doves coo from wicker cages on the beams and at the eaves of the house. In the garden, by a well and rows of umbrella-shaped cassava bushes is another hut with the *mandi* in it, a square tiled trough full of water where everyone sluices themselves with a plastic ladle – a daily rebirth in that clammy heat – and, discreetly screened from the *mandi*, a hole in the ground with a porcelain surround, connected, five years ago, to proper sewage pipes. Before the pipes were installed, Hendra confides with a giggle, she had to crouch over a pool behind the house and the little fishes nipped her bum.

Titik, one year older than Hendra, lives on the opposite side of the ruined palace by the open baths where eleventh-century Javanese ladies performed their ablutions and where Titik now does her washing in her bra and pants, beating away on the boulders as she chats to her friends, sheltered from prying male eyes by a high stone wall. Titik spends her days a mile away in one of Indonesia's largest factories along with 45,000 other girls and women from the neighbouring villages. The steel hanger in which they work vibrates to their chatter like a vast cage of starlings, the dark heads stretch away into the distance, each face dissolving into a Seurat stipple of pale oval discs. Squashed among them, Titik's hands never stop their rolling, rolling, rolling. She is making the Indonesian Gudang Garam cigarettes and the hot air is heavy with their sweet clove scent. Black damp strands of hair are plaited away from her sweat-beaded face. She, too, is married and has left her eleven-month-old baby with her mother; she has worked for seven years here. If she keeps up the pace and meets the target of 3,000 cigarettes a day, she earns about £6 a week. She can swim in the evenings in a huge swimming pool fed by great cement dragons vomiting water, and there is a clinic, too, where she can go for contraception, for medical treatment or just to lie down if she feels unwell during her six days' work a week.

All around the factory complex are the rice fields, glowing green in the golden sun. There, Ambar – her slanting eyes shaded by a wide coolie hat – is bent double raking out dry stooks from the ankle-deep water. She lives in the same village as Hendra and Titik and can harvest a kilo of rice in a morning, of which the owner of the field gives her 10 per cent to take home to her one-year-old son and her husband who is one of the many men in Indonesia's 'informal' sector, for which read unemployed. The sun is unforgiving and the hard rice stubble scratches at her bare feet. Ambar straightens up for a moment with harsh groans and says her back aches and her head too, from the sun, but the work is better paid now because of the two-crop kind of rice; there are more good grains per plant. With the old kind, too many stooks were empty.

Back in the village, by the entrance gates with their dancing painted family, is the primary school where Hendra, Titik and Ambar went

for four years of mornings as little girls, regularly or less regularly
depending on how much they were needed at home to care for
younger brothers and sisters while their mothers did a stint in the rice
fields or went to market or lay sick with a fever or recovering from
childbirth. Today, as in their day, the one-storey cement building
hums like Titik's factory with high starling squeaks, you can hear the
noise 200 yards away, rising to a crescendo of ear-splitting shrieks at
the entrancing sight of a visitor. Inside, dark heads line every low
hardboard partition between classrooms and the narrow alleys that
divide them fill with screeching, laughing little figures who mob the
stranger and fall back, clutching at each other in excitement and
delight.

The two teachers, a mild and melancholic man and a woman with a
large flat bun of hair and heavy spectacles, advance with dignity from
their blackboards, quite unfazed by the clamour. They stand talking
on the steps outside as their pupils ricochet back and forth, stolid and
patient, only raising their voices to make themselves heard over the
babble. Never, once, do either of them attempt to rebuke the cluster-
ing children or try by word or gesture to hush them. Soon, unrepri-
manded, the children settle at their wooden desks again and begin, as
the teacher's pointer moves from word to chalky word on the blackboard, the high monotonous chanting of an Islamic prayer.

Here, eight years ago or so, Ambar, Titik and Hendra learned what
they learned of reading and writing – because all three are classified as
literate. Three girls from the same village leading much the same lives
as their mothers except for their reproductive past and future. Each
has two children or less, each uses contraception, each says she will
not have more than two children and none expects to have or has had
the grief of losing a child. Hendra's mother had eight children, two of
whom died. Titik's mother had ten, five of whom died, and Ambar's
mother lost one of her six. Evidently, then, the magic key, carved with
all the letters of the alphabet, is literacy. Opening the door to a better
life, it sets women free to control their own fertility, unshackled by
endless pregnancies and the fear of infant deaths. Hallelujah!

But hark, who comes here? Yuri, twenty-three, and Rukiyah,
twenty-five. Yuri who works with Titik at the cigarette factory and
Rukiyah who harvests rice alongside Ambar in the noonday sun. Both
these young women – and others like them in the village – are more
obviously poor. Their sarongs are grubby, their feet bare, their faces
boney, their legs patched with sores. Like the skinny hens scratching
around them in the dirt, they have a hard job keeping body and soul
together, their huts at the fringe of the better houses are soiled and
torn in places, the thatched roofs sag. Though both of them smile the

obligatory Javanese smile when spoken to, their eyes, already a little sunken, shift nervously about. Yuri went to school for a year or so but the demands of her family were constant, two younger brothers needed education more and the money ran out. Rukiyah spent her childhood in another village – she points a stubby broken-nailed finger towards the blue mountains – and the school was too far away and too expensive. Though Indonesian primary education is compulsory and free, on paper, it costs about 50,000 rupiah (£50) a year all told, including the essential uniform (standard throughout the country to emphasise the unity of the nation) and Rukiyah's parents, with five children, earned at best £400 annually.

Yet Yuri has been married for three years and has only one child while Rukiyah, married five years, has two. Both of them come from families of six and five respectively and neither of them, like their parents before them, can read or write. Will they have more children? Solemn as owls, both recite together the words painted on the village gates: *Dua anak cupuk*, two children are enough. And they, too, do not expect any child of theirs to die, despite the evidence of the stonemason's shop outside the village with its rows of tiny tombstones waiting for occupants.

Curious, this. UNICEF's 1985 report, *The State of the World's Children,* says that research in many countries shows a clear correlation between female literacy, smaller families and lower levels of infant mortality and this in spite of rural/urban variations and even income differences. It concludes that maternal education acts as a powerful *independent* force, no matter what other disadvantages a woman may have. In other words, if girls can be got into school and taught to read and write, this alone empowers them to take more control of their lives so that when they are married they have a better chance of winning an argument with their husbands or in-laws about having children.

Well, that makes sense. In fact, it seems a glimpse of the obvious. The more a woman knows, the more say she has in her own reproductive life, the better she can take care of the number she decides to have. Literacy is concerned with choice, after all, and the relevant statistics from Indonesia prove it:

	Years of education			
	0	1-3	4-6	7+
% of married women in Indonesia who have never used efficient contraception	30	36	40	53
Infant mortality – deaths per 1,000 live births – in Indonesia	103	109	82	55

Add to that a 17 per cent drop in birthrate in Indonesia as a whole and a spectacular 34 per cent drop in the island of Bali alone, plus a 75 per cent female primary school enrolment and we have, do we not, a QED situation.

But statistics are funny things. Like iron filings following the pull of a magnetic field, they can fall into the oddest configurations depending on the hand that controls the magnet. If you want to make a link between female education, lower birthrates and lower infant mortality, you can always do so and in many cases you might well be right. There is no doubt that women are having fewer children, and healthier ones too, in Indonesia. Yet such statistical links sometimes turn out to be entirely fortuitous or lacking some vital piece of the jigsaw that, if included, would make quite another picture. In Queen Victoria's time, when every male from the richest landowner to the scruffiest mudlark wore a top hat, fogs were the bane of London life, suffocating the city in a choking blanket of grit and foul smoke. But as men began to discard their top hats, the pestilential fogs began to lift. Should we conclude that tall headgear caused fogs or that fogs in some way influenced the height of hats?   Another example of rogue statistics, rather more to the point, occurs in Ireland. The Republic leads the world in primary school enrolment for both boys and girls and its secondary and tertiary education matches that of the United Kingdom. But infant mortality rates are higher and Irish mothers near-legendary for the numbers of their children. Given these facts in isolation, could we not assume a link between female literacy, families of eight to thirteen children and more infant deaths?

The missing piece of information here, as you are doubtless aware, is the fact that the Catholic Church runs all primary and secondary schools, forbids contraception and abortion and preaches the evils of both daily, in every school. That, in itself, far outweighs the effects of female literacy. Is there, then, such a missing link in Indonesia's statistics?

One morning, people gather at the entrance to Hendra's village staring across at a bungalow flapping with banners. Two helmeted policemen, their hips slung with guns, truncheons and handcuffs, stand with their legs apart cheerfully grinning as groups of young women are shepherded inside by stripling youths in flared trousers and high wedge heels. On the wide verandah village elders sit cross-legged between lines of golden gongs and wooden xylophones, tapping and chanting in reedy old men's voices while the women take their places on rows of chairs, as solemnly agog as the infants bundled at their sides.

At the top of the room, focus of the women's most absorbed attention, numbers of substantial males lounge at flower-decorated tables, their pastel safari suits immaculate. Flanking them, along each wall, sit the younger men and soldiers. The elders beat their gongs and wail, the men of substance shake each others' hands, the young men chat and smoke. Only the women sit quiet as mice in the soupy heat and no child whimpers.

After a while, a man with a wispy moustache takes possession of a microphone and talks at some length to the top tables, flashing his teeth now and again into a flashing camera. He introduces the village headman, who has a flat, amiable, pock-marked face and is marvellously garrulous, speaking for many minutes without notes. His wife, resplendent in an orchid bodice and skin-tight sarong, pouts her glossy lips at a compact, pats the dark pancake of hair at her neck, dabs her winsome nose with powder and, as her husband ends his speech, lifts two graceful hands towards the women and leads their applause.

More chairs are set up and more women squeezed in. The safari suits surge to the microphone, gold rings and watches gleaming, and talk on and on. The headman's wife gossips with the soldier at her side and the heat becomes palpable, blue with the clove smoke of Gudang Garam cigarettes made by Titik and her friends. The stubs lie everywhere except where the women are, because no woman smokes. Instead they fumble at their bodices and ease out pale breasts for the infants, but their small round faces, open-mouthed, never leave the talking men.

At a gesture from the floor, three older women leave their seats to be given large brass plaques. They bob their heads meekly in thanks and one, overcome by such exposure, grins madly with fright. Time passes, flies dance, corn and peanuts and glasses of jasmine tea are brought to the head tables and the compère announces a fashion show. Silver teeth glint as the women's mouths open even further.

There are five models: a beauty swaddled in traditional Javanese dress, a figure wrapped in Moslem veils, a secretarial female in sensible blouse and skirt and two bright butterflies in jaunty Western frocks. They sidle in, quivering with nerves, pause for two seconds before the audience and scuttle off, backs bent, arms swinging, like pretty miners making for the coal face. Kindly, the men of substance clap but the women can hardly find their hands, so stunned are they by the spectacle.

To wind up the proceedings, the one European present is beckoned from her sweaty corner and urged to speak. She looms over the women, shifting uneasily on heat-puffed feet, mouthing politenesses.

Then the flock of dignitaries gather at her waistline and all are trapped on film to join, eventually, the other framed photographs hanging on the walls. The event is over and the women back out, smiling the wild endearing smiles of those with rather more than their share of teeth.

These occasions, into which the peasant women are ushered, are repeated in villages and towns all over Java and Bali and, to a lesser extent, across most of the 13,500 islands that make up the long archipelago of Indonesia. Called 'Smiling Family Safaris', they are the cornerstones of the country's family planning drive and every ingredient occurs again and again. Local bigwigs, along with functionaries of the BKKBN – that part of the Civil Service concerned with co-ordinating family planning – proclaim the inestimable benefits of contraception, promise health, wealth and happiness to those who limit their fertility (*Dua Anak Cupuk,* Two Children Are Enough), describe in dramatic detail the squalor in store for those who do not and chart the progress of the particular village towards that promised land where smiling nuclear families will live happily ever after. Those in charge of anything local – factory, school, market, mosque – are exhorted to redouble their commitment to the cause; stalwart women pioneers of contraception are awarded their plaques and the village elders, custodians of the traditional *gamelin* bands and puppet plays, cunningly insert into familiar songs and stories the blessings of unfruitful wombs. Fashion shows, market stalls, balloons, pop groups and the starry presence of any passing foreigner complete the gilt on the gingerbread.

Afterwards, health workers swarm round the women, busily weighing the babies to monitor their growth, immunising them, while behind screens and partitions their mothers lie on tables, patiently waiting to be transformed into angels. *Apsari* is the Indonesian word for angel, and that is what you become when you accept contraception – sometimes the pill, more often Depo-Provero and most often, on account of its low maintenance, the inter-uterine device or IUD. New angels are given some immediate reward, perhaps four kilos of rice prettily tied with blue ribbon. Other rewards take the form of community incentives. If enough women in a village use contraception, the village may get an irrigation pump, new wells, funding to help the women start income-generating projects. In devoutly Moslem villages, long-term angels sometimes receive a more spiritual bonus – a trip to Mecca, all expenses paid. *Per* IUD *ad astra.*

Not so much a programme, more a religious crusade, population control in Indonesia. Under their navy baseball caps and neat blue suits its officials crackle with fervour, their eyes burn with an evangelical flame and they smile upon the women as the Archangel Gabriel smiled upon Mary, full of glad (though very different) tidings. This hearts-minds-bodies operation began after President Sukarno and his 'pro-natalist' policies led to a baby boom and his downfall in 1965. It was given fresh fuel in 1975 with the personal backing of President Suharto. His faded fleshy face looks down upon his flock from a million plaster walls and rattan huts, gravid with his revelation that the future greatness of his country had less to do with land reform or job creation or education (first, contraception, *then* a new school) than with the closure of wombs as fast as possible and in almost any way bar physical force. 'The Indians were too brutal,' says one of his officials. 'We have learnt from them.'

Indonesia is the fifth most populous nation on earth and each of her nubile girl-children conceals beneath her sarong the wherewithal to overturn all patriotic hopes and dry up World Bank monies along with many other Western funds. Upon her forebearance (that *mot* so literally *juste*) depends some part of the workings of whole international structures, the investments of multi-national companies, the network of development agencies, the livelihoods of innumerable far-flung academics, scientists, researchers, journalists, medical men, bankers and politicians, the mortgages of a million lesser folk and even the position of the leader of the nation himself.

But the girl is amenable, she is docile and smiles a lot as everyone smiles here, constantly, radiantly and with a wondrous armoury of teeth. No matter how forbidding, at first glance, the piratical forehead-banded street-wise faces of hordes of scavenging street men, one smile from a visitor causes an instant outbreak of dentures all round and the broad grins of old women, their mouths a disaster area of betel-stained gums, would warm the cockles of an ice queen's heart. The young women smile, too, though more shyly. They conform to the traditional view of the second sex, where a voice above a murmur or a glint of opinions too strongly held is considered profoundly unfeminine. Even apparently emancipated female pop stars, singing on television, can reduce a hard rock beat to something lyrical and cute with one decorous click of little fingers. The babies are amenable, too. They curl contentedly at their mothers' sides, passive spectators of their passive world, a breast always ready for their comfort. Nor does there appear to be any tension between the sexes. The men show no sign of aggression, let alone machoism. Compared to the smooth-skinned, doe-eyed Javanese male, the odd Dutch, German or Australian tourist seems oppressively masculine: huge, hairy, bristling presences devoid of charm. This contrast, however, does not conceal the fact that the Javanese male also rules every roost. Or, at least, his own and those on the rungs below him.

In the old palace at Yogyakarta in Central Java and at countless ceremonies in Bali, young men and women dance. But that word does not adequately convey the infinite slowness of movement involved, the stoic control over every muscle in every limb from the delicate arch of a little finger to the careful placement of a big toe. Western tourists come and go in their dozens between each unfolding gesture, unable to stay the snail's pace during which a small bronze statue of a man shifts his weight from the ball of his foot to the heel and a smaller woman stands still as a flower in the dead still heat. This subtle grace is the outward and visible manifestation of a complex civilisation, an ancient pyramid once crowned by kings who now gaze from their portraits on the Palace walls, caught in amber beside their vanished queens and princesses, whose stiff little figures cocooned in gold lie tip-tilted in the arms of servants. For thousands of years each individual in that serried hierarchy has known his place and his hereditary duties, gazing upwards in trust, obedience and the hope of reflected glory to his betters above and down on those beneath him like a father upon his children. Curiously, the last King of Java is Indonesia's Minister for Sport and millions of his erstwhile subjects who once kow-towed to him now touch their toes and jog to his command. *Plus ça change.*

This finely-layered pyramid has its strengths, but it is also hugely vulnerable to the foreign invader or the home-grown dictator who has only to indoctrinate or pluck out and replace existing male lynchpins and all will continue as it was, the chain of dependencies unbroken though each lynchpin has undergone a sea change. So the Buddhists and the Hindus from South India found it in the first century AD, and the Arabs spreading Islam 800 years later, and the sixteenth-century Dutch who ruled until the Japanese drove them out in the Second World War. The pyramid is now at the service of President Suharto and his military men, who thread policies from Jakarta through loop after loop of provincial governors and regency heads on down through sub-districts and village leaders to the hamlets and, in Bali, even further, into the *banjars* or hamlet councils and finally to each individual.

Suharto's educators use the same conduits, galvanised in the capital city and spidering outwards and downwards, co-opting each governing patriarch and mullah as they go until their present targets, the little girl in her school and her mother knee-deep in the mud of the rice fields, hear the same message from every one of their gods and mentors. And the message is not 'learning is good' but 'what we teach you is good'. Literacy in Indonesia, as in many developing countries (and many developed, too) is not seen as a key to opening the

ndividual mind but a potter's wheel for moulding it, and the young
newly literate are, quite simply, easier and more flexible material to
work with than the already hard-baked clay of their elders. In the
government's view, there are more pressing tasks to accomplish than
the teaching of the three Rs – that is only the means to their ends. And
one of the most important ends is spelt FEMALE and filed under
CONTRACEPTION. Once you know that, mere reading and writing ceases
to cast quite the same light on a girl's future reproductive life. Literacy
does not happen in a vacuum, leaving its possessor to pick and choose
her learning where she will. It is only the first and tentative step on
that long road whose goal, distant and veiled in mist, is the ability to
winnow grains of truth from the chaff of lies. Until that goal is in sight,
though, there are many hazards to overcome and many obstacles in
the path of the newly literate, like Hendra and her friends. The irony
is that those on the first lap are actually more vulnerable to the lies and
the half-truths than those who never entered the race, because their
very skills render them temporarily defenceless against all those
techniques of modern propaganda that their mothers, concealed
behind a mask of illiteracy can happily ignore.

A majority of women under forty in the Indonesian 'home' islands of
Java and Bali are accounted literate. When asked if they can read and
write, they nod cheerfully 'yes', though it must be said that if they
cannot, they nod as cheerfully 'no'. But quite what statistical literacy
means in Indonesia is unclear. To begin with, there are 350 different
languages on the archipelago. 'My mother,' says one young Javanese
woman, 'is illiterate.' Then she adds, 'but she can read some
Javanese.' And adds, again, 'And she understands Indonesian and
Arabic; she can write Arabic.' Disentangled, this reveals that her
mother understands the non-Latin calligraphy of her own language,
Javanese; can speak some Indonesian; can copy out passages of the
Koran in Arabic and chant Arabic prayers which, as a Moslem, she
does five times a day. Not bad going for a so-called illiterate woman.
For her daughter, literacy means a combination of all these things and
also, if she goes on to secondary school, the reading and writing of the
Latin-lettered Bahasa Indonesian, the Malay-based language now
official all through the islands. Such polyglottism is confusing to the
visitor and must, to some extent, bewilder the inhabitants too.

Also, if you come from a country where literacy is more or less
taken for granted and the judgements passed on the education of
individuals tend to be crudely divided into those who are 'stupid' and
those who are 'clever', it is difficult to make out exactly what the word
literate' means. Certainly Hendra, Titik and Ambar, after leaving

school, could lead their daily lives without ever needing to read o
write again. Their particular village is innocent of letters, there are n
books or documents or even road signs, and literacy has no obviou
use in the rice fields or the cigarette factory. Indeed, the only printe
matter for miles around appears on the village gates in the form o
governmental exhortations to greater patriotism, harder work
cleaner living and smaller families. After constant exposure to this, i
is hard to avoid a certain envy of the illiterate, her mind gloriousl
uncluttered by slogans that are, like most slogans, actual impediment
to thought.

Hendra's mother, like most women of her age, never went to schoc
and calls herself, without the slighest embarrassment, 'illiterate'. Sh
sits on the steps of her house, this illiterate person, with the dove
cooing over her head, a wiry woman with no ounce of spare flesh an
cheekbones like small boulders under the skin, smiling the luri
purple smile of the dedicated betel-gum chewer. She is totally unprac
tised in the art of introspection. Like most peasant women, she ca
chat happily for hours about things that are happening around her an
about other people, but questions to do with her own thoughts an
feelings are a novelty. She squints in concentration, as if she wer
trying to interpret the emotions of a stranger. The furnishings of th
Western mind, clogged with self-awareness, self-analysis, self
centredness, crammed with facts and factoids and fictions, layere
with hypocrisies and so clouded by past and future that the presen
hardly exists, do not encumber hers, which seems weightless b
comparison and roomy, so that she must hunt about inside like
housewife suddenly asked to find traces of her own footprints on
clean floor.

Finally she answers the visitor's question. 'No. Not being able t
read or write has never made any difficulties in my life. No . . .' sh
shakes her head, 'I never wanted to go to school.'

Had she ever felt, well, inferior, left out, because of being illiterate
'No, why should I? No one else could read or write then. None of th
women I grew up with can.'

Well, does she feel the lack now, with literate daughters? Anothe
shake of the head. Was it difficult, not being able to help with thei
homework? 'But I did,' she says. 'I was angry with them if they didn'
do it.'

Everyone laughs. What pointless questions this visitor asks. This i
just the way of things, they all know that. Older women have whit
hair, wrinkles and cannot read; younger women have black hair, n
wrinkles and can read. It is natural.

Well then, if she were in her daughter's place now, would she like t

:arn to read? She nods, of course. And how does she think that bility would change her life? She looks puzzled for a moment, aware hat there ought to be an answer to this because, otherwise, why ould the government be teaching her daughter? But she can't think f it and, shrugging politely, she goes off to make tea. When she omes back with the tray of glasses she says, smiling with satisfaction t having solved the riddle, that reading and writing is modern and ese are modern times.

Hendra, handing round the tea, smiles in pleased agreement. That's right,' she says, 'it is modern. Like the pipes that go from the ole in the ground, better than being nipped by the fish.'

Everyone laughs again, though they avoid comment. Instead, Hen-a's mother launches into praise of modern medicines, the ones she n get at the clinic, they are so *easy* compared to the days when she ad to make her own brews, searching for the plants, chopping them, ounding them, boiling them. How much easier to have an injection. ut did they work, those herbal medicines? Oh yes, they worked. She metimes buys them still, at the market. But the injections – so *easy*. nd learning to read and write is not so easy, is that it? Hendra and er mother splutter into their hands and the air vibrates with nspoken words – 'nor so useful, either.'

In a country like Indonesia, teaching is not confined to children at chool, though they are the most receptive targets. When Hendra's other goes to the clinic for medicine, she as a grandmother will be ught the blessings of birth control and the need for spacing out ildbirth so that she will no longer urge Hendra and her other aughters to have more than two children, as she would have done efore. They teach the village midwives too. There are four dukuns king the new-fangled test today, old women with filed teeth, faces uckered into deep seams and twenty-five years of delivering the abies of the village to their credit, though not in the modern way that now required. The four grey heads line a table opposite a girl half eir age who asks them to pick out from a strange assortment of jects what they would use at a delivery. Watch it, old ladies! Don't oose anything familiar, discard every sort of traditional herb and ntment, plump for the metallic and shiny, the things you've never ed before.

The women stoop and peer with cloudy eyes, their hands, blotched ith the freckles of age, hovering uncertainly. But they choose right d they're on to the next hurdle: the delivery. First they pour water n gnarled fingers and wash and wash, peeping sideways at the aminer to see if they've used the modern soap and disinfectant long ough. No real woman in labour here so they make do with a cotton

sack and a doll inside. The rheumatic hands pat the shape of the do
slowly down within the sack till its plastic face pops out, bright painte
eyes staring, painted eyebrows raised. There is a piece of twisted cor
linking its tummy to a cotton placenta dyed blood red. Carefully th
women dip scissors into pretend-boiling water, tie off the preten
umbilical cord and ceremoniously snip in between. The doll is bor
and held tenderly to shrunken shoulders while the young woman noc
approvingly and children gawp at the door, children the old wome
themselves midwived into the world.

Do they mind, these four dukuns, learning all over again what the
have spent their lives doing? Does it upset them, being told they'v
been doing it wrong all that time, and their mothers before them, the
mothers who taught them? Peeping again at the young woman, the
shake their white heads. No, no. It is good, the new way. Better, muc
better. And how does it differ from the old way? Confounded for
moment, the hooded eyes flicker from side to side. One of them pick
her nose in anxious concentration. Nothing is different, they say. /
pregnant pause, more peeps. The faces brighten, remembering th
lessons. Ah! We are clean now. We wash our hands, we boil thing
That is the difference! Everyone in the room smiles, everyone
pleased. The young woman says, 'You see, they understand, they wi
pass the test.' Which is just as well because, otherwise, their livel
hood, the practice of their ancient trade, would be taken from them

But one of them, at least, is not so modern, not so perfectly in tun
with the modern world. At the flash of a camera she throws he
withered arms up in the air, her cheeks sink inwards in despair and sh
wails aloud, squeezing her eyes tight shut. The young woma
explains, with a tolerant smile, that the dukun thinks having he
photograph taken will shorten her life. The old dukun beside th
wailing one looks hard at her and gives a scornful burp. Nevertheles
they have learnt something valuable, the need for cleanliness tha
could save lives. How many mothers of those they have delivered ove
all those years have died as a result of their former ignorance? All fot
of them say with pride, oh none, no, they have never lost a mother. N
one disputes this. Perhaps they are too polite.

The headmistress of the local secondary school, a plain sturd
woman in her late thirties, her eyes earnest under pebble glasse
came from an illiterate family and studied hard as a girl 'because I wa
poor and the other girls looked down on me, also I was not pretty and
think I never marry'. She is married now, to a man younger tha
herself who appears to do very little all day. 'It is difficult when yo
are educated,' she says. 'You must work hard when other girls ar
getting married and then there are no men left. When I was twenty

eight I pray to my God, please find a husband for me, because I long
for children. And He found . . .' she jerks a brisk thumb to where her
husband stands feeding the dove in its cage '. . . *him*. But I say to
myself that my God has chosen him for me so I must think that he is
the man for me. My God cannot be wrong and I have my two
children.' She smiles resignedly.

In her school, as in all the other schools, the children are taught by
rote, parroting their teachers' words or leaving their desks in groups
of six to stand by the blackboard and recite whatever is written there.
Rote learning, long fallen into disrepute in the West (except in
Ireland), gives the children a somnolent glaze, their eyes turn inward
as they quack away, pleasurably anaesthetised, their minds in a coma.
But all the village people and many of the grander folk in Jakarta, too,
communicate in the same way. Whenever two or three are gathered
together, the recitations begin, echoing that ancient oral tradition of
story-telling by which information has always been passed from one
generation to the next. The children chant at the blackboard and,
outside, in the streets and the markets, their mothers stand chanting
at each other, their hands and their voices weaving and reweaving the
tales of yesterday and today, one spinning out a saga of something that
happened to her or her husband or her neighbour or her children,
looping back the embroidery to add a stitch here or there and passing
the skein to her friend who puts her own touches of colour on it and
hands it back to its owner, now in a happy trance.

'The day my mother fell ill, I went to the well and while I was
washing my clothes my neighbour came and told me. . .'

'The day your mother fell ill, you went to the well and while you
were washing your clothes, your neighbour came and told you. . .'

'The day her mother fell ill, I saw her pass to the well and while she
was washing her clothes, my grandmother came and told her . . .'

Interminable, infinitely soothing and ever more deeply etched on
the mind, that tale, with each retelling. It lies at the core of all human
learning and has served its purpose well since time began. Unfortunately, it is not so finely tuned to the needs of the twentieth century, as
anyone who has tried without success to keep their eyes open through
the endless speeches of Indonesian bureaucrats can testify. The
indigenous audience lapses contentedly into the familiar swoon, leaving the Western visitor alone and twitching, apparently the only
person present more concerned with questions than with hypnotic
form.

Questions, however, are not encouraged, either from adults or
from children. In school, they simply recite, though the recitation has
changed. There is the students' vow, Islam's prayers and promises

and the Pancasila – Indonesia's Constitutional chant.
'Freedom is the right of all members of society in the world
Colonialism must be wiped out, it is not in accordance with humanity or justice
The struggle of the Indonesian people for freedom has now been achieved
With happiness we proclaim our country
Our government stands for justice, humanity and prosperity
With the blessing of God and the will of the Indonesian people
We proclaim our independence.'
But Indonesia is a military dictatorship . . . what about East Timor? What about . . .? *Quiet.*
'We must follow God's rules
We must respect and obey our teachers and parents
We must be clean and strong in heart and body
We must be diligent in study and in charity
We must do good for our society, our nation, our country
We must carry on the good deeds done by Mohammed.'
Ho hum.
'Two children are enough
Go for Family Planning body and soul
It's good for you, body and soul
It'll keep you well preserved.'
Quite.

The headmistress, blinking with zeal behind her glasses, explains that children must have their consciousnesses raised (how, one wonders, when they are all fast asleep?) and that task belongs to the school.

'For instance, I teach birth control in every class, in every subject. The Indonesian language, reading, writing, art, sport, arithmetic, science, religion and the Pancasila. Also in geography and history. Always there is the opportunity to say how bad it is, too many people.'

Listen to her in an arithmetic class in the primary school, second grade – teachers are in short supply and she is everywhere. Fourteen little girls in white blouses and red skirts and nineteen little boys in white shirts and red pants. She places a shelled egg on the pencil runnel in the desk of a small girl. The other children crane their necks to see.

'How many brothers and sisters do you have?' she asks the child.

'One brother,' she whispers.

'Good,' says the teacher. 'Now if you and your brother want an equal share of this egg, what must you do?'

She lays a knife on the desk and the child, taking it up, cuts the egg in half.

'Yes!' The teacher claps her hands. 'One half for you, one half for your brother.' Her voice deepens. 'And suppose you had two more brothers. What would you have to do then?'

The child saws clumsily away at the two halves of the egg.

'Very good. Each of you would have a quarter of an egg. Not very much, is it?'

The child pokes at a bit of egg and the hard-boiled yolk crumbles, shedding yellow flakes.

'So!' A rap of the pointer on the side of the desk. 'You must go home and tell your mother she mustn't have any more babies or you will be hungry!'

She pulls a comical face and rubs her stomach. A bird flaps out of the beams above, startled by the peals of childish laughter.

In the rough pictures and the words of the children's reading books, there is little or no discrimination shown between girls and boys. A girl picks bananas, a mother irons and her son puts the linen away. A father walks in the rice fields with his daughter, a sister reads a book with her brother. For older children there are comic books depicting the difficulties families have if there are more than two children and the prosperity attendant on small families. The headmistress teaches sex education but only in terms of family planning and only in terms of what the girl-children must do. IUDs, injections, the Pill, this is Indonesian sex. No one will instruct the girl, ever, about sex itself, the act or its pleasures. 'We think,' the headmistress says, 'it is not decent to talk about sex openly. Maybe she will learn from her friends.' Whatever she learns, however short the time she spends at school, however sketchy her reading and writing, one thing is sure – a female child will become very literate indeed in the lingua franca of family planning. There are no love songs for her to sing, she may hold no man's hand in public, she will see no erotic carvings on any temple, however old, and there are no antique Javanese sexual epics like the *Kama Sutra* over which she can giggle and learn with her friends. But with any luck she will be able to read the contraceptive forms and fill them in and, if she lives in Bali, be numerate enough to chalk up on the board over her door the number of her children, so that all who run may read.

Asked what she thinks her pupils need in the future, the motherly headmistress, gently smiling, says, 'More discipline.'

More discipline?

'Ah yes. Otherwise . . .' she lifts her hands, moving them sadly in the air.

Otherwise . . .?

'. . . they will have no moral ground. They might do anything.

Breakdancing perhaps.' She sighs deeply. 'Or drinking brandy.'

But she is a good woman and has her pupils' best interests at heart. Avid for any nugget of foreign ideas, she listens far into the night as the geckos trumpet on the wall beside her and her visitor rambles on about Western ideas of education. In the early morning, red-eyed, she returns to the subject.

'All night I think and think of what you told me. About how, maybe, children should be taught everything about a subject, the good and the bad, the different ideas other people have and then work out what they think for themselves. Make their brains *move*, you said . . .' one finger twists furiously at her temple '. . . *move!* And I think you are *right!*' The Western banality illuminates her face, haggard with lack of sleep. 'My niece who married a Dutchman and lives in Holland, she come back on a holiday here and say she would not like to be here any more. She say too hot. And also too bor-ing all the time. But if we make the brains move, perhaps not so boring?'

Perhaps not. Perhaps the young woman student at Yogyakarta University, met in passing, who whispered, looking nervously around her, 'I cannot talk here . . . I am not free . . . the military . . .' and then did not turn up at a rendezvous, will not give up entirely, will not turn into a bor-ing Jakarta lady, chanting her empty speeches to a drowsy audience for the sake of her photo in the next day's newspapers and her husband's eventual promotion, so that she can afford a few more illiterate maids.

Not that you have to be illiterate to be a maid. All that can be seen of Ani is a soft cherubic face and round black startled eyes. A starched white lace-edged veil covers her ears and every last lock of her hair; spotless grey cotton shrouds her body from throat to toes. She looks like a tiny pretty nun. Until this day, Ani has never been further from home than the rice fields that surround her village in Central Java, where she lived for all of her twenty years with her mother, her father and three younger brothers.

But that is now in her past. Today she sits far up in the air in a Boeing 747 with twenty-eight other shrouded girls, in a world as unknown to her as the dark side of the moon. Never before has she sat in a padded chair, never before has she used a knife and fork or eaten the sort of food she is eating now or heard a language she cannot understand or tried to use a Western lavatory. She stares gravely out of her veil at the bustle around her, the huge white people, the swinging curtains, the film flickering on the screen ahead, the sky at the window. In her hand is a crumpled document drawn up by an employment agency back home. It says that she is contracted to work for two years as a housekeeper for a family in Jeddah, Saudi Arabia, the family who have paid for her flight. It does not say what hours she must work or what her duties are or what time off she may have or what can be done if she wants to leave before the two years are up. Only that she will be paid 20,000 rupiah (£20) a month, all of which she will send back to her family, to pay for the education of her younger brothers. She does not speak Arabic, though she can chant Koranic verses, and she says she trusts in Allah that she will be well-treated. We must trust so, too, because there is no one on earth to come to her aid if she isn't.

So there goes Ani, thunder-struck, flying off to a strange land and stranger people, to earn money for three more Indonesian children to be educated. Her small brown nail-bitten hands lie in her lap, clasped tight over the document of her employment. She can read what is printed on it and she has signed her name at its end.

It is not by literacy alone that women shall enter a Queendom on earth. Admitted, to render 160 million people literate on slim resources is no easy task. Admitted, women are better off when freed from the burden of endless pregnancies. Admitted, children survive now in Indonesia who would not have survived a mere ten years ago because of the dedicated campaign of health care, nutritional advice and immunisation – one glimpse of a young man limping down a Bali road on a leg withered by polio is enough to convince the most sceptical observer of that.

But the idea that literacy alone gives women autonomy over their own bodies remains an illusion. Today, Indonesian women are dragooned towards contraception as, once, they were doomed to uncontrolled fertility. This is, without doubt, a kind of beginning but it falls a long way short of choice and also seems, particularly to the Western observer, unnecessary. In every society in the world, women have been, are and always will be diligent in their search for ways to avoid constant childbearing and reckless in the risks they are prepared to take with their own health to achieve that end. In Indonesia, contraception is freely available and emphatically approved. Why, then, is it not possible simply to clear the way for them by removing the one obvious obstacle in their path – the objections of men – so that they may avail themselves, without coercion, of what they have always wanted, literate or not?

Jill Tweedie was born in Cairo, and spent her childhood in the Middle East. She was educated at schools in England and Switzerland, and after her marriage spent ten years living in Canada. When she returned to England she approached the *Sunday Telegraph* and in 1968 began writing a column for the paper's women's page; in 1969 she transferred to the *Guardian*, and for fourteen years wrote the articles for its women's page which have made her a household name. She has published a series of non-fiction works connected with women: *In the Name of Love* (1979), *It's Only Me* (1980), *Letters from a Fainthearted Feminist* (1982), and *More from Martha* (1983). The latter has been made into a comedy series. In 1984 Jill Tweedie wrote her first novel, *Bliss,* and is currently working on a second. She has two sons and a daughter and lives and works in London.

POLITICS

t is still unusual to see women's faces among the ranks of men that
omprise the world's governments. Women's entry into politics is
ampered by their lack of education and confidence. But even more
f an obstacle is their lack of time. A woman who must work in field
nd factory as well as in the kitchen has less energy than a man to
ommitt herself to political action.

From Egypt, Nawal el Saadawi travels to the United Kingdom, to
ne grey, slush-filled, winter streets of London and Oxford and the
olythene tents on Greenham Common, where women are
ncreasingly involved in political action for change both inside and
utside their families. Here there are women standing on picket
nes, occupying factories and hospitals to protect jobs and services,
aubing slogans on pornographic advertisements, and pioneering a
ew kind of peaceful protest against nuclear weapons.

From Australia, Germaine Greer travels to Cuba, to the land of
ne cigar and the rhumba, where women fought beside men in the
evolution, where they have spearheaded literacy, health and
ygiene campaigns, where they paint nail varnish on hands that hold
ifles, and where the demands of being a class of superwomen –
ctive comrade and sex object simultaneously – leave them little
me for a career in politics.

Nawal el Saadawi

I can still remember that day, still remember there was no sun, and that the black clouds crept over the sky from the north in a slow, heavy movement. An icy shiver went through me as I sat on an ancient tree trunk, lying there as though it had been cut down centuries ago.

She squatted on the ground, as old and as wizened and as powerful as the tree trunk. Her face looked out at me from under the tent – stone white with a bluish tinge of cold, its lines deeply curved as though with a knife, her chapped lips almost bloodless, under the strong nose lifting sharply upwards. Her voice resounded with an inner strength hidden somewhere in the tired body: 'Their Cruise missiles will have to cross over our bodies.'

A circle of eyes looked at me through the open door of the tent, gleaming with a strange light in the semi-darkness – the young eyes of girls under twenty, the old eyes of women over seventy. When I lifted my head, I could see through the steel wire mesh an endless space of ground covered by trucks and machines of various kinds. Further away were houses for the families of the Americans occupying the base, with schools and gardens.

I could imagine children playing in the grey morning. I could see them but could not hear their voices. There was something terrible in this vision of silent children, on the playground of nuclear war.

All I could hear was the heavy pacing of the sentinels behind the wire fence, and the occasional click of metal drifted across to where we sat. Through the wire their eyes looked out at us like coloured glass, and under the helmets the skins were white and sometimes black. Now and then I glimpsed the occasional fullness of a female breast.

Outside the wire the women had erected their tents. Every group of tents was designated by a different colour, so there were the yellow tents and the blue tents and the green tents. The old woman had dug a small pit in the ground and filled it with dry wood from the tree. Now she lit a fire. A young woman was scraping the mushrooms she had collected with a small knife and throwing them into the cauldron. A dark-haired girl wearing a long full dress went off into the neighbouring forest to collect wood, and came back carrying it in her lap. A third woman who had been warming her big rough hands at the fire stood up, went into the tent, came out with a plastic jerry-can and disappeared somewhere to look for water.

Close to the fire a number of women gathered for the weekly meeting of delegates from the various groups of tents.

My eyes followed what was going on around me in some bewilderment, but each time they would return to the woman sitting in front of me, like the trunk of a powerful tree.

'My name is Mary,' she said. I followed the deep lines in her face, wondered at the vitality in her voice and eyes and thought: 'The soul inside has defied the passing of time.'

'At night we listen carefully for the sound of wheels. They try to get the Cruise in when they think we cannot see them,' she said.

'But how can you stop them?' I asked.

'With our bodies. As soon as we hear the wheels, we lie down on the ground. Their rockets will have to pass over us if they want to get in. I prefer to die here rather than alone in my room. Then at least there will be some meaning to my death. Maybe my grandson will be proud of me. I have lived for seventy years but no one has ever been proud of anything I have done.'

Her voice still echoes in my ears, and her wrinkles speak to me at different times, in buses, and planes, or when the night is silent. I remember now her body was thin, without flesh, and around her shoulders she had wrapped a dirty yellow shawl. When I looked down I could see her feet swollen in their grey stockings, and wet with the rain and the mud of the forest.

I shivered with cold, but I felt the warm blood flow under my ribs. She brought her feet close up to the fire: 'The first winter here in 1981 was really bad, but in 1982 things were easier. This is the third winter we have been here and you can see . . .' She broke off, closed her lips tightly, and stared at a big metal sign through the iron gate leading into the military base. I followed her glance and read the black letters: 'We have orders to shoot . . .'

She brought her head close to the fire and blew into it until the embers flared up again. I heard her chuckle like a child: 'During the night we crawled up to the gate and dismantled it. They were obliged to use the other gate, and there we made a rampart with our bodies.'

She leaned over a hole in the ground. It contained a number of huge iron scissors. She pulled one of them out, put it in my hand, and gave me a piece of steel wire.

'Try and cut it,' she said.

I put the wire between the two edges of the scissors and pressed down with all my might. Immediately it broke into two pieces.

I heard her chuckle again: 'That's what we do at night. Yesterday they saw four of us cutting the wire and put them in jail. But next

Saturday we will assemble five thousand men and women to cut the whole fence. Do you know,' she added, 'that in England now there are 102 military bases? We have become an occupied land. If we want to be free these must be closed down.'

'Which part of England do you come from, Mary?' I asked.

I heard her swallow with difficulty and pause for a moment before answering: 'I was born in South Africa, of an English mother and an English father. I used to see my father beat my mother at home, then go out to work where he would beat the blacks on the farm. My mother killed herself in front of my eyes. And I learned to hate my father, and to hate those who colonise others. Then I married.' She paused for a moment. 'My husband taught me to hate marriage, to hate any form of oppression. As the years went by I realised you can't distinguish between different kinds of oppression, that imperialism, colonial, racial and sexual oppression are all linked together in one way or another.'

And so, at Greenham Common[1] were confirmed some of the things my life had led me to realise. Before the winter of 1983 I had been to London several times, but that was the first time I visited the women at Greenham Common. From that winter onwards, each time I came to London, I returned to the peace camp, to the women I had seen before on the common, to Mary and Karen and Liz and Sue, and many others. I wanted to look into their eyes once more, to feel their strength, their will, and watch their common effort. To listen to the things which the media never spoke of.

'We lived through two world wars. We're determined there'll never be a third.'

'In the past our men left home to go to war, now we women are leaving home for peace.'

Year after year, winter and summer, they laid their bodies down on this patch of Berkshire scrubland. Step after step they built up a new force, against nuclear war, resisted police harassment, trials, periods in jail. Month after month they grew from a small movement into a vast protest which numbered tens of thousands of people, mainly women. The initial group was constituted under the name 'Women for Life on Earth'. They carried out a 110-mile march which started from Cardiff and ended at Greenham Common where the women's peace camp was established. This peace camp later became the spark which inspired many of the recent peace movements in Britain, Europe and the United States.

When I was asked to contribute to this book the women of Greenham Common were the reason why I chose to write about 'women and politics in Britain'. For I felt that they represented something totally new, a novel political movement of women full of a great human potential, a movement destined to develop and to grow even if it did not survive in its initial form. I realised that women in Britain would continue to play an increasing role, become a catalyst and driving force which would contribute to a vast movement of all the oppressed, whether they be oppressed by class, or race, or sex, or for any other reason.

For in their camps and tents these women stood up and resisted the most powerful and dangerous forces the world has ever known, the forces trying to build up and prepare a nuclear war.

For months and years they stood the hardship of this primitive life on Greenham Common. Through months and years of effort they succeeded in mobilising the 50,000 women who surrounded the nuclear base on 11 December 1983, formed a human barrier around the nine-mile fence, and with their sheer weight made substantial parts of it collapse. They suffered rough handling by the police who carried large numbers of these women off to jail. And although they failed to stop the installation of Cruise missiles in the base, yet the final result of their action has been the development of a peace movement in Britain that today numbers more than 400,000 men and women.

Again it was winter. This time two years later during the month of February 1985. No sun, no black clouds, just an icy cold, and a world where everything seemed to be made of lead except the buses and the young faces that hurried over the pavements or rode bicycles swiftly through the streets. My companion this time is an English girl of Turkish origin. Her name Algin, her occupation, unemployed for the last year – one of the 12 per cent looking for work. One of the four million reserve army who serve as a threat to those who have a job.

'Which are the most active feminist groups these days?' I asked Algin.

'The lesbians,' she answered with a smile.

'I meant active politically,' I hastened to clarify.

'Lesbian activities are political activities,' she replied.

'I heard that a group of women have occupied one of the hospitals, and are running it, and that another group have occupied a church.'

'Yes, that's true. You probably mean the South London Women's Hospital. The women took it over last summer and it's still in their hands. As regards taking over the church, that goes back to the spring of 1982.'

'I'd like to see them,' I said.

So we took the underground to Clapham South. As we approached the hospital I caught sight of the banners hanging on the walls. I liked them. They said a lot to me. As I walked up my feet were light, rapid, eager over the steps. The banners said:
- South London Hospital – Women Will Not Close
- No Cuts of National Health Services
- Stop this Racist Attack on Women
- Fight back – we can win
- Women Need the South London Hospital
- Centralised Hospitals Treat People Like Sardines
- Building Medical Empires

In the entrance hall I saw women sitting on the floor. Some of the faces I had seen before, maybe at Greenham Common or elsewhere. But most of them were new. To the left of the entrance was a room with a glass panel facing the hall. Behind it were men wearing blue helmets. Their eyes watched us through the glass panel as we walked in. One of the men held a telephone receiver in his hand and we could hear him informing the District Health Authority about the situation in the hospital.

In one of the rooms I found a group of women sitting on cushions arranged on the floor. As soon as I walked in one of them stood up and shook hands with me warmly. I recognised Mary, my friend from Greenham Common. There was something motherly in the way she embraced me, in the touch of her arm on my shoulder, in her voice so soft and yet so strong.

'I was at Greenham Common when we heard that an order had been issued to close the hospital. We held a meeting composed of delegates from the groups and decided to occupy the hospital and run it on our own, so that the patients could continue to get the care they needed. Many of the members of the staff, whether women doctors or nurses, decided to continue working. One of the nurses called Ruth was at the head of this movement, and when the authorities tried to transfer her she resigned from her job and decided to stay on with us. We have been running the hospital since June 1984, that is for the last seven and a half months. We're beginning to feel the strain. There's so much to do. We have to clean this huge hospital ourselves. We are against the closure of this hospital because it serves the women in this district. Most of them are immigrant women belonging to racial minorities from Africa and Asia, including Moslem women whose husbands refuse to allow them to go to male doctors. The decree to close down is not only against women. It is racist and it's directed against the poorer classes of working women or housewives married to working men.'

One of the women I met there was Jane, a dark English woman born in India. She was carrying a magazine called *Mokti* which is published by a group of Asian women (mainly from the Indian subcontinent).

'I live in this district of South London. My four children were born in this hospital and have been taken care of ever since by the doctors and nurses who work here. There is no other place where I can go for medical services,' she told me. In answer to my questions she replied: 'Yes, I am a feminist and I carry on political activities together with other Asian women who live in England. We issue a magazine, and participate in marches and demonstrations. We lived for some time at Greenham Common, and joined the miners' wives in their activities to support the miners' strike.'

Lying on her back in one of the corners was a woman. Her body was covered with a grey blanket and she wore an old black shawl. 'If they want to close this hospital they will have to move in over our bodies,' she said. I remembered the women at Greenham Common – the same words, and the same look on her face, the face of someone who is being driven beyond fear.

Caroline was standing near us, her greying hair hanging over her shoulders, her eyes gazing straight ahead with a strange absorption. 'We expect them to expel us next month,' she said. 'They want to sell the hospital and found a company which will make huge profits. Now we know that sooner or later we will be evicted. It took us some time to realise that they are stronger. That's what happened too at Greenham Common. But we are learning, and as time passes, when we get over the setbacks, resistance will grow.'

I spent two nights in the hospital, talking to women of different professions and races, to whites and blacks, Asians, West Indians and Africans. Names and faces crowd in on my memory: Vicky, Viv, Ruth, Caroline, Mary, Karen, Suzy, Sue and many others. We gathered around as though seeking warmth in the cold night. An English girl of Pakistani origin made us some strong tea. The heating in the hospital was not functioning, but as the night went on exhaustion got the better of us, and the women dropped off to sleep one after the other in rooms which had been emptied of everything except a few medical appliances. But I was unable to sleep.

I walked along a deserted corridor looking for the kitchen. I was thirsty and needed a glass of water. Coming back I lost my way and ran into a black girl sitting with her back to the wall. A white girl huddled up close to her. She said her head was spinning and that her hands and feet were icy cold. The words she spoke in a weak voice served to remind me that I was a medical doctor. I dropped down on my knees and I felt her pulse. It was distant, scarcely to be felt, and her lips were almost blue. Then I heard her say: 'I came from Greenham Common this morning and have had nothing to eat for two days.' Together with her friend I helped her to walk down the corridor. We lifted her on to an empty bed and wrapped her in a shawl, then covered her with three blankets. Two cups of tea and coramine drops gradually brought some warmth back to her body. I looked in my bag and found a bar of chocolate. As she munched it we started talking.

'I've been out of a job for over two years,' she told me. 'When I'm hungry I go to the market and steal food, and when I want to read I go to a bookshop or a stall and steal books. I come from a working-class family in Kent. My mother wanted me to have an education. But my father was a hard man and treated both my mother and myself very badly. So I ran away at the age of seventeen, and worked as a secretary. Then I fell in love with a man and we lived together. But he was just like my father, and the day came when I could stand it no longer. I left him and never went back. Then I got to know women in the feminist movement and joined the Women's Health Group. I fell in love with a girl and realised I was a lesbian. Now I live on social security which is £28 a week, and at the same time work here in the hospital as a cleaner. I work more than the others because I am younger and have no higher education and because I am black.'

During this time the white girl who sat with us had said nothing, but now she joined in. 'My life is no better than hers,' she said. 'My real mother was a Catholic. My father and mother lived together without marrying and as soon as she became pregnant he left her. After I was born my mother left me in a home, and there I remained until my adoptive mother and father came along. They made me work in the house like a servant, so I ran away at the age of twelve. After a short while I started to live with a friend but he left me soon as I became pregnant. It was after this that I became friends with some members of the feminist movement. They came to my rescue and helped me to get an abortion.'

As we sat chatting around the bed a dark girl called Helen came into the ward and sat down beside us. I wondered for a moment where she had suddenly sprung from. She was very slight with short hair and big childlike eyes. It did not take long before she started to tell her story. She was born in Cyprus of a Turkish Moslem mother and an English father. When she came to England with her father she was only eleven. He married her off to an Indian businessman from Bengal. She bore him two sons but after four years of marriage he divorced her. She joined the feminist movement and started to work in a shop so that she could bring up her children. Now at the end of each day's work she comes back to the hospital to spend the night with the other women.

Suzanne was a woman who had given birth to her child during the period when the women took over the running of the hospital. She had named her daughter Scarlet and the child was now five months old. The mother was only twenty years old and was born in Canada. She worked as a nurse in the hospital, struggling with the other women to keep it open.

As the night went on our group kept growing all the time. Marion told us she was born in Jamaica, and had five children by an English man. But he had abandoned his family and now she lived with the children in a small room close to the hospital and was dependent on social security. I could see her staring at me with her big eyes, big enough to carry all the sadness of these lives. Yet somehow in her voice there was something like joy when she described the political action she was undertaking with the other women. She was black, she was poor, unemployed, abandoned first by her father as a child, then by her husband when she had become a mother of five children. Yet her eyes carried a message of pride as she sat there between her women friends.

The mornings have not changed. Still grey, still icy, infusing energy into my body accustomed to the warmth of subtropical sunshine. Now as I walk there is ice under my rubber shoes, it crunches with a sound like desert sand, takes me back for a moment to those I have left behind.

Two days earlier in the *Observer* I read an item of news. A mother and her child were reported to have died of cold. The mother, Helen Smith, was found dead in her flat in the south of London. Near her lay Natasha, eleven years old. The boy Michael, just turned thirteen, was in an advanced state of hypothermia.[2]

I felt suffocated in the underground, felt I was breathing in stagnant air breathed out by thousands of men and women who had breathed it in from others before. A never-ending vicious circle of intoxication, of queues, and crowds, and sallow unhealthy faces, with the sallowness that shows through white, black, brown and yellow skins. Exhaustion looked out from the faces yet the feet moved quickly over the stairs and along the passages underground.

I had put on my woollen coat, and wrapped my neck in my woollen shawl but below my feet were cold. I walked as fast as I could, rising from the tube into the fresh air, breathing in oxygen again, chasing the fumes from my head. I was going to the King's Cross Women's Centre, and as I approached I could see crowds of men and women closely packed around it, carrying banners and singing in chorus: 'Arise you prisoners of starvation, arise you wretched of the earth.'

I asked one of the women: 'Why the demonstration?'

'We're picketing the Ferndale Hotel,' she said. 'The people of the National Front have made it into a headquarters for themselves, and it's close to our King's Cross Women's Centre. During the past months, on several occasions they have attacked individuals and organisations in the area, including our centre. Police and councillors have said that the Ferndale Hotel is a base for Nazis.'

The demonstration advanced like a slow-moving human river, surrounded by lines of policemen, then came to a halt in front of the Ferndale Hotel. I heard hundreds of voices clamour in one breath: 'Sweep out the Nazis. Smash the National Front.'

The police pressed in more thickly around the demonstrators. Over their heads I could see the banners flapping in the wind:

'Youth in Unity', 'Women against Apartheid', 'King's Cross Women's Centre', 'Black Women for Wages for Housework', 'South London Women's Hospital', 'Arab Women's Group', 'Miners' Support Committee Hackney', 'English Collective of Prostitutes', 'Women Against Violence', 'Students' Union', 'Irish Women's Group', 'Federation of Bangladeshi Youth Organisations'.

There were many others. As I looked round I saw the same pallor showing through the skin of the faces, the same tired features, the same old threadbare coats. Blacks and whites, women and men, youths and children, housewives, women teachers, women with jobs and women without, prostitutes, lonely mothers and divorced wives, women living with men and women living without men, women living with other women, Asian women, African women, Arab women, Irish women and American blacks. Women of all ages and colours and professions, but all from the poorer ranks.

As I had come to see women in Britain and to know more about them, next morning I was back at the King's Cross Women's Centre before their clock had struck nine.

The room was neither big nor small. The windows were covered in faded curtains and the legs of the chairs swayed slightly when anybody sat down on them. A group of women had gathered there, most of them immigrant blacks or Asians. On the dark walls they had hung posters and photographs. My eyes were attracted to a big photograph hanging on the wall in front of where I sat, showing a group of women wearing black masks and underneath them a caption in block capitals:

'Occupation of the Holy Cross Church by the English Collective of Prostitutes and supporters to protest against police illegality and racism in King's Cross. They occupied the church for twelve days and nights (from 12–29 November 1982).'

I asked why they were wearing black masks and the women next to me said, 'So that the police should not be able to distinguish between those who are prostitutes and those who are not and so be able to arrest the prostitutes.'

On the same wall was a poster bearing the words of Virginia Woolf: 'To sell a brain is worse than to sell a body, for when the body seller has sold her momentary pleasure, she takes good care that the matter shall end there. But when a brain seller has sold her brain, its anaemic, vicious and diseased progeny are let loose upon the world, to infect and corrupt and sow the seed of disease in others.'

I turned back to the group. A dark-faced woman was speaking in a low but clear voice: 'Feminists who belong to the middle class do not understand the problems of women like us who have to live under the very different conditions imposed on people from the working class who have immigrated from other countries. We are faced with poverty, unemployment, racism, with police brutality, the threat of deportation and racist immigration laws. They think that their enemy is the man. They are against prostitutes because women who practise the profession have sexual relations with men. They are against pornography because it leads to rape, and rape in their view is in the nature of men. Can you imagine that at the Women's Place they do not allow boys over the age of twelve to enter the centre?!'

At the head of this group are two women, Selma James and Wilmette Brown. Selma is an American Jew but is against Zionism and considers that it is a racist movement just like apartheid in South Africa. 'That's why the relationship between the two is so close,' she said.

Wilmette is a black American born in a New York ghetto. She lives in London and is active in the black feminist movement in Britain.

'Racism makes black women the poorest, and the most deprived,' she said, and punctuated her words with a sweeping movement of her long, beautifully chiselled hand.' Many of us have been forced by the international arms trade, the arms race, NATO, and foreign aid in support of military dictatorships, to migrate. It's the poorest classes in the States who pay the price for these policies, and when we fought back they tried to make life impossible for us. So we came to Britain as migrants and refugees. The struggles in our home countries are contributing to the defeat of the war machine here and there. Our struggle against police powers in Britain has opened a way for the peace movement's challenge to the nuclear state. For us black women, sexism reinforces the racism which upholds and is upheld by nuclear weapons. Apartheid in South Africa is inseparable from the US-British military industrial complex. Struggle against racism is also a struggle against the mining of uranium in Namibia for Trident nuclear submarines.

'Women and men, black and white in our countries do owe something to women and men in the so-called Third World. Not only do the multitude of daily struggles for survival and liberation there confront the issues which are crucial for survival and liberation elsewhere, but they give power to us here by challenging the military industrial complex which rules us both, and which is based on plundering the Third World in our names.'

I sat there taking notes as the discussion went on. Selma took over and started to summarise what in her view were the differences between their group and some other groups of what she called 'white feminists'. 'We fight politically side by side with other oppressed people like black women, immigrants, black men, the mine workers and their wives. We struggle against racism, class oppression and sexual oppression. We do not postpone our fight in any of these three areas. And our enemy is never the man, as the 'white feminists' seem to think. That is the first difference between us and these other groups.'

'What are your other differences?' I asked.

'Our second difference,' she replied, 'is that we demand wages for housework. Sheila Rowbotham was one of the first women who drew attention to this question in her article entitled *Women's Liberation and the New Politics*, published in 1969.[3] In our group we are struggling so that women should be paid as of right a living wage for physical and 'emotional' housework, and this money is to come from the military budget of the government. We working-class women have worked enough. Every time they have 'let us in', it was to find for us some traditionally male enclave, some new level of exploitation. Here we can make a parallel between under-development in the Third World and underdevelopment in our countries. Capitalist planning proposes to the Third World that

it develop, that in addition to its present agonies, it too suffer th
agony of an industrial revolution. We women here have bee
offered the same 'aid', but those of us who have gone out of ou
homes to work have warned the rest: inflation has riveted us to th
bloody typing pool or to the assembly line and in that there is n
solution. We refuse the development they are offering us. But th
struggle of the working woman is not to return to the isolation of th
home, any more than the housewife's struggle is to exchange bein
imprisoned in a house for being chained to desks or machines. Th
challenge is to find modes of struggle which, while helping u
liberate ourselves from the home, at the same time avoid a doubl
slavery and another degree of capitalist control and regimentation
This is the dividing line between reformism and revolutionar
politics within the women's movement.'

24 February, 1985. The sky was a deep blue and the sun shone dow
on London. Now and then a white billowing cloud intervened
turning the bright green expanses into a dark olive, almost metalli
colour. I stood on the soft green grass enjoying the sunshine, an
the feeling of being and yet not being a part of the ocean which ha
flowed down into Hyde Park. They had come from different parts o
England, Scotland and Wales. Miners from villages, cities an
towns, workers from industrial districts all over the country
representatives of the trade unions and their federations, of th
political parties, of different people's organisations, of women fron
the feminist groups, and of the miners' wives.

The miners' wives. They were anonymous women at one time
like millions of other women who go about the hard daily job o
looking after the house, and the children, and the man, on a
working wage. But in the Britain of today, irrespective of what ha
happened in the year-long strike, they have carved a place fo
themselves in the history of the miners' movement, in politics anc
most likely in the shaping of future events.

That day they had come from many parts of the United Kingdon
carrying their banners. One of them was carrying a huge poste
depicting a working man and a working woman holding hands anc
marching together. At the bottom of the poster were the words
'Miners' Wives Action Group'. My eyes quickly ran over some o
the street banners: 'Cardawan Women's Support Group'
'Cumnock Miners' Wives', 'Miners' Wives – Kent Area'.

The demonstrators marched along. Column after column of men
women, youths and children filed past. On the coats and jackets

sweaters, blouses and dresses were yellow badges or tags printed with black and red letters: 'Coal not Dole', 'Support NUM' (National Union of Mine-workers), 'Keep Fighting', 'Stop Pit Closures'.

Lines of policemen, mounted or on foot, hemmed them in on either side, trying to control the masses of people as they marched like an unending human tide. Thousands of voices shouted in union: 'The workers united will never be defeated', 'Maggie out, Maggie out, Maggie Maggie Maggie, out out out'.

Trade union leaders, politicians, workers followed one another on the rostrum. I could hear the voice of one of them soaring above the clamour of voices that kept breaking out. Tony Benn, the Labour politician, spoke, followed by Dennis Skinner, another Member of Parliament and a one-time mine-worker himself. Then there was a roar and the thunder of clapping hands.

I saw a column of women approaching under a banner which floated high above their heads. Their eyes lit up as a white cloud fled over the sky letting the sun through again. One of them, a tall blonde woman, full of vitality which showed in the way she moved and talked and shook her head, was Margaret Holmes. She spoke to me of many things, and I confined myself to taking notes. She said, 'I started as an agricultural worker and become active in a trade union in the Kent area. I was the only woman in the regional committee for general transport workers. Agricultural workers are not politically aware and they discriminate against women. They push them into low-wage work, or into work under thirty hours a week to deprive them of many rights. I have been married to a miner called Joe Holmes for the last twenty years. We have four children. Miners' wives depend on their husbands' jobs since there is no work for them in the mines. After the strike started we formed a miners' wives group, to support our husbands, then later we formed our committee in the Kent area. I am the vice-chairman of this committee. At the national level we have constituted the committee known as "Women against Pit Closures" and Ann Lilburn is its president. Our strength comes from the local communities. If we are defeated it's going to be very bad not only for us here in England but for the whole of Europe, and for the working-class all over the world. We are looked upon as a leading force.

'I was born in 1942. I have no college education, only a secondary school education. I participated in workers' demonstrations in 1972, 1974 and 1984. What is new in the miners' strike is that women, for the first time perhaps, are in the front ranks. We formed our own women's committees, and these activities helped us to gain a new awareness of our rights as members of the working class, but also as women. Most of us have joined local union organisations and are now active in the trade union movement. This has broken down barriers between us and other women and helped us to find out more about their problems. We began to understand the meaning of women's solidarity, and built up relations of mutual help and cooperation with the feminist groups. On 8 March we are going to Germany and Denmark to celebrate International Women's Day.

'For many of us women, this struggle started in the kitchen. But instead of catering for our families we were catering for hundreds. We left our homes, organised women, raised money, spoke at meetings and demonstrations and travelled in this country and abroad. When our husbands were arrested we went on picket lines with the men. We risked imprisonment ourselves. But through all these activities we have united women and whole communities against pit closures and Thatcher's policies.'

After we had finished, I talked to a number of miners' wives as we walked along in the demonstration which led us from Hyde Park to Trafalgar Square.

One of the most interesting women to whom I talked was a miner's wife named Anne Marie Norris. Very white-skinned and rather fat, she nevertheless did everything with a smooth quickness. Together with one of her colleagues she was carrying a banner and yet managed at the same time to carry on a lively discussion with me as we walked. Her friend said to me, 'Anne collected money for the miners' families in a very novel way.' When I asked her how, she replied: 'She made a bet that for £50 she could reduce her weight by one pound every week. She succeeded in reducing her weight by twenty pounds in twenty weeks and collected £1,000 this way.'

Anne smiled and said, 'I still have 80 spare pounds that are worth £4,000.'

I heard the women laugh merrily. They reminded me of my relatives in the village of Kafr Tahla on the banks of the Nile. For the voice of village women, or of those who live away from the big cities have much in common. They are not cultured voices, nor do they pronounce words in a sophisticated way. But they are voices full of life. They ring true and they carry with them that good humour and readiness to fight that make certain moments in life so beautiful.

It was the miners' wives who helped the strike to survive for almost a year. It was these laughing, almost child-like voices that lived through the harsh struggles and rarely weakened. But a minute later they were drowned in the sound of galloping horses closing the vay to Trafalgar Square.

When it was time to leave we sat for a few moments at the kerb. Anne looked at me in her naive smiling way and said: 'If the miners' union declares the strike at an end this will not mean that we have ailed. We will continue to fight by other means until we win.'

Look,' said Hilary to me. 'Look how some people sleep their nights n London during the winter months.' I followed the angry gesture of her hand as she pointed to the human bodies, to the men and women and children sleeping in cardboard boxes in the shelter of he Royal Festival Hall. My eyes strayed to the beautiful building lit up in the night, to the opulence that still hangs over the rich quarters of London, to the waters of the Thames flowing by, then back to hese people lying on the ground. I felt my heart held in a vice.

'A few days ago,' she went on, 'the *Daily Express* published an tem about a woman called Hadow who died recently. In her will she lonated £1.75 million, which was all she possessed, to the care of animals. [4] I'm not against being kind to animals, but I'm against a ystem which permits animals to inherit millions of pounds and obliges human beings to sleep on the ground during the icy winter nights.'

Hilary is a professor at Oxford. She describes herself as a socialist eminist, and 'not belonging to Oxford society'.

'Oxford University,' she says, 'is one of the most conservative, and this makes me very proud of the fact that last week the Oxford authorities refused to bestow an honorary doctorate on Margaret Thatcher.'

My first meeting with Hilary took place in Oxford, in the house of a woman named Anne, after a one-hour train ride from Paddington tation and a short drive by car.

Anne is the daughter of a rich family, and her father is a conservative. In Oxford she started to read about socialism and became interested. She joined the Labour Party and married a Marxist. 'One of the problems we have,' she said to me, 'is that I have become a vegetarian, whereas my husband loves meat, and ries to provoke me by filling the freezer up with quantities of choice cuts which I have to cook for him.'

'Why doesn't he cook them himself?' I asked.

She shrugged her shoulders. 'He's really too busy to be able to cook, you know. Politics take up a lot of his time.'

We sat near the fire, chatting. 'I don't think women can be liberated under a capitalist system. Socialism for me is not only a question of class struggle. Women must struggle not only against class oppression, but against patriarchy also. We concentrat essentially on fighting the oppression exercised against women, an I think that the women's liberation movement has made importar contributions to some of the sciences and helped to change mar concepts which at one time were considered fundamental. This true not only of the medical sciences but of other areas such a biology, psychology, philosophy, history and the social science Now in many universities there are sections for women's studies She stood up, went off to the kitchen to bring the tea, and cam back with a tray.

Meanwhile Hilary was explaining: 'In more progressiv universities like Essex, Kent, Warwick and Sussex, establishe relatively recently, sections for women's studies have bee established. But in the more conservative ones like Oxford they d not exist, and most of those in charge are resisting such a step.'

Anne picked up from where she had left off. 'We started ou activities by establishing a natural childbirth trust.'

'What does that mean?' I asked.

She went to get the teapot and the sugar and came back balancin them in her hands, answering my questions as she filled up our cup

'It means having a baby without medical intervention and trainin women to do it themselves.' I heard her laugh in a ringing voic before she went on. 'In the Victorian era doctors refused to us anaesthetics during child labour because the Bible says that wome will give birth to their children in sorrow and pain. But later o Queen Victoria issued directives permitting the use of anaesthetics Now her laughter rang out again. 'We have discovered that woman can give birth to a child without pain or anaesthetics c sorrow.'

That day there were other women present at the gathering i Anne's house. Some of them lived in a village called Cholse fifteen miles away from Oxford. Ginny, Caroline and three othe women, all of whom were housewives, came from this village. The had started a group called 'National Housewives Register fc Lively-Minded Women'. Working together had helped their idea to develop further, and led them to join first the Labour Party an later the peace movement. Some of them had also been arreste during the March 1982 demonstration against the installation c atomic missile bases in Britain.

One of the members of this group, Marlene, was also a membe of the Communist Party. She was born in the same village and bot her parents were members of the Communist Party. Later on he father left it to join the Labour Party but her mother stayed on as member.

'In 1968,' Marlene said, 'there was a split in the Communist Party and we formed the Communist Party of Britain. The main area of disagreement with the orthodox party is on the issue of what we call the British Road to Socialism. We believe that this road will necessarily be extra-parliamentary. Although I work with the group of women we have been talking about, I also share in the activities of the Committee for Women within our party.'

Marlene's words launched a long discussion about the relationship between the women's movement and socialist parties. During the demonstration in support of the miners' strike organised in Hyde Park I had met a woman named Bea Campbell who is one of the leaders of the Communist Party, and I now remembered the views she had expressed on this subject. To her, being a party member and being involved in the activities of the women's wing within the party were very important for whatever work she undertook in the women's movement in general. There was no contradiction between the two. On the contrary, they were mutually supportive. She said that problems of class, sex and race were interlinked. 'Yet we cannot give the same emphasis to all three at all times. There are moments when one of the three is a priority and race or sex are pushed in the background. At other moments race or sex could come to the foreground.' My contention with her had been that left-wing movements tended to push sex into the background at all times, in other words to neglect it, to avoid giving it a rightful place. The fear among left-wing movements was that problems related to women's status and women's róle could militate against the development of the class struggle and confuse its issues. It was a matter both of understanding and of practice. The women at the Oxford meeting considered socialist feminism as a movement which refused to postpone or alleviate the struggle for women's liberation in order to give emphasis to the class struggle. They believed that both had to go hand in hand.

Later on, when I met Joan Ruddock, chairwoman of CND (Campaign for Nuclear Disarmament), she expressed the same views. We had lunch together in a small restaurant opposite her office in Reading.

'Yes,' she said, 'I am a socialist feminist. But I am also active in the peace movement and in the struggle against nuclear war. I am a member of the Labour Party and intend to stand for parliament in the next elections which will be held in 1988. Political activity in the area of women's movements should be undertaken through parliament and also by extra-parliamentary means.'

I found the same concepts reflected again in my discussion with

Glenys Kinnock, who is the wife of the Labour Party Leader Neil Kinnock. I felt she was a woman who had made her way in the political movement as an independent personality and through many years of effort. She is active in the women's movement as well as the peace movement and has done a lot in support of the miners' wives. She invited me to her house in South Ealing and we had a long talk over tea and biscuits.

'I am a wife and a mother but I am not dependent on my husband in any way. I became a member of the Labour Party at the age of sixteen, long before I married. My father was an active member of the Labour Party and played a role in my anti-colonialist position. In 1956 when the British invaded Egypt I heard my father say angrily: "It's their canal." ' I asked about her job and she told me that she was a teacher but had not gone to work because the teachers were on strike. 'The government has reduced the wages of teachers by 33 per cent,' said Glenys. 'Thatcher can hit out at the miners' strike because coal can be imported from Poland or the States. But she can't import teachers from abroad. We need a change of government, and I think that in the coming elections, a new Labour Government will take over and will implement policies intended to serve the interests of the people.'

Valerie Wise is the chairperson of the Women's Committee of the Greater London Council. She's a tall blonde woman, twenty-nine years old. Her mother, Audrey Wise, is an active Member of Parliament, and she was brought up in a family where politics were a part of daily life. As a result she joined the Labour Party at the age of fifteen.

I met Valerie in her big office at County Hall. We had lunch together in the cafeteria situated on one of the floors of the huge building. She also calls herself a socialist feminist and for further precision added, 'I am anti-sexist, anti-racist, anti-imperialist, anti-Zionist. But I'm also against heterosexism,' she added with a laugh, 'meaning that I'm not opposed to lesbian groups. Through the Women's Committee we give financial support to more than 600 women's groups. But the Government wants to abolish the Greater London Council. I am therefore engaged in the campaign which has been launched against the abolition of the GLC. I believe in political action through parliament and by other means.'

Many women in Britain belong to the movement which calls itself socialist feminist. And most women writers in the country seem to be favourable to the idea of socialist feminism. That is what I was given to understand by Michèle Roberts, who is herself a writer and whom I met in a café near Piccadilly. She sat opposite me, tranquil and yet as nervous as a butterfly. I heard her say in a quiet voice: 'But the problem which faces most feminist women thinkers and writers is not the choice between capitalism and socialism. We know that women can never be liberated under capitalism. But socialist women need a new "consciousness" or, to put it differently, a new "unconsciousness".' We have to shift from raising feminist "consciousness" to raising feminist "unconsciousness".'

The following evening I met a group of women writers at dinner in a Covent Garden restaurant. Present were Germaine Greer, Marilyn French, Debbie Taylor and myself. Marilyn French was very much in favour of the idea that feminists need to shift from raising 'consciousness' to raising 'unconsciousness'. But Germaine Greer saw things differently. 'We have to shift from the First World to the Third World.' 'To do what?' asked Debbie Taylor with the disarming charm she brought to everything. And thus we found ourselves launched on one of the discussions which I have heard whenever an international conference brings women from different parts of the world together.

This on-going discussion between feminists in the so-called First World and feminists in the so-called Third World is no doubt important, but it is too complex an issue to be dealt with in a few lines. One thought, however, it is perhaps necessary to retain. Nobody can deny that feminist writers and in particular socialist feminist writers (like Sheila Rowbotham in England) have, starting from the sixties, played an important role in developing feminist thought, not only in their countries but also in other parts of the world.

However, many of them believe that feminist struggles in the practical and ideological fields are limited to the Western capitalist world, and that women's liberation movements in other countries owe their impulsion and their ideas exclusively to what has been done or said or written by feminists of the First World. For example Sheila Rowbotham herself writes: 'Demands like monogamy, birth control, education, the right to organise were borrowed from Western capitalism.'[5]

But this is not correct. Methods of birth control were known and utilised by women in Egypt, as well as in other Arab and African countries, many centuries ago. This also applies to the struggle for monogamy and against other patriarchal customs and values.

Sheila in a later passage goes on to say: 'In the 1920s an incipient feminism emerged in developing countries which resembled the early "equal rights" feminism of middle-class women in capitalist countries.'[6]

But Victoria Brittain, a journalist on the *Guardian* and a friend of mine, does not agree with this view. Over a glass of wine in the living-room of her house she said to me, 'Such sweeping statements are liable to lead us astray for two reasons. Firstly, ideas and their practices take different forms according to the societies in which we live. The struggle of women in the Third World countries took forms which are perhaps not recognisable by the criteria which Western families use. Secondly, the Third World is not a homogeneous bloc, and to reach such a conclusion without making a concrete study of the historical movement of women in each country is rather a hasty way of dealing with social movements.'

Tindle Manor Building is a huge modern construction with corridors and numerous rooms, where groups of women were meeting, or talking, or moving around, and constantly busy.

After a while I felt that I was visiting a feminist hive. But this time the feminists were very different from the ones I had met before, although in all cases there remained this common stand against the Conservative government, and against the policies that have now come to be known as Thatcherism.

The previous groups, whether they were socialist feminists, miners' wives or immigrants, were groups opposed to the monetarist policies of Thatcher. The groups I met at Tindle Manor, however, were opposed to another category of policies implemented by the Thatcher government, namely those know as moralist policies.

We were sitting around a table in one of the numerous rooms – a group of about twenty women of different ages, some of them still young girls while others were middle-aged or older. Nicky, a short blonde woman, explained to me what they meant by moralist policies: 'The revival of Victorian values that the Tories are fostering means that women are left holding the baby while the men go off to war.'

One of the women around the table intervened: 'Doesn't this remind you of Hitler?' Then she added, 'Perhaps we should tell you a little about the groups in this building.'

I soon discovered that my earlier impression of a feminist hive was correct. For Tindle Manor houses a large number of feminist groups including Rights of Women (ROW), Women's Aid Federation, Women's Aid Refuges, Rape Crisis Centres, Battered Women Group, Prostitution Group, Lesbian Group, Health and Therapy Centre, Legal Advice Group, Women Against

Pornography, Women Against Rape, Women's Reproductive Rights Group and others.

I spent several hours in the building, moving from one to the next. Each one of them was involved in one form or another of activity aimed at providing services to women, and helping to solve many of the problems they faced. Such groups have spread rapidly, not only in Britain but in many countries of Europe, and in the United States. Amongst the most recent is a group constituted in England under the name Women's Reproductive Rights. When I asked what she meant by women's biological rights, a phrase which often came up during the discussion, the woman who seemed to be in charge of the group said: 'We women have the right to determine our own sexuality, the right to decide if and when to have children. We must also have the right to comprehensive national health services. They are necessary in enabling us to back up our decisions, whatever these decisions may be, and irrespective of whether we are married or not, black or white, poor or rich, heterosexual or lesbian.'

When these women used the word lesbian, it came naturally in their conversation, without a hint of reservation, just like anything else which was an integral part of daily life. And as I moved from room to room one of the groups which I met was Lesbian Mothers' Rights. It had been constituted with the aim of defending the rights of lesbian women and particularly those who had children. Among the main issues was custody of the children and their rights as mothers to bring up children, but there was a whole range of other matters, including defending lesbians against discrimination in legal matters, education, social services and social security.

A long discussion about lesbianism and the lesbians ensued. I noticed that the lesbians are divided into two main groups. One group considered that lesbianism is the way to women's liberation and that the political and sexual future of women lies in lesbianism. The second group considered lesbianism as a transitional stage, the aim of which was to rid women of their need for men and replace this with an alternative. To them this alternative was not only sexual but also emotional, social and familial. I found that there were a growing number of families which can be considered 'new female families', in which the two female partners rear the children together. The central idea in the thinking of this second group is that the absence of an alternative to the male makes men authoritarian and irredeemable (meaning recalcitrant to any change or improvement).

I asked, 'And now are men any better than before?'

One of the young women present, a tall blonde girl, laughed before she replied. 'Not at all. Now the men are bypassing their need for women by building up relations with one another. That's why the gay movement is growing and gay families and clubs are spreading all over the country.'

Another young woman intervened. 'I was lesbian but I discovered that inequality also exists in lesbian relationships. One partner tries to dominate the other. That's why I have become bisexual. This gives a woman more freedom.'

I also attended a meeting with the group called Women Against Rape. The women present were exchanging ideas about the causes of violence and rape, and I noticed a tendency to consider aggression as being a male characteristic. When I asked, 'Aren't women sometimes violent and aggressive too?' a white-skinned woman with short grey hair answered, 'Of course, but it's always a reaction to the aggression of men. Violence in men is an intrinsic part of their nature, it's biological instinct. Men love war but women love peace. That's why the peace movement is mainly composed of women.'

I said that I found it difficult to accept such statements –otherwise we would find ourselves prisoners of Freud's concept that 'anatomy is destiny.'

A tall slender girl who had been silent all the time now intervened. 'I agree with you completely, Nawal. And I must tell you that there is a split in the women's movement around this issue. One sector of the movement considers that violence is a male characteristic and that man is therefore the enemy. The spokeswoman of this group is Lilian Mohin, who maintains that the women of Greenham Common and the political movement against nuclear war have diluted the feminist movement because women have diverted their attention and efforts to issues; that the danger that faces women is not nuclear war. Nuclear war is only one of the symptoms of male supremacist culture, and women should not put their energies into attacking the symptom, but instead should attack the fundamental cause, which is perhaps too dangerous to confront ie the man next door.'[7]

'But,' the young woman went on to say, 'I and many other women do not believe that violence is solely a male biological characteristic and peace and gentleness exclusively female qualities. Otherwise it would be difficult to explain Thatcher.'

There was a silence in the room. Perhaps many felt that peace and war are linked to issues of social justice rather than to the hormones we have in our bodies?

I moved on to another group sitting around a long table. One of
he pamphlets I picked up from the table was entitled *Surrogate
1otherhood*, and when I asked if this was a new 'biological right' a
oung girl sitting by my side said, 'Not yet. But we try to protect
urrogates from any form of exploitation which could be exercised
gainst them by private profit-making organisations. Poor women
an be used for reproductive purposes, as wombs for producing
abies, and a black market situation could then be created. This is
specially so since under current British law any woman who carries
 pregnancy to term is legally the mother of the resulting child, no
natter whose egg is used.'

One of the women asked me: 'Have you followed the discussion
oing on about embryo research on the television?' I nodded my
ead so she added, 'What do you think about it?'

'I think it's a false issue although I support research which gives
omen more freedom.'

'I agree with you. They only talk about the right of life when they
liscuss embryos and foetuses. They have never made a fuss about
housands of black people who are killed and maimed in South
Africa.'

A woman sitting at the other end of the table commented:
Defending the rights of the unborn means denying the rights of
vomen. All the issues related to this question are being raised to
leprive women of some rights, such as abortion.'

'Yes,' said the young girl by my side, 'but the problem is that
eproductive technology such as artificial wombs, sperm banks,
:mbryo-freezing, tran-species fertilisation, cloning of embryos etc –
.ll these can be useful to some women if properly directed. But
cientific research is male-dominated and is usually directed to serve
nen and not women.'

The woman sitting at the head of the table made a final remark:
Anyhow, unless some clear justification is found and has clear
ublic approval, we see no reason to spend money on cloning of
:mbryos in a country which cannot afford to provide adequate
ealth care out of the national purse.'

Feminist groups in Britain, no matter what the issues to which they
iddress themselves, have been unanimous in condemning the
oolicies of Mrs Margaret Thatcher's government and in considering
hem prejudicial to the cause of women's rights and women's
iberation.

I therefore thought it would be appropriate for me to meet Mrs
Thatcher in person and ask what she thought about the views the

different feminist groups had expressed to me when we discusse
the policies of her government. But by the time my trip was comin
to an end, Mrs Thatcher had left for the states to meet Mr Reaga
and I could not prolong my stay in London to meet her.

However, I was able to meet Mrs Linda Chalker, who is th
Minister of Transport and is considered to rank second after th
Prime Minister as far as the women ministers are concerned.

I walked over to the main entrance of the Ministry. I could se
Parliament House and Big Ben and the statue of Churchill with th
characteristic hunch of his shoulders and the dogged face of a man i
battle.

Linda Chalker took me into her big room. We sat at th
conference table and it took only a few moments before we wei
plunged into the subject for which I had come.

'Mrs Thatcher is the first prime minister since Churchill with rea
courage, with a courage that even men do not have. I am saying th
today although in 1975 I was not one of her supporters, and differe
with her on various issues. But today I am in complete agreemei
with what she stands for.'

'What made you change your mind?' I asked.

'She raised the political debate above the level of purely loca
issues to what is necessary if the United Kingdom is to become grea
again. Her horizon is not limited. She thinks of long-term solutions

'But most of the women I met are against her,' I said.

'Those who are against her do not know the anguish of change

'What do you mean by the anguish of change?' I asked.

'I mean the price of change,' she said. 'We want to move forwarc
to change for the better, and this change has its effects on som
people. But sacrifices are inevitable. Our most important goal a
this moment is production. But can anyone produce withou
encouragement, without incentives? Even in communist countrie
like China they have started to believe in material motivation an
are now giving incentives to the workers. We have moved over to
stage where we must produce and work. We are no longer at th
stage where people can earn a salary without doing anything.'

'Women complain that unemployment has been forced upo
them because there are no jobs. They say that housework is work
They also say that there is a continuous cut in national expenditur
on health services, education, social services and benefits. This ha
affected women more than men because they are the ones who bea
children and care for them. They also care for the sick, the old an
the disabled,' I said.

'Social services have become greatly inflated,' said Lind
Chalker.

'The women say it's the military budget which is swallowing a substantial part of your resources.'

'But the social services consume a quarter of our national income. I am not against social services, quite on the contrary. When I was Minister for Social Services in 1979 I introduced child benefit. But I'm against laying too much emphasis on social amenities at the expense of production and work. We must build a great United Kingdom and become what we were at one time.'

'But the great United Kingdom was "great" because of the empire and the exploitation of colonies in Asia and Africa. Is that what you want to go back to?'

'No, of course not. We must build up our industry and production here in Britain. This cannot be done unless we work and work and produce all the time.'

'Do the mine-workers want to stop production, to stop working? They and their wives are opposing the closure of the pits.'

'The miners are not realistic. Coal mines are no longer economic. And their wives too do not understand these new economic facts. In addition we oppose the violent means to which the miners have had recourse in defending their demands. Violence and destruction are not a way to solve problems. They must respect order and return to their work in the mines.'

And so we went on with ease and informality, one point leading to another. From behind her spectacles Linda Chalker looked at me with lively eyes reflecting the vitality which characterised the way she moved and talked and laughed. She kept standing up every now and then, half-sitting on the edge of the desk, or the table, then returning to her chair only to stand up again after a little while, for, like myself, this white-skinned slightly stout woman suffered from a prolapsed disc which caused her severe pain whenever she sat down for some time. I advised her to buy a 'balans' chair like the one I had purchased from Oslo, and which I found relieved much of the pain of sitting at my desk for a long time.

'Do you know you are the third person who has spoken to me about the "balans" chair during the last week,' she commented with some surprise before going on to answer the questions I asked her about her life. 'My father was a lawyer and tried to get into parliament but failed. So I kept dreaming of doing what he had failed to do. While still in school I decided to become a doctor, but abandoned the idea later on because I did not like the look of the cockroaches which students dissect in the pre-medical years. I joined the volunteer wing of the Conservative Party when I was still fifteen and became a Member of Parliament in 1974, then minister in 1979. Margaret Thatcher is the first woman prime minister in Britain and now we have four ministers who are women. There are twenty-five women in the House of Commons and fifty women in the House of Lords. I am one of the founding members who established the 300 Group. It aims to increase the number of women who are in parliament. I am enthusiastic about women's rights and do as much as I can to make women participate more actively in political life and in parliamentary activities. We named our organisation the 300 Group because we want the number of women in parliament to reach 300. This to my mind is the correct way of envisaging feminism. If we do not succeed in getting more and more women into parliament we will never become an influential force in British society.'

'That is true, of course,' I said, 'but it seems to me that here in Britain you have a women's movement which is active in many areas outside parliament, and exercises a notable influence on what is happening in your society. To give only one example I cite the women's peace movement which has had a considerable influence on the peace movement directed against the danger of nuclear war.'

'We are all opposed to the unleashing of a nuclear war. But to impose peace we have to be strong, we have to build up the strength of the UK in the economic, technological and military spheres, so that we can protect our country from any danger menacing it. The building-up of military bases in Eastern Europe is a menace to our security.'

'Which side is menacing the other?' I asked.

'It's a struggle between the superpowers and it endangers everybody, hence the need to build up our own strength so that we can defend ourselves and not lose our freedom. I believe in my freedom as a human being and as a woman, and in democracy, and I am against the systems that destroy the freedom of the individual. Women in the Soviet Union are not free, whereas in our country woman is free and can become a head of state, or a prime minister.'

When she spoke about these issues it was with enthusiasm. After a little while I started to ask her about the more personal aspects of her life. In answer to my question she told me that she had been married twice and had divorced her first husband because they disagreed over her involvement in political activities. 'But my second husband helps me in everything, including the kitchen. Margaret Thatcher's husband also helps his wife and so do the husbands of all the women ministers. When I married I did not take my husband's name. I have always been Linda Chalker.'

It was dark by the time I left. I walked through Westminster, along the broad pavements, and Big Ben struck eight with its booming chime. I had spent about two hours discussing many things, and despite our differences of opinion I could feel that Linda Chalker all along had been deeply convinced of what she said.

The night was icy cold but I felt warm in my coat, the blood was flowing through my veins and my body seemed to tingle with the thoughts and experiences of the past few days. I had seen so many women, heard so many voices, watched the play of feelings on their faces. But one thing I had perhaps known before I arrived, and now it had impressed itself indelibly on my heart and mind. Here I was in a country where the head of state and the prime minister were both women. And yet the rights of British women were more in jeopardy than they had ever been in recent times. This confirmed what I had learnt from my own experience in Egypt. What really matters is the economics and the policies of the system under which women live. What matters is the interests of the class or classes which hold sway over the system. What matters is the political awareness of women, the strength of their organisations and their ability to fight.

I rested my head against the back of my seat, and left my body to enjoy the deep feeling of relaxation which comes after effort, the gentle lift of the plane rising higher into the sky, the sensation of abandoning myself to the care of other people. I stretched my legs over my handbag swollen with books and magazines from feminist bookshops, like Silver Moon, Sisterwrite and others. Feminist bookshops and publishing houses have multiplied in Britain during the past few years and are a reflection of the growing interest in feminist ideas.

Feminist magazines – *Spare Rib, Outwrite* and others – have played a role in reflecting different aspects of the women's movement for liberation both in Britain and in some of the developing countries of Africa, Asia and Latin America.

Feminist films and Cinema for Women (COW) have succeeded in breaking the monopoly of men where the visual arts are concerned. I had seen a film called *A Free Country* which deals with the subjugation of Irish women and the efforts they were making to liberate themselves and their country from British oppression.

Through my mind flashed the many faces I had seen, and the many things I had heard during the past two weeks. Now I knew more than at any previous time that the feminist movement in Britain as a whole was a progressive and liberating force which continued to enrich the political and social life of the country with new ideas and new forms of struggle, and which was also

contributing to the development of the feminist movement in othe
countries through its experiences, through its successes and it
failures, through the painful birth of new concepts, of new ways o
seeing the problems of women and men and solving them.

The feminist movement is an independent, innovative and ye
related part of the total struggle against violence and exploitation,
whether in society or in the micro-unit of the family.

Parts of this movement might show a tendency to adopt extremis
positions either in the area of conceptualisation, or in the dail
political and social struggle, or in both. But this is natural, especiall
for a movement which has a relatively short history and is involvec
in a very complex and difficult struggle. With time, and by dint o
effort, even though setbacks are inevitable, issues will become
clearer, and forms of action more effective.

Revolution and change are a break away from all that is usual
customary and known. They are necessarily accompanied by ange
against all forms of oppression and by great enthusiasm for justic
and freedom. At all moments I felt myself involved both mentall
and emotionally with what is happening in the feminist movement i
Britain, even though I disagreed with some of the views expressec
to me. It made me more optimistic, more confident, happy to fee
that we women of Egypt and the Arab countries were not alone, anc
that we have friends in Britain and in many other countries of th
world.

As the plane crossed over the Mediterranean shores of Egypt th
sun shone brightly and the sea was an azure blue. I was happy to b
home. I was happy to have lived this rich experience with m
feminist sisters in Britain, and looked forward to the future which
knew was full of hope.

Notes

1. Greenham Common in Berkshire is one of the sites chosen for 160 Cruise missiles. (See: *Greenhan Common, Women at the Wire,* Barbara Harford and Sarah Hopkins, The Women's Press, London 1984, p. 7.)

2. *Observer,* 17 February 1985, p.1.

3. 'Women's Liberation and the New Politics', in *Dreams and Dilemmas,* Collected Writings of Sheila Rowbotham, Virago, 1983, p.20.

4. *The Daily Express,* 14 February 1984, p.1.

5. *Women, Resistance and Revolution,* Sheila Rowbotham, Penguin, 1972, p.202.

6. *ibid,* p.203.

7. *Breaching the Peace* (a collection of radical feminist papers), Only Women Press, London, 1983, pp.18 – 21.

Nawal el Saadawi was born in the village of Dafr Tahla in Egypt. She trained as a doctor of medicine and rose to become Egypt's Director of Public Health, a remarkable achievement for a woman in her country. She began writing thirty years ago, producing novels and short stories, and in 1972 published her first study of Arab women's problems and their study for liberation, *Women and Sex*. She has suffered at the hands of the Egyptian censors, being forced to shift publication of her works to Beirut, and earning her dismissal from the Ministry of Health. She writes in Arabic, but has published two books in English, *The Hidden Face of Eve* and *Women at Point Zero*. Nawal el Saadawi currently lives and works in Cairo.

Germaine Greer

came to Cuba with my heart in my mouth. Ever since my first contact with the 'Third World', in Jamaica in 1971, I had been aware how burningly important it is for the developing nations that Cuba not be a fraud or a failure. As the years passed and I wandered through slums in Bombay, past windowless huts in Morocco, Tunis and Yucatan, through the dust of Uttar Pradesh and the infested dirt of the Brazilian north-east and the menace of Bogota and the Guatemalan highlands, every step showed me that paternalist development aid is worse than useless. In the eighties, as the external debts of the developing countries mushroom over them while their people grow steadily poorer and the number of landless multiplies daily, the need of a genuine alternative is agonising. If Cuba had shown me nothing but the institutionalised poverty and bureaucratic rhetoric and repression that Western megamedia taught me to expect, a brain-washed militarised population living by hypocrisy and fear, the dark future would show no sign of dawn. If Cuba's was really a revolution of the people, then even if a malignant power should blast Cuba out of the Caribbean, its people will be invincible.

My arrival coincided with the fourth congress of the Federation of Cuban Women, the FMC. Billboards and posters announced it all over Havana. *Toda la fuerza de la mujer en el servicio de la revolución.* The logo was an art-nouveau-ish montage of Kalashnikov rifles and Mariposa lilies. I was not keen on the implications of either. On the Rampa, the floodlit exhibition pavilion was turned over to the exploits of women. Banked television sets showed colour videos of the history of Cuban women, and a succession of booths displayed everything from the techniques of screening for breast cancer to scent and hair curlers. Women whose bottoms threatened to burst out of their elasticised pants tottered round the exhibits on four-inch heels, clutching their *compañeros* for support. Their nails and faces were garishly painted. Their hair had been dragged over rollers, bleached, dyed and coloured. Their clothes, including their brassières, were all two or three sizes too small and flesh bulged everywhere. Most people rushed past the educational exhibits to where a painted, conked, and corseted trio bumped and ground its way through an amorous rhumba. At the sight of an unattached woman, the loose men began psst! psst! and beckoned to me, as if I had been a dog.

The next day, my minder from the Ministry of Exterior Relations (MINREX) came to take me to the Palacio de Congresos for the first

session of the FMC Congress. Security was tight. I was directed to
press box in the back of the vast auditorium, with no facilities f
simultaneous translation. A policeman ordered me not to put n
tape-recorder up on the parapet. Later I discovered that one suc
instrument had been accidentally knocked off and narrowly misse
braining a delegate seated thirty feet below, but then and there
seemed that Cuba was determined that I would see little and unde
stand less. The whole day was taken up with the reading of the *inforn*
central, the 157-page official report to the congress. The reader w;
Vilma Espín, president of the FMC, alternate member of the Poli
buro, member of the Central Committee of the Communist Part
and wife of Raul Castro, Fidel's brother. She read correctly ar
quietly, a calm, matronly figure hard to associate with the slender gi
who had organised the medical support system during the *lucl*
clandestina and joined the guerrilla fighters in the Sierra Maestra.
complained that she was hardly a charismatic speaker. 'She doesn
have to impress us,' answered one of the delegates. 'We know he
She is our Vilma.'

Alongside her, in the front row of the serried ranks of officebeare
on the dais, sat Fidel Castro, quietly reading through the report.
expected him to make some formal rhetorical statement, as befits
totalitarian figurehead, putting in a token appearance for the Ass
ciation of Townswomen's Guilds, before leaving to take care of mo
pressing matters of state. To my surprise, he sat there quietly tl
whole day long, reading, caressing his beard, thinking and listenin;
The next day he was there again. As one of the delegates waxe
eloquent on discrimination against women in the workplace, a man
voice interjected. 'This is the heart of the problem, isn't it? Women
access to work!' I looked about, wondering who owned these mil
slightly high-pitched tones. It was Castro, whom I soon learned to ca
what every Cuban calls him, Compañero Fidel. He was leanin
forward earnestly, intent on participating in the debate, not leadir
but participating. If anything, the discussion became less formal ar
more spontaneous, as delegates held up their hands for recognitic
and described precise problems of access to work. The wome
claimed that they were considered more likely to absent themselv
from work, because of their family responsibilities. Fidel pointed o
that men still refuse to shoulder their part of the burden of housekee
ing and child-rearing as laid down by the Cuban Family Code. Tl
women pointed out that in fact the *ausentismo* of women workers w;
often less than that of men, and certainly no greater. Fidel pointed o
that women shoulder a double duty, which is unequal, and the wome
argued that they were not prepared to give it up. Sometimes when tl

head of state wagged his hand for recognition, the chairperson ignored him. At other times, the delegates noisily disagreed with him, crying, 'No, no!', some even booing.

I had been prepared for the chants of Fidel! Fidel! but nothing had prepared me for this. I thought ruefully of Margaret Thatcher and Indira Gandhi, each incapable of listening, especially to someone who disagreed with her. And all the time Fidel made jokes, selected funny comparisons, continually pressing the delegates to give concrete, living examples. Their carefully prepared statements went all to pieces. We discovered that women did not want men to have the same leave to absent themselves from work for family reasons, because they would abuse it and use the time to visit other women – or at least the delegates thought they might – and thus one of the most fascinating contradictions in Cuban sexual politics was drawn out in a public forum of 1,400 participants.

All afternoon the debate surged on, with Vilma at the helm steadily working through the order paper. And all the next day. When delegates complained that if the day-care centres closed down for any one of a hundred reasons – lack of water, pollution of the water supply, sickness of staff, deterioration of the building, communicable illness – women were called away from hospitals and factories, schools and voluntary work, to take care of their children. Because the day-care centres did not operate on the free Saturdays, which fall every two weeks, women were effectively prevented from undertaking the extra voluntary work that led to distinction and party membership. Fidel noticed that the Minister of Labour and Employment and the Minister of Education had not bothered to attend the Congress. 'They should be hearing this,' he said. 'Watch,' said one of the Cuban journalists. After lunch the chairs on the dais had all been moved up, and lo! the ministers in question had appeared to answer the women's demands. When the Minister for Education complained of lack of trained infant teachers, Fidel reminded him that he was using statistics from the Second Party Congress and up-dated them for him, thus destroying his excuses. Everyone but the ministers, who could fall back only on silly compliments and party slogans, enjoyed it enormously.

When the sessions rose, the women leapt to their feet, waving the coloured nylon georgette scarves and matching plastic flowers they had all brought with them, pounding maracas, bongoes, conga drums and cowbells, clapping their hands and singing fit to bust, *Para trabajar, para estudiar, para defender nuestra libertad! Firmes con Fidel! Firmes con Fidel!* Hips gyrated, scarves flashed, flowers wagged. The syncopated thunder roared round the huge building, sucking the tiredest professional congress-makers out of their offices to watch as the women put on a turn that would have shamed a Welsh football crowd into silence. They were so delighted – with the occasion, with Fidel, but above all with themselves – that I forgot how clumsy some of the women looked in their harsh-coloured and badly-made synthetic suits and the crippling high heels they thought appropriate to the situation. I abandoned my posture of superiority and let myself be impressed.

Each lunchtime, 1,400 women swarmed into the commissaries of the vast building and forty minutes later they swarmed out again into group and regional meetings in preparation for the afternoon sessions. They gave hundreds of interviews for Cuban television, to be used gradually over the ensuing months, for daily papers, for women's magazines, for regional newsletters, for books. The youngest delegate was sixteen, the oldest ninety something. They were ready to work all day and all night if necessary. My questions to Vilma Espín had to wait ten days for answers, but late on a Saturday afternoon I was called to her office, to spend two hours discussing what the questions meant. The written answers and tape-recording of our discussion were delivered to me first thing on Monday morning.

The first evening the delegates were taken to a ballet. They arrived stomping and chanting, sat chatting eagerly about the day's doings, and when the dancing had started and silence was finally imposed, a good proportion of them went straight to sleep, waking up only to applaud wildly. While exhausted *delegadas* slumbered around me, I watched Dionea, a man-eating plant composed of Josefina Menendez and the *cuerpo de baile*, to music by Villa-Lobos, as it ate three male dancers dressed as glittering mothy creatures, with horribly erotic gestures. This was followed by the world *première* of *Palomas*, a ballet choreographed by the Chilean exile Hilda Riveros especially for the 4th Congress of the FMC. The story ran straight down the party line; the dancers mimed birth, the mother mimed ecstatic admiration of her child. She was joined by her mate and mimed ecstatic admiration of him. They simulated spontaneous conjugal relations on the floor. She then went off for her militia training, and mimed something rather like *kung fu* in strict unison with the *cuerpo de baile*. Then she and her fellow soldiers were joined by their mates and mimed heterosexual fulfilment in unison.

The delegates snored through the whole thing but woke up with a start to watch the eighth wonder of the world, Alicia Alonso, sixty years old and virtually blind, dance a *pas de deux* with Jorge Esquivel to music by Chopin. Her line was exquisite, and if once or twice things went slightly wrong, such as when she slid out of a lift and down Jorge Esquivel's nose, so that his eyes streamed with tears, the audience had no intention of feeling, let alone showing, any dissatisfaction. Alicia Alonso came back to Cuba at a time when artists and skilled technicians were leaving in hordes. She promised her people a world-class ballet and she kept her promise. She danced in complete confidence on a stage she could no longer see, borne up less by Esquivel's strong arms than by the love and loyalty that surrounded her.

This was early days, but already I could feel something unfamiliar and very special about Cuba. The absence of theatricality that I noticed in Vilma and Fidel was part of a complex of attitudes. People did not sell themselves as they do in consumer society. Life was not soap opera, but real. There was no competition or character assassination, as people jockeyed for limelight. They spoke not to persuade or bamboozle, but to explain. They had not our prurient interest in domestic and sexual affairs. No one was quite sure how many children Fidel might have had, or, for that matter, Vilma. Public functionaries were assessed on their performance of their public duty, and did not have to drag their bed partners around with them, miming domestic bliss. Life without gossip magazines and advertising seemed wonderfully uncluttered. There was no equivalent of Princess Diana's latest outfit or Elizabeth Taylor's latest wedding or the American president's haemorrhoids. Doubtless there are some Cubans who think life would be more interesting if murder and rape were reported in the newspapers and convicted criminals were paid a working man's earnings over ten years to describe their activities in lurid detail, but most of the people I met know the other culture from glimpses of Miami television and find it crazy and perverse. The slice of American culture they get from Miami includes late-night pornographic videos, which do nothing to improve the US image. Some Cubans, the ones who steal designer jeans off foreigners' clotheslines in Miramar and offer to change pesos for dollars, giving five times the official exchange rate so that they can buy ghetto-blasters in the dollar shops, obviously envy the hyperstimulated lifestyle of capitalism, but all the Cubans I met and talked to were more interested in Ethiopia and Guatemala than in Michael Jackson. A Chilean exile explained to me, 'I could have stayed in West Germany. They were paying me a fortune, but what could I do with it? Invest in the latest parsley cutter? Life is exciting here, even if I have very little money. There is always something to do, and it's exciting. People are creating their own future. If I got sick in Germany I could lie and rot. Here, if I don't show up at the *tienda* for my rations, people are straight round to help.' Her bath was kept permanently full of water to flush the lavatory, for Havana has a chronic and crippling water shortage, just another minor inconvenience that women have to deal with, but it made no dent in Elisabeth's fierce loyalty to Cuba. As we sat on her tiny balcony, drinking *añejo sobre las rocas*, while people flowed in and out of the tiny apartments above, beside and below us, and the old red buses, affectionately known as *guaguas*, groaned and shrieked down the hill, disgorging streams of workers, she said, 'It's a hard life, but a good life.'

The Cubans are involved after all in a much bigger adventure than sex, speed and smack could possibly supply. Their morale is towering, even if their energy should occasionally flag, as they negotiate the daily obstacle course which is life in a poor country, cursed by an irreplaceable investment in a single crop – sugar – and strangled by the American blockade which has cut off the only cheap source of supply for all the goods a single-crop economy does not produce. Every Cuban will tell you that underdevelopment is a feature of minds and hearts as well as economies. As Cubans struggle to develop logistical and communicative skills, they encounter inefficiency and confusion at all levels of social organisation. The response is not irritability and hostility, but tolerance and mutual assistance. Because of rationing, limited supplies of essential commodities and the unreliability of transport (given shortage of vehicles and spare parts), queueing is a way of life, but Cubans do not try to jump queues or stand guard to see that no one else does. Instead they have developed a characteristic solution to an intolerable situation. When you arrive at the *tienda*, to find fifty people already waiting for their ration of rice, beans, oil, crackers, fruit juice or whatever other commodity is on sale that day, you simply ask who is *el último*. When another person arrives, and you are asked the same thing, you are free to go about other business and return when the queue has moved up. People less pressed chat, criticise the authorities, flirt and clown around. When you come back the person who was behind you will call you to your place. This ad hoc system involves co-operation and a degree of awareness of other people, neither often found in rich countries. Even on my last day in Cuba, when I found a hundred people queuing at the hotel cashier's desk, I could hardly prevent myself from panicking, thinking I had no time to pack because I would be queuing for two hours or so (given the mean speed of such transactions in Cuba). However, I tried asking *el último* and went about my other chores, When I came down, the honeymooners behind me waved me to my place, by now only four from the head of the line. As I had screamed and ranted at the hotel management about their inefficiency, while they politely defended a system I condemned as hopeless, I felt truly ashamed.

It may seem that all this has little to do with women and political power in Cuba. In fact, it has everything to do with it. The people meet constant daily frustrations with calm and co-operation because they do not feel that they are the result of corruption, caprice or incompetence on the part of a separate ruling class, but aspects of problems which afflict a 25-year-old nation with a heritage of ignorance, disease and poverty.

The first priority of the Cuban revolution was to combat illiteracy, disease, and malnutrition, thus bringing the Cuban population to a condition in which they could exercise the duties of popular government. Despite the enormous drain of human and other resources in maintaining a convincing defence posture, they have achieved those basic aims, largely by voluntary work undertaken alongside the desperate struggle to make the sugar economy profitable despite falling world prices, and to cope with the effects of the US blockade. My first duty in Cuba was to check the validity of Cuban claims about health and education, so I hired a car and slipped off into the countryside driving through town after small town, checking the *policlinico*, the water supply, the electricity cables, the health status of the inhabitants, the intensity and productivity of the industry and agriculture. I turned up back streets, wandered into sugar mills and factory forecourts, stopped to watch militia training and the volunteer brigades grubbing up garlic and packing tomatoes in boxes. Nobody stared, nobody tried to beg, but people by the roadsides cheerfully accepted lifts. *La guagua esta mal*, was the usual explanation. Everyone I saw was healthy, busy and quietly self-confident. Occasional unpleasantnesses helped me to realise that I was not dreaming. A boarding-school cook, coming back from collecting his daughter who spent the weekend with her psychologist mother and lived with her father during the week, told me he would not let her marry a negro. 'Oh, popi,' said the ten-year-old indulgently, shaking her head at his foolishness. Everyone was interested in the progress that was being made. They explained to me about the difficulties of industrialising sugar production, 'humanising the work' they called it. Questions about plant genetics and animal diseases got intelligent answers, if not from parents then from the children.

In all Cuba's struggles women have been in the front line. During the *lucha clandestina* women organised medical supplies and treatment and taught school in the Sierra Maestra. Fidel has always acknowledged that without the help of women in building up the underground organisation which victualled, supplied and protected the guerrillas in the fifties, they would never have been successful. Celia Sánchez, who was waiting with supplies, petrol and transport for the arrival of the yacht, *Granma,* which brought Fidel back to Cuba in 1956, became his aide in the closing years of the war, and took part in several battles. She chose to work as Secretary to the Council of State when the Revolutionary Government was set up. Every little girl in Cuba grows up with an impressive series of role models, going back more than a hundred years before the revolution: Rosa La Bayamesa, a captain in the war of independence; Paulina Pedrosa and Carolina Rodriguez, supporters of José Martí's revolutionary party in the 1890s; Emilia Rodriguez, leader of the Partido Popular Obrero in the 1920s, and dozens more. The struggle to oust Batista threw up more still, like Lydia Doce and Clodorinda Acosta Ferrais, who were only twenty years old when Batista's police threw their bullet-riddled bodies into the sea. The all-woman Pelotón Mariana Grajales, formed in September 1958 and named after the mother of the *maceo* who led the Revolutionary War of 1868–78, held one of the most exposed positions on the highway between Havana and Santiago de Cuba and was involved in some of the bitterest fighting of the war. Women fought at the Bay of Pigs; Cira García Reyes, leader of the FMC in the region, lost her life there.

On 23 August 1960, the female network which had contributed so much to the rebel effort was officially instituted as the Federation of Cuban Women, the FMC. By spreading out over the countryside, they were to consolidate the revolution by convincing the passive and fearful that they could construct a new society. Peasant women like Nadividad Betancourt Marten led groups of women who travelled from village to village in their regions, politicising women like them-selves. The FMC organised the push for literacy in Cuba, working as volunteer teachers in peasant huts up and down the island, teaching more volunteers who taught others. Women conducted the 'Battle for the Sixth Grade' and when that was won, they went on to help all kinds of people achieve the standard of ninth-grade education.

The US blockade is a disaster which popular endurance and initia-tive have turned into a blessing, for nothing less brutal could have protected Cuba from becoming another impoverished would-be con-sumer nation. The ridiculous attempt to invade, known by the Cubans as the Victoria de Girón and the Americans as the Bay of Pigs débâcle, gave all Cubans a sense of external threat and national heroism. The strangely explosive epidemic of haemorrhagic dengue fever, involving a mutant strain similar to one that is normally found in Asia, which swept through the province of Havana in 1981, produc-ing thousands of cases within a week, was met by mobilising all the mass organisations to isolate cases and run improvised field hospitals in all kinds of public buildings. The hypothesis of germ warfare was obvious, but the Cubans wasted no time in investigating whether it was another gift from the CIA dirty tricks department; they were more interested in their own preparedness and efficiency in overcoming it, as they did. The disease vanished from Cuba as suddenly as it came.

It would be quite wrong to imagine, however, that there was no resistance to the full incorporation of women in the development process. For many people the only notion of the good life was derived from the bourgeois example; moreover, the legacy of the past included male unemployment, especially during the seven months of the year when the cane was not being cut, while women struggled to feed their families by domestic work, by working in the tobacco industry, and by prostitution. Slave women had not been protected from brutalising toil, therefore the right to manual labour was not one that Cuban women were on the whole particularly anxious to win. There had been opposition to the presence of women fighters in the Sierra, but for some reason, perhaps his dependence on Melba Hernández and Celia Sánchez, Fidel insisted on women's full participation in the struggle, in the victory and in the glory. In 1965 he was already defining women's liberation as 'a revolution within the revolution'. It is generally assumed that the authority for the revolutionary Cuban conception of women's role is the writings of Marx and Lenin, against 'the base, mean and infamous denial of rights to women' and inequality of sexes. To be sure, Cuba follows the Russian line on abortion, contraception, neo-malthusianism, women in the workplace, divorce, child care, education and maternity leave. But there are aspects of sexual politics in Cuba that are distinctly Cuban, and owe nothing to the Russian paradigm.

Sexual politics in Cuba are complex. It is not enough to say that the Cuban man is macho or even extremely macho. Chances are that whatever the Cuban male is, his mother has had far more to do with the development of his personality than his father. A joke in a Cuban girls' magazine sums the conundrum up perfectly. 'Your boyfriend is terribly macho,' says one. 'Yes,' simpers the other. 'Aren't I lucky!' Cuban sociology does not express itself in detailed examinations of the psychopathology of everyday life, so it was difficult for a visitor to gain any clear idea of the reality behind the body language of male-female interaction. Officially, Cuba is a totally heterosexual country. There are no homosexual unions, no people living alone, no one-parent families. There are no published figures to illuminate the reality behind this impossibility, just as there are no figures on rape and crimes against women or sex-related offences generally. Certainly, when work is over, the streets of Havana fill with couples, hand in hand, kissing, giggling, wandering through Coppelia (a complex of pavilion and garden covering a whole block and totally given over to the sale and consumption of ice cream) or attending any of the dozens of free amusements that socialism supplies – museums, aquaria, literary *tertulias*, concerts. . . . The situation is complicated by a severe housing shortage, with a typically Cuban solution. People in need of privacy to make love can go to one of several *posadas*, where at very reasonable rates they can hire a room, a bed, and clean sheets by the hour and order food and beverages to the room. Nobody asks questions about the couples, who may be married to each other, married to others, unmarried, engaged or one-hour stands. The only inconvenience is that, as with everything in Cuba, there is a wait, sometimes a three- or four-hour wait. Couples sit in the waiting-room, smoking, necking, chatting, until the next horizontal space becomes free. Anyone who remembers Lenin's scornful dismissal as bourgeois the demand of feminists like Inessa Armand and Alexandra Kollontai for the right of free love will see that, in this matter at least, the Cubans have gone their own way.

The Cubans have accepted that adultery is their national sport. Men boast of it. A man otherwise intelligent, cultivated and reasonable, will tell you that when a pretty girl works for him or near him, he will do his best to get near her and 'be with her' as often as he can, but his attentions to his wife will continue at the same intensity. The implication is that he can satisfy both, and there can be no significant objection to the spreading of so much happiness by his so potent art. The men seem to be totally caught up in this fantasy, which explains why they have the temerity to call unattached women across to their sides as if they were loose puppies. A foreign woman alone in Havana might well interpret the staring and gesturing of men as signs of aggression, hostility and low esteem for women, especially if she is accustomed to the North American or North European version expressed in whistling, cat calls and sexist comments.

Cuba's boast of advances in their progress towards complete equality for women seemed to me invalidated by the overt interference by Cuban men in my freedom to sit in a darkened cinema by myself or stand waiting for the lift in a hotel lobby. However, after a few days I began to realise that male aggression in Cuba was different. If I clearly expressed my displeasure or lack of interest in the proceedings, the men appeared startled and embarrassed and tended to disappear or, indeed, flee. Men told me that Cuban women quite enjoy approaches of this kind and often flirtatiously provoke them, and I did see some evidence for the truth of this claim. Women on the other hand told me that if I had protested, when I was harassed in the cinema, the people sitting around me would have taken my part. One of the men involved might have found himself the victim of a citizens' arrest and eventually subject to up to fifteen years' detention in a work centre. This is a rather different reason for not creating a scene than what prevails in England, where the people around me would most likely dismiss the uproar as evidence of my hysteria and exonerate the man for lack of evidence other than my protest.

It stands to reason that male aggression towards women would be modified by the salutory reflection that any woman may be a salaried officer of the Fuerzas Armadas Revolucionarias. Most women are trained in the militia and actively involved in the public surveillance duties of the Comités para la Defensa de la Revolución. However, male-female relationships in Cuba are different from those I grew up with principally because, like Cuba itself, they are Afro-Latin. The Africans who were shipped to Cuba left behind them intricate family structures in which the relationships of siblings and cross-cousins through the female line were at least as important as patrilineal relationships, and the mother-child relationship possibly the most intense and durable of all human bonds. In the slave society, where men and women were bought and sold like cattle, women were used as brood animals, often fecundated by their owners rather than the men of their choice and prevented from setting up any viable, legitimate family structure. The legacy of this persists in all Afro-American societies where first births are often very early, where the nuptial bond is fragile and mothers and mothers' mothers supply the only stability in the child's experience. Doubtless, feminist chauvinists will sneer at an impression based on two weeks' acquaintance; nevertheless I must say that there seems to me to be less hostility in male-female relations in Cuba than, say, in Northern Europe. Cuban women would agree. They staunchly refuse to entertain a notion of sexual politics which postulates any significant degree of male-female hostility. Even when Compañero Fidel suggests that the greatest obstacle to women's complete equality is the attitude of men to the work traditionally done by women, the women prefer to stress other 'objective' factors. Cuban men, for all their flirtatiousness, seem to like and respect women. One way of interpreting the emphasis on men's strength, 'machismo' as Cubans are themselves ready to call it, is as an attempt to counter-balance the dominance of women in family and kin relations.

It is notable that one of the sources of friction in the day-to-day workings of the friendship between the Cuban cockerel and the Russian bear is the Russians' treatment of women. Almost more important than Marx and Lenin in the genesis of the Cuban revolution is the figure of José Martí, the National Hero of Cuba, a man of high culture and clear and coherent political ideology, who adored women. He died fighting with the Mambi Army in 1895, but his personality permeates Cuba still. When accused of being a Marxist after the attack on the Moncada Barracks in 1952, Fidel claimed that the sole designer of the attack had been José Martí. Martí believed that no cause that women supported could be defeated, and no side could be victorious which did not have the support of women. Martí's feminism was based on a chivalrous ideal of the pure, cultivated, disinterested woman, an ideal drawn from bourgeois notions of women as weaker, nobler and less sexual than men, but which had a special relevance in a society in which women had never been protected from degrading physical toil. His notion of male/female complementarity relied upon an extreme polarity, but he also argued that one source of the brutality of capitalist society was that it suppressed feminine feeling in women *and* in men. He found American feminism erring in its over-emphasis on the same coarse self-seeking that characterised the perversion of the American dream of a free and egalitarian society. If they achieve their aims, he asked, *Dónde estará el aroma de las rosas*? Present-day Martí scholars argued with me earnestly that society needs the feminine qualities, which when pressed they defined as self-abnegation, sensitivity, enthusiasm, 'espírito' and tenderness. *Cuál es la fuerza de la vida su úmica raíz sino el amor de la mujer?*

To Martí's enduring influence, then, we may attribute the emphasis that Cuban feminists lay on feminity. Women who have been trained to kill will be wearing pearlised nail polish and lipstick when they do it. The perennial shortage of acetone in Cuba probably means that the nail polish will be chipped, unless the soldier has had time to go to the beauty parlour, for acetone is supplied to the nation's manicurists. Even the heroines of work, who cut cane, go down the mines and drive huge cranes, are depilated, deodorised and scented. One of the first problems tackled by the FMC was devising a way of supplying Cuban women with the resources for making pretty clothes out of the scanty fabric supplies. Seamstresses and tailors were trained and given the facilities for carrying on trade as licensed artisans in a state scheme. At the FMC Congress, some of the foreign journalists were intrigued that so many women were wearing suits of various styles in a particular shade of kingfisher blue Courtelle. Was it a uniform of some sort, they asked. In fact it was simply that the blue was one of the few vivid shades available, and literally hundreds of women had chosen it.

For a feminist like me who considers that the combination of dazzle with drudgery is one of the most insidious ways in which women in our society are subject to stress, the multiplication of contradictory demands upon the Cuban woman is a cause for concern. Women who are expected to be prepared to kill are also expected to be flower-like; the Mariposa must accompany the Kalashnikov. The brain surgeon, the politburo member and the chief of police must also be ready to sit by their children's beds in hospital, comforting and caring for them, their attention for the moment undivided. The Cuban women are proud that they can handle all this. They see theirs as the force of the flower that in growing towards the light shatters the rock. To Martí's question, *Hay hombres que se cansan, cuando las mujeres no se cansan?* (do men tire when women do not?) they answer *yes*.

As I travelled around the provinces of Havana, Matanzas and Pinar del Rio, alone in a hired car, I talked to dozens of women, hitch-hiking without fear in their own country, to join their parents, their *novios*, their husbands, separated from them by the demands of the revolution. They were shy, but not frightened to talk.

Pilar was typical. She is twenty-three, nearly finished her studies in medicine at the University of Havana. Next will come work in a remote part of the island or *internacionalismo*. She had hitched a ride with me to visit her husband, studying a hundred kilometres away at the University of Matanzas. When I suggested that so much separation now and a prospect of indefinite separation to come was a bit hard on a marriage, she said, 'We can handle it. We were sweethearts for eight years, and it was always like this.' I pushed a little harder, saying how hard it was to give men the attention they demanded after a week's hard work. She grinned and I noticed how pale she was and how white her gums. 'Sometimes, I've been in the operating theatre all night and I have to grab my bag and get out here on the road. I haven't time to wait for the *guagua* and it's always so crowded, I just can't face the trip standing up.' I probably should have concentrated on the pot-holes and let her go to sleep, but instead I asked if she might not have been anaemic. She seemed slightly startled by the thought. 'Possibly. I've got an IUD.' She knitted her brows. Cuban girls can be fitted with IUDs on demand if they are sixteen or over. Pills, some made from steroids derived from locally-grown hennequin (sisal) are also available, and there is a move to switch. IUDs in a young population are always problematic, but absolutely no publicity is given to such matters in Cuba. Juvenile pregnancy is such a pressing problem that the emphasis is all on prevention.

We talked about housework. 'A man wants a wife, doesn't he? Not a maid,' she said stoutly. I got to know other women like her, hard-working party members, serious and committed in everything, including their sexual relationships. As I watched her walking towards her husband's dormitory over the burnt grass, I hoped she would find his room clean and his clothes washed when she got there. The older women told me, 'Oh no. If she wanted to be at all comfortable, she would have had to set to and clean him up.' The young women said, 'Of course,' but it sounded more like ideology than fact. As she walked away, I called out, 'Take care of yourself!' She gave me a white smile, and a slightly ironic shrug.

It would be perfectly possible to argue that Fidel Castro's revolution exploits women. Socialist revolution exploits everybody. 'From each according to his capacity, to each according to his need.' Every ounce of courage, patience, energy, determination and intelligence is needed if Cuba is to realise her own aims.

The burden ought to fall on men and women impartially. In addition to their salaried and professional work, men and women both undertake voluntary work in the service of the revolution. Men and women are involved in the constant watch kept in Cuban streets by day and night, so that the Cuban people can be mobilised from the street up in the event of an attempted insurrection or invasion or an epidemic, and, as a by-product, crime has disappeared off their streets. Men and women volunteer to clean the streets and plant public gardens in their free time; on a Sunday morning in every town in Cuba, you may see gangs of women, gangs of men, and mixed gangs sweeping away leaves, burning waste paper, hauling trash. Such voluntary work is particularly onerous for women because in addition to their paid work, they are also working unpaid in the home. As the level of general culture and the standard of living has risen, the amount of housework to be done has increased exponentially. Cubans are fanatically clean. When it became possible to wash garments every time they were worn, because water, soap and garments were all present in sufficient supply, all Cuban garments were so washed. The traditional Cuban diet involves a good deal of preparation and long cooking, as well as the hours of waiting at the *tienda* for the monotonous supplies. The state helps by providing meals at the place of work, and in schools and day-care centres, where pre-school children stay from seven to seven pm and eat two full meals and two snacks. Working women carry a card which enables them to go to the front of the food queue, not because they deserve some free time but to make it possible for them to cram all the duties expected of them into the inelastic 24-hour day.

There is very little time left over for even more voluntary work in the grass roots organisation of the *Poder Popular*, the ultimate legislative power in Cuba, even if we do not take into account the time and money the Cuban woman must spend on her other duty of keeping pretty and attractive. It is the more remarkable then that two million members of the FMC voted to be allowed to train with the *Milicia de las Tropas Territoriales*, the volunteer home guard, who train one Sunday a month. Women's record as *cumplidoras*, with full attendance at work and invariably fulfilled production quotas is consistently higher than men's. And yet at the first sign of *fiesta*, the Cuban woman is ready to stick a frangipani behind her ear and rhumba the night away. Even the Cuban sugar allowance, four pounds of sugar per person per month, could not generate this kind of energy in a disaffected population, although it clearly goes some way to causing a serious health problem of massive obesity, especially in women over forty.

Those people who ask, 'But in Cuba are men relinquishing political power so that women can take it up?' are projecting a curiously corrupt notion of political power on to the post-revolutionary process in Cuba. Revolutionary socialists are involved in re-making political power in such a way that it is genuinely wielded by the masses. While enemies of the revolution may persist in believing that power is still concentrated in the hands of an oligarchy, the people themselves are working hard to create the administrative structures which will promote the expression of the collective will and translate it into state policy.

Outsiders may assume that Cuba is actually a dictatorship masquerading as a democratic republic and that real power is vested in the politburo or the Central Committee of the Communist Party; such in fact is not the case. In 1976, Cubans voted in a referendum to accept a socialist constitution which enunciated the principle by which the popular assemblies became the ultimate legislative power in the land. Those of us accustomed to seeing democratic processes subverted by lobbying, patronage and secret government would assume that the huge machinery of *Poder Popular* could do little but rubber-stamp legislation originating in the inner recesses of the Communist Party. In fact, the grass-roots-level assemblies do originate the legislative process, follow it through and participate actively in the drafting of legislation. For such a cumbersome system to work, the enthusiastic participation of large numbers of people for frequent and long sessions is indispensable, yet the system has produced the new housing law in Cuba, which has less to do with socialist ideology than the pragmatic expression of the people's will. Rather than nationalise housing, the Cubans have chosen to own their own homes, amid a multitude of special considerations regarding leasing, letting, inheritance, all designed to protect the right to own one's home and prevent speculation or profiteering.

Democratic centralism, if earnestly undertaken, is the system which produces the least return for the most massive expenditure of human resources. Frequent long meetings, with the intervening struggle to study unfamiliar matters, such as housing law, contract, equity, conveyancing, and alternative administrative systems, as in the case of the 1985 Ley de las Viviendas, must arrive at unanimity, much as juries do, by long argument and counter-argument. The amateur legislators – for only the full-time functionaries are paid – must struggle to keep the process under control, agreeing agendas and then following them through. The process demands what Cuban women have least of – time – yet, even so, 27 per cent of delegates in *Poder Popular* are women. This is more significant than the presence of women on the Central Committee of the Communist Party; nevertheless of 119 members and 71 alternates, 27 are women, 17 of them full members. Women formed 22 per cent of the delegates at the Second Party Congress, which elected them, an increase of 50 per cent over the First Party Conference. The Third Party Congress this year will probably be attended by a high proportion of women and elect more female members of the Central Committee.

If we look at the profile of women's participation in leadership activities, contradictory trends emerge. From their first participation in the youth movement of the José Martí Young Pioneers we will see that little girls are 50 per cent of the members and 66.3 per cent of the troupe leaders. In the Federacion de los Estudiantes de las Escuelas Medias, women are 57 per cent of the membership and 61 per cent of the leadership, while at university level they are 59 per cent of the student enrolment but only 48 per cent of the leadership. Thus, as women become numerically dominant in the rank and file, they are outnumbered in the leadership. Women are only 41 per cent of the Young Communists, the highly selective organisation and training ground for future members of the Communist Party of Cuba. The disparities can be understood in two ways: the increasing proportion of female leaders in the younger age groups may reflect a general tendency to increasing female participation in the future; the troupe leaders among the Young Pioneers may continue as leaders until they find themselves on the Central Committee of the CPC. (In December 1984 the FEEM elected a national committee composed of six women and three men with women for president and vice-president.) The negative interpretation of the same data leads to the conclusion that as little girls approach puberty their ascendancy over the boys, who develop social and communicative skills more slowly, disappears, to be replaced by passivity and participation only in an ancillary capacity, in proportion as they become aware of and involved in sexual activity.

The price Cuban women pay for teenage sexual activity is very high: analysis of statistics supplied in the Anuario Estadístico de Cuba (1981) shows that not only were nearly 52,000 of the nations 187,500-odd births in 1976 to mothers aged between fifteen and nineteen, a further 10,000 of the total were unaccounted for, probably to mothers below the age of fifteen, the only category not specifically mentioned. Abortions have settled at about 100,000 per year, and about a quarter of them are carried out on women under nineteen; more than 400,000 girls of less than nineteen years old are already married, accounting for the largest proportion of divorces, currently running at about 3.2 per thousand per year, while marriages stand at about 13 per thousand. Of the nation's 3,371,000 women over fifteen, about 1,400,000 are legally married, while half as many are living in informal unions. Of Cuba's 575,000 or so girls under nineteen, 52,000 are already legally married, while 87,000 are living with a man, and a further 25,000 describe themselves as divorced or separated. The data are incomplete, but they point to a situation in which young women find themselves with domestic and family responsibilities just at the time when they should be gaining professional experience and qualifications. To the problems of evolving sexuality and the contradictoriness of the female role as both active comrade and sex object, are added the divided attention of the young mother and the unavoidable drain upon her time and energy. The state gives all the help that legislation can provide, with free birth control, free abortion on demand, and free day-care facilities, but it cannot alter the emotional reality of juvenile marriage, parenthood and divorce and the young women's own attitudes towards them. Babies are accepted in day care from forty-five days old, but mothers are not and should not be constrained to give them up for twelve hours a day, an impossibility in any case if they wish to breast feed.

It must not be thought that it has taken an outsider to detect the series of interlocking factors militating against women's full incorporation in the development of the Cuban state. The FMC is a high-relief organisation, with vociferous representation at all levels of local, provincial and state administration. Las federadas are known throughout the country, and although their demands may cause consternation, as does their present campaign to allow husbands to be granted leave from work to accompany sick children in hospital, it is understood that they will eventually have to be met. Cuba's commitment to the full social, political and economic equality of women is a fundamental aspect of Cuban socialism. Insofar as the system is not one of draconian imposition but of pragmatic accommodation of the people's will and transformation of social realities at a pace with which the ordinary people who are the ultimate cause and purpose of the revolutionary process can keep up, women's full emergence into political life depends upon their own redefinition of their life aims with a consequent alteration of the psychopathology of everyday life. Put in the simplest terms, this means that women will have to demand more of men.

There are some indications that the young Communists are leading the way in this. In sex education discussion groups involving both sexes it is generally agreed that emotional relationships should be built on a more intimate and committed basis. Cuban feminists have begun to reject the idea that men should help with women's work, and have begun to demand sharing all aspects of family building, involving men much more in the activities of parenting than has traditionally been the case. It is understood that progress towards women's equality is a struggle against entrenched attitudes and obsolete but enduring concepts of appropriate sex roles. An older Cuban man may tell you that he accepts the idea of his responsibility towards his children and their mother or mothers, and yet give curiously vague answers to direct inquiries about how often he sees his children and how much time he spends with them. He may tell you that his wife accepts his absenteeism and his sporting attitude to extra-marital conquests, but it is unlikely that his wife will agree with him. The *delegadas* stoutly maintain that as women have economic independence they no longer have to tolerate humiliation and would reject any husband whose infidelity was discovered, but their anxiety about male fickleness could not be concealed. When I argued that male adultery was impossible without serious flaws in female solidarity, they refused to see the point. They would not agree either that if women were really monogamous, men would be unable to find partners for adultery or that men's promiscuity was anything but 'natural'. *El es hombre* is the sexist explanation they give for male perfidy. They could not see that women's vulnerability to men's infidelity was an aspect of sexual colonialism. The Cuban woman has all her emotional eggs in one basket; she is psychic one-crop economy, direly threatened by male sanctions, in particular the withdrawal of affection and intimacy, but the suggestion that she protect herself by cultivating other kinds of emotional satisfaction and other sources of esteem was not taken. There was very little emphasis placed by the FMC on sisterhood. No one ever discussed the single woman, a rare creature in Cuba in any event.

There is an inherent contradiction in Cuba between the socialist ideals of the revolution and the bourgeois paradigm of the nuclear family, which is what most Cubans take as the basic unit of the modern state. In the nuclear family the child is confronted by only two adults contrasted by sex. The tendency towards polarisation is unavoidable. The duplication of effort in the nuclear family is directly connected to the family's role as the principal unit of consumption in consumer society. Each household is destined to acquire a complete set of all the consumer durables considered necessary for the good life, and *per capita* consumption is therefore maintained at its highest level. In sex as in consumption the nuclear family emphasises possession and exclusivity at the expense of the kinds of emotional relationships that work for co-operation and solidarity. Even the best-educated Cubans seem unaware of the arguments of Marx and Engels against monogamy. They regret the instability of marriage, and work towards enculturating young people to delay the formation of exclusive sexual partnerships until they should be mature enough to undertake long-term commitment, when perhaps they ought to be spending more time reducing the psychic damage done to young people, young women especially, by the breakdown of these early relationships, so that they are less vulnerable in future. One of the heroines of the revolution, Haydee Santamaria, killed herself after her husband began a public affair with a younger, more glamorous woman. Although she was the founder of the Casa de las Americas, and widely respected throughout Latin America, she could not recover from this blow to her self-esteem, yet Cuban feminism shows no signs of any attempt to reduce women's psychic dependence upon their success in heterosexual relationships by strengthening cameraderie among women or teaching them that in order to live with men they must learn to live without them. As the standard of living rises women's work increases and their dependence upon the sexual relationship with their husbands will increase as households diminish in size.

There are difficult days ahead for the Cuban woman, but as long as the ideology of revolution is lively and sincere, ways will be devised to deal with the new stresses. In the meantime Cuba remains the only country in the world where women may take any job they wish to do at the same rate of pay as a man, earn any qualification they are prepared to study for, carry their own weapons in the army and rise to the rank of colonel, dress as they please and accept or refuse men's attentions as they please, terminate or continue a pregnancy as they think fit, knowing that they will have help to carry out whichever course they should decide to follow.

Perhaps the true extent of women's power in Cuba is best illustrated not by quoting numbers on the central committee, but in a homely example which shows how important women are to Cuba. Every sexually active woman in Cuba at risk of contracting cervical cancer is given her smear test every six months. Every year hundreds of women's lives are saved by prompt treatment, while in England, Equal Opportunities Commission or no, women are dying because they have not had their smears, because they did not have them often enough, and because they were not informed when the cells were seen to be abnormal. The British health service could not cope with the demand if all the women who should asked for smear tests and presented themselves for further treatment. Yet little Cuba manages it. Follow-up and recall are carried out at street level by the FMC and the Committee for the Defence of the Revolution, while the state institutions supply the technical facilities. This may not be evidence of power as it is commonly perceived by capitalist societies, but access to the technology in order to save your own life is the kind of power women want. It is real power, unlike the authoritarian fantasies that pass for power in most of the world. And the women of Cuba struggled for it, defined it and exercise it on their own behalf. It remains to be seen now whether Cuban women will raise their own standard in the world forum and show the other emergent nations how to harness the strength and tenderness of women in the remaking of our tired and guilty world. As Cuba's leaders have always realised, survival is too desperate a matter to be left to half the world's population. We need to see Federations of Women of every nationality mobilising in the streets of every city, town and village in the world, *para trabajar, para estudiar, para construir nuestra libertad!*

Germaine Greer was born in Melbourne, Australia, and studied at Melbourne and Sydney Universities in Australia, and at Cambridge University in England, where she wrote her doctoral thesis on Shakespeare. She became a university teacher, but after the publication of *The Female Eunuch* in 1970, a book which was enormously influential in the debate about women's roles in sex, love, and society, she increasingly moved to writing rather than teaching. She has written *The Obstacle Race*, a study of women painters, and most recently, in 1984, published *Sex and Destiny*, a challenging study of the politics of human fertility. Dr Greer has lived in England since 1964, as a full-time writer and broadcaster.

SEX

There are few societies in the world where women's enjoyment of sex is encouraged and expected. Men's almost universal control of sex – by tradition and religion – means that, for the vast majority of women, the experience of intercourse is at best inhibited, at worst filled with guilt and pain, fear and shame.

From Mexico, Elena Poniatowska travels to Australia, to Adelaide, Melbourne and Sydney, basking in the aftermath of the sexual revolution. Here pornography, the pill and exotic sex aids are available in every town. But beneath this façade of freedom runs an undercurrent of dissatisfaction. Brothels, rape crisis centres, incest survivor organisations, refuges for battered wives, show that the sexual revolution has not necessarily been good for women.

From the Unites States, Angela Davis travels to Egypt, to the bustle of Cairo and the quiet of sand-baked villages. Here a woman's virginity is so highly prized that – until recently – most young girls had their clitoris removed to prevent them from enjoying sex. Here many women must cover their bodies in a veil when they venture out of the house, and sex with a husband is sex with the stranger chosen by their parents, who moves in a completely separate world and only comes home to eat and to sleep.

SEX – AUSTRALIA

Elena Poniatowska

– So how is it?
– Oh, it's okay.
– Do you like making love?
– Yeah, it's okay.
– But why do you do it if it isn't great, wonderful, marvellous?
The four of them look at me from behind their cigarette smoke. I must be some kind of exalted 'oldie'.
– Why do you do it?
– I dunno, the tallest one says.
– I dunno, answer the others.
– You don't know?
– Dunno, dunno, dunno, dunno.
Four teenagers are sitting around the table in a house in Melbourne, like those you see in magazines, those that have a kettle and a rocking chair. It's home sweet home after all. The four girls look fresh and clean in their light sleeveless dresses, pink, white, blue. They're wearing bows in their hair, and fringes, and they have soft giggling voices. One of them, Kathy, has just come in from a dancing class and has already devoured a carton of vanilla ice cream, two slices of ham, potato salad from a Tupperware container, a glass of chocolate milk, a tomato the size of an apple, and now she's sipping on a Coke and stuffing dry-roasted peanuts into her mouth. These she passes round. It's her house after all, she can offer me what she wants. She lives here with her oldest sister, Sheila, and her father, who is divorced. The other three, Gail, Joyce and Gwen, are just friends but their parents are also divorced (in Australia, two out of three marriages end in divorce). Kathy and Sheila have chosen to stay with their father because, as Kathy says, 'He has the house. My mother wanted us kids to be together. She remarried and moved to a flat. I've got a stepsister now. My father hasn't married again. He cooks dinner when he gets home from work. Other times we just go to the fridge. It's always full. No, we're not lonely, not even my kid sister – she's nine – she stays with the neighbours most of the time. We all go out sort of in groups.'
– And what do you do when you go out?
All four giggle in chorus.
– Oh, movies, dances, picnics, parties, discos, tennis (along with cricket, it is the national sport), beaches, surfing. We watch

television, drink Coke, or beers for the boys, eat hamburgers and
lollies.

Lollies. Other voices resound in my ears on hearing this word
Susan White only allows her children one lolly each a week, on
Sundays. There's only healthy, near-vegetarian food, fresh from her
garden, on her table. No salt and pepper. No sweets but for the
Sunday lolly. No television. Like many other Australians, the
Whites are self-righteous, living on a low income, and with the same
concern they apply to their food, they opt for a vasectomy. ('For
George, it meant only being away from work half a day
Sterilisation would have meant two days in the hospital for me and
no one to take care of the children.') George has always helped
Susan with the housework and the cooking. When their son
Charlie, was born and yelled all night long because he was a difficult
baby, George would take him into the living-room so Susan could
sleep. Never a quarrel. Never a harsh word between them. They
work together in the office of a local charity. They have a terrific sex
life that gets better year after year and George is only too sorry
Susan is not prepared to make love all the many times he would like

Punctuality, keeping fit and glowing, bright and beautiful, is their
way of life. 'We are people who do what we like and know what we
are doing.' For me, someone forever making mistakes, arriving late
and not being too sure what tomorrow will bring, this efficiency has
an element of terror. 'My children,' Susan says proudly, 'have never
been into McDonald's.'

McDonald's are sprinkled like salt throughout Melbourne
Sydney and Adelaide. Kentucky Fried Chicken is nearly as popular
On the whole, Australia seems to be a mixture of England and the
United States. They drink tea and turn out to welcome the *Queen
Elizabeth* when it sails into Adelaide harbour, but the spirit of
enterprise and big business ethic is entirely American. In Australia
sex does not seem to be an activity, an urge, a desire, not even an
organ (Mexicans call their penis '*mi sexo*', '*mi animal*', it's the best
thing they possess, what they value the most), but rather a
glamorous, money-making business. In fact, Australia is one big
commercial set-up where, in one way or another, everything is
stored, sold, or disposed of. People have to have a purpose in life
'What do you do for a living?' I am asked. But nobody asks me
'Are you happy?' or 'Do you enjoy life?' Money talks and the élite
are those who earn and save it.

The four girls prefer giggling to answering my questions. They
look at each other. Who's going to speak first? Then they talk about
steady boyfriends as if the word 'steady' were something to look

forward to. Joyce covers her mouth with her hand as she explains that the best time in life is when their parents are away, Kathy and Sheila's father or Gail's or Gwen's, because they can take over the house, there is a bedroom for everyone in the gang – beds, and not the back seat of a car or drive-ins – and from there they can go down for a swim in the river which is nearer than the sea.

The fridge (the fridge is God in Australia) is continually at their mercy. It gives them everything they want, from beer to cheese-cake. The boys play cards, smoke, spread themselves everywhere, watch television, turn the stereo on loud. The girls play mother: they cook, they even bake cakes and wash and clean up after the boys. They mimic traditional parental behaviour and follow the pattern of a patriarchal society. All the girls I interviewed made love for the first time in their parents' homes. Mum was out. Dad was out. (Parents generally travel a lot in Australia: to Honolulu, Hawaii, Oakland, New Zealand, Borneo, Indonesia, the beaches and jungle of New Guinea.) Kathy and Sheila told their mother and she immediately put them on the pill. 'If my parents hadn't separated,' Kathy says, 'I wouldn't have got to know them as individuals. Dad is pretty conservative. He knows I'm on the pill but we've never spoken about it.' 'I have sex,' boasts Joyce. 'I'm seventeen. I spoke to Mum beforehand. She's not the big bad wolf, she has a life of her own, she understands. The pill has been great. Before I used to have a lot of trouble with my periods and that's all gone now, the pains, the headaches. I like the pill, it works.' 'Oh no,' Gail says to another of my questions, 'boys don't use any kind of contraception. They leave it to us. If I weren't on the pill, the boy I'm going out with would probably use a condom, but since he knows I'm on it there's nothing to worry about. The pill's very safe.'

Australia has the highest usage rate of the pill and the mini-pill in the world. In Mexico, women keep such things to themselves. Girls never say they are menstruating and if they do, they find other ways of saying it, like 'the little donkey knocked me over', 'I'm riding on horseback', 'my aunt is visiting', 'the painter came', 'I'm carrying a red flag', 'I'm a little sick', 'I'm indisposed', 'it's that time of the month', and other vague explanations.

'I got my period when I was eleven,' one of the girls says. 'Gee, God, poor you,' the others exclaim, laughing. 'But most of my friends had it later. I used to get very sick before my period. I'd be in tears, in absolute agony. The pill is great. We all knew all about menstruation.' Yet the Melbourne newspaper *The Age* shows in a survey that 24 per cent of girls thought menstruation rid the body of wastes, that you shouldn't take a shower or wash your hair while menstruating. Kathy says her period never stops her swimming. 'Exercise helps it. The more you exercise, the lighter your period is. I put in a tampon and do everything I usually do – tennis, basketball, dancing lessons, swimming, hiking, everything.' Gwen says: 'I don't like working when I have my period because I feel weak in the knees. I do part-time child-minding. Forty little children. I hug them and change their nappies. We're all paid 5 dollars an hour. We get 220 dollars a week, 1000 a month.'

I nearly pass out. In Mexico, 75,000 women workers in factories, in Ciudad Juarez, very near the border with the United States, earn 816 pesetas a day, exactly 4 dollars, less than in Singapore and Taiwan where cheap labour is the rule. Kathy, Gail, Joyce and Gwen express little interest in studying. Their school grades were low and the kind of work their boyfriends do ('mine cleans swimming pools', 'mine works in a pet shop') is not at all specialised. Their own jobs require no particular skills either. They certainly do not need a university degree. And yet they earn huge sums of money. *Girls for Trades for Girls* advertise watchmaking, welding, printing, retail butchery, radio mechanics, bricklaying, auto-electrics, wood machining, optical mechanics, scientific instrument making, upholstery, jewellery, and so on. Practical skills are in demand. These girls receive in a month what Mexican women workers do not earn in a year. Perhaps the Mexicans have no schooling, but Kathy, Gail, Joyce and Gwen are no longer at school nor do they have any intention of going back. Still, they are very assertive about themselves.'Oh, yes, you should have sex before marriage,' says Kathy. 'It would keep down the divorce rate. I know exactly what I'm doing with my sex life,' says little Gwen, and the others nod their heads in agreement.'To have sex is my choice, of course. Everyone else is having it, so you feel lost if you're not. I wouldn't like to be secretive about it. I'd feel bad if I couldn't talk to others about it. Before I'd say I was having sex even if it wasn't true, so the gang wouldn't make fun of me.'

According to New South Wales's Family Planning Association, by the age of sixteen, 50 per cent of girls have had sexual intercourse, usually without any kind of protection. And according to an article written by a medical correspondent, Barry Hailstone, in Adelaide's *The Advertiser*, about 50 per cent of teenagers become sexually active by the end of high school and of these possibly as few as 10 per cent use some form of birth control. Sarah McCarthy, a doctor's wife who is now in her seventies, says that Australia is a very contradictory country.'It's crazy. For instance, girls believe that if they have intercourse standing up they won't get pregnant or if they only do it once nothing will happen. They have never ever heard about the hymen. Sex in my time was taboo. My mother would never talk about menstruation and there was no disposable stuff at all then. She would just say: "Don't worry about it. It's bad blood going away, don't worry about it." But all this sexual education is not true. There are many unwanted pregnancies because there are all kinds of funny theories and stupid ideas, a tremendous amount of ignorance. In my time girls were afraid of getting pregnant. Now, there are many things they can use. Even if they are not, girls say they are having sex, so their contemporaries won't look down on them. There is a lot of pressure from radio and television and magazines on sex; it's so silly the way they carry on. All this contraception doesn't really work. Why would there be so many single mothers if it worked?'

The four girls from Melbourne whom I interviewed were the stable ones. We never brought up the topic of abortion, rape, incest or sexual assault. They said they would love kids 'later on'. And with respect to lesbianism, they felt it was okay as long as lesbians 'keep to themselves'. It wasn't for them, that was for sure.

In Sydney, girls might start having sex even younger than in Adelaide or Melbourne, but they are a lot tougher. They wear baggy clothes called 'survival fashion' and they have punk haircuts. Two of them, Ginny and Tania, have had their heads shaved except for the top part which sticks out like a rooster. The other girl, Barbara, has her hair short on one side and long on the other. They're all wearing black T-shirts. One says 'Cocaine' and another shows the mushroom of Hiroshima's atomic bomb. In Mexico, we are not conscious of the atomic bomb because we have no nuclear power. It is one of the few advantages of being a Third World country. Here in Australia, as in the United States and Europe, especially West Germany, young people's lives are tainted by the belief that everything will be reduced to ashes. So they start carrying their chains and death's heads before it happens. The three girls were beautiful and tough and looked down on me. There was no giggling this time. They hardly even smiled.

Tania fills the silence with her humming and I jump on the opportunity and ask her about rock. She lists the groups she likes methodically: Duran Duran, Mental As Anything, Midnight Oil, Australian Crawl, Little River Band (because of a spot between Melbourne and Geelond called Little River Creek), The Eurogliders, Red Gum (an Australian gumtree, red is the ideology), The Honey Drippers and 10cc (the average amount of sperm in male ejaculation).

Besides being lovers of rock, heavy metal and that kind of thing, these three are surf fanatics. The topic brings a broad smile to Barbara's face. Surfing for them is sacred. Is sex too? No, sex is for fun. Sex is whatever the surfers want it to be. They describe surfing to me and later I have a chance to see it for myself. It seems a purely sexual act, the surfer cutting back into the wave towards the beach after having gone deep into the sea. In Sydney, boys surf from early morning to late evening. Surfing is not a woman's sport, but surfers are. A girl waits on the beach and keeps her eyes pinned to the small black spot way out there, her boyfriend on his surf board. He has taken his board out as far as the open sea (the board is looked after with much greater care than is the girlfriend) and now waits for the freezing water to rise. Then, astride the tallest wave, he comes riding in on the crest, sustained at this peak of pleasure, taking the utmost care not to slip, coming in and in on this semen-white foam that eventually dies as it hits the sandy beach. He has penetrated the wave with his board, he has flown on top of the great marine womb, he has cut through it like a peasant cuts through the earth with his plough. Above all, he has run the risk of being swallowed by the ocean – for many have been – and instead has conquered it in a dazzling feat of skill.

All this time, the girls have awaited their heroes, their Ulysses, and while waiting, they have embarked upon their own odyssey. This voyage, more often than not, involves drugs. However, the surfers themselves frequently take drugs so as to find the courage to cast their boards out into the ocean and keep them there. It involves a great deal of courage, endurance and ability to stay on the board, up there on a nine-foot wave. Marijuana helps, provides an initial stimulus, but when that is not enough, some go as far as heroin.

Under a blue Sydney sky, the girls speak openly of dope, unwanted pregnancies, abortions and single mothers putting their children up for adoption, although few Australians do this anymore. Barbara even knew where Mexico was. 'I drink tequila, that's why.' At some point in the conversation there was a discussion between Ginny and Tania about the 'hole'. 'It's called the anus.' 'No, stupid, it's not the anus, that's the ass hole. It's the uterus.' 'You don't know what you're talking about,' Barbara says. 'It's the cervix.' I listen to all this somewhat stunned. Sarah McCarthy was right. What a contradictory mixture: dope, tequila, abortion – and ignorance of anatomy, not a clue. Nor of geography for that matter. The most they know about Mexico is that tequila is good and marijuana is to be found everywhere: 'Plenty of fields covered with dope, whole plantations of the stuff.'

The first sexual revolution in the world? Women far more liberated than others, especially we Latins? Oh yes, I would like to take all Mexican women over there. Australian women have gained sexual independence and assertiveness because of contraception, they have gained economic independence because they know how to work (in 1980, 42 per cent of married women worked and were not ready to be kicked out of their jobs and forced back into the kitchen). Still, Australia is a large consumer of tranquillisers and the number of women with mental disorders such as depression is higher than that of men. Valium, Triptanol and Tofranil are several anti-depressants prescribed with great frequency. In a chapter of her well-known *Damned Whores and God's Police*, Anne Summers talks about the number of suicides by women who take large doses of barbiturates and pills prescribed by doctors. Mary Leunig, who was born in Melbourne in 1950 and who has had her pictures (as she calls her very wonderful drawings) published in *Nation Review* and then compiled into a book, *There's No Place Like Home*, draws in anguish and with a desperate sense of humour. In *There's No Place Like Home*, women's dissatisfaction leads to madness. The universe beckons the housewife to get out of the house and the doormat on the floor says 'Go Away'. Girls who start their sex lives as early as twelve rarely end them at eighty-three, as many sex therapists propose. On the contrary, an account shows that many beach girls turn into unmarried mothers, nervous wrecks, heroin addicts. I don't wish to sound like a moralist, but Eros and Thanatos are opposite sides of the same coin and if orgasm is a 'little death' as we say in Mexico, the big death is always waiting on the street corner.

Women who have chosen to do what they want seem to be very hard not only on their children but also on themselves and without ever realising it. They are so intent on building up their new personality that they unwittingly reveal their tension about that new self.'Life doesn't revolve around my children. They don't need minding all the time. I'll do what I want to do first and then worry about the kids. Sacrificing means you can't live the kind of life you want.' Geraldine Matthews, one of my contacts, has two daughters. They are slim, pale adolescents who look much younger than their age. The eldest, who is already fifteen, looks eleven in her little yellow shorts and pony-tail, with her thin thighs and lips; she speaks as little as possible, doesn't want to bother anyone and never raises her eyes. The second one is also silent. I ask Geraldine if they have already started to menstruate and she answers: 'Oh, sure. I showed the oldest one how to put a tampon in by putting one in myself in front of her.'

– A tampon? Straight up like that?

– Of course.

– But what if she loses her virginity?

She looks at me with absolute contempt.

– Who cares? I couldn't give a damn about her virginity.

– And what will happen when a boy – ?

She interrupts me impatiently; she is, in fact, always impatient most women are in Australia:

– What about the boy? To hell with the boy. It's his problem. No one gives a damn about a thing like that anymore. On the contrary, the quicker she loses it the better.

For me – a Latin – this was hard to swallow. I come from a country where the idea of virginity is the rule, not the exception. The Virgin of Guadalupe appeared before an Indian, Juan Diego (in Australia, he would be an aborigine), and all the girls are told that they should be virgins like Our Mother of Guadalupe, who is more highly revered by Mexicans than the best football player or the most famous television entertainer. 'Protect your integrity', girls are taught at school. Virginity is lost in marriage when most men exert their violence as is expected of 'machos'. In Oaxaca and Juchitan, the stained sheets are taken out to the window for all the village to see.

In Australia the hymen is a nuisance, like tonsils and appendix. Everyone's attention centres on the clitoris. Dr Elsie Koadlow, who treats patients with psychosexual marital difficulties at the Queen Victoria Hospital, talks freely about coital response, lubrication and swelling, followed by orgasm, vaginal dilation by inserting fingers during love-making, fears about absent clitorises and longing for vaginal orgasm. Vaginal stimulation and the Grafenberg Spot – a sensitive area on the front wall of the vagina which causes a deeper orgasm than the clitoral one – are often mentioned by sex therapists. Dr Elsie Koadlow teaches and encourages women to explore their vaginas, to know their genitals and, most of all, to insert vaginal tampons.'What do you use? Pads or tampons? If only the former, have you ever considered inserting the latter?' She believes the doctor's role should also be an educational one and that practitioners and gynaecologists should invest time and experience in sexual counselling, because patients sometimes have such strong anxieties about sexuality that they become overwhelmed and deny all erotic feelings. To accept manual erotic stimulation in marital cases is a gain, but Dr Koadlow does not advise mechanical aides ke vibrators: 'To encourage a girl to use mechanical aids will only ncourage her to further denigrate her husband's role.'

Jeraldine Matthews is probably the contact with whom I spend most ime. She is quick, competent, competitive, sure of herself, a very ood tennis player, and in her conversation she keeps hitting verbal ennis balls into my face. Her backhand drive is especially good and ve play about 227 sets. She believes she has made the right choices nd tells me: 'I'm a worthwhile person.' She is proud of her university career, started after her dull marriage.'For me going to university and getting my degree was very important. I did it after ny girls were born and would never give it up, not even for them, ot for anything.' In fact, now she is looking for someone who will ake charge of them for six months while she goes to Indonesia to do esearch. She has learnt Indonesian at the university and on a recent rip to Borneo. As she sees the dismay on my face, she adds: 'Once ny girls get settled anyway, I probably won't see them more than once or twice a year.'

In Mexico, numerous families meet at least once a week, usually on Sundays, and they all sit down to eat at a huge table. Grannies ook after grandsons and granddaughters. There is always an aunt, a sister, a cousin, to watch over the children, and even in the poorest amilies adults accept responsibility for infants who are not always heir relatives. Poor Mexicans are very quick at picking up stray dogs and children, even if they live a 'dog's life'. Where two people eat five can also get a tortilla. So women always have children hanging around their necks or pulling at their skirts. In that aspect, Australian women's loneliness is sad. Alone with her children, Geraldine has no one to fall back on. Even married women usually have only their husbands or their neighbours to ask for help. In new societies like Australia, there is no tradition of big family groups, and mothers without family support can become very isolated. Bringing up children by themselves without much contact with other women is very hard, and there is a severe shortage of day-care facilities.

Geraldine chooses her career in reaction to her parents who had no such possibility.'They are working class and very poor and that restricts their lives in many ways. My father was a labourer and he earned the minimum wage. He worked in a factory and had no schooling. My mother was unschooled too and cleaned hospitals and schools. I left school at sixteen because there was no money. The university cost money in those days; now it's free and it's easier to do housework. You go to the supermarket and it's all done in an hour.

'After my marriage I got my degree and now I've finished m
career. I divorced my husband ten years ago because he couldn
keep up with my intellectual interests. I was a virgin before marriag
and when we had sex it was all right but boring as we were bot
naive. He wanted sex more than I did but we never tried anythin
new and I was too embarrassed to ask then. Sex isn't abou
performance but coming close and having a release. Once he aske
me: Do you love me? I said no, and that was it. I took th
opportunity – as a rule I never miss opportunities – and we split up
He moved out and I asked for the divorce. As easy as that. M
mother is very traditional and disapproved so I haven't seen her i
ten years. But before that I hadn't seen her for seven years, and onl
sent her a Christmas card, one that she didn't answer.'

After divorcing, Geraldine didn't have another man for a year a
she was busy working and studying and 'sorting herself out'. She ha
more confidence and assertiveness, and joined a consciousness
raising group. This attitude she transmitted to her children, teachin
them to be on their own.

After the first year, Geraldine began to have lovers, at first 'on
night stands' with married men she'd meet at parties. Now she has
steady boyfriend, Danny, who stays at her house at the weekend
and comes for lunch or dinner during the week. She locks the doo
of her bedroom. The girls have to knock if they want to come in
'Once they started getting moralistic but I haven't hidden anythin
from them.' She and Dan pay their own way at restaurants, shows
movies, concerts, anything. She gets 180 dollars a week governmen
pension for the three of them and the only thing she seems to worr
about is leaving Dan's trousers or shirts on the clothesline in th
backyard. If an inspector saw them she'd lose her pension.

The maintenance cheque arrives in the mail and the women wh
have custody of their children in many cases depend on thi
government pension: 15 to 20 dollars a week would be the averag
contribution for a divorced mother. The father is obliged to giv
60 dollars a week for the upkeep of two children. 84 per cent of singl
female parents are on a pension and wait eagerly for the white
envelope to come through the letter-box.

Not all Australian women are as sure of doing the right thing a
Geraldine Matthews, but it is a general belief that children –
particularly males – should be encouraged very strongly to do thing
for themselves, because women who spend their lives looking afte
men have great difficulty in getting men to do work in the home
Australian mothers do not want to bring up their boys to sit aroun
while the girls do all the work for them. Even Bettina Arndt

Australia's best-known sex therapist and former editor of *Forum*, says: 'Australian women are very active, most women are working while their children are still reasonably young, but mothers feel very uncomfortable about the fact they might be depriving their children by working. Nevertheless, guilt doesn't make them leave their work and come home because when they look back at their mothers who stayed at home and sacrificed an awful lot, it didn't necessarily produce happier children as a result. Young mothers who have to decide whether they are going to work or not look at their mothers and say: "Maybe I would have been happier if my mother had been working." '

When I was asked to go to Australia, two things immediately came to mind: kangaroos, of course, and surfing. This was an adventure I couldn't possibly let my sixteen-year-old son miss. So I took him out of school and had visions of him learning how to surf on Bondi Beach. I could see him swimming far out to sea and then, after a few hours practising on a rented board, would gaze at him as he came towards me on top of the highest wave, all the way into the sandy beach where girls stretched out in their monokinis would view his arrival. It was a good beginning. He would surf and swim while I interviewed long-legged golden-haired Australian women about sex. We would see kangaroos running freely, and koalas, platypusses, parrots, all as promised in the technicolour advertisements. Our trip would be the closest thing to heaven.

So Felipe and I travelled sixteen hours from Mexico to London, then another thirty hours from London to Adelaide. We left Mexico on the tenth of February and landed in Adelaide on the fourteenth. 'Your son treats you very warmly,' Jonathan Stone from the Tourist Office remarked to me, 'and that's very good, because tenderness is also another part of sex.'

I thanked him and went arm in arm with Felipe through Gawler Street, King William Street, Rundle Mall and Hindley Street in Adelaide. We weren't very happy; we felt isolated, we were always looking at each other or one of us was following the other, as we ate hamburgers on a park bench or walked around staring at shop windows. This was our only form of entertainment because I conducted thirty interviews, each at least an hour long, during an eleven-day period (the trip from Mexico took four) and in many of the interviews it was felt that Felipe's presence might inhibit the women although I assured them he did not speak English and therefore would not understand anything. (Actually, this isn't true because he understood so much that when we returned to Mexico he was able to deliver two lectures on sexology in his school, replete with diaphragms, condoms, loops, IUDs, pills, vaginal douches, spermicides, jellies, foams, Kotex, Tampax and Lord knows what other contraptions that aided him in his most eloquent conference for which he received top marks. Everybody was stupefied that this little round adolescent knew, or was willing to say, more than most Mexican gynaecologists.)

When Felipe wrapped his arms around me or held my hand while we were walking in Melbourne, Geraldine would look disgusted. I felt as if I were committing incest. This seemed to me a glaring contradiction within the broad expanses of their immense sexual freedom. But in Australia, the family unit *per se* lasts only a short time. By the age of sixteen, a son no longer keeps his mother company and a fourteen-year-old daughter is already leading her own sex life.

If Felipe was not allowed to sit in on the interviews at the women's counselling and family planning centres lest the women felt uncomfortable, for me it was also disappointing because a revolution is supposedly outspoken and revolutionary ideas can be expressed in front of everyone (sex in the media certainly is). In the conversations, all the women except the counsellors, sex therapists and lesbians asked me to change their names. The fact that young girls would not give me their real names seemed normal, but what is this so-called sexual revolution which no woman will back up with her name? Working mothers and housewives, after telling me their husbands had had a vasectomy (currently more than 30,000 done a year in Australia, each at a cost of 1,000 dollars) would say: 'But please change my name because Adelaide is such a little town, everyone talks.' Students didn't want me to use their names because they feared the reaction of parents and peers. Even Bettina Arndt told me I couldn't quote her in my interview unless she could first see what I had written. She reminded me of a school mistress. So the only real names in this article are those of the three lesbians: Joan Russell in Adelaide, Jane Richards and Maureen O'Connor in Melbourne; Margaret Valedina and Natascha McNamara from the Aboriginal Training and Cultural Institute in Sydney; the aborigine playwright, Eva Johnson; Dr Elsie Koadlow, medical psychotherapist from Melbourne; Lesley Barclay from the Family Planning Association; Anne Jackson from the excellent Biological Centre in Melbourne; Helen Boyle and Carla Craney from Sydney's Women Unit at the Premier's Department; Nuria Vidal from the Women's Health Centre in Flood Street, Sydney; Julie Ewington, Sue Walpole, Cathy Carey, Peggi Job and Barbara Wigan from

Sydney; Clare Byrt and Rhonda Sharp from the Women's Advisory Office at the Premier's Department in Adelaide; Olive Mettyear of the Marriage Guidance Council in Adelaide; and finally, the woman with whom I identified most strongly in less than an hour, Beatrice Faust, who looks like Beatrice d'Este, with her dark hair shaped delicately around her white face, whose house was as warm and welcoming as her books were familiar – from Proust to Raymond Chandler.

Many of the women's meeting rooms, workshops, development networks, headquarters, refuge referral services and rape crisis centres in Sydney, Melbourne and Adelaide look like girl guide hang outs, with posters and enlarged photographs of extremely poor women from India, Latin America and Africa, workers in the fields, breast-feeding, black madonnas, bulletin boards, hooks, bookshelves, coat racks and old chairs and tables. Good intentions are evident everywhere: documentation on rape, incest, sexual assault, domestic violence, sexual harassment, junior biology, menopause, contraception; Germaine Greer's books and Anne Summers'; *Women, Sex and Pornography* by Beatrice Faust; Miriam Dixon's *The Real Matilda*; Kate Englis' painful research into adoption called *Living Mistakes*. I read tags and announcements: *'The money required to provide adequate food, water, education, health and housing for everyone in the world has been estimated at 17 billion dollars a year. It is a huge sum of money, about as much as the world spends on arms every two weeks'* or *'Don't be an ostrich, Make sense or sex, Born to win, Taught not caught, A happy child is a wanted child, Our situation is not good even if somebody else's is worse.' 'Because women's liberation is a movement of the powerless for the powerless and by the powerless, its attraction is not immediately clear to the powerless who feel they need alliance with the powerful to survive.'* Equal opportunities board: *'If you feel that you have been treated unfairly on the basis of your sex and marital status, speak up. Value self-esteem, value self-respect. Right to say no.'*

In all the guidance councils, I saw a printed credo by Joyce Stevens written in *Women's Liberation Broadsheet*, International Women's Day 1975: *'Because women's work is never done and is underpaid or unpaid or boring or repetitious and we are the first to get the sack and what we look like is more important than what we do and if we get raped it's our fault and if we get bashed we must have provoked it and if we raise our voices we are nagging bitches and if we enjoy sex we are nymphos and if we don't we're frigid and if we love women it's because we can't get a "real" man and if we ask our doctor too many questions we're neurotic and/or pushy and if we expect community care for children we're selfish and if we stand up for our rights we are aggressive and "unfeminine" and if we don't we're typical weak females and if we want to get married we're out to trap a man and if we don't we're unnatural and we still can't get an adequate safe contraceptive but men can walk on the moon and if we can't cope or don't want a pregnancy we're made to feel guilty about abortion and . . . for lots and lots of other reasons, we are part of the women's liberation movement.'*

The buildings which house marriage guidance councils, family planning associations, the Women's Switchboard and the Women's Advisory Office at the Premier's on King William Street, Victoria Place or Goodsell Building in Chiffley Square, in Sydney, are functional, beautiful, wealthy. Flower vases, sofas and chairs, desks, are arranged with the neatness of hospital operating theatres. Quiet and lovely women rise from their chairs in a soothing manner and ask if you want tea or coffee, revealing no hurried movements, no awkward angles, no dissonance. Is this Dior's or Nina Ricci's? I ask myself. When are the fashion models coming in? Such softness and luxury I have seldom seen. In Mexico, only very expensive beauty parlours are as sumptuous. I am propelled into a big room and there I find a wide range of books and magazines that speak of women's issues and sex. Again Germaine Greer and her *Female Eunuch*, her *Sex and Destiny*, Mercer's *The Other Half: Women in Australian Society*, Abbot's *Sappho was a Right on Woman* and Altman's *Homosexual Oppression and Liberation*. Most of the other book covers are of boys and girls who look like gods and goddesses, blonde and tanned, smiling and satisfied. A sailing boat in the background. Everyone is young. Australia is a young country, it's a very youth-oriented society. I do hope that elderly women are treated in the same way as young people. Older women walking down Gawler Street and streets around Randle Mall appear out of place in their old-fashioned flowery dresses and black shoes alongside those plastic people strolling barefoot in their shorts and T-shirts. Even in Sydney, people go barging into hotels, restaurants and shops like conquerors. Mexico is also a barefoot country but for other reasons. The supreme self-confidence, even arrogance, of the Anglo-Saxons leaves one queasy. Mexico, where's that? How can Mexicans have blue eyes? Do they speak English over there? When I told a young woman in the Koala Motor Inn, in Sydney: 'I hope you come to Mexico,' she exclaimed: 'I wouldn't dream of going on a vacation to a Third World country.'

The women in charge of networks and offices are called

'femocrats', feminist bureaucrats, I was told by Cathy Carey. Still, in the councils or the Advisory Office at the Premier's, advisers and their secretaries are uniformly sweet and courteous. No one looks like they are in a hurry. Women are self-confident, they all have bank accounts. 'Would you tell your partner how much you have in your bank account?' asks the magazine 'Cleo' in its March 1985 issue, revealing in its survey that two-thirds of women in marriages or partnerships have separate accounts, that until 1969 a male guarantor was required for a woman who wanted to borrow money and now 67 per cent of women have full-time jobs, 69 per cent have part-time jobs, and having their own personal fortune makes them feel secure and independent top-tigers. Virginia Dowd, the financial consultant, advises them: 'Single or separated, married or divorced, take the time to make a will. Otherwise, your hard-won assets may be lost in legal tangles.' Australia – one is constantly reminded – has the highest rate of home ownership in the world.

All these women have a keen sense of self-preservation and they know how to achieve recognition. Life rewards them well. They walk past me and smile politely and I can smell their toothpaste. Only a very rich country could treat its women this way. I'm sitting on top of the world down under. From particularly cute rectangular machines that hang on the wall you can get a condom by simply inserting a coin that displays the face of Queen Elizabeth. In ladies' rooms you can also purchase Kotex and Tampax and hygienic containers are provided for their disposal. Everything is conceived, prepared and arranged beforehand.

From 14 to 25 February, 1985, I listened to words that repeated themselves in my ears day in day out: pads, periods, diaphragms, tubal ligation, IUD, vaseline, pleasure, sexual harassment, refuges, enjoyment, vasectomy, orgasm, professional help, Decade for Women's Meeting, missionary position, tricks, facilities, lack of imagination, the Lesbian Coffee Shop, Salvation Jane, Right to Choose, vagina, performance, superior women, free style, feel my body, self-directed pleasure, sisterhood is powerful, cock, cunt, premature ejaculation, self-fulfilment. And even in the toilets of women's networks, phrases jump off the doors at you: 'War is menstruation's envy', 'The only good men are dead men', as well as the usual graffiti of penises and respective testicles cut into the wood with hairpins next to this statement: 'A woman needs a man like a fish needs a bicycle'. André Breton would certainly have subscribed to that. I was also happy to read in Sydney, perhaps as a reaction to the sexual revolution: 'Santa Claus beats his wife' and 'Santa Claus' wife prefers the reindeer.'

In Mexico and Latin America we don't have much leisure time. Most women dedicate their entire lives to trying to find food for their children, washing other people's clothes, sweeping someone else's home, all this simply to survive. For many men sex is a quick and violent release and women are there to receive their ejaculation. Others don't even wake them up: *'Tú dormidita, dormidita'* (stay asleep, stay asleep). And then they are soon as soundly asleep as their wives. Sex is closely linked with leisure and it is only because Australians have such a high standard of living and are so comfortable and affluent that they have time and energy and means to analyse at length their relationships to find out if they are happy or not.

Compared to countries where economic survival is the main question, Australian women as well as men, children and animals, are in a privileged position and there have been extraordinary gains for women. In fact, no country has done for its women what Australia has achieved in this decade. The Labour Government, in the early '70s, was very positive about women; it was sympathetic towards abortion and also supplied contraception. In 1975, International Women's Year, the Australian Government could be considered a progressive and feminist one, having given an enormous amount of money to women's issues. This Labour Government, even though it did not last long, made a tremendous difference to the women's movement. The Women's Electoral Lobby, begun by Beatrice Faust, interviewed all the electoral candidates at this time and published their opinions on women's issues – abortion, equal pay and child care – and gave the politicians marks (some of them, the conservatives, got – 3), and continued to do so for several elections.

Australia is a strong and competent country, and it seemed to me a country for women, where everything is taken care of: pensions for single mothers, pensions for divorced women, for widows, rape crisis centres, refuges, work shops, health centres, development networks, welfare. There are social security offices in all the urban towns of New South Wales, Victoria, Queensland, Western Australia, South Australia, Tasmania, the Northern Territory. The State takes over and assumes responsibility for all the problems that in Latin America are part of an intimate (or should I say 'tragic') relationship between men and women. Australians believe that sex is one of the pleasures that men and women have been placed on this earth to enjoy, so they expect it to be very good, while we (the Latin American continent) haven't found out yet if it is really one of life's joys or not. An ordinary Mexican woman would never imagine that she is on earth for sex but in Australia sexual pleasure is a right. Women demand an orgasm.

Olive Mettyear of the Marriage Guidance Council in Adelaide is a sex therapist who says that women are fighting for their rights and searching for higher quality sex. Women demand more from sex now than ten years ago when they did not expect to enjoy it. They simply tolerated it because it was their duty, but with today's greater sexual freedom women expect orgasms and will help themselves to achieve it through the technique of self-stimulation or masturbation. 'First of all,' says friendly and attractive Olive, 'we teach a woman to do it on her own because it is more relaxing for her to discover she is orgasmic this way; then she can show her husband how to do it so that she can get the same from him she gets from herself.' Olive Mettyear regrets that couples only visit her when in difficulties. 'People don't like to admit they don't run their own sex lives any more. We have interviews and hold workshops and conferences for couples six times a year because the first thing about sex problems is to communicate them. . . . No, no, please don't call it frigidity. We don't use that word anymore. We call it general sexual dysfunction. This dissatisfaction can be caused by myriads of problems. Some women think that after a child is born there is no need for sex anymore; others feel they are being used. Sexual problems are the root of personality problems and if the sexual side of marriage goes wrong the marriage goes wrong too. In general women who come here feel that men are fairly selfish in bed and I think this causes a lot of sexual problems; it makes a woman feel that she is being used and not appreciated. Then she tries to avoid sex.

'We use the Masters and Johnson three-stage programme. In the first stage there is no sexual intercourse, no touching of the erogenous zones (genitals, breasts). In the second stage there is no pressure on the woman, so there can be fondling and cuddling without sex, and in the third and last stage, when she is enjoying the massage, the physical contact, and is willing to relax, the man can then touch and caress her whole body, and after this fondling and tenderness, she is free to move naturally into intercourse again, because she herself is asking for it. This programme has worked well. The mutual anger disappears and the woman, who felt mistreated in some way, now feels valued. Last month, in January, we had 150 people who came to us with sex problems.'

The Family Planning Association in Sydney makes an important point which many of the women interviewed stressed again and again: 'Now there is much more freedom and assertiveness on the part of women to enjoy sex and get pleasure from it by learning about their bodies. Before it was only important that men enjoyed it, now men feel they have to satisfy women and give a good performance.' Similarly, many Australians talk about the importance of choices for women: to have or to refuse to have sex, to marry or stay single, to have children or not (Australia has the lowest birth rate in the world: 'we are not even replacing ourselves'). Only one mother told me: 'My child is my greatest accomplishment.' Women choose to accomplish themselves in ways that were not thought of ten years ago: working, studying or by choosing male or female partners.

At first, I listened with surprise to women who told me about their husband's penis or their lover's low sex-drive.'They think you are a psychiatrist,' my son said, but then it dawned on me that everyone does the same, everyone speaks openly of sex. Nothing similar has ever happened to me before and details descended on me like the Niagara Falls. I was inundated with oral sex, anal sex, petting, touching; after a while penises were dancing in my Latin American sense of guilt as I absorbed the unemotional plain and slow voices of sex therapists and counsellors repeating: 'Relax, sex for recreation, not for procreation, the link between sex and babies has been cut, relax, here are the sexual techniques, don't hesitate to be specific: harder! slower! wait for me! stroke me here! I am as responsible for my pleasure as you are.'

When I told Olive Mettyear I used to believe masturbation was not only a sin but it was bad for people's health, and that boys who masturbate in Mexico are told they will end up like the idiot who sticks his tongue out in one of Goya's paintings, she answered: 'What you believed is not true. It is not only harmless but it is healthy.' Later in Melbourne, I learned that most doctors recommend masturbation before going to sleep. Women who seek sexual release and look out for their own sexuality feel capable of claiming the right to be what they want to be, and not to be downtrodden any more. They are also freer to see homosexuality as just another form of sex.

Certainly Sydney probably matches San Francisco now as the two best cities in the world for gays. The night Felipe and I arrived, there was a demonstration in Sydney – thirty thousand gays marching in the streets, thirty thousand out of a population of three and a half million! There was pride in their claims and their high voltage clothes, their hair that stuck up in separate stiff, high tufts like goats' horns or unicorns.

In Adelaide, Joan Russell (who, along with Sandy Loffler, probably helped mc the most with this article) took me to a sex shop (in Mexico such a thing does not exist) and to me it looked like a movie from the Wild West, with all those fake plastic gadgets, black leather belts and bracelets with iron spikes for executioners, muzzles for raging dogs, girls turned into tormentors, enormous penises, porno-videos, records, posters, cassettes and little pieces of clothing meant to be burnt. It was like going into a big bad wolf's mouth and I kept asking why the dildoes were so big, the lips so red, the leather so covered with studs, the teeth so long, the panties so full of holes, the ears so large, the magazines (mostly from the Philippines and Japan) so well protected in plastic bags, the vibrators so expensive, the images so brassy.

And yet there was something infantile about this sex shop, as if it were a fairy godmother's tale turned upside down and inside out – every muscle dislocated and out of proportion, like a gross caricature of men and women who have become self-parodies, unconscious clowns. Afterwards, at a fair in Sydney, I bought a red clown's nose and Felipe and I each put it on in turn. Surely I did it because of the sex shop. It seemed to me a bolder and more nurturing (a word often mentioned in the conversations on sex) device than all the gadgets offered to adults whose fantasies and whims soon turn stale.

Undies, tidies, minis, panties, bras, beedees, topsy turvy, dinky drawers, dollies, sweeties, shorties, softies – everything to do with women is reduced to the first sounds of infancy. In Spanish we call underpants *calzones* and to a little girl we can say '*Ponte los calzoncitos*' (put on your panties) using the diminutive, because the pants are actually small. But in English, North American and Australian magazines, everything to do with women employs this infantile language as if women were mentally deficient. Daddy do, good girl, as if a sleeping puppy were having her head scratched. The magazines *Cleo*, *Dolly* and *Australian Women Monthly* are full of deodorants and hair removers (as a threat to convention, lesbians don't shave their legs or armpits) and sprays of all kinds, while *Australian Penthouse*, *Australian Playboy* and others written for men show females no longer as puppies but rather as gorgeous, glowing apricot and peach slices, called sexual objects by the feminists.

The media supposedly has a very strong impact on liberating women by clearly portraying and airing the problems of loneliness experienced by mothers and housewives, but what predominates are all the commercial products that surround a woman, not the serious articles or surveys about self-fulfilment. Stay Free, Maxi Pads, Eve, Carefree, Panty Shields, Pregnancy Testing Kit, New Freedom, Lovable, Satin – all these products (good or bad) need buyers, and women have proved to be insatiable consumers. Sex in Australia has been commercialised in advertising, fashion and pornography. Clare Byrt of the South Australian Women's Advisory Unit thinks that the media 'treat women as faces or bodies rather than people having minds or personalities. There's a new form of condescension in this.' In her view the link between sex and money is like nail and flesh and any attempt to change sexual attitudes comes up against powerful special interests.

Australia feels that everyone is fit for sex, that sexuality is a very great life force and that old people should not be afflicted by ageism – on the contrary, society should not allow them to feel old. Sexual interest seems never to die in Australia. But the thing I admired the most was sex for the handicapped. Cerebral palsy, infantile arthritis, childhood accidents, paralysis – despite impairments of many kinds, everyone is given a sense of self-worth. In Mexico, we are barely starting to care for our handicapped: there are no special bathrooms, no ramps, no parking spaces; so sex for the disabled – as a government goal as it is in Australia – would be completely out of proportion.

Even if Australians criticise, even if counsellors and feminists keep telling me: 'It's not enough, it's not enough,' Australians are so far ahead of any Latin American country that sometimes I felt their continuing demands were like eating a wonderful roast for dinner, and then complaining that the dessert was not sweet enough. Yet almost all the advances that women have achieved have brought problems and these have made many women question to what extent they have really benefited from the sexual revolution. Carla Craney points out, 'There are nine methods of contraception and seven involve controlling the fertility of women. Therefore the responsibility for taking preventive measures is more on girls, so there is not really total equality.' On a *per capita* basis, the pill is used more widely in Australia than in any other country in the world, but many of the women I interviewed criticised the pill or the IUD or their husband's or lover's penis or the health institutions of all Australia. Perhaps they are right and we Latins should follow their example, and express our needs more explicitly.

When I think of all the care given to a woman who is raped in

Australia, I could cry out in sheer despair for the Mexican women. Why does one country have so much and another so little? Australians have sexual assault centres, rape crisis centres, legal advice, self-defence classes, community groups, yet we have nothing and we even believe rape is pleasurable. *Las viejas se lo buscan.* Mexicans live on myths and rape is one of them: the myth that all Mexican women want is to have a man on top of them at all times. The myth that men are not attackers, women are always responsible – after all rape is as much a sexual experience as any other.

In Australia, a court cannot question a raped woman about her past sexual history. The booklet says it clearly: 'Evidence about a woman's sexual reputation (for example, what other people say or think about her) is not allowed. . . . Rape is an attack on a woman's body, her senses and emotions, her whole self. It is an attempt to humiliate, hurt and destroy her. *No one* wants or invites that. It doesn't matter what women look like, how they dress, where they go, where they live, how old they are, whether they are married or not. . . . Rape in marriage is common. Through physical force or emotional or other blackmail, women are forced by their husbands to engage in unwanted sexual acts, including oral and anal sex. Since the recent changes in the sexual assault law, a husband can be charged with sexual assault of his wife. The law recognises that a woman is not the property of her husband, to be sexually used and abused as he likes.'

Weak, passive mentalities are not encouraged in Australia.'A woman's greatest protection lies in her own strength, her confidence in herself, her respect for her own body and her life.'

Thanks to Joan Russell I had the opportunity of interviewing Dolly, a Madame who loves publicity and appears on television talking about 'women's issues'. Her house is full of lace frills: cushions with lace frills, curtains lined with lace, lace on the furniture, lace on the dining table, cupboards covered with porcelain figures, teacups, china plates and plastic flowers. A big picture of Dolly in a golden frame hangs over the television and her set of rules to keep the business going is written on the wall next to the telephone:'Black stockings and suspenders must be worn and not kept in bags. If not worn, no work. If wearing white, wear white ones. Girls who don't turn up for work in the afternoon will be docked seventy dollars. No drugs or dope in the flat at any time. No Greeks, drunks or lepers, etc.'

Facilities and tricks cost more. 'The nursing mother' and 'the woman in flames' are some of the stereotypes men look for. Dolly says: 'Some want to play horse and others want to be kicked and slapped or whipped. Leather we don't do, none of my girls go for it.' And she adds: 'The legal age to start is seventeen, that's when the girls go on the game, but kids today go in for six months then move out. The younger generation has no standards. They should keep on for at least three or four years. I feel a little sorry for them. They should see it as I do – as a trade, a business with morals and a standing.'

Dolly pays them 120 to 130 dollars a week. She has sixteen girls working for her now. 'I have my own drivers to take them home. We are all exploited. My girls work either five nights or three nights a week and this business depends on advertising in the phone book or in the local papers. Look, here's my card.'

Prostitution is illegal in Australia but in Sydney and Melbourne girls can be picked up on the streets. Brothels, massage and gym parlours, health and photographic studios, night clubs, model agencies are no competition for call girls.

Was Dolly thinking of retiring? Oh, no, she wasn't ready to turn off. 'This business is like a drug. It's a habit, it's a challenge. Most of the girls miss it if they get out. I am a top entertainer. Members of parliament, senators, politicians, they all dial my number – so do Japanese men, they have a special liking for very tiny blondes!'

Dolly, now a grandmother, is not tired of fighting and believes God has put her on the earth to be a Madame, even if prostitutes are not allowed to believe in God.

There is in Australia a new breed of strong independent women who care for each other and do not want to fit in, who sometimes enter into lesbian relationships. Joan Russell is one of them. As the mother of Christie, her twelve-year-old daughter ('Above all I am a mother'), she maintains that 'to be a lesbian is not against the law and there is no law that says that lesbians cannot keep their children, but if a man is left by his wife, he has to prove that her lesbianism makes her unfit to be a mother.

'After six years of a bad marriage in New Guinea, I came back to Adelaide and lived seven months alone, put my two-year-old child in care, learnt how to drive a car and started to grow. Before, I had been simply surviving. From that moment on I went on a pension and retrained for a new career. My experience as a lesbian is very privileged because I have a large measure of control over my own life and feel very secure about my choice. I am a highly respected citizen, pay my dues, own this house, earn a good living. My child, Christie, is nearly thirteen and knows I am a lesbian. My mother is hateful of my lesbianism and recently my daughter sided with her and declared she hated my being a feminist and a lesbian. I answered her: 'What harm has it done you? I put it to you it has done you a lot of good.' Christie was jealous when I had partners other than her father who were men and now she is jealous of my partner who is a woman. Do you want to speak to her and see how she feels?'

Joan called her daughter. Christie told me that she couldn't accept her mother's being a lesbian, that she had only told her best friends. But she didn't think lesbians were perverted or bad or a moral danger as society said, and that perhaps this experience of a different life style made her a better human being. 'Hardly anyone is normal. My school is straight, square, very aristocratic; disabled children came in for a visit and everyone was laughing and making fun of them behind their backs. I could not.' Christie Russell sounded older than her mother.

Jane Richards and Maureen O'Connor live together openly in Melbourne. Although they have no money whatsoever, they served my son and me a lovely dinner: wild rice, shishkebabs, cheese cake, and wanted to take us back to our motel in Ridgewood along a road next to the sea shore so Felipe could see it. They were very sceptical about the sex lives of teenagers. 'What does a little girl who has just gotten her period know about caring, really caring about someone else?' It seemed to infuriate Maureen: 'If you've got somebody who is thirty-five years old who doesn't know what caring about someone is all about, how do you expect a twelve-year-old to? This is all rubbish.'

'So you don't think there's a sexual revolution at all?' I ask.

'I would say there was a revolution and we lost,' answers Jane Richards. 'The influence of the American media actually built up this so-called revolution. It's all in the media, the media can do anything. Still, twenty years ago, it would have been difficult to share a house with another woman openly; even if Gertrude Stein shared hers with Alice Toklas. They were famous, that makes a lot of difference. For my mother it was hard to accept and when I told her, she said she had always suspected my father had been a fag and wondered if it wasn't hereditary.'

Peggy Saunders only came to terms with her lesbianism when she was twenty-five. 'I tried to be heterosexual when I was seventeen and knew nothing else but wasn't comfortable. It didn't work but I didn't know why. It's natural to want to fit into something that's easy rather than into something for which you're going to be called sick, degenerated, deviant, ready to be shown in the zoo. I said to myself: I'm going to try and have a decent, honest life, true to myself, instead of gaining approval in an heterosexual world in which I don't belong. Lesbianism is still not accepted as an alternative.'

Jane Richards and Maureen O'Connor cried out in protest: 'It is definitely an alternative.' Neither they nor Peggy Sanders were Marxist lesbians or radicals or man-haters and they argued: 'The only thing the public sees are the radicals, the ones that get into the papers – drags, dikes and transvestites – but there are a lot of male homosexuals who would not dream of dressing like women. They are happy with their maleness, their loving bond is with a male instead of a female.'

Maureen O'Connor, Jane Richards and Peggy Sanders have made their choice. They are lesbians and are not afraid of saying so or of allowing their real names to be used. They suggest that in spite of the sexual revolution lesbians frighten other women who think they might be after sex with them. Lesbianism, like homosexuality, is 'treated by the media as a kind of disease'. There is also a tendency towards stereotypes that suggests a heterosexual relationship means love and warmth and that lesbians are only out for sex. Ironically, statistics show that lesbians are the least sexually promiscuous group in Australian society. These women also argue that they are more independent since they are 'not threatened as much as other women economically and socially and they can fight back more'. They also attribute this independence to the fact that they 'do not socially nor economically depend on men'. While in varying degrees the lesbians are breaking away from men or the traditional male image of women, they suggest that the sexual revolution has backfired. It was intended to produce a more loving, enjoyable relationship but has been distorted and commercialised. They are sceptical about how far down the social scale changes in attitudes sexuality have gone, and while accepting that there is more sexual freedom, they question if men have accepted responsibility in sexual relations. 'This new freedom has also resulted in problems with venereal disease and pressure on women to have sex, and parents giving young girls the pill without sufficient orientation about sexual relationships.'

Like the lesbians, the aborigines are also a thorn in the flesh of Australia. I met eleven aborigine actresses and four musicians who were willing to speak about their sex lives (aborigines are supposed to be loose sexually). Most of them had children much whiter than themselves. 'Yes, all that men ever want is to throw their white shit into us.' The aborigine names sprang up: Ernabella, Amata, Indulkana, and the girls' names which have their white equivalents: June (Gunluckii), Allyson (Arjibuk).

Warata Telver, born in Kalgorila, was a descendant of the Narumba Tribe. Christine Williams, from the Kaunra, was one of fifteen children who grew up in the Point Pearce Aborigine Reserve in York but was freed because of good conduct under the Assimilation Act. They spoke spitefully of their white lovers. One of them had been raped, others picked out by the head of the Mission because they had a nice ass (aborigines are not considered pretty from the Anglo-Saxon point of view, but sexy, just like black women).

I asked Eva Johnson, the aborigine playwright: 'Do aborigines appeal to whites?'

'Oh yeah, we are supposed to be very hot. We really turn them on.'

The naked actresses surround me, with their straw skirts, like hula-hula, their earnest faces, and breasts hanging on their stomachs because they are fat and nobody minds (what a rest from the magazines), and the sweat that washes out the deep yellow, black, red and white lines painted on their bodies. They have just performed a dance that describes the birth of the spirit of the Women of the Sun and when I watched them I had the sensation of a woman panting, pushing and crying. They wailed and moaned and started moving rhythmically as in the act of love. It's the creation of the earth, the beginning of all times, the birth of man: Australia is an enormous womb. Ayers Rook with its crevice could be the world's vagina and the Mount of Venus with its scanty pubic hairs rises up to meet the sky. During the whole stay I had the feeling of a void. Even if there were sheep and children being born, the postmen delivering letters, and apples and peach trees in Sandy Loffler's backyard, I felt this country had no past and that its only possible past, the aborigines, had been trodden on and were destined to disappear just like the dinosaurs.

Australia felt as though it had popped out of the sea and that men, like ants, were trying to cover it; but it isn't like Europe or Latin America, where man feeds the soil with his own flesh and blood. In Mexico, under every Catholic an idol appears or a jug or a piece of pottery, wearing the face of your ancestors. In Australia, if you dig you will find the first fire of the universe. For me, it would not have been strange to see, coming down any street of the prudent, coy and homely city of Adelaide, a mammoth or some

other antediluvian animal with a terrific erection to prove that the
sexual revolution was meant to take place in Australia from the
beginning of time, as Jesus was meant to be born in Jerusalem.

The Women of the Sun (in Mexico, we also call ourselves the
people of the sun) were named aborigines and could as easily have
been called spidermonkeys, gorillas or apes. The word 'aborigine'
has an echo to it. We are all aborigines. My children are my
aborigines. I myself am an aborigine. If the first Australians
baptised the inhabitants as aborigines, the mistake has been passed
down through generations. From now on, I will call my son my little
aborigine, until he insists: 'Then let me buy a bottle of gin in the
store next to the Grosvenor Hotel,' because we have seen very poor
blacks (are there any rich aborigines?) coming out of there with
their liquor wrapped up in brown paper and taking a swig as soon as
they get on to the sidewalk. Eva Johnson reminds me it was the
white men who brought alcohol to Australia.

Are Australians Anglo-Saxons? I asked Eva. 'Of course. The
Anglo-Saxons are racists, they hunt down not only the aborigines
but the Chinese, the Kanakas (islanders from the Pacific) brought
into Queensland on the cotton and sugar plantations, the people
they recruit as cheap labour in the wool industry, the women who
work themselves to extinction under the tropical sun. But if
Australians feel Anglo-Saxon now, they certainly will not twenty
years from now. There is a constant shift in the population. People
arrive here from Europe, Asia, and every migrant group in its turn
is discriminated against. Throughout Australian history, the group
that arrives discriminates against the next to arrive. Twenty years
ago it was the eastern Europeans, the Germans, the Hungarian Jews
who were discriminated against. Now they are the discriminators,
the victims being which new group arrives on the island, for example
the Vietnamese refugees in recent years.

'To discriminate is an Australian trait. They are now trying to
make up to us, make up for the whole of Australian history of
discrimination, but aborigines are still worse off than any migrant.
Even the migrants discriminate against us after a while. The Greeks
that come over here are not exactly Onassis, you know, but still the
poor Greeks, the poorest Turks, the Jews who immediately make
money and move to richer suburbs look down on the others. These
actors were only willing to speak to you because you come from a
Third World country. If they had told us you were European we
wouldn't have seen you. We've had enough of them bitches.
Immigration was first offered to the Dutch, German, Maltese and
other Europeans, but when they did not come in sufficient numbers,

the government had to lower its standards and put up with less desirable immigrants. If the Asians are now the lowest on the scale we are lower still. More than 200,000 people have settled in Australia, even though it is not exactly paradise. They are trying to make it up to us now, but for the aborigine it has been sheer hell.'

Because of the immigrant population in Melbourne, there are more than 78 women's refuges there. The battered women come in with their children, spend the night and are helped in many ways. I was asked to tear up the piece of paper with the address lest an angry husband found out its location and set the refuge on fire.

The refuge I was taken to was cosy, full of sunshine, cushions to sit on, blankets, beds and Kleenex for the weeping women, toys for the children, bunk beds, cradles and a big kitchen, tasks assigned on the notice-board for women to do, the same they had at home: clean, cook, sweep and garden.

Similar refuges have sprouted up all over Australia, to give women and their children a place to get away from severe domestic violence, a home where they have emotional and physical support for four months, a lawyer, an understanding counsellor, help in getting a divorce, a house, in looking for a job, a doctor, while social workers take the children to school, feed them, play with them – all this paid for by the government. Ethnic radio, television and newspapers also advertise the extensive phone-in service that is available. Experienced counsellors from different countries (twelve languages spoken) attend the non-English-speaking women. The predominance of working-class women does not mean that they have the monopoly on domestic violence, and as Melanie Blake explains: 'Domestic violence is common to all social classes but richer women have money for a hotel or another house.' Margaret Valadian states: 'Australia is still a male-dominated society so the revolution has to work through that dominance to be a real revolution. There is no revolution if there is still a need for women's refuges.'

Aborigines and immigrants and poorer Australians don't have much to do with the sexy, healthy, dynamic, multi-orgasmic, highly successful Australian women who jog, drink cocktails and relax in their bath-tubs. Male masseurs and clitorises are, for them, words without meaning and they would be surprised to find out in *Forum* that erotic massage is highly recommended for women.

I listen and read, read and listen, and feel more and more unhappy about my trip to Australia. Why didn't I find out earlier in my life about orgasm? Orgasms and penises flying high in the sky wave goodbye to me as I leave and I remember Simone de Beauvoir's bitterness at the end, having dismissed all the books she had written, all the work she had done, only to cry out in the last sentence: *'Plus jamais un homme.'* Never again a man.

To be happy and fulfilled you should have planned your sex life, your orgasms, your family, the children you wanted and what you were to eat the day after tomorrow. I felt as if some kind of disaster had befallen me. I was quite content with my unexciting fate before coming to Australia.

A Mexican writer who went blind lamented: 'Why did it have to happen precisely to me?' And after some time, she asked herself: 'Why not to me? Why shouldn't I receive the same as all the other men and women on this earth just because I write?' We are all in the same boat, I share the destiny of the women of my time. In the 1950s we were afraid of pregnancy, shy in bed, sentimental. There was no Olive Mettyear on the horizon to teach masturbation or squeezes ('hold the penis very tight and squeeze it once or twice, dear, so as to avoid premature ejaculation'). Sexual relationships were part of domestic life. But now magazines have made them a separated, glamorous item. Women in their fifties have never looked at themselves below the waist. Now a woman falls into a trance because she can insert a speculum into her vagina and observe her organs in a mirror. Exciting, wonderful, overwhelming, exhilarating, enchanting, vaginal lips, mount of Venus, clitoris, vulva, everthing can be depicted, nothing is missing, genitals stare back.

For a Latin, like me, for whom sex is secretive, intimate and sinful (and not frantic, garish and noisy) all this was a shock and I felt as if I had suddenly missed life, missed love and could not go back. Perhaps I should have a nice cup of 'lost time' tea (Australians consume 133 tons of tea every day, 8 cups each), go to sleep and dream about Australian kangaroos' flying penises, or better still, count the sheep and have the wool willingly pulled over my eyes.

Elena Poniatowska was born in Paris of a French-Polish father and a Mexican mother. At the age of nine she moved to Mexico, where she still lives. She started her career as a journalist in 1954 with *Excelsior*, a major Mexican newspaper, and after a year transferred to the periodical *Novedades*, to which she has contributed articles on social and political subjects for thirty years. Since her first novel, *Lilus Kikus* (1954), she has written many books, fiction and non-fiction, including *Massacre in Mexico* (1971) and, most recently, *The Last Turkey* (1985), which deals with the festivities of the poor. Elena Poniatowska's main concern as a writer is the exposure of poverty and injustice throughout Latin America.

SEX – EGYPT

Angela Davis

Twelve years ago, I had passed through Cairo en route to Brazzaville to celebrate the tenth anniversary of the Congolese Revolution. I remembered how frustrated I had felt then, being in Egypt, yet unable to catch even a glimpse of that country's life. This time, as I prepared to go through customs, I thought about the women in Africa and indeed the many thousands of women scattered all over the globe who, like their sisters in Egypt, were getting ready to celebrate the end of the UN Decade for Women in Nairobi. It felt invigorating to be a part of this.

Three women representing the newly established Arab Women's Solidarity Association had come to the airport. Since TWA had lost my luggage (which I did not retrieve until the night before returning home), we were soon on our way to the hotel in Giza. Driving through the city, I was unexpectedly shaken by the sight of a vast and ancient cemetery consisting of unending rows of small sand-coloured mausoleums. When I asked about this enormous city of the dead, I was told that it also housed at least a million living beings as well. So critical is the housing shortage in Cairo that people are forced to live in the shelters that have been constructed for the dead members of their families. Right away I began to realise that the issue of adequate housing was high on the list of priorities for women in Egypt.

When I initially decided to travel to Egypt for the purpose of writing an article on my experiences with women there, I did not realise that I would be expected to focus quite specifically on issues relating to the sexual dimension of women's pursuit of equality. I did not know, for example, that I would be expected to write about the practice of clitoridectomy. When the topic was made known to me, I began seriously to reconsider whether to proceed with the project, since I was very much aware of the passionate debate still raging within international women's circles around the efforts of some Western feminists to lead a crusade against female circumcision in African and Arab countries. Being an African-American woman myself, I was especially sensitive to the underlying racism characterising the often myopic emphasis on such issues as female circumcision – as if women in the twenty or so countries where this outmoded and dangerous practice occurs would magically ascend to a state of equality once they managed to throw off the fetters of genital mutilation. Or rather once white Western feminists – whose appeals often imply that this is the contemporary 'white woman's burden' – accomplished this for them. As the Association of African Women for Research and Development pointed out: 'This new crusade of the West has been led out of the moral and cultural prejudices of Judaeo-Christian Western Sociology: aggressiveness, ignorance or even contempt, paternalism and activism are the elements which have infuriated and then shocked many people of good will. In trying to reach their own public, the new crusaders have fallen back on sensationalism, and have become insensitive to the dignity of the very women they want to "save". They are totally unconscious of the latent racism which such a campaign evokes in countries where ethnocentric prejudice is so deep-rooted. And in their conviction that this is a "just cause", they have forgotten that these women from a different race and a different culture are also *human beings*, and that solidarity can only exist alongside self-affirmation and mutual respect.'[1] In an analogous situation in the United States, the birth control movement has frequently been viewed with justifiable hostility by African-American women, since that movement often portrayed us as bestial and oversexed, producing not only children, but the means with which numerically to challenge the rule of white supremacy.

In lecturing on various university campuses throughout the United States, I have encountered not a few women who know nothing at all about women in Egypt or in the Sudan except the fact that they suffer the effects of genital mutilation. And this fact often causes them to recoil in horror, although they rarely admit that they are also appalled by the lengths to which some women in the US will go in order surgically to alter their bodies in accordance with male supremacist standards of beauty. Might not Maureen Reagan, the misguided daughter of the US President, who is leading the governmental delegation to the Nairobi Conference, be quite willing to raise this issue, while simultaneously arguing that disarmament, apartheid and Zionism are not proper 'women's issues'? I realised that if I were to follow my own convictions, I could not write about sexuality and the predicament of Egyptian women without acknowledging its manipulation by those who refuse to recognise the larger political context of male supremacy.

The Arab Women's Solidarity Association had agreed to host my visit, so I was naturally disappointed to learn that Nawal el Saadawi, the president of the organisation, would be abroad during the week I spent in Cairo. In fact, she was scheduled to deliver a series of lectures in the United States during the only period I was free from my teaching responsibilities in San Francisco. Since she planned to remain in the country for an extended period, I made plans to meet with her after my return. Having met her the previous year during a lecture tour in the San Francisco Bay Area, and having been thoroughly impressed by her personality as well as her brilliant writings, I looked forward to seeing her again in New York.

The itinerary arranged by the Arab Women's Solidarity Association was conceived with the idea of permitting me to make contact with as wide a range of women as possible. Large, relatively formal meetings, small discussions and individual interviews had been included in the schedule. Among the scores of women were political leaders, social scientists, writers, artists, trade unionists, students and peasant women. When my travelling companion and I sat down to discuss the itinerary after the seventeen-hour plane trip and an unsuccessful attempt at an afternoon nap, my mind felt rather fuzzy. For a brief moment, I began seriously to doubt whether it would be possible to absorb all the information I would receive over the coming days. I suggested to Debra, who had accompanied me on this trip, that we rise early the next morning to take a walk down the Nile before breakfast. I thought this might clear my head before we plunged into the day's interviews and meetings. But the stroll down the Nile gave me a lot more to think about than I had expected. It was not the contrast between the bareheaded women and those attired in a variety of veils that struck my attention, but rather a dusty make-shift tent we stumbled upon. Suddenly, out of the dark interior of this tent, which was pitched on the bank of the Nile in the middle of one of the busiest sections of the city, emerged two men just awakening from their night's sleep. My mind flashed back to the million people who had set up house in the cemetery. This was the legacy of Sadat's Open Door economic policy. The trans-national corporations which had greedily rushed into Egypt under the guise of promoting economic development had created more unemployment, more poverty, and more homelessness. In one of the many meetings to take place during the coming days, this comment would be offered on the relationship between sexual relations and poverty: 'Take a family here in Cairo with five or six children. They all live in the same room. If there are two sofas and a bed in the room, then with a child on each sofa, the mother and father will sleep on the bed and three children will sleep under the bed. Try to imagine the kind of sexual relationship the parents have under this pressure. Even though there are sexual problems, these problems are of secondary importance.'

After breakfast, we crossed El Tahrir Street, where our hotel was located, and walked a short distance to the apartment of Shahira

Mehrez, who had greeted us at the airport the previous day. The Secretary-General of the Arab Women's Solidarity Association, Mona Aboussena, was waiting to accompany us to the National Centre for Sociological and Criminological Studies. A group of women was expecting us there and we immediately sat down to begin the discussion. As I had anticipated, there was an instant and incisive response to my description of the project I had undertaken. The most outspoken of the group, Dr Shehida Elbaz, hastened to point out that the campaign against circumcision under way in the West has created the utterly false impression that this is the main feature of Muslim women's oppression. 'Women in the West should know,' she asserted, 'that we have a stand in relation to them concerning our issues and our problems. We reject their patronising attitude. It is connected with inbuilt mechanisms of colonialism and with their sense of superiority. Maybe some of them don't do it consciously, but it is there. They decide what problems we have, how we should face them, without even possessing the tools to know our problems.' Dr Elbaz went on to describe a public debate in England during which she had challenged a number of women who attempted to argue that the eradication of female bodily mutilation was the pivotal issue in the quest for women's liberation in such countries as Egypt, the Sudan and Somalia. 'I originally came from the countryside, I said to them, but all my life I have lived in Cairo. I can't assume that I have the right to talk about women in the countryside without conducting field research. So how can you decide for us, so far away? You know nothing about our culture, our background, our level of development.'

Having spelled out her irreconcilable differences with the most publicised proponents of the Western anti-circumcision campaign, she generously shared fascinating information on the recent historical evolution of attitudes toward sex in Egypt, often recounting her own personal experiences, but always meticulously connecting her observations with their appropriate economic and political background. There was one emphatic point which was a recurring theme of her remarks: during the period of the sixties, prior to Sadat's government – and particularly before the Camp David Accords and the Open Door policy – women were far freer from male tutelage than they are today. Women have suffered a retrenchment of economic, political and even sexual oppression as a direct result of Egypt's new ties to the US and to Israel. I was impressed by this woman's frankness and found myself feeling far more at ease than I had expected.

Perhaps I had begun to feel a bit too relaxed. After all, I had

slipped into a cultural continuum whose acquaintance I had previously made through mental excursions alone. In any case, the
events which transpired that evening during a dinner at Shahira
Mehrez' home took me unawares. When Debra and I arrived, a
good number of women were already there. At first I tried to
converse individually with several women about their work – and
virtually everyone there was involved in some way in the effort to
elevate women's status. Moving from one seat to another around a
traditional circular brass table, I talked first to a sociology professor,
then to a journalist and afterwards to the well-known artist and
peace activist, Inji Efflatoun, who presented to me a catalogue
containing a portrait of me she had painted during the period I spent
in jail. After more guests arrived, Mona Aboussena suggested that I
formally address the thirty-five or so women who were attending the
dinner. I prefaced my remarks with comments about the importance
of the end of the Decade for Women forum in Nairobi and went on to
say that I had been asked to make this trip – as other women from
around the world were visiting a variety of countries – in order to
write an account of my experiences with Egyptian women. But when
I mentioned that the specific topic was 'Women and Sex' – and just
as I was about to explain the particular approach I wanted to take –
pandemonium erupted. The palpable hostility arising from every
corner of the room made me silently chide myself for not having
formulated my ideas with greater care. Yet I had not known that
the very mention of the word 'sex' would of itself elicit such
spontaneous outrage.

At first I simply listened, trying to repress my own emotional
responses. When I was finally able to get a word into the discussion,
I reacted rather defensively. However, it soon became clear that the
very idea that sex might be the focus of an article on Egyptian
women was so disgraceful that the great tide waters of anger were
not to be stemmed simply by qualifying my own position on the
subject. I laboured to convince myself to refrain from attempting to
defend my own position. Was I not in Egypt to learn about the way
Egyptian women themselves interpreted the role of sexuality in their
lives and their struggles? Was I not especially interested in their
various responses to the unfortunate chauvinism characterising
attitudes toward the sexual dimension of Arab women's lives in the
capitalist countries. I tried to persuade myself that even in the
attacks clearly directed at me, there was something of significance to
be learned.

'Angela Davis in the Third World,' one woman said. 'Your name,
your personality is known because of your struggle. You can be used

by your society, a wealthy society, which is trying to exploit our country.' Dr Latifa Zayat, to whom I had been previously introduced added: 'I have come to see you this evening because you are Angela Davis. If you were simply an American research worker, I wouldn't have come to see you. I would have even boycotted this meeting, because I know that through this research we are being turned into animals, into guinea-pigs. I would boycott any American who is doing research on Arab women because I know that we are being tested, we are being listed in catalogues, we are being defined in terms of sexuality for reasons which are not in our own interests.' Dr Zayat, a highly respected veteran leader in progressive causes, explained that she made those remarks so that I might better understand the reactions of the women. Eventually another woman summed up the discussion by saying: 'You would be doing a great service to the women's cause in the Third World if you tell people that women in the Third World refuse to be treated as sexual objects or as sexual experiments. We want to be liberated, we want to be emancipated, we want to be equal – but from an economic point of view, not from a sexual point of view.' I don't think she meant to imply that inequality on the sexual level was of no importance whatever, but rather that an isolated concern with sexual equality would not solve the problems connected with women's state of economic dependency and their exclusion from the political process, not to speak of the exploitation and poverty suffered by women and men alike.

In reflecting on the discussion that had transpired that evening, I began to wonder whether it would be possible within such a short period of time to move beyond discussions centring on the problematic posture of researchers from the capitalist countries dealing with issues of sexuality. Two days later, in a meeting convened at the headquarters of the Hoda Shaarawi Association, named after the founder of the Egyptian women's movement, there were similarly intense reactions. Dr Shehida Elbaz, whom I had previously interviewed, argued during this meeting that I should not have agreed to write – even critically – on the topic of sexuality. 'I am outraged by the assignment of these topics. Although you have defended yourself very well, it raises in my mind another question: the role of the revolutionary woman in the West. Because it is so obvious from this assignment that it reflects the international division of labour imposed on the Third World by the Western capitalist countries. To make the topic of England, "Women and Politics" and in Egypt, "Women and Sex" shows that they assume that women's participation in politics in England is more important than in Egypt. Whereas although women may be more involved in politics in England, in prospect and destination it is much less radical, much less revolutionary and it does not threaten the international capitalist system.' It seemed to be the consensus of the gathering that the politics underlying the distribution of topics for this anthology – whether consciously or not – misrepresented the cause of Egyptian women. Why, indeed, was not sex investigated in England or in the United States? Did the prevalence of female circumcision or the widespread adoption of the veil among urban women indicate that the most salient features of women's oppression in Egypt was sexual? Or was it simply in the interests of sensationalism that this topic was suggested?*

Several women, however – and a man as well – argued that sexuality cannot be ignored by those who are authentically concerned about the emancipation of women. The young man said very sharply, 'Women cannot become creative agents without being freed from sexual oppression.' Dr Nadja Atef, to whom I was later introduced, spoke about Egyptian women's responsibility to confront and publicly represent their own positions on questions involving sexuality: 'The fact is, we must be sensitive to the question of sexuality. Otherwise we would not have argued so happily and for so long and totally forgotten to talk about other issues. In and of itself, this is a touchy area in our society and I think we have to look at ourselves in order to find out what our responsibility is to represent ourselves. It may be our duty actually to write about this. It may be our duty to start putting forth our position at forums and to publishers abroad. If this topic upsets us, let us speak it openly. Why does it upset us? Every time you say "sex", people respond like a stimulus response test – they go crazy.' After this comment, Nadja Atef received extended applause. Later that evening, when I spoke with Dr Sheriff Hetata, the husband of Nawal el Saadawi, I asked him to comment on the relationship between the sexual and the political. His response was concrete and to the point. The sexual oppression imposed on so many women results, for example, in the

---

*In fact Elena Poniatowska, from Mexico, has written about 'women and sex' in Australia precisely to counter such (otherwise totally justified) accusations of misrepresentation and voyeurism. And Germaine Greer went to Cuba to look at 'women in politics' in a developing country. The whole purpose of these exchanges was to ensure that the women writers, and the women about whom they were writing, could express themselves in detail on a specific topic as freely as possible. If sex is low down on the list of priorities for Egyptian women this is something that readers in other countries need to know and something we intended to be brought out clearly in this essay. We are very sorry if the aims of the project were not communicated adequately to Angela Davis or to the women to whom she spoke in Egypt.   *Debbie Taylor*

prohibition of women's participation in political activities. 'If you want to hold a political meeting for young women and the young women can't go out after seven o'clock in the evening, there is no meeting.' As long as women are viewed as the sexual property of their present or future husbands, their ability to bring about the institutional transformations which will lessen the burden of sexist oppression will be severely limited. This dialectic condemns an isolated focus on sexual issues, but demands that these issues take place as prerequisites for the larger struggle.

The overwhelming majority of the women with whom I spoke were urban, educated women. While many of them had come from poor village backgrounds, their lifestyles were very much removed from those of the masses of Egyptian women. 'I met a thirteen-year-old girl in Upper Egypt,' one woman recounted, 'and this girl said: "As far as the government is concerned I have not been born at all. I have no birth certificate. I do not go to school. I have no official document at all. I was born and I will die, but as far as the government is concerned, I'm not there. I have never been there.' The practice of female circumcision is gradually becoming obsolete in big cities like Cairo and Alexandria. However, the degree to which it is still prevalent in the country often goes unrecognised. Most of the women with whom I spoke were absolutely opposed to the practice of genital mutilation. Many of those of my generation and older, who spoke about their own personal experiences, said that they had themselves been circumcised, but that they had broken the cycle with their daughters. And indeed, the young women I met – primarily students – had not suffered under this practice.

In her pioneering work on Arab women, *The Hidden Face of Eve*, Nawal el Saadawi – who was one of the first publicly to raise the issue of female circumcision – described her own experience at the age of six years. She was seized from her bed by family members she thought were thieves in the night and taken to the bathroom where the operation was performed. '... I realised that my thighs had been pulled wide apart, and that each of my lower limbs was being held as far away from the other as possible, gripped by steel fingers that never relinquished their pressure. I felt that the rasping knife or blade was heading straight down toward my throat. Then suddenly the sharp metallic edge seemed to drop between my thighs and there cut off a piece of flesh from my body. I screamed with pain despite the tight hand held over my mouth, for the pain was not just a pain, it was like a searing flame that went through my whole body. After a few moments, I saw a red pool of blood around my hips.'[2] Research carried out by Dr Saadawi about ten years ago indicated that some

97.5 per cent of uneducated families and 66.2 per cent of educated families continued to sanction the performance of clitoridectomies on their daughters. I visited a village outside the city of Mansoura and while I could not directly engage in conversations with the village inhabitants because of the language barrier, I was able indirectly to conduct a number of interviews. All of the five women with whom I had contact there had been circumcised. They were all in their twenties. This was one of the most difficult moments of my visit. The masses of women in Egypt are peasants, yet I was spending all of a few hours attempting to communicate with women with whose language I had no familiarity whatever. How could I honestly view these as anything more than token encounters with peasant women? I thought about a book I had recently read, Nayra Atiya's collection of oral histories of Egyptian women from peasant backgrounds, entitled *Khul Khaal*. She is herself Egyptian, yet it was five years before she could develop the material for this book, in which the women talk frankly about their lives and unabashedly present their own interpretation of such sexual initiation rites as circumcision and defloration.

The key question, it seems – at least among progressive women and men – is not whether circumcision is an acceptable contemporary cultural practice, but rather how to initiate a viable process of relegating it to historical obsolescence. Nawal el Saadawi has pointed out that 'amputation of the clitoris and sometimes even of the external genital organs goes hand in hand with brainwashing of girls, with a calculated merciless campaign to paralyse their capacity to think and to judge and to understand. For down the ages a system has been built up which aims at destroying the ability of women to see the exploitation to which they are subjected, and to understand its causes.'[3] At least one woman with whom I spoke during my stay in Egypt was directly involved in a campaign against female circumcision: Azziza Hussein, president of the Family Planning Association. She has delivered papers on the subject, at various conferences, and attempts, through the family planning network, to educate mothers and the midwives who perform circumcisions about the need to obliterate the practice. Perhaps because she is involved in direct action with respect to the dissemination of contraceptive measures, she also believes in direct action campaigns to eradicate genital mutilation. 'I am trying to do something about the problem, which reflects itself in so many ways in our society. We've studied it and we are taking action. We are trying to reach those who have the possibility of doing something about this practice, which means the nurses, the midwives. We formed a national committee in 1979.... The taboos that we have with regard to sex, we've broken them because we've dealt with family planning. This is why we are the ones who are able to tackle female circumcision.' While Azziza Hussein aggressively advocated tackling the problem head on, she would not consider isolating it from its larger social context.

Even if it were possible to envision the success of an isolated campaign targeting female bodily mutilation, the fact that Egyptian women represent barely 10 per cent of the labour force would remain unchanged. That 71 per cent of the female population suffers from illiteracy would not have been altered. The personal status of women with respect to polygamy, divorce and guardianship would remain one of socially enforced powerlessness. Actually the relationship between this salient sexual issue and the socio-economic elements of women's oppression is quite the contrary. It is not really possible to foresee the universal abolition of female circumcision unless the process of integrating women into the labour force moves forward, unless female illiteracy is significantly defeated and unless the personal status of women within the family is elevated. These specific changes in the condition of women cannot themselves be considered in isolation from far-reaching transformations in the society as a whole – economic development and progressive social change, which would indeed fundamentally alter the lives of men as well as women in Egypt.

Many women whom I encountered emphasised the centrality of the current struggle to defend the status of women within Egyptian family law. When the National Assembly approved a series of amendments to the law on personal status in 1979, this marked the first changes in this area to have occurred in fifty years. At issue was the man's unilateral right to divorce his wife and to engage in the practice of multiple marriages, thus his right openly to treat women as sexual property. The amendments did not change the husband's right to obtain a divorce from his wife at will – and without having to go through the courts – but it did provide that the wife be immediately informed of the divorce. Likewise, while the man retained his right to marry up to four wives – as is his perogative according to the Sharia – he was compelled by the amendments to inform his present wife of his intentions and his future wife of his marital status. Obviously the fundamental inequality of the woman within the family remained unaltered. Nevertheless, there are presently efforts under way, encouraged by Islamic fundamentalist elements, to abrogate the new law on the grounds that it is unconstitutional. If this occurs, what meagre rights women have managed to acquire in relation to marriage would be annulled.

Divorced women would no longer be entitled to alimony amounting to two years' maintenance (or more if the marriage were especially long), but rather for one year, as was the case prior to the amendments. Moreover, divorced women, who retain custody of their children, would no longer be guaranteed the right to living quarters, which their ex-husbands must presently provide for them, and must move out of the home they had shared together. They would be once again compelled to return to their parents' abode. Women's right to sue for divorce, while it is by no means comparable to men's corresponding right, became less rigidly restricted. Now there is a nine-month waiting period during which the court attempts to mediate (yet there is no waiting period for men) and in the event that this attempt fails, the divorce is finalised. In 1979 amendments also extended age limits of child custody for the wife, previously seven for boys and nine for girls (with possible extensions to nine and eleven respectively). Presently, automatic custody is given to the mother until the boy is nine and the girl eleven, subject to extensions of fifteen for male children and until marriage for female children. Azziza Hussein has pointed to the amendments' important implications for women's ability to move toward economic independence. 'Another important and new aspect of the amendments is the confirmation of the woman's right to work. This right is not contingent any more on the husband's approval. In the past, a woman who worked against her husband's wishes was legally placed in the category of *nashez*, meaning "disobedient". As such, she lost her right to maintenance by her husband, who had the right to neglect her. The wife's right to a court divorce was very much jeopardised by the "disobedient" status.'[4]

The Arab Women's Solidarity Association recently organised a meeting of representatives from various political parties in order to pressurise Parliament to reject the fundamentalists' bill. However, as Nawal el Saadawi has pointed out, although they are opposed to the new bill, they are not, therefore, satisfied with the 1979 amendments. If women are to move in the direction of achieving an equal status within the family, polygamy must be outlawed altogether and the woman must have equal rights to divorce. Moreover, as many women emphasised, women must eventually be capable of achieving economic equality if they wish to enjoy equality in their personal status.

As far as women's role within the family is concerned, important structural changes are occurring as a result of the migration of Egyptian labour abroad. About two million Egyptians are working abroad – primarily in the Gulf countries. Among them are men from the working and peasant classes. As Sheriff Hetata pointed out, for the first time in the history of Egypt, with the exception of military service, large numbers of married men are leaving their families to go abroad. 'The women take over the responsibilities of looking after the fields and responsibilities within the family as a whole. Because the men are not present, the women are becoming the decision-makers. Therefore when they return, there are often serious problems in the relationships.' Certainly this economic pheno-menon must be affecting the structure of sexual dominance within the family.

On several occasions I asked about the prevalence of rape in Egypt and was told that in recent years there has been a rising incidence of sexual assault. However, there was a universal response of incredulity when I mentioned in a meeting that one out of every four women in the United States will experience at least one episode of sexual assault before reaching the age of eighteen. One in every three women will be raped during her lifetime. Amina Shafix, a journalist and leading member of the Progressive Unionist Party, tied the rising incidence of rape to the overall deterioration of the status of women since the end of the Nasser era and specifically with the dissemination of such capitalist cultural commodities as pornography. Rape is a capital offence in Egypt, but cases against rapists are frequently dismissed on the grounds that the victims are sexually promiscuous. Mona Aboussena told me about a recent case of a woman who was raped by four men, who also stole her money. The case was dismissed because of the 'conditions of the woman', meaning that she was considered to be either a professional prostitute or sexually familiar with men. The problem, of course, is hardly peculiar to Egypt or to the Arab world. The dualistic representation of women as virgins and whores is an integral element of the ideology of womanhood associated with the Judaeo-Christian tradition. Some years ago, a judge in the state of Wisconsin dismissed a rape case because the young woman was 'provocatively dressed' – in jeans and a loose-fitting tee-shirt.

Among the young urban population – and especially among students – new problems are arising, problems involving social attitudes which have only begun to be superficially resolved in the capitalist countries. While the need for a woman to be a virgin at marriage has begun to be questioned, women often suffer from the clash between new, emerging values and the old culture. Although this double standard with respect to sexual activity must eventually be eradicated, during this transitional period, women are often lured into relationships, under the guise of expressing their sexual freedom, only later to discover that their partners do not wish to marry them because they are no longer virgins. Young women of the petty bourgeoisie therefore often feel compelled to undergo surgery to repair the hymen in order to be considered suitable marriage partners. There is indeed a great danger of representing sexual liberation as 'women's liberation', as women of my generation came to recognise in the United States during the sixties. Precisely as a result of the widespread dissemination of the pill, women were represented as moving in the direction of sexual liberation. Actually they suffered disguised sexual exploitation because if they took the pill, the excuse that they wished to avoid becoming pregnant was no longer accessible to them. It is not coincidental that the women's liberation movement erupted directly on the heels of the so-called 'sexual revolution'.

As the reliance on birth control measures in Egypt becomes more widespread, and especially since this is occurring within the context of an omnipresent cultural invasion from the Western capitalist countries, problems relating to the sexual conduct of young women will no doubt increase in severity. While the right to exercise control over the reproductive process of one's body should be enjoyed by every woman, problems will inevitably result from the tendency to tie the technology of birth control to the overall influence of capitalism. Not long ago, condoms were promoted by television commercials – the very same commercials that offer a plethora of capitalist-promoted commodities to the Egyptian public, the overwhelming majority of whom, of course, cannot afford them. Protests resulted in the cancellation of the television commercials, but there are still billboards all around Cairo advertising 'Tops' condoms. One afternoon, driving through the streets of the city, I noticed one of these billboards adjacent to an advertisement of *The Seven-Year Itch* starring Marilyn Monroe, who was depicted in her usual strapless attire. Although abortions are illegal in Egypt, they are shrouded in far less controversy than in the United States. Shahira Mehrez told me, in fact, that many women will not hesitate to tell you how many abortions they have had, but they will never admit to having a lover.

That enormous numbers of women are compelled to live under male tutelage, which is so terribly slow to give way to change, is rendered symbolically visible by the increasing popularity of the veil. Most of the women with whom I spoke – and all except a few had opted against wearing the veil – volunteered observations on the dramatic increase in the number of veiled women in recent years.

The veil, of course, has long been considered a symbol of the oppression of women in Islamic culture and it is frequently assumed that because of it, sexism is qualitatively more injurious for Moslem women than for their Western counterparts. The fixation on the veil among Western scholars – like the contemporary myopic focus on female circumcision – has often distorted attempts to analyse the condition of women in Arab countries. As Irene Gendzier pointed out in her forward to the American edition of Nawal el Saadawi's *The Hidden Face of Eve:* 'Wearing the veil, the much emphasised symbol that has become a substitute for the analysis of women's work and status, is often associated with the petty bourgeois urban sector. Peasants do not practise seclusion, and the use of the veil is an obvious impediment to certain aspects of their work, notably as agricultural producers.'[5] Nawal el Saadawi herself, in discussing the history of the women's movement in Egypt, points out that the leaders of the first women's organisation, founded by Hoda Shaarawi in 1923, did not really grasp the class character of the veil. Thus, in concentrating their energies on the campaign to eliminate the veil – to the exclusion of issues directly related to the conditions of working women – they managed further to widen the gap between them and their sisters of the poorer classes. 'One of the demonstrations organised by working women ended in a gathering at the premises of the new Women's Federation, but the aristocratic leaders, who were responsible for its activities, paid no attention to the grievances of these poor women, and concentrated on the issue of abolishing the veil, which was unlikely to evoke much enthusiasm amongst them since in any case the working women in factories and fields had never known what it was to wear a veil.'[6]

While it would be a misconception of the nature of Muslim women's oppression to attempt simplistically to equate it with the veil, the prevalence of the veil in urban areas functions nonetheless, I think, as a metaphor for the ideological representation of women, which is imposed – even in contradiction to the realities of their lives – on those who have never known what it means to be secluded behind the veil. In the words of Fatna Sabbah, 'the veil has a very precise meaning: it represents the denial of the economic dimension of women, who, according to the tenets of Muslim orthodoxy, are exclusively sexual beings.'[7] The traditional veil, covering most of the woman's face, is worn only by a small minority. Yet the modern veil, which reveals the face, but covers all the hair and sometimes drapes around the chest, is very much in evidence. Although I was aware of the recent resurgence of the veil, I was truly astonished by the sight of so many women in the streets of Cairo attired in various versions of this headpiece.

The majority of women in the Parliament's People's Assembly are veiled, I was told, as are a large proportion of young women studying at the university. On several occasions, I spent time with a group of students, all of whom were unveiled. During an auto-mobile trip to Mansoura, several hours outside Cairo, I had the opportunity to hear about their attitudes toward the veil. We drove to Mansoura in a three-car caravan and at one point or another I rode in each of the three automobiles. I sensed that this might be one of the most provocative discussions of my stay – this was truly the only time we could squeeze it in – but I found myself feeling frustrated as we talked, my eyes continuously drawn to the sights along the way. The road to Mansoura followed the tortuous route of the Nile, where unending groups of colourfully dressed women were at work on the river bank. Not only were they unveiled, but their dresses were frequently pulled up above their knees as they waded in these ancient waters, cleansing their family's vestments for the coming week. These images flew aggressively in the face of the notion that women's bodies are always to be camouflaged so as not to provoke sexual desire in the men whose eyes might behold their nakedness. I also saw numerous women working alongside men, picking cotton in the fields and working in the brick-making plants on the side of the road, transporting and stacking the heavy bricks no less efficiently than the men with whom they worked.

One of the young women with whom I spoke during this journey along the Nile wore jeans and sweatshirts each time I saw her. She looked very much like the students I am used to seeing in my classes at San Francisco State University. When I posed a question to her about the relationship between the veil and social perceptions of women's sexuality, she said that men generally seek women whose sexual conduct is precisely the opposite of their own. 'The veiled woman covers herself and is guaranteed to be of good morals. This creates a problem for me, because I have to prove that I am as good as she is. I have to prove that I am not a bad girl, that I don't go around with men, and that I can be interested in serious things.' I asked her why she had opted against wearing the veil and she hastened to point out that her reason for rejecting the Islamic head covering was quite unique. 'Maybe I am only one out of ten or one out of a hundred girls who does not wear the veil because I do not believe in God.' This explanation took me by surprise because I had been previously warned that of all the prevailing taboos, the one surrounding religious belief was respected by virtually everyone. However much one might be prepared to criticise the Islamic fundamentalists, one would hardly go so far as to express openly doubts about the existence of God. Of all the women I encountered in meetings, interviews and informal conversations, she was the only one who announced herself as an atheist. Her friend Randa presented a different side – she said that to interpret the veil simply as a visible mark of adherence to the tenets of Islam was bound to be misleading. 'The veil now doesn't mean anything but the norm. It's the majority who is wearing the veil. If you wear the veil, you have no problems. Before, it was the other way around. The veil was the challenge. My aunt was one of the first girls who wore the veil and everyone was against it, even her mother, who was quite religious. But now it is the other way around. I decided not to wear the veil because I believe that to be religious is to do everything that the religion says. It is not how I dress but rather how I behave.'

Abir, a recent sociology graduate, argued that it should not be assumed that the veil possesses an unambiguous religious significance. 'It is a societal question, not only a religious question. It is the only thing you can cling to during turbulent conditions. It is something solid for some people.' Her friend Naula argued that the veil calls attention to women's readiness to consider themselves sexual objects for men. 'In this day and age, it is not an expression of religion. It is an expression of being ashamed of your body. How can women consider that they are not sexual objects if they cover their hair, their arms and their legs? The body is still there, the contours are still there. A man who wants to enjoy a woman's body will still enjoy it whether or not she is wearing a chador.... The veiled women still have men walking behind them in the streets making comments.'

But Abir spiritedly disagreed. 'If you saw the expression on a man's face looking at a woman's behind who is wearing a short, tight skirt, you would really envy a veiled woman. It's terrible the way that men now look at women's bodies.'

Indeed Naula recalled a situation in which she confessed that she was made to feel utterly embarrassed by a veiled woman. 'I remember once we were standing in front of the university and it was a particularly hot summer day. This girl passed by us. She was not wearing the veil around the face, but the one that covers the face. She was also wearing gloves. Actually, she was totally covered except for her eyes. Someone in our group remarked that it must be unimaginably hot for her. After she walked a few steps, she turned around and said: "It's hot here now, so you can imagine what it must be like in hell." Her tone was so self-righteous that it made us feel this small.'

It was suggested that the veil was occasionally adopted as a matter of expediency. As one of the students said, 'Sometimes the veil is a practical convenience. It is not just a symbol of retardation. If a girl wants to go out to work or to study, it is much more convenient.' A young woman who cannot afford to spend a great deal of money on clothes or who cannot afford to go to the hairdresser may choose to wear the veil for these secondary economic reasons.

Sheriff Hetata had told me that I might have the opportunity to meet several young veiled women who were members of the organisation Bint Alard – Daughters of the Earth – in Mansoura. The last time he had visited Mansoura with his wife, Nawal el Saadawi, several members of the group were still veiled. Once they become members of this activist women's group, however, the usual tendency is to abandon the veil. And, indeed, all of the women attending the gatherings in Mansoura were unveiled. But I did have a brief encounter with a number of veiled women at the Ains Shames University in Cairo, where Mona Aboussena is a professor of English Literature. During the trip to Mansoura she had jokingly said, 'Sometimes I feel ashamed being unveiled – because so many of my students wear the veil.' It was she who pulled together a brief informal discussion with some of her students after I delivered a lecture there on 'Education and the Struggle for African-American Equality'.

As an outsider, I felt I should proceed as cautiously as possible, so I was careful not to begin by blurting out a question on the significance of their veils. I began by asking a woman who wore one of the more austere versions of the veil whether she planned to teach after receiving her degree in English Literature. 'No,' she answered, in halting though meticulously correct English. 'I'm going to stay at home. I'm going to read literature at home.' An abbreviated discussion on women and work ensued, the women with veils generally asserting that they did not want to work outside the home. Just as this discussion began to take on the character of an animated argument between the unveiled women, who felt work was quite important to them, and their veiled counterparts, Mona asked the woman to whom I had initially spoken in a rather point-blank manner why she had donned the veil. The young woman, her blue cotton long-sleeved dress covering the entire length of her legs, her white headpiece falling around her shoulders, answered matter-of-factly, 'It is in accordance with my religious order.' She had first adopted the veil upon reaching puberty.

'Who convinced you to wear it?' Mona asked. 'Your parents, the radio...?'

'My reading of the Koran,' she responded. 'That was enough for me.' She went on to explain that 'the veil is an order from God. We must obey God in all his orders without any refusals.' Throughout the entire meeting, this young woman tightly held a small Koran in her hand.

When I later spoke to Nawal el Saadawi in New York, she harshly criticised those who attempt to justify the rising popularity of the veil by representing it as a symbol of resistance to the invasion of Western influences. There is an uncamouflaged message in the popular television programmes during which El Sheik Shaarawi praises the veiling of women as an emphatic challenge to the imposition of Western values, followed by a commercial depicting a swimsuit-clad woman advertising a shampoo made in the USA. When Nawal el Saadawi lectures in the United States, she invariably feels compelled to criticise Elizabeth's Fernea's film, *The Veiled Revolution*, which represents the veil as a positive step on the road to liberation. The film argues that Egyptian women made a profound mistake when they took off the veil at the beginning of this century. Now they have embraced authentic Arab culture and are thus capable of moving forward on their own terms, rather than on the terms established by Western capitalism. This is an erroneous, apologetic position, according to Nawal el Saadawi. The veil does not represent the authentic culture of her people – and indeed, in her book, *The Hidden Face of Eve*, she offers a historical analysis of the veil as a product of the Judaeo-Christian tradition – but rather is, in its contemporary expression, a direct result of prevailing socio-economic conditions in Egypt. As unemployment began to rise in connection with Sadat's Open Door policy, so the veil began to be resurrected. One of its essential purposes was to remove women from the job market at a time when domestic production was declining in response to the saturation of the market with imported goods from the capitalist countries. Rather than functioning as a means of resisting the invasion of Western, capitalist values, the veil serves to consolidate and confirm them as it strengthens the sexist social attitudes which facilitate neo-colonial economic fetters in Egypt.

Dr Hoda Badran, a professor in the School of Social Work at the University of Cairo, described the problem in this way: 'The economic system in Egypt, because it is tied to the West, and in particular to United States capitalism, is hindered from being productive. Egypt is being transformed into a consumer society. It is not productive and it does not generate jobs. In a situation where you don't have jobs, there is competition ... and people try to find scapegoats.... That is why there is more prejudice against women than before.... Also, in a country which has been transformed into a consumer society, it is easy, through the mass media, to use women as sex objects. At the same time, as Awatef Abdel Rahman's study of women and the mass media in Egypt confirmed, both the print and electronic media almost exclusively present women in the traditional roles of wife and mother.'

In a meeting with women writers and artists, the well-known playwright Fathia al Assal argued that Egyptian women should seriously examine problems revolving around sex, if only to understand that the seeming overemphasis on sexual liberation, which originates in the West, is directly related to the call for women's return to the home – and thus to the donning of the veil. I recalled Fathia al Assal's observation when Nawal el Saadawi said that 'women in the West wear nudity like Arab women wear the veil.' A widely publicised proposal, in fact, calls for working women to be paid half a salary for returning home, thus confining themselves to their mothering, housekeeping and sexual roles. The playwright asserted that if women permit themselves to become preoccupied with the isolated question of sexual liberation, they might indeed loose sight both of the larger issues involved in women's emancipation and those related to the overall national liberation of their people. Having made this point, however, she went on to say that Egyptian women should not be afraid of discussing sexuality. After all, she argued, if one examines the historical development of human societies, it becomes clear that private property emerged at the moment when women became the sexual property of their husbands. Just as the sexual oppression of women coincided with the oppression of social classes, in order for women's bodies to be fully liberated, the social system responsible for that oppression must be eliminated.

Fathia al Assal dramatically illustrated the degree to which the cumulative frustrations of women who have been held captive as sexual property can dangerously erupt, by describing a widely publicised criminal case involving a woman who had recently been charged with killing her husband. This case must have fundamentally shaken the Egyptian public, for many of the women with whom I spoke during this trip made reference to it. After twenty-two years of marriage, this woman stands charged with killing her husband and cutting his body into twenty-two pieces, first carving out his eyes, then severing his penis from his body. If newspaper accounts are true, after killing him, she began to tell him all the things about which she had remained silent for twenty-two long years. In directing her rage towards her husband's eyes and his sexual organ, she was perhaps attempting symbolically to annihilate the means with which women are transformed into sexual objects. If indeed she did kill her husband, she did not even succeed in scratching the surface, for the true culprit is the underlying social system, of which her husband was unfortunately also a victim.

I was extremely impressed by Fathia al Assal's presentation in the meeting and felt quite excited when she agreed to talk to me in a more informal setting. After the tumultuous discussions at the Hoda Shaarawi Association, we met at Shahira Mehrez' flat and – with Shahira graciously acting as the interpreter – we talked late into the night. I had not known that Fathia has the distinction of being one of the first woman playwrights in the Arab world, but I had sensed something profoundly great in her presence. Fathia al Assal comes from a family which rapidly acquired wealth in the aftermath of World War II. Her father was married twenty times and while he made a special effort to educate all his sons, he did not consider knowledge to be an asset in the case of his daughters. Her family moved to Cairo when she was quite young and although she attended school for a while, her family withdrew her at age nine because of an early puberty. By the time she was fourteen she began to receive marriage proposals and, after being engaged twice, she married at sixteen. She told me that one important factor which made her husband so attractive to her was his political activism. Prior to their marriage, she herself embarked on a long era of activism in progressive political causes. Her husband spent two years in prison during the fifties and in 1981 she herself was detained by Sadat.

Fathia al Assal's career has not been without its difficulties. In fact, Sadat himself was responsible for having her fired after she wrote a serial about a shyster lawyer which was scheduled to be aired on television. The lawyer in the serial was romantically involved with a young woman, who discovered and exposed his fraudulent activities. Because Sadat assumed that he himself was the underlying inspiration for this character, he was responsible for barring Fathia from writing television scripts for two years. When she returned to television, she wrote scripts sharply focused on the predicament of women in Egypt. Modelled after American soap operas, serials on Egyptian television generally explore the lives and loves of the middle and upper classes. Fathia al Assal, however, decided to create women characters who could serve as popular models for resistance to the traditional behaviour of women in family relationships. *She and the Impossible*, for example, revolves around an illiterate woman chosen by a landowner as his bride so that she might care for his mother while he studies in Cairo. Upon his return, he informs her that he no longer wants to remain with an ignorant woman. Refusing to divulge to him that she has become pregnant, she leaves unprotestingly and decides to study, work and bring up her son alone. Twelve years pass before the husband discovers that he has a son. When he proposes that they resume their marriage, she refuses, saying, 'The woman you married is not the same as the woman I am today.' Moreover, she continues, 'My son is a child of circumstances and I will not come back to you.' Initially, the censors categorically rejected this script, insisting that the woman return to her husband for the sake of the child. Five years passed before the programme was actually produced and aired.

In another of her serials, *Moment of Decision*, the leading character was divorced by her husband after twenty years of marriage, because he decided to take another wife. Instead of remaining economically dependent on her former husband, this woman took a job in a library. Seeking to escape the emptiness of her new solitary life, she began to read library books and in the process not only became a literate woman, but was inspired to write an autobiographical account of her life. When her book won an important literary prize, her husband attempted to return. But like the younger woman in the previous serial, she did not surrender to his wishes. In the meantime, she had fallen in love with someone else – and as the serial concluded, she faced the man she loved, pressing her prize to her bosom.

I could have spent many more hours listening to Fathia al Assal describe her work, which she did in the manner of the ancient story-teller. Her commitment to the cause of women's freedom permeated every word of her narration. Her most fascinating story summarised the plot of her pivotal play, *Women Without Masks*, which she described as a synthesis of all the women she had ever known. It is dedicated to 'my friend and daughter, one among a generation to come in a free society yet to be realised. I didn't inherit my mother's bonds and I hope you don't inherit mine.' It is a play which explores the truth of women's condition. The main character is a woman writer who initially fears the consequences of this truth. As she visualises what she wants to write, a ballet evokes the historical period of humankind when man and women were one. 'But the woman is unable to face the beast on an equal basis with the man and he directs her to the cave where she gives birth. Afterwards he forbids her to leave the cave. The playwright then announces that she wishes to express the condition of this woman when she entered the cave.'

A circumcision is performed on stage and out of an enormous womb, four women are born – a single woman, a married woman, a divorcee and a widow. By the end of the first act, the playwright has rendered the stories of the four women. However, she has not told the entire truth and the characters harass her until she confesses: 'In the past we were symbols of life. Our children were named after us. The moment of creation was the moment of love and the moment of love had no other end. Then the whole world was fenced in and we were fenced in with it and named after those who could own land. We were separated from our children and they were named after the master. We were dethroned and our entire history was falsified. We became simply a woman that reproduces. We became a factory that reproduces human beings. One night I woke up and they took me, my hands tied together, like an animal to be slaughtered. "What are they going to do?" I asked my mother. "They are going to butcher you as they have butchered my mother and my mother's mother." I screamed, but the knife butchered me. My blood was running red before my eyes. I became two people, one bleeding and the other on the edge of the knife. "Now you are ready for marriage to a man," said my mother. "Now I am half a human being. Who needs a man, unless he is half a human being? I am a body without feeling. Who needs a body without feeling unless he is a body without feeling?" Men shout: "You were circumcised." ' When the writer's characters ask her why she didn't tell the truth, she answers that she was terrorised. One of the characters responds: 'If you are afraid to tell the truth, then you don't deserve to be a writer.' The writer then proceeds to tell the truth about the married woman, the single woman, the divorced woman and the widow.

As Fathia al Assal would certainly acknowledge, the speaking of the truth is only the first step in a protracted process of challenging the forces responsible for the oppression of women. The battle for women's equality in Egypt, as throughout the Third World and in the capitalist countries as well, must be waged on many fronts. It must target specific areas such as the disproportionate burden of poverty shared by women, employment discrimination, illiteracy, inadequate health care, genital mutilation, the Personal Status Law, and the distorted images of women in the media. As the campaign against sexist discrimination must be waged in the political arena, I was particularly interested in meeting with representatives of the major political parties in Egypt. At various times during my stay in Cairo, I engaged in discussions with prominent women in Mubarak's National Democratic Party and in the major opposition parties – the Progressive Unionist Party (Tagamo), the Socialist

Labour Party and the New Wafd Party.

Fathia al Assal is a member of the Tagamo, which is a coalition of the Marxists, Nasserites and people of various progressive political orientations. According to this party's analysis, there has been a significant regression in the status of women since the end of Nasser's era. While the Revolution of 1952 accorded Egypt a leadership position in the national liberation movement in the Arab World, and while the non-capitalist economic path resulted in a visible amelioration in the economic status of women, important areas were left unchanged. Amina Shafix, the chairperson of the Women's Federation of the Tagamo, pointed out that even under Nasser, no attempt was made to bring women into an independent mass democratic organisation – just as there were no independent peasant or youth federations. When Sadat came to power after Nasser's death, it was thus easier to reverse Egypt's previous progressive path. 'He declared the Open Door policy, our non-commitment to the national liberation movements and the non-aligned forces (by entering into the Camp David Accords).... The old problems of the sixties helped him in implementing these policies.' Women were directly affected as they found doors closing on job and educational opportunities. Women in the peasant and working classes began to feel the effects of the immigration of labour to the Gulf countries. Sexual crimes became more prevalent, and as a direct result of the socio-economic crisis Islamic fundamentalism began to become increasingly influential.

Because women's destiny is tied to the larger political situation, they certainly have a stake in the development of a strong political opposition. And indeed many of the women whom I met were militant activists, a good number of them having suffered repeated arrests and imprisonment. At an informal gathering of the National Culture Defence Committee, every single woman in the room had been arrested at one time or another. Just a few days prior to this meeting, in fact, several women had been arrested as they peacefully demonstrated against the presence of Israeli representatives at the International Book Fair. Two members of the committee, Dr Awatef Abdel Rahman and Dr Latifa Zayat, had personally received letters from Meir Kahane containing uncamouflaged threats on their lives. The Mubarak government had done absolutely nothing in response. Moreover, preparations were under way for an important trial of thirty leading political activists, trade unionists and working-class peasant and youth leaders. It is known as the case of the Egyptian Communist Party and among the accused is the progressive journalist Farida al Naquash.

As I prepared to leave Cairo, I felt that I was still at the very beginning of my journey. The week's sojourn had passed far more rapidly than I had imagined and I was just beginning to understand some of the elementary features in the complex structure of oppression suffered by Egyptian women. The larger, global context certainly involved a resolute battle for peace and for the New International Economic Order. And I carried home with me the nourishing memories of a brief encounter with Palestinian women who were justifiably concerned that the issues of Zionism and apartheid remain on the Nairobi forum's agenda. There were specific domestic issues relating to Egyptian women which certainly bore similarities to our issues in the capitalist countries and there were struggles which might benefit from the experiences of the socialist countries. But there were also unique issues which women in Egypt would have to work out themselves. The goal of women's equality in their country may not be on the verge of immediate realisation, but I felt profoundly touched by the determination of so many women to keep the fires of struggle alive.

Angela Davis was born in Birmingham, Alabama. She studied at Brandeis University in Boston, and at Goethe University in Frankfurt. She is well known as an activist in the struggle against racism, sexism, and class oppression, and as a result has found herself in both courtrooms and jails in the USA. She is a campaigner on behalf of political prisoners throughout the world, and has written an autobiography and a study entitled *Women, Race and Class* which was published in 1982. Angela Davis now teaches women's courses and courses in Black Philosphy at San Francisco State University, the San Francisco Art Institute, and the California College of Arts and Crafts.

1 'A Statement on Genital Mutilation' by Association of African Women for Research and Development. in Davies, Miranda, ed. *Third World, Second Sex.* London Zed Books Ltd. 1983, pp. 217-218.
2 Nawal el Saadawi, *The Hidden Face of Eve*, London: Zed Books Ltd., p.7.
3 Saadawi, p.5.
4 Azziza Hussein, 'Recently Approved Amendments to Egypt's Law on Personal Status' in Michael Curtis, ed., *Religion and Politics in the Middle East*, Boulder, Colorado: Westview Press, p. 128.
5 Saadawi, *The Hidden Face of Eve*, Boston: Beacon Press, p.xi.
6 Saadawi, p.175.
7 Fatna A. Sabbah, *Women in the Muslim Unconscious*, New York: Pergamon Press, 1984.

Part Three

Women

THE FACTS

NOTES TO THE TABLES

These tables were compiled by the Statistical Office of the United Nations Secretariat, in co-operation with the International Labour Office, the United Nations Educational, Scientific, and Cultural Organisation, and the World Health Organisation, for the United Nations World Conference on Women, Nairobi, Kenya, 15-26 July 1985. Users should consult the statistical sources cited for detailed technical notes on the underlying data.

THE FAMILY

1. Percentage of population by age, sex and marital status

Based on census results provided by national statistical services to the UN Statistical Office and published in the *Demographic Yearbook*[6]. 'Never married' is the percentage of persons of each sex aged 15-19 and 20-24 who are not, and have not previously, been married. 'Not cur-recently married' aged 45-59 includes never married, widowed, divorced and separated persons. For countries where consensual unions are counted in the population census, the concepts 'never married' and 'not currently married' exclude persons reported as living in such unions.

2. Percentage of currently married women of child-bearing age using contraception

Compiled by the Population Division of the United Nations Secretariat from the results of national surveys associated with the World Fertility Survey and other surveys[5].

3. Total fertility rate

Estimates of fertility are prepared every two years by the Population Division of the United Nations Secretariat[4]. The total fertility rate refers to the average number of children which would be born to each female if the fertility patterns of a given period were to stay unchanged. This measure gives the approximate total number of children an average woman will bear in her lifetime, assuming no mortality.

4. Average household size

From statistics in the *Demographic Yearbook* and a working paper prepared by the Population Division of the United Nations Secretariat [3]. Household size statistics in the *Demographic*

Yearbook are from population census Population Division estimates are based on population census data available up to 197 supplemented by other national sources. T internationally-recommended definition of household is one or more persons 'who ma common provision for food or other essentials f living ... They may be related or unrelat persons or a combination of both'. Persons livi in institutions are not considered to be living households. In most censuses persons n resident in a given household cannot considered members of the household.

WORK

5. Percentage of total labour force which is female

Compiled from ILO sources[1], which define person as belonging to the labour force if they a working for pay or profit, or seeking such wor at any time during a specified reference perio The labour force comprises all employed a unemployed persons, including those seeki work for the first time. It covers employe persons working on their own accou employees, unpaid family workers, members of producers' co-operatives, members of the armed forces and part-time workers. This definition may, however, differ substantially from country to country: the choice of the time reference period, minimum hours of work, criteria of seeking work, and the extent to which unpaid family work is included, can all affect the assessment of women's participation in economic activity.

6. Percentage of total population of each sex in 1980 who are unpaid famil workers or employees

From ILO sources[2]. The classification used is recommended by the UN for use in censuses and by the ILO for labour force statistics generally. The percentages are calculated on the basis of total population of each sex, not just persons of each sex in the labour force. This approach has been used because there are major unresolved problems in the coverage of women in labour force statistics, particularly in agriculture and in rural areas generally. Use of the total population rather than the labour force as the denominator for these indicators lessen problems of comparability and reliability.

7. Percentage of the total population ir professional and administrative

occupations, 1980 (a), and percentage of total labour force in industry 1980 (b)

Compiled from ILO statistics[2]. The occupational categories are based on the revised International Standard Classification of Occupations issued by ILO in 1968. Members of the armed forces and persons seeking work for the first time are not included.

HEALTH

8. Life expectancy at birth

The expected average number of additional years to be lived by a female or male born alive. These figures are prepared by the Population Division of the United Nations Secretariat[5]. Many developing countries lack reliable statistics of births and deaths so various estimation techniques are used to calculate life expectancy using other sources of data, mainly population censuses and demographic surveys. Life expectancy at birth by sex gives a statistical summary of differences in male and female mortality across all ages. However, infant and child mortality rates are the predominant influence on these life expectancy statistics in most developing countries. Thus life expectancy at birth is of limited usefulness for assessing male and female mortality rates at other ages in these countries.

9. Child survival rate

Percentages of the cohorts aged 0 (that is live births in a given year) and aged 15 which are expected to survive to ages 5 and 45 respectively. For example, 97 per cent survival of males aged 0 to 5 means that 97 per cent of persons born in a given year will survive to the age of 5[6]. Life expectancy and survival rate calculations assume age-specific mortality levels will remain unchanged for the life of the cohort. Inasmuch as mortality rates are generally declining over time, the actual life expectancy and survival rates are likely to be higher than those given by the present indicators.

10. Percentage of pregnant and non-pregnant women with nutritional anaemia

Estimates prepared by WHO of women with haemoglobin concentration below norms laid down by WHO experts[7]. The causes of anaemia are multiple, but there is no doubt that young children and women are specially affected because of their relatively high requirements for iron. The amounts needed often exceed the quantities of iron available from the daily diet, especially when this contains few animal products. This, compounded with the high parasitic load observed in tropical and subtropical areas, explains the higher prevalence of iron-deficiency anaemia in developing countries. Anaemia may affect productivity and work capacity, and aggravate many other disorders; it contributes to the overall mortality associated with malnutrition; in the case of anaemia in pregnancy, it poses a threat to the life and health of the mother at the time of delivery and may affect the viability of the infant.

11. Maternal mortality rate per 100,000 live births

From the *Demographic Yearbook*[6], calculated from maternal deaths and live births for a given year, based on statistics provided to the UN by national statistical authorities.

EDUCATION

12. Percentage of population which is illiterate, by age

Compiled from statistics prepared by UNESCO from national population censuses and surveys[9]. UNESCO recommends defining a person as illiterate when they cannot, with understanding, both read and write a short simple statement on their everyday life.

13. Number enrolled at primary and post-secondary level (in thousands)

Compiled mainly from statistics published by UNESCO in its *Statistical Yearbook*[8]. UNESCO prepares enrolment statistics from data provided by governments in response to UNESCO questionnaires. Projections to the year 2000 are based on the assumption that the trends observed between 1960 and 1980 will continue to 2000[10]. The coverage and quality of these educational data vary considerably, not only across countries but also across years.

14. Enrolment ratio, combined primary and secondary levels

From the UNESCO *Statistical Yearbook*[8]. The gross enrolment ratio is calculated on the basis of age-specific enrolment data from countries, the normal age of enrolment in each country at primary and secondary levels, and age-specific population estimates prepared by the Population Division of the United Nations Secretariat. The combined primary-secondary enrolment ratio is defined as the ratio of total primary and secondary enrolment (without regard to age) to the total population of the primary and secondary age groups. Since the latter does not cover the entire range of ages covered by the former this indicator may overstate the actual percentage of population of primary and secondary age enrolled.

POLITICS

15. Membership of national legislative bodies

Figures refer both to elected and appointed members of national legislative bodies.

SYMBOLS

Data not available is signified by a blank space.

Because of rounding, 'O' indicates magnitude of 0 or less than half of whatever unit is employed. '100' as a percentage indicates 99.5 - 100.

Data for 1970 and 1980 may refer to any year in the periods 1965 - 74 and 1975 - 83, respectively, for which the series is available.

REFERENCES

1. ILO *Labour Force Estimates and Projections, 1950-2000, 5 volumes,* Geneva 1977.

2. ILO *Yearbook of Labour Statistics,* Geneva, annual.

3. ILO "Estimates and projections of the number of households by country, 1975-2000 (1978 assessment)" ESA/P/WP.73.

4. *World Population Prospects, Estimates and Projections as Assessed in 1982,* UN publications, Sales No. E.84.XIII.8.

5. *Recent Levels and Trends of Contraceptive Use as Assessed in 1983,* UN publications, Sales No. E.84.XIII.5.

6 UN Department of International Economic and Social Affairs (DIESA), Statistical Office, *Demographic Yearbook,* UN sales publications, annual.

7. WHO "The prevalence of nutritional anaemia in women in developing countries: a critical review of available information", by E Royston, *World Health Statistics Quarterly,* Geneva 1982/2.

8. UNESCO *Statistical Yearbook,* Paris Annual.

9. UNESCO *Statistics of Educational Attainment and Illiteracy, 1970-1980,* CSR-44, Paris, 1983.

10. UNESCO *Trends and Projections of Enrolement by Level of Education and by Age, 1960-2000* CSR-E-46, Paris, 1983.

THE FAMILY

1. Percentage of population by age, sex and marital status

| Country (or area) | Aged 15–19, never married | | | | Aged 20–24, never married | | | | Aged 45–59 not married or living in a union | | | |
| | 1970 | | 1980 | | 1970 | | 1980 | | 1970 | | 1980 | |
	M	F	M	F	M	F	M	F	M	F	M	F
Afghanistan			91	46			63	9			8	24
Algeria	95	54			54	11						
Argentina	98	89			79	56			17	27		
Australia	99	91	99	93	64	36	67	40	16	21	16	21
Austria	99	93	100	96	74	45	81	57	12	31	13	28
Bahamas	99	90			72	48			21	37		
Bahrain	97	71			57	17			11	20		
Bangladesh	92	24			60	3			4	35		
Bolivia			96	84			61	43			14	29
Botswana	95	87			88	56			20	40		
Brazil	98	87	98	83	75	51	68	45	13	32	12	27
Brunei	98	85	98	87	77	44	79	52	10	24	10	22
Bulgaria	96	82	96	82	63	25	63	28	5	14	5	14
Burkina Faso			96	46			75	7			10	21
Burma	94	78			57	36			13	30		
Burundi	97	88										
Byelorussia									3	38		
Canada	97	89	99	96	63	44	76	55	13	22	13	19
Chile	98	91	98	90	74	56	74	54	17	34	18	33
Colombia	97	86			75	51			17	36		
Costa Rica	98	85			71	49			15	31		
Cuba	95	70			63	30			19	25		
Cyprus	99	96	100	95	82	61	83	60	5	15	4	16
Czechoslovakia	99	92	99	92	66	35	68	33	11	23	13	24
Denmark	100	96	100	99	73	45	92	78	17	24	20	23
Dominican Rep.	94	78			76	39			26	32		
Ecuador	96	81			66	41			16	29		
Egypt			96	78			80	39			7	32
El Salvador	97	80			67	44			18	37		
Ethiopia	27	9	94	39			53	5			5	40
Fiji	98	83	97	86	65	32	65	37	9	24	8	25
Finland	99	95	100	98	74	54	87	70	17	30	22	30
France	99	94	100	95	67	45	74	51	15	23	16	22
German Dem. Rep.	99	94	99	95	64	35	68	39	6	30	10	24
Germany, F.R.	86	66	93	81					9	28	12	22
Greece	99	89			86	53			8	24		
Guadeloupe	100	96							19	32		
Guatemala	93	72			55	33			13	29		
Guyana	98	85			72	47			23	37		
Haiti	99	95	99	95	88	62	88	62	17	33	17	35
Hong Kong	100	97	99	97	92	68	89	71	9	17	12	17
Hungary	99	88	98	86	66	32	66	31	9	24	12	25
Iceland	99	96	100	98	70	50	81	64	23	25	23	25
India	82	43			50	9			12	32		

Table 1 *continued*

Country (or area)	Aged 15–19, never married				Aged 20–24, never married				Aged 45–59 not married or living in a union			
	1970		1980		1970		1980		1970		1980	
	M	F	M	F	M	F	M	F	M	F	M	F
Indonesia	95	63	96	70	59	18	60	22	8	41	6	33
Iran	96	54	94	66	69	13	61	21	5	28	4	21
Iraq	91	68	95	68	65	31	70	33	10	28	7	23
Ireland	100	98	99	97	85	69	82	66	30	30	28	27
Israel	99	91	99	92	76	46	78	46	7	18	3	2
Italy	99	93			86	56			12	25		
Japan	99	98	100	99	90	72	92	78	5	24	6	18
Kenya	96	64			73	19			11	25		
Korea, Rep.	100	97	100	98	93	57	93	66	4	32	4	27
Kuwait	97	62	97	71	75	21	75	29	6	42	5	33
Lesotho	99	78			76	21			13	41		
Liberia	98	50			74	16			14	27		
Libyan Ar. Jm.	98	60			68	12			4	24		
Luxembourg	99	94	99	94	76	44	76	50	16	27	15	24
Macau	99	98			89	72			15	21		
Madagascar	93	61	91	66	52	23	53	31			13	32
Malawi			94	49			49	7			5	12
Malaysia	97	84			75	43			10	29		
Maldives			88	44			43	7			21	31
Malta	100	97			84	67			21	33		
Martinique	100	97							21	33		
Mauritius			99	87			84	46			97	98
Mexico	95	79	95	79	61	38	61	38	11	26	11	26
Morocco	96	66			68	18			6	33		
Nepal	73	39			33	8			9	26		
Neth. Antilles	100	97			86	71			21	36		
Netherlands	99	95	100	98	72	45	85	61	10	19	13	19
New Zealand	98	90	99	96	68	39	76	52	14	20	18	21
Nicaragua	96	78			64	38			15	36		
Norway	99	94	100	98	73	47	86	65	17	21	19	20
Pakistan	94	69	93	69	67	18	64	24	13	23	11	17
Panama	94	73	96	79	66	33	69	39	24	34	18	23
Paraguay	99	88			80	55			15	32		
Peru	94	83			69	45			15	29		
Philippines	98	89	97	86	69	50	67	45	9	23	9	26
Poland	100	95	100	96	76	47	75	46	7	24	9	23
Portugal	98	93			76	55			10	22		
Puerto Rico	95	84			62	45			22	33		
Reunion	99	91			73	53			13	30		
Romania	98	78	97	84	68	24	71	34	6	25	7	20
Rwanda	97	82			45	18			5	35		
Saint Lucia	100	99			95	87			28	42		
Samoa	99	90	98	91	75	38	74	41	9	22	11	22
Senegal			99	61			88	24			9	32
Seychelles	99	94			88	70			35	44		
Singapore	100	95	100	98	89	65	92	74	10	29	10	24
Solomon Is.	98	84	95	74	79	41	67	32	16	27	16	26
Spain	99	97	99	95	90	68	86	62	11	24	11	21
Sri Lanka	99	89	99	90	87	53	84	55	12	22	10	21
Sudan	96	57			71	15			12	51		
Sweden	100	98	100	99	87	66	95	85	21	22	26	26

Country (or area)	Aged 15–19, never married				Aged 20–24, never married				Aged 45–59 not married or living in a union			
	1970		1980		1970		1980		1970		1980	
	M	F	M	F	M	F	M	F	M	F	M	F
Switzerland	100	96			81	55			18	27		
Syrian Ar. Rep.	96	72			76	30			5	21		
Thailand	96	81			65	38			9	26		
Togo	98				74				12	31		
Tunisia	99	81	100	89	82	27	86	45	7	28	6	23
Turkey	92	80	92	78	41	13	61	27	6	18	4	16
Uganda	93	50			57	13			25	37		
UK	98	91	99	96	63	40	75	54	13	19	15	19
Untd. Arab Em.			91	44			69	12			7	32
U. R. Tanzania	93	48			57	9			11	27		
Uruguay			98	88			73	49			21	29
USA	96	88	97	91	56	36	68	51	14	24	17	26
USSR									5	39		
Vanuatu	99	82			76	32			16	25		
Venezuela	97	84			75	51			19	37		
Yugoslavia	97	84			68	37			8	26		
Zambia	97	59			64	10			10	35		

2. Percentage of currently married women of child-bearing age using contraception

Country (or area)	1970	1980	Country (or area)	1970	1980
Afghanistan	2		Lebanon	53	
Bangladesh		13	Lesotho		5
Barbados		46	Malaysia	9	35
Belgium		85	Martinique		36
Benin		18	Mauritania		1
Cameroon, U.R.		2	Mauritius		46
China		71	Mexico		39
Colombia	21	49	Nepal		7
Costa Rica		66	Netherlands	59	75
Czechoslovakia	66	95	Nigeria		6
Dem. Yemen		1	Pakistan	6	3
Denmark	67	63	Panama		64
Dominican Rep.		42	Paraguay		36
Ecuador		34	Peru		41
Egypt		24	Philippines	15	39
El Salvador		34	Poland	60	75
Fiji	41		Portugal		66
Finland	77	80	Puerto Rico	60	69
France	64	79	Senegal		4
Ghana		10	Singapore	60	71
Guatemala		18	South Africa		37
Guyana		31	Spain		51
Haiti		19	Sri Lanka		55
Honduras		27	Sudan		5
Hong Kong	42	72	Syrian Ar. Rep.		20
Hungary	67	74	Thailand	15	59
India	14		Trinidad Tbg.	44	54
Indonesia		27	Tunisia		27
Iraq	14		Turkey		38
Italy		78	UK	69	77
Jamaica		55	USA	65	68
Japan	53	56	Venezuela		49
Jordan	22	25	Yemen	32	40
Kenya	6	8	Yugoslavia	59	55
Korea, Rep.	25	58			

3. Total fertility rate

The approximate magnitude of 'completed family size', that is, the total number of children an average woman will bear in her lifetime, assuming no mortality

Country (or area)	1970	1980	2000	Country (or area)	1970	1980	2000
Afghanistan	7.13	6.9	5.75	Bangladesh	6.91	6.66	4.3
Albania	5.09	4.18	2.88	Barbados	3.3	2.63	2.07
Algeria	7.48	7.17	5.13	Belgium	2.34	1.71	1.71
Angola	6.38	6.39	6.13	Benin	6.86	7.0	6.7
Argentina	3.04	3.37	2.74	Bhutan	5.89	5.74	4.51
Australia	2.88	2.1	2.0	Bolivia	6.56	6.4	5.5
Austria	2.53	1.65	1.69	Botswana	6.48	6.5	6.23
Bahrain	6.97	5.23	3.38	Brazil	5.31	4.2	2.91

Country (or area)	1970	1980	2000	Country (or area)	1970	1980	2000
Bulgaria	2.16	2.25	2.1	Kenya	8.1	8.22	7.31
Burkina Faso	6.51	6.5	6.23	Korea, D.P. Rep.	5.64	4.53	2.95
Burma	5.73	5.53	3.83	Korea, Rep.	4.49	3.38	2.05
Burundi	5.82	6.44	5.7	Kuwait	7.48	6.46	4.41
Cameroon, U.R.	5.78	5.79	5.32	Lao P.D.R.	6.13	6.15	4.26
Canada	2.51	1.87	1.85	Lebanon	6.05	4.3	2.83
Cape Verde	5.07	3.04	2.13	Lesotho	5.67	5.73	5.54
Cent. Af. Rep.	5.69	5.89	5.64	Liberia	6.27	6.9	6.27
Chad	6.05	5.89	5.64	Libyan Ar. Jm.	7.48	7.38	5.84
Chile	4.08	3.1	2.5	Luxembourg	2.22	1.54	1.56
China	6.13	3.07	1.9	Madagascar	5.83	6.09	5.85
Colombia	5.94	4.3	3.0	Malawi	6.91	7.0	6.7
Comoros	6.29	6.29	5.28	Malaysia	5.91	4.26	2.46
Congo	5.93	5.99	5.77	Mali	6.65	6.7	6.11
Costa Rica	5.8	3.73	2.85	Malta	2.18	2.03	2.03
Cuba	4.3	2.18	2.1	Martinique	4.96	2.63	2.08
Cyprus	2.78	2.31	2.27	Mauritania	6.87	6.9	6.4
Czechoslovakia	2.09	2.36	2.14	Mauritius	4.25	3.07	2.09
Dem. Kampchea	6.22	4.1	3.48	Mexico	6.7	5.39	3.0
Dem. Yemen	6.97	6.97	5.84	Mongolia	5.89	5.35	3.16
Denmark	2.24	1.71	1.44	Morocco	7.11	6.87	4.37
Dominican Rep.	7.01	4.8	2.81	Mozambique	5.87	6.09	5.6
East Timor	6.16	4.3	4.3	Namibia	6.08	6.09	5.6
Ecuador	6.81	6.29	4.72	Nepal	6.17	6.54	4.92
Egypt	6.46	5.33	3.79	Netherlands	2.75	1.59	1.48
El Salvador	6.62	6.01	4.45	New Zealand	3.22	2.21	1.99
Eq. Guinea	5.66	5.66	5.36	Nicaragua	7.09	6.31	4.5
Ethiopia	6.65	6.7	6.41	Niger	7.1	7.1	6.8
Fiji	4.57	3.59	2.46	Nigeria	7.1	7.1	6.8
Finland	2.06	1.64	1.64	Norway	2.72	1.81	1.54
France	2.61	1.87	1.81	Oman	7.17	7.17	5.94
Gabon	4.07	4.36	5.58	Pakistan	7.21	6.29	4.1
Gambia	6.4	6.39	6.13	Panama	5.62	4.06	2.65
German Dem. Rep.	2.3	1.81	1.77	Papua N.G.	6.18	6.25	4.3
Germany, F.R.	2.34	1.44	1.54	Paraguay	6.4	5.21	3.75
Ghana	6.57	6.5	5.77	Peru	6.56	5.37	3.5
Greece	2.37	2.3	2.26	Philippines	6.01	4.62	2.87
Guadeloupe	5.18	3.04	2.08	Poland	2.28	2.27	2.11
Guatemala	6.4	5.68	4.31	Portugal	2.84	2.4	1.97
Guinea	6.41	6.19	5.92	Puerto Rico	3.4	2.77	2.25
Guineabissau	5.19	5.38	5.24	Qatar	6.97	6.76	5.84
Guyana	5.3	3.91	2.19	Reunion	5.11	2.84	2.11
Haiti	6.15	5.92	5.15	Romania	3.06	2.55	2.24
Honduras	7.42	7.13	5.0	Rwanda	7.0	7.31	6.94
Hungary	1.99	2.13	1.88	Saudi Arabia	7.26	7.28	5.94
Iceland	3.16	2.29	1.79	Senegal	6.42	6.5	6.23
India	6.04	5.0	2.87	Sierra Leone	6.12	6.13	5.85
Indonesia	5.57	4.81	2.46	Singapore	3.42	1.84	1.74
Iran	7.55	6.05	3.79	Somalia	6.1	6.09	5.85
Iraq	7.17	6.97	4.82	South Africa	5.61	5.07	4.44
Ireland	3.85	3.46	2.47	Spain	2.91	2.61	2.16
Israel	3.79	3.5	2.47	Sri Lanka	4.65	3.87	2.25
Italy	2.49	1.92	1.71	Sudan	6.68	6.68	5.56
Ivory Coast	6.63	6.7	6.11	Suriname	5.94	4.63	2.77
Jamaica	5.43	3.96	2.25	Swaziland	6.45	6.5	5.95
Japan	2.02	1.82	1.83	Sweden	2.12	1.65	1.46
Jordan	7.17	7.28	6.76	Switzerland	2.28	1.52	1.48

Table 3 *continued*

Country (or area)	1970	1980	2000
Syrian Ar. Rep.	7.79	7.44	5.43
Thailand	6.14	4.27	2.51
Togo	6.17	6.09	5.85
Trinidad Tbg.	3.89	3.07	2.28
Tunisia	6.83	5.64	2.97
Turkey	5.8	4.96	3.18
Uganda	6.91	6.9	6.27
UK	2.53	1.73	1.83
Untd. Arab Em.	6.76	6.76	4.0
U.R. Tanzania	6.87	7.1	6.8

Country (or area)	1970	1980	2000
Uruguay	2.81	2.93	2.38
USA	2.55	1.93	2.09
USSR	2.42	2.37	2.34
Venezuela	6.01	4.74	3.27
Vietnam	5.5	5.48	2.87
Yemen	6.76	6.76	5.84
Yugoslavia	2.49	2.2	1.95
Zaire	6.07	6.09	5.85
Zambia	6.65	6.76	6.48
Zimbabwe	6.61	6.6	6.31

4. Average household size

Country (or area)	Average household size		
	1970	1980	2000
Afghanistan		6.2	5.27
Albania		5.25	3.83
Algeria		6.14	5.22
Angola		4.8	4.76
Argentina	3.8	3.9	3.07
Australia	3.3	3.1	2.61
Austria	2.9	2.76	2.35
Bahamas	4.1		
Bahrain	6.4		
Bangladesh		5.98	5.21
Barbados	4.0	3.57	2.76
Belgium	2.9	2.85	2.55
Belize	5.2		
Benin		4.78	4.76
Bhutan		5.4	4.88
Bolivia		4.4	4.08
Botswana		6.79	5.65
Brazil	5.1	4.2	4.22
Bulgaria		3.1	2.66
Burkina Faso		4.85	4.79
Burma		5.11	4.49
Burundi		4.86	4.8
Byelorussia	3.6	3.8	
Cameroon, U.R.		4.52	4.29
Canada	3.5	3.1	2.47
Cape Verde		4.3	3.21
Cent. Af. Rep.		4.04	4.23
Chad		4.14	4.25
Chile	5.1	4.42	3.33
China		4.44	3.31
Colombia	5.9	5.39	4.15
Comoros		4.79	3.43
Congo		4.71	4.41
Costa Rica	5.6	5.2	4.01
Cuba	4.5	4.28	3.38

Country (or area)	Average household size		
	1970	1980	2000
Cyprus	3.9	3.62	2.97
Czechoslovakia	3.1	2.8	2.65
Dem. Kampchea		5.62	4.27
Denmark		2.63	2.31
Dominican Rep.	5.3	5.14	3.92
Ecuador		5.96	5.24
Egypt	5.2	4.85	4.05
El Salvador	5.2	5.08	4.17
Eq. Guinea		4.52	4.29
Ethiopia		4.98	4.68
Fiji	6.3	6.0	3.19
Finland	3.0	2.7	2.37
France	3.1	2.9	2.64
Gabon		4.05	4.28
Gambia	8.3	4.89	4.75
German Dem. Rep.	2.6	2.5	2.13
Germany, F.R.	2.7	2.58	2.26
Ghana		5.14	4.85
Greece		3.26	2.85
Guadeloupe	4.4	3.66	2.74
Guatemala	5.2	4.76	4.06
Guinea		4.71	4.52
Guineabissau		4.09	4.21
Guyana	5.4	4.96	3.57
Haiti		4.9	4.83
Honduras	5.7	5.38	4.59
Hong Kong	4.5	3.9	3.19
Hungary	3.0	2.8	2.45
Iceland		3.39	2.68
India	5.6	5.27	4.41
Indonesia		4.8	4.17
Iran	5.0	4.9	4.65
Iraq		5.83	4.92
Ireland	3.9	4.09	3.41
Israel	3.8	3.6	3.16

Country (or area)	Average household size			Country (or area)	Average household size		
	1970	1980	2000		1970	1980	2000
Italy	3.3	3.23	2.75	Philippines	5.9	5.9	4.51
Ivory Coast		4.52	4.47	Poland	3.4	3.1	2.67
Jamaica	4.3	4.25	3.07	Portugal		2.9	3.05
Japan		3.2	2.78	Puerto Rico		3.96	3.03
Jordan		5.69	4.84	Reunion	4.9	4.98	3.43
Kenya	5.6	6.16	5.61	Romania	3.2	3.02	2.63
Korea, D.P. Rep.		5.66	4.28	Rwanda		5.16	5.1
Korea, Rep.	5.2	4.5	3.62	Samoa	5.9		
Kuwait	6.2	6.5	5.1	Saudi Arabia		5.53	5.16
Lao P.D.R.		5.29	4.62	Senegal		4.85	4.8
Lebanon		5.25	4.13	Seychelles	4.7		
Lesotho		4.4	4.15	Sierra Leone		4.81	4.76
Liberia		5.75	5.15	Singapore	5.3	4.7	3.25
Libyan Ar. Jm.	6.0	5.11	4.68	Solomon Is.	5.1	6.7	
Luxembourg	3.1	2.93	2.54	Somalia		5.09	4.52
Macau	5.0			South Africa		5.11	4.47
Madagascar		4.71	4.52	Spain	3.8	3.8	3.17
Malawi		4.9	4.72	St. Christopher	4.0		
Malaysia		5.22	3.71	St. Vincent	4.0		
Maldives		6.1		Sri Lanka		5.2	4.04
Mali		5.1	4.9	Sudan		5.29	4.81
Malta	4.0	3.74	3.02	Suriname		6.89	5.07
Martinique	4.4	3.76	2.8	Swaziland		4.98	4.6
Mauritania		5.5	4.81	Sweden	2.6	2.4	2.32
Mauritius	5.3	4.87	3.45	Switzerland	2.9	2.81	2.36
Mexico	4.9	4.91	4.39	Syrian Ar. Rep.	5.9	6.0	5.01
Mongolia	4.4	5.01	4.02	Thailand	5.8	5.73	4.33
Morocco	5.4	5.91	4.79	Togo		5.63	5.58
Mozambique		4.68	4.53	Trinidad Tbg.	4.8	3.98	2.9
Namibia		4.8	4.42	Tunisia	5.1	5.28	4.03
Nepal	5.5	5.83	5.29	Turkey		5.2	4.79
Netherlands		2.88	2.42	Uganda		4.91	4.66
Neth. Antilles	5.1			Ukraine SSR		3.7	
New Zealand	3.7	3.0	2.68	U. R. Tanzania	4.4	4.95	4.79
Nicaragua		6.9	5.94	Uruguay	3.4	3.53	3.18
Niger		5.16	5.12	USA	3.1	2.87	2.48
Nigeria		5.26	5.15	USSR	3.7	4.0	2.76
Norway		2.7	2.51	Vanuatu	5.0		
Oman		5.52	5.15	Venezuela		5.35	4.25
Pakistan	5.7	5.66	4.95	Vietnam		5.12	4.39
Panama	4.9	4.6	3.08	Yemen		5.78	5.2
Papua N.G.		4.58	3.97	Yugoslavia	3.8	3.42	2.79
Paraguay		5.31	4.52	Zaire		5.01	4.46
Peru	4.8	4.81	4.12	Zambia	4.6	4.78	4.41

WORK

5. Percentage of total labour force which is female

Country (or area)	1970	1980	Country (or area)	1970	1980
Angola	16		Japan	39	37
Antigua Barb.	38		Korea, Rep.	35	39
Argentina	25		Kuwait		12
Australia	32		Libyan Ar. Jm.	7	
Austria	39		Luxembourg	26	
Bangladesh	4		Malaysia	32	
Barbados	55		Mauritius	20	
Belgium	30		Morocco	15	
Belize	19		Nepal	29	
Bolivia		22	Neth. Antilles	35	
Botswana	54		New Zealand	30	32
Brazil	21		Nicaragua	22	
Bulgaria		47	Norway	28	
Cameroon, U.R.		40	Papua N.G.	31	
Chile	23		Paraguay	21	
Costa Rica	19		Philippines	31	
Czechoslovakia	45		Portugal	26	
Dem. Yemen	18		Saint Lucia	36	
Denmark	37		Samoa	14	
Ecuador	17		Seychelles	33	
Fiji		17	Singapore	26	
Finland	42	44	South Africa	34	
France		37	Solomon Is.		17
German Dem. Rep.	46		Spain	20	
Germany, F.R.	36		Sri Lanka	26	
Greece	28		St. Christopher	38	
Guatemala	14		Sweden	35	42
Guyana	21		Switzerland	34	
Haiti	47		Syrian Ar. Rep.	11	
Honduras	16		Thailand	47	
Hong Kong		35	Togo	44	
Hungary	41		Trinidad Tbg.	25	
India	17		UK	37	
Indonesia	33		Ukraine SSR	50	
Ireland	26		Uruguay		29
Israel	31		USA	37	
Italy	27		Vanuatu	45	
Jamaica	33		Venezuela	22	

6. Percentage of total population of each sex in 1980 who are unpaid family workers (A) or employees (B)

Country (or area)	(A) M	(A) F	(B) M	(B) F	Country (or area)	(A) M	(A) F	(B) M	(B) F
Algeria	1	0	19	2	Austria			46	25
Australia	0	1	46	26	Bahrain	0	0	53	10

Country (or area)	(A) M	F	(B) M	F
Bangladesh	11	1	15	0
Barbados	0	0	42	30
Belgium	1	2	41	22
Bulgaria			50	43
Cameroon, U.R.	5	10	11	1
Canada	0	1	50	36
Czechoslovakia	5	4	51	43
Denmark	0	3	48	41
El Salvador	6	2	30	13
Finland	1	3	42	35
Fr. Polynesia	1	1	31	16
Germany, F.R.	0	2	50	27
Greece			25	9
Hong Kong	0	1	51	33
Hungary	0	1	46	33
Indonesia	7	9	20	10
Iran	3	3	24	3
Ireland	1	1	34	17
Israel	0	1	31	20
Italy	1	3	38	17
Japan	2	9	46	23
Korea, Rep.	3	11	23	11
Kuwait	0	0	48	11

Country (or area)	(A) M	F	(B) M	F
Mali	22	9	3	0
Malta			46	17
Nepal	7	10	9	3
Netherlands	0	2	44	18
New Zealand	0	0	43	25
Norway	1	2	46	35
Panama	2	0	25	13
Philippines	6	8	19	11
Portugal	3	9	41	21
Puerto Rico	0	1	48	25
Seychelles			41	25
Singapore	1	1	47	29
Sri Lanka	3	3	29	11
Sweden	0	0	50	44
Syrian Ar. Rep.	3	4	22	3
Thailand	15	30	13	8
Trinidad Tbg.	2	2	45	21
Tunisia	3	3	24	4
Turkey	10	23	24	4
UK			48	33
Untd. Arab Em.	0	0	66	5
USA	0	0	47	34
Venezuela	1	1	28	13

7. Percentage of total population of each sex in professional and administrative occupations, 1980 (a) and percentage of total labour force in industry, 1980 (b)

Country (or area)	(a) M	F	(b) M	F
Afghanistan	1	0	3	0
Australia	10	5		
Bahrain	7	3	11	3
Bangladesh	1	0		
Barbados	7	5		
Bulgaria	9	11		
Cameroon, U.R.	2	0	3	1
Canada	12	9		
El Salvador	2	1	5	8
Fr. Polynesia	5	4		
Germany, F.R.	10	5		
Guyana	23	8	43	39
Hong Kong	6	3	13	10
Indonesia	1	1	8	6
Iran	2	1	6	0
Ireland	6	4		
Israel	9	8	8	9
Japan	7	4	27	15
Korea, Rep.	3	1	10	7
Kuwait	8	4	10	2

Country (or area)	(a) M	F	(b) M	F
Mali	1	0	1	0
Nepal	2	1		
Netherlands	10	5		
New Zealand	10	6		
Norway	13	10	6	13
Panama	5	4	4	5
Philippines	2	3	4	6
Portugal	3	3	9	7
Puerto Rico	12	7	8	8
Seychelles	4	4		
Singapore	8	4	14	12
Sri Lanka	2	2	7	1
Sweden	15	15		
Syrian Ar. Rep.	4	1	7	1
Thailand	2	1	4	5
Turkey	5	2		
Untd. Arab Em.	6	3	12	1
USA	16	9	7	16
Venezuela	5	4	9	6

HEALTH

8. Life expectancy at birth

The expected average number of years to be lived by a newly-born baby, assuming a fixed schedule of age-specific mortality rates

Country (or area)	1970 M	1970 F	1980 M	1980 F	2000 M	2000 F
Afghanistan	35.1	35.8	36.6	37.3	42.5	43.5
Albania	65.1	67.4	68.0	71.5	71.4	76.4
Algeria	50.4	52.5	54.4	56.3	64.0	66.3
Angola	34.5	37.5	38.5	41.6	46.4	49.7
Argentina	62.8	69.3	65.4	72.1	68.7	75.4
Australia	67.6	74.3	70.1	77.0	72.7	80.0
Austria	66.5	73.4	68.5	75.6	71.8	79.1
Bahrain	58.1	62.0	64.1	68.1	69.6	75.0
Bangladesh	45.6	44.1	47.1	46.1	53.8	52.8
Barbados	65.3	70.3	67.9	73.2	71.3	77.5
Belgium	67.8	74.3	69.1	75.7	72.2	79.0
Benin	36.0	39.1	39.0	42.1	46.9	50.2
Bhutan	41.4	39.9	44.6	43.1	52.6	51.1
Bolivia	42.9	47.3	46.5	50.9	57.0	62.0
Botswana	46.9	50.2	50.8	54.2	58.8	62.2
Brazil	55.9	59.9	59.5	64.3	64.7	70.4
Bulgaria	68.8	73.0	68.7	73.8	71.9	78.0
Burkina Faso	34.5	37.5	38.5	41.6	46.4	49.7
Burma	46.1	49.0	51.0	54.1	60.1	63.8
Burundi	37.5	40.6	40.4	43.6	48.3	51.7
Cameroon, U. R.	40.4	43.6	44.4	47.6	52.2	55.8
Canada	68.9	75.3	70.5	78.1	72.9	80.3
Cape Verde	49.0	52.4	53.1	56.2	61.6	65.1
Cent. Af. Rep.	35.5	38.6	39.4	42.6	47.4	50.7
Chad	35.5	38.6	39.4	42.6	47.4	50.7
Chile	57.6	63.6	62.4	69.0	67.4	73.9
China	50.6	53.7	62.6	66.5	69.1	73.0
Colombia	56.3	60.7	60.0	64.5	64.7	69.3
Comoros	43.4	46.6	46.4	49.7	54.2	57.8
Congo	39.0	42.1	43.0	46.1	51.0	54.1
Costa Rica	63.9	67.5	69.0	74.0	71.8	77.2
Cuba	66.8	70.3	71.1	74.4	72.7	76.7
Cyprus	68.7	72.0	72.0	75.5	73.6	78.8
Czechoslovakia	66.9	73.4	67.0	74.1	70.8	78.0
Dem. Kampchea	44.0	46.9	30.0	32.5	51.9	55.0
Dem. Yemen	38.5	40.0	43.0	45.1	53.0	55.0
Dominican Rep.	53.6	57.2	58.4	62.2	66.1	70.2
Denmark	70.6	75.3	71.3	77.3	73.2	80.1
East Timor	36.9	38.1	30.0	32.5	46.4	48.7
Ecuador	52.9	56.4	58.0	62.0	67.0	71.0
Egypt	48.9	49.5	53.9	55.6	63.2	65.7
El Salvador	54.1	57.8	60.0	64.5	69.4	73.3
Eq. Guinea	36.5	39.6	40.4	43.6	48.3	51.7
Ethiopia	37.4	40.5	39.3	42.5	47.3	50.6

Country	1970		1980		2000	
(or area)	M	F	M	F	M	F
Fiji	66.4	69.9	69.5	73.1	72.6	77.9
Finland	65.9	73.5	68.0	76.6	71.4	79.7
France	67.9	75.4	69.8	78.0	72.6	80.3
Gabon	41.4	44.6	45.4	48.7	53.2	56.8
Gambia	30.2	33.1	32.0	35.0	39.4	42.6
German Dem. Rep.	68.8	74.0	68.8	74.6	71.9	78.4
Germany, F.R.	67.4	73.4	69.0	75.8	72.1	79.2
Ghana	44.4	47.6	48.3	51.7	56.3	59.7
Greece	69.3	72.8	71.3	75.0	73.3	78.6
Guadeloupe	63.5	68.4	66.5	71.8	70.6	76.5
Guatemala	50.4	52.0	56.9	58.8	66.8	69.3
Guinea	33.7	36.7	36.7	39.8	44.6	47.8
Guineabissau	36.5	39.6	39.4	42.6	47.4	50.7
Guyana	60.3	64.7	64.1	68.9	69.3	75.0
Haiti	44.9	47.6	49.1	52.2	56.7	60.2
Honduras	49.2	52.7	55.4	58.9	66.0	69.7
Hungary	66.7	71.9	66.7	73.3	70.7	78.3
Iceland	70.7	76.3	73.4	79.3	74.6	80.6
India	46.8	45.4	51.2	50.0	59.0	58.3
Indonesia	44.1	46.1	48.7	51.3	58.1	61.4
Iran	53.5	52.9	58.4	58.0	65.6	66.0
Iraq	51.5	54.6	57.2	60.9	64.8	69.5
Ireland	68.9	73.4	69.6	74.6	72.5	78.4
Israel	69.2	72.4	71.4	74.9	73.4	78.1
Italy	68.2	73.9	70.4	76.9	72.8	79.9
Ivory Coast	39.4	42.6	43.4	46.6	51.3	54.8
Jamaica	64.5	68.1	67.0	71.0	70.7	76.1
Japan	68.5	73.9	73.1	78.3	75.0	80.4
Jordan	50.2	53.2	58.3	62.0	68.0	71.8
Kenya	43.0	47.0	48.9	52.3	57.8	61.5
Korea, D.P. Rep.	56.0	59.4	60.5	64.6	67.0	71.3
Korea, Rep.	56.0	59.4	62.4	68.8	68.9	75.0
Kuwait	62.5	66.4	66.9	71.6	71.6	78.2
Lao P.D.R.	43.9	46.9	46.1	49.0	55.5	58.4
Lebanon	61.1	64.8	63.1	67.0	68.1	73.4
Lesotho	41.7	44.9	45.7	49.0	53.7	57.0
Liberia	41.4	44.6	45.4	48.7	53.2	56.8
Libyan Ar. Jm.	49.0	51.8	53.8	57.0	63.6	67.0
Luxembourg	66.8	73.2	68.2	75.7	71.6	79.0
Madagascar	42.1	45.3	47.0	48.5	54.0	55.9
Malawi	37.5	40.6	41.4	44.6	49.3	52.7
Malaysia	57.8	61.0	63.5	67.1	68.4	73.1
Mali	35.5	38.6	38.5	41.6	46.4	49.7
Malta	67.5	71.4	68.4	73.0	71.7	77.4
Martinique	64.3	68.5	67.4	72.2	71.0	76.0
Mauritania	37.5	40.6	40.4	43.6	48.3	51.7
Mauritius	59.7	63.5	62.6	67.3	68.0	73.4
Mexico	58.5	62.2	61.9	66.3	67.1	72.1
Mongolia	56.3	59.8	60.5	64.6	67.0	71.3
Morocco	49.0	51.8	53.8	57.0	63.6	67.0
Mozambique	41.6	44.8	45.8	49.1	53.6	57.2
Namibia	42.0	44.5	45.0	47.5	53.0	55.5
Nepal	41.1	40.1	44.6	43.1	52.6	51.1
Netherlands	71.0	76.4	72.1	78.6	73.5	80.4

Table 8 *continued*

Country (or area)	1970 M	1970 F	1980 M	1980 F	2000 M	2000 F
New Zealand	68.3	74.4	69.3	75.7	72.3	79.1
Nicaragua	50.5	52.8	55.3	57.3	67.0	70.1
Niger	36.0	39.1	39.0	42.1	46.9	50.2
Nigeria	40.9	44.1	44.9	48.1	52.7	56.3
Norway	71.1	76.7	72.2	78.6	73.6	80.4
Oman	41.4	43.3	46.2	48.4	56.0	58.5
Pakistan	46.7	44.3	49.0	47.0	57.0	55.5
Panama	63.1	65.5	67.6	70.9	71.2	75.5
Papua N.G.	45.4	44.9	50.5	50.0	61.5	61.0
Paraguay	57.5	61.7	61.9	66.4	65.3	70.5
Peru	50.1	53.0	55.2	58.8	65.1	69.0
Philippines	56.1	59.0	60.9	64.3	68.3	72.0
Poland	66.9	73.0	67.0	75.0	70.8	78.6
Portugal	63.1	69.3	66.1	72.9	70.4	77.3
Puerto Rico	68.2	73.5	70.3	77.1	72.5	79.5
Qatar	60.7	64.4	66.7	71.6	70.9	76.7
Reunion	58.7	62.4	63.0	66.7	68.2	71.8
Romania	66.4	70.6	67.5	72.2	71.1	76.8
Rwanda	43.1	46.3	45.9	49.2	53.7	57.3
Saudi Arabia	45.8	48.3	51.5	54.6	62.9	66.6
Senegal	37.2	40.3	39.7	42.9	47.7	51.0
Sierra Leone	28.8	31.7	30.6	33.5	38.5	41.6
Singapore	66.0	70.0	68.6	73.1	71.5	77.6
Somalia	37.4	40.5	39.3	42.5	47.3	50.6
South Africa	45.8	49.2	49.8	53.2	57.8	61.2
Spain	69.1	74.3	70.6	76.5	72.9	79.6
Sri Lanka	63.5	65.0	63.5	66.5	70.0	74.0
Sudan	39.8	42.1	43.9	46.4	54.3	56.7
Suriname	61.5	65.7	65.5	70.2	70.0	75.6
Swaziland	40.1	43.3	42.9	49.5	51.7	58.3
Sweden	71.9	76.5	72.3	78.3	73.6	80.4
Switzerland	69.4	75.1	72.0	78.6	73.5	80.4
Syrian Ar. Rep.	53.8	56.2	63.2	65.6	69.6	74.1
Thailand	54.6	58.9	59.3	63.2	64.8	68.9
Togo	41.0	44.2	45.0	48.2	53.1	56.8
Trinidad Tbg.	63.7	67.7	66.5	71.0	70.6	76.0
Tunisia	51.6	52.6	57.6	58.6	66.2	68.5
Turkey	52.8	56.1	58.3	62.8	66.8	71.7
Uganda	44.4	47.6	48.3	51.7	56.2	59.9
UK	68.3	74.6	69.7	76.0	72.6	79.3
Untd. Arab Em.	60.7	64.4	66.7	71.6	70.9	76.7
U. R. Tanzania	42.5	45.7	47.3	50.7	55.3	58.7
Uruguay	65.5	71.9	66.4	73.0	68.8	75.6
USA	66.9	74.1	69.4	77.2	72.4	80.1
USSR	65.5	74.0	65.0	74.3	69.9	78.2
Venezuela	59.3	64.5	63.6	69.0	68.1	73.8
Vietnam	45.7	50.2	53.7	58.1	62.7	67.1
Yemen	37.3	38.7	40.4	42.2	50.5	52.5
Yugoslavia	64.5	68.9	67.6	72.9	71.1	77.3
Zaire	40.4	43.6	46.4	49.7	54.2	57.8
Zambia	43.7	46.9	47.7	51.0	55.6	59.1
Zimbabwe	47.4	50.8	51.3	55.6	59.4	64.2

9. Child survival rate

Country (or area)	0 to 5 years				15 to 45 years			
	1970		1980		1970		1980	
	M	F	M	F	M	F	M	F
Australia	97	98	98	99	94	97	95	98
Austria			98	98			94	97
Argentina	93	94			91	95		
Bahamas	95	96			89	92		
Bangladesh	77	78			79	79		
Belgium	97	98			95	95		
Bermuda	96	97			93	96		
Brazil	88	89			88	90		
Brunei	92	93			93	90		
Bulgaria	96	97	97	97	95	97	95	97
Burundi	67	72			76	71		
Cameroon, U.R.	72	76			68	72		
Canada	98	98	98	99	94	97	94	97
Chile	91	92	89	91	89	93	89	92
Costa Rica	93	94			93	95		
Cyprus	97	96	97	98	95	98	98	98
Czechoslovakia	97	98	97	98	93	97	94	97
Denmark	98	99	99	99	96	97	95	97
Ecuador	89	90	85	86	88	89	85	91
Finland	98	99	99	99	92	97	94	98
France	98	98	99	99	93	97	94	97
German Dem. Rep.	97	98			94	97		
Germany, F.R.	97	98	98	98	94	97	94	97
Greece	95	96			96	98		
Guadeloupe	93	94	97	97	90	92	91	95
Guatemala	84	85			85	86		
Hong Kong	97	98			94	96		
Hungary	96	97			93	97		
Iceland	98	99	99	99	94	100	95	98
India	81	81			79	75		
Ireland	98	98			95	97		
Israel	97	98	98	98	95	97	96	98
Italy	97	97			95	97		
Japan	97	98	99	99	94	96	96	98
Kenya	80	82			80	83		
Korea, Rep.	93	94	96	94	91	93	91	95
Kuwait	95	95			93	96		
Liberia	80	74			75	84		
Luxembourg	98	98			94	97		
Madagascar	77	80			83	84		
Malawi	61	70			81	75		
Malta	97	98			97	97		
Martinique	94	94			91	92		
Mauritius	91	92			93	93		
Mexico	89	90	91	92	87	91	89	92
Netherlands	98	99	99	99	96	98	86	98
Neth Antilles	92	94			86	92		
New Zealand	98	98	98	98	94	97		
Nigeria	68	69			76	73		
Norway	98	99	99	99	95	98	96	98
Pakistan	81	81			89	81		

Table 9 *continued*

Country (or area)	0 to 5 years				15 to 45 years			
	1970		1980		1970		1980	
	M	F	M	F	M	F	M	F
Panama	92	93			91	92		
Poland	95	96			93	97		
Portugal	93	94			92	96		
Puerto Rico	96	96	97	98	92	92	92	97
Reunion	89	90			87	91		
Samoa	90	92			86	89		
Singapore	97	98			94	96		
Spain	97	97			95	97		
Sri Lanka	92	93			92	93		
Sweden	99	99	99	99	95	98	95	98
Switzerland	98	98			95	98		
Syrian Ar. Rep.	84	85	91	92	88		92	91
Trinidad Tbg.	95	96			93	94		
USA	98	98	98	98	92	96	93	97
Venezuela			94	95			91	95
Yugoslavia	94	94			98	97		

10. Percentage of pregnant and non-pregnant women with nutritional anaemia

Country (or area)	Pregnant	Non-pregnant
Algeria	65	
Argentina	61	34
Bangladesh	66	70
Barbados		45
Bolivia		15
Botswana		20
Brazil	20	8
Burma	55	
Cape Verde	42	
Chile	32	3
Colombia	22	6
Costa Rica	44	30
Dominica	46	60
Egypt	75	
El Salvador	15	
Ethiopia	6	8
Fiji	68	72
Gambia	80	80
Ghana	64	
Guatemala	34	

Country (or area)	Pregnant	Non-pregnant
Guineabissau	85	85
Guyana	55	41
India	68	60
Indonesia	65	55
Iran	50	
Israel	29	29
Ivory Coast	34	
Jamaica	24	
Jordan		25
Kenya	48	
Lao P.D.R.	62	
Lebanon	50	44
Libyan Ar. Jm.	47	24
Malawi	49	
Malaysia	77	
Mali	50	
Mauritania	24	
Mauritius	80	70
Mexico	38	17
Morocco	46	

Country (or area)	Pregnant	Non-pregnant	Country (or area)	Pregnant	Non-pregnant
Nepal	33		Sri Lanka	62	
Nicaragua	20		Thailand	48	
Niger	57	36	Togo	47	
Nigeria	65	50	Trinidad Tbg.	56	21
Pakistan	65		Tunisia	38	31
Papua N.G.	55		Turkey	74	
Peru	35	22	Uganda	35	46
Philippines	47	37	U. R. Tanzania	59	
Sierra Leone	45		Uruguay		7
Singapore	26		Venezuela	52	18
South Africa	25	12	Zambia	60	
			Zimbabwe	27	

11. Maternal mortality rate per 100,000 live births

Country (or area)	1970	1980	Country (or area)	1970	1980
Angola	113.4		Jamaica	105.6	
Argentina		84.5	Japan	51.6	22.9
Australia	24.5	8.1	Jordan	46.9	49.8
Austria	25.8	12.7	Kenya	203.9	
Bahamas	93.9	61.6	Kuwait	19.9	14.9
Barbados	143.4	69.7	Luxembourg	66.5	24.5
Belgium	20.4	10.6	Malta	18.0	68.2
Bulgaria	44.7	12.6	Mauritius	171.1	99.4
Canada	20.2	6.4	Mexico	143.0	108.2
Cape Verde		134.0	Netherlands	12.1	6.9
Chile	179.1	66.0	New Zealand	30.5	11.5
Costa Rica	112.5	49.0	Norway	12.4	13.6
Cuba	70.5	45.7	Panama	135.1	90.5
Czechoslovakia	22.3	12.9	Paraguay	159.5	
Denmark	8.5	11.8	Philippines	149.9	141.6
Ecuador	229.8	198.5	Poland	28.0	14.6
Egypt	107.4	84.8	Portugal	54.4	42.9
Fiji	57.9	40.7	Puerto Rico	28.1	5.3
Finland	7.7	7.6	Romania	129.3	129.2
France		15.7	Singapore	31.4	7.4
German Dem. Rep.	44.7	23.4	South Africa	90.1	
Germany, F.R.	52.2	22.0	Spain	32.2	13.0
Greece	28.3	14.0	Sweden	10.0	1.0
Guadeloupe	74.5	106.4	Switzerland	23.2	11.1
Guatemala	157.0	120.8	Trinidad Tbg.	135.7	78.9
Guyana	63.3	153.4	UK	18.0	11.6
Hong Kong	19.0	8.6	Uruguay	83.8	58.6
Hungary	39.5	15.5	USA	21.5	9.6
Iceland	46.8		Venezuela	92.1	65.1
Ireland	32.6	11.7	Yugoslavia	53.4	14.6
Israel	22.3	10.6	Zimbabwe		45.8
Italy	52.9	24.1			

EDUCATION

12. Percentage of population which is illiterate (by age)

Country (or area)	Aged 15–24 1970 M	Aged 15–24 1970 F	Aged 15–24 1980 M	Aged 15–24 1980 F	Aged 25–44 1970 M	Aged 25–44 1970 F	Aged 25–44 1980 M	Aged 25–44 1980 F
Afghanistan			54	89			71	97
Algeria	35	70	15	41	63	94	56	84
Argentina	4	4			5	6		
Bahrain	23	45	10	18	55	78	20	42
Bangladesh	53	78			64	88		
Barbados	0	0			0	0		
Belize	3	3			8	8		
Benin			54	82			83	94
Bolivia			9	24			21	50
Botswana	46	36			60	52		
Brazil	26	25	14	12	29	37	23	29
Brunei	9	18	6	7	23	61	10	29
Burkina Faso			77	93			86	98
Cameroon, U.R.			20	41			45	78
Chile	5	4			9	10		
China			5	18			14	43
Colombia	13	12			17	21		
Costa Rica	5	5			12	13		
Cuba			2	1			5	6
Dominica	1	1			5	3		
Dominican Rep.	22	21			27	34		
Ecuador	12	16	5	7	21	30	11	18
Egypt			37	62			46	80
El Salvador	27	30	27	29	41	49	40	51
Ethiopia	88	100			92	100		
Fiji			6	9			14	27
Ghana	31	60			60	89		
Greece	2	2			4	13		
Grenada	1	1			1	2		
Guadeloupe			2	1			6	4
Guatemala	38	52			47	64		
Guineabissau			40	82			70	95
Guyana	2	2			5	9		
Haiti	64	72			74	86		
Honduras	29	28			43	49		
Hong Kong	3	5			10	31		
Hungary	1	1	1	1	1	2	0	1
India	38	67			50	81		
Indonesia	13	26	10	18	29	59	18	40
Iran			29	58			54	80
Israel	3	6			7	21		
Italy	1	1			3	4		
Jamaica	2	1			4	3		
Korea, Rep.	1	1			2	10		
Kuwait	28	40	19	24	33	55	26	41

Country (or area)	Aged 15–24 1970 M	F	1980 M	F	Aged 25–44 1970 M	F	1980 M	F
Libyan Ar. Jm.	9	62			37	93		
Macau	9	14			14	25		
Maldives			16	13			15	17
Mali			73	87			90	97
Mexico	15	18			20	29		
Morocco	47	77			70	95		
Mozambique			36	75			54	91
Nepal	67	94	55	85	80	98	69	92
Neth. Antilles	5	3			4	4		
Nicaragua	37	34			43	46		
Pakistan	59	82	55	75	69	90	62	86
Panama	12	13	5	4	20	22	11	11
Paraguay	8	11			14	22		
Peru	7	20	3	10	16	42	17	38
Philippines	8	8	9	8	13	16	13	13
Portugal	3	4			16	26		
Puerto Rico	5	3			6	8		
Reunion			6	2			20	13
Rwanda			40	55			41	77
Saint Lucia	6	4			21	18		
Sao Tome Prn.			9	26			25	61
Seychelles	28	18			44	39		
Singapore	8	15	4	4	16	49	5	18
Spain	2	2	1	1	4	8	2	4
Sri Lanka	10	16	9	10	11	30	7	14
St. Christopher	2	1			2	2		
St. Vincent	2	2			4	4		
Swaziland			24	25			41	47
Syrian Ar. Rep.	22	65			38	83		
Thailand	4	8	2	4	10	21	5	9
Togo	51	83			76	95		
Trinidad Tbg.	1	1	1	1	3	9	2	3
Tunisia			10	37			36	74
Turkey	13	44	9	32	28	69	18	59
Untd. Arab Em.			34	44			40	61
U. R. Tanzania			19	46			33	72
Uruguay			2	1			4	3
Venezuela	13	13			18	26		
Vietnam			4	6			5	12
Yugoslavia	2	7			10	32		

13. Number enrolled at primary and post-secondary levels (in thousands)

Country (or area)	Primary Level 1970 M	F	1980 M	F	Post-Secondary level 1970 M	F	1980 M	F
Afghanistan	519.5	84.4	883.6	179.0	6.6	1.1	21.2	4.7
Albania	261.1	235.4	291.8	260.9	17.2	8.3	7.3	7.2
Algeria	1179.2	707.9	1845.9	1340.0	15.3	4.2	51.7	17.2
Angola	279.5	154.9	670.3	588.5	1.4	0.9		
Antigua Barb.	5.0	4.7	4.9	4.7				
Argentina	1713.1	1672.7	1953.7	1887.3	157.3	117.3	244.9	249.9
Australia	933.4	878.6	864.3	823.9	120.9	58.8	177.0	146.7
Austria	273.3	258.6	205.3	195.1	42.2	17.5	79.3	57.5
Bahrain	22.4	16.3	26.6	22.2	0.1	0.2	0.9	0.6
Bangladesh	3590.7	1693.1	5182.0	3037.3	106.1	11.5	215.0	35.0
Barbados	19.9	19.1	16.2	15.9	0.5	0.3	1.7	1.3
Belgium	525.8	495.8	432.2	409.9	79.6	45.2	109.2	86.9
Belize	16.1	15.5			0.0	0.1		
Benin	119.4	54.5	245.0	134.1	0.3	0.0	2.9	0.6
Bhutan	8.5	0.5	17.3	7.7	0.0	0.0	0.2	0.1
Bolivia	402.5	276.6	521.8	456.4	25.3	10.0	38.8	18.2
Botswana	38.9	44.1	78.1	93.8	0.0	0.0	0.8	0.5
Brazil	7990.6	7904.0	11406.8	11040.6	268.3	162.2	818.4	832.7
Brunei	14.6	13.4	16.0	14.5			0.2	0.3
Bulgaria	539.8	510.0	511.8	482.3	49.2	50.4	44.4	56.9
Burkina Faso	67.1	38.3	122.7	73.1	0.2	0.0	1.2	0.4
Burma	1685.7	1492.0	2104.5	1946.0	28.6	17.5	62.0	64.6
Burundi	122.0	59.8	102.3	66.3	0.5	0.0	1.6	0.4
Byelorussia					67.5	72.6	78.8	95.0
Cameroon, U.R.	530.4	392.8	721.4	621.4	2.5	0.2	10.8	2.3
Canada	1919.2	1817.3	1120.4	1064.5	384.2	257.8	443.2	445.2
Cape Verde	14.4	13.5	29.9	28.9	0.0	0.0		
Cent. Af. Rep.	118.6	57.7	163.3	96.5	0.2	0.0	2.3	0.4
Chad	143.5	48.3	183.5	70.6	0.0	0.0	1.5	0.1
Chile	1029.5	1010.6	1143.3	1091.2	48.3	30.1	85.1	55.0
China			81096.0	65174.0			891.2	270.3
Colombia	1633.2	1652.9	2151.7	2166.5	62.7	22.9	179.7	119.3
Comoros	10.3	4.7	34.9	24.8				
Congo	135.2	105.9	199.4	183.6	1.7	0.1	5.8	1.0
Costa Rica	178.5	170.9	179.3	169.4	8.8	6.7	34.0	27.0
Cuba	781.7	748.7	796.7	719.7	15.9	10.4	101.4	88.1
Cyprus	35.7	33.5	24.9	23.8	0.4	0.3	0.8	0.8
Czechoslovakia	1004.2	962.2	967.2	937.3	81.4	49.7	115.1	82.0
Dem. Kampchea	591.0	398.5			5.9	2.2		
Dem. Yemen	107.9	26.6	166.8	94.4	0.1	0.0	4.1	1.6
Denmark	224.5	218.6	222.7	212.0	48.1	27.9	54.3	51.9
Dominica	9.3	8.5	8.4	8.1			0.1	0.1
Dominican Rep.	384.0	380.1	534.0	532.7	13.4	10.1	37.4	31.8
Ecuador	506.9	477.1	732.8	699.3	27.1	11.6	179.7	101.8
Egypt	2361.6	1433.3	2786.9	1875.9	171.5	61.8	381.0	179.0
El Salvador	293.5	266.1	461.7	445.1	7.0	2.5	24.3	12.3
Eq. Guinea	17.7	13.9			0.0	0.0	1.0	0.1
Ethiopia	449.7	205.7	1262.4	681.6	4.1	0.4	12.4	2.7
Fiji	63.0	58.4	65.9	63.7	0.3	0.1	2.7	0.9
Finland	202.8	183.5	191.5	181.9	30.9	28.9	63.8	59.4

Country	Primary Level				Post-Secondary level			
	1970		1980		1970		1980	
(or area)	M	F	M	F	M	F	M	F
France	2527.3	2412.4	2374.4	2236.0			571.9	488.5
Fr. Polynesia	12.4	11.7	15.1	13.9			0.1	0.0
Gabon	52.7	47.9	72.3	69.3	0.2	0.0	1.0	0.3
Gambia	11.8	5.3	25.9	13.0	0.0	0.0		
German Dem. Rep.			1042.5	1064.0	172.9	130.3	168.5	232.3
Germany, F. R.	3233.1	3111.7	2638.9	2405.5	368.5	135.3	719.8	503.4
Ghana	537.3	429.6	809.9	639.5	4.6	0.8	8.9	1.4
Greece	472.0	435.4	466.5	433.1	58.8	27.0	71.3	46.1
Grenada	15.4	15.0	9.4	8.6			0.2	0.4
Guadeloupe	36.0	34.2						
Guatemala	282.1	223.6	441.3	362.1	12.7	2.9	43.0	17.0
Guinea	130.7	60.6	180.3	96.9	1.8	0.2	20.2	5.3
Guineabissau	19.6	8.4	55.0	26.5	0.0	0.0	0.0	0.0
Guyana	66.6	63.9	69.1	66.8	0.9	0.2	1.7	1.5
Haiti	204.0	162.8	327.6	279.0	1.5	0.2	4.2	1.6
Honduras	191.9	189.8	295.0	272.9	3.5	1.3	20.2	12.0
Hong Kong	389.2	350.4	286.8	263.6	17.9	7.6	43.5	18.2
Hungary	577.7	538.3	597.0	565.2	46.1	34.4	50.9	50.3
Iceland	13.9	13.2	13.5	12.9	1.3	0.4	1.9	1.1
India	35739.1	21306.3	43769.2	27848.7	2270.6	633.0	4087.4	1435.1
Indonesia	8089.4	6780.8	12164.5	10740.1	185.8	62.4	277.9	116.8
Iran	1937.8	1072.3	3310.1	2261.0	55.7	19.0	148.9	70.9
Iraq	780.4	318.5	1403.1	1212.8	33.0	9.4	76.0	35.0
Ireland	266.6	253.6	214.6	205.4	18.7	9.8	32.5	22.2
Israel	249.0	229.9	308.2	297.7	30.9	24.6	47.1	41.7
Italy	2505.6	2351.3	2316.7	2189.9	428.2	259.0	641.7	476.0
Ivory Coast	320.0	182.9	609.1	407.3	3.8	0.6	11.9	3.1
Jamaica	177.6	176.9	179.7	178.5	3.7	3.2	7.8	5.9
Japan	4851.9	4706.2	5985.8	5764.8	1306.6	512.8	1620.9	791.3
Jordan	155.5	122.1	235.4	213.0	3.2	1.3	17.2	12.9
Kenya	836.3	591.3	1843.3	1677.2	6.7	1.1	11.6	2.7
Korea, D.P. Rep.			1318.7	1243.0	152.6	48.9	467.4	148.1
Korea, Rep.	2994.7	2754.6	2912.6	2745.4	152.5	48.9	467.4	148.1
Kuwait	43.7	31.8	81.0	72.5	1.4	1.3	6.3	8.4
Lao P.D.R.	154.3	90.5	261.7	219.2	0.3	0.1	1.5	0.6
Lebanon	237.9	197.2	203.0	182.9	32.6	10.0	66.4	22.6
Lesotho	73.4	110.0	99.8	143.3	0.3	0.1	0.8	1.3
Liberia	80.6	39.6	135.2	83.8	0.9	0.2	3.9	1.5
Libyan Ar. Jm.	220.6	129.6	348.3	314.6	4.6	0.6	11.6	3.7
Luxembourg	17.6	17.0	12.7	12.0	0.2	0.2	0.5	0.3
Macau	13.3	11.8						
Madagascar	504.9	433.1	743.3	671.5	3.9	1.8	12.3	6.4
Malawi	227.8	134.8	487.4	340.5	0.8	0.2	1.6	0.5
Malaysia	895.6	788.7	1038.8	974.1	10.6	3.9	27.7	15.3
Mali	131.0	72.7	210.0	123.7	0.6	0.1	6.3	0.9
Malta	20.7	19.3	16.7	15.7	1.2	0.6	1.0	0.4
Martinique	35.1	33.7						
Mauritania	23.0	8.9	60.4	36.2	0.0	0.0	0.7	0.1
Mauritius	77.4	73.0	66.4	63.2	1.9	0.1	1.5	0.5
Mexico	4814.8	4433.5	7582.4	7037.5	197.8	49.8	589.2	297.3
Mongolia	57.2	56.4	73.6	70.1	3.6	3.3	5.4	7.8
Morocco	777.3	398.0	1379.1	810.2	13.4	2.7	76.2	24.6
Mozambique	328.9	168.0	797.1	590.1	1.1	0.9	0.5	0.3

Table 13 *continued*

Country (or area)	Primary Level				Post-Secondary level			
	1970		1980		1970		1980	
	M	F	M	F	M	F	M	F
Nepal	279.9	53.0	761.8	285.9	14.4	3.3	40.7	9.0
Netherlands	745.2	717.2	674.8	658.5	167.1	64.1	217.0	143.1
New Zealand	206.6	193.8	195.4	185.8			45.5	31.1
Nicaragua	141.9	143.4	209.5	215.4	6.4	3.0	22.4	10.7
Niger	58.0	30.6	136.2	80.9	0.0	0.0	1.1	0.3
Nigeria	2216.2	1299.6	6313.8	5369.7	18.8	3.2	89.4	17.3
Norway	188.3	197.3	199.9	190.3	34.9	15.1	42.0	36.4
Oman	3.0	0.5	60.4	31.5	0.0	0.0	0.0	
Pakistan	2931.1	1061.7	5493.4	1889.1	90.5	24.5	136.9	50.0
Panama	132.8	122.5	179.8	167.2	5.1	3.8	18.1	21.6
Papua N. G.	121.4	69.7	176.0	123.8	0.8	0.2	7.0	1.5
Paraguay	224.7	199.5	271.4	245.4	4.8	3.4	13.9	10.6
Peru	1266.8	1074.3	1659.8	1517.9	82.9	43.3	195.0	101.2
Philippines	3580.6	3388.4	4083.3	4191.6	289.3	362.2	597.6	673.1
Poland	2726.7	2530.2	2141.5	2025.8	209.2	188.7	260.7	328.4
Portugal	509.5	483.0	635.8	584.3	27.8	22.2	47.9	43.4
Puerto Rico	241.5	231.2	226.3	235.3	29.8	33.3	50.5	62.1
Qatar	8.3	6.7	15.4	14.3	0.0	0.0	0.8	1.5
Romania	1461.2	1417.5	1658.4	1578.4	86.5	65.4	109.2	81.7
Rwanda	234.2	184.9	338.7	314.7	0.5	0.1	1.3	0.1
Saint Lucia	11.4	12.1	14.5	15.1			0.3	0.2
Samoa	15.2	14.3	17.3	15.7	0.1	0.0	0.6	0.0
Sao Tome Prn.	5.0	4.0	7.5	6.7				
Saudi Arabia	290.4	132.3	564.9	365.0	7.8	0.7	43.7	15.6
Senegal	161.2	101.7	249.6	167.1	4.2	0.8	9.4	2.8
Seychelles	4.6	4.6	7.1	7.4	0.0	0.1	0.0	0.1
Sierra Leone	99.4	66.7	157.9	106.9	1.0	0.2	1.5	0.3
Singapore	193.8	169.7	151.3	138.5	9.6	4.2	12.5	9.3
Solomon Is.	13.5	7.7	16.9	12.0				
Somalia	32.3	10.4	190.2	113.3	0.9	0.1	2.7	0.3
Spain	1970.0	1959.5	1856.1	1753.5	164.9	60.1	382.0	299.0
Sri Lanka	884.4	787.0	1082.2	999.2	7.0	5.3	13.0	7.0
St. Christopher			4.2	4.1			0.0	0.0
St. Vincent	14.3	13.9	11.1	10.4			0.1	0.2
Sudan	513.7	311.9	889.0	621.4	12.4	1.9	21.6	7.9
Suriname	47.7	44.1	43.5	39.9	0.3	0.0	1.0	0.6
Swaziland	35.6	33.5	54.4	54.7	0.1	0.1	0.7	0.4
Sweden	313.2	302.2	341.6	325.1	81.4	59.9	109.8	91.2
Switzerland	253.4	247.1	230.0	220.9			59.4	25.8
Syrian Ar. Rep.	589.1	335.9	886.8	669.6	34.2	8.5	87.1	37.6
Thailand	2859.0	2541.0	3866.6	3504.2	55.1	35.2	325.0	250.0
Togo	157.7	70.8	300.8	193.5	0.8	0.1	4.2	0.9
Trinidad Tbg.	114.5	111.2	83.3	82.2	1.5	0.9	4.8	3.1
Tunisia	570.8	364.9	616.1	437.9	8.2	2.1	21.5	10.5
Turkey	2891.6	2120.3	3223.3	2707.5	137.8	32.8	279.9	91.5
Uganda	663.7	446.3	889.6	656.2	3.5	0.7	5.9	1.9
UK	2972.5	2833.9	2517.7	2393.0	401.5	199.8	529.3	302.8
Ukraine SSR	3398.0	3270.0			420.6	386.0	422.5	408.8
Untd. Arab Em.	16.5	9.4	46.3	42.3	0.0	0.0	1.0	1.0
U. R. Tanzania	558.4	363.7	1826.0	1624.3	1.7	0.3	3.4	0.7
Uruguay	184.9	169.2	169.2	159.3	12.2	9.0	19.0	20.7
USA			14087.0	13361.0	4991.0	3507.2	5874.4	6222.5

Country	Primary Level				Post-Secondary level			
	1970		1980		1970		1980	
(or area)	M	F	M	F	M	F	M	F
USSR					2333.7	2247.0	2405.4	2448.6
Venezuela	890.8	878.9	1271.6	1241.7	59.7	41.1	169.1	144.4
Vietnam	3787.2	3305.2	4215.5	3892.8	96.0	31.6	135.9	50.1
Yemen	79.9	8.3	403.4	57.2	0.1	0.0	5.4	0.8
Yugoslavia	825.3	753.7	739.5	692.1	158.2	103.0	225.0	187.0
Zaire	1952.4	1135.6	2384.9	1893.9	11.7	0.7	30.3	6.2
Zambia	385.7	309.0	546.1	485.4	1.2	0.2	10.4	1.8
Zimbabwe	404.9	330.9	604.0	503.3	0.8	0.2	0.9	0.5

14. Enrolment ratio, combined primary and secondary levels

Country	1970		1980		Country	1970		1980	
(or area)	M	F	M	F	(or area)	M	F	M	F
Afghanistan	32	5	41	10	Eq. Guinea	57	39		
Albania	90	81	97	89	Ethiopia	15	7	37	20
Algeria	57	34	74	54	Fiji	84	79	92	93
Argentina	80	83	91	95	Finland	91	93	94	99
Australia	101	100	99	100	France	90	93	92	100
Austria	84	84	80	82	Gambia	23	10	42	22
Bahrain	94	71	85	75	Germany, F.R.	78	78	78	80
Bangladesh			48	26	Ghana	61	43	61	44
Barbados	90	88	96	99	Greece	90	81	94	89
Belgium	93	92	94	95	Guatemala	38	32	48	41
Benin	33	15	55	25	Guinea	34	14	35	16
Bhutan	7	0.4	10	4	Guineabissau	40	18	82	36
Bolivia	72	50	76	64	Guyana	80	79	77	78
Botswana	44	49	66	79	Haiti			47	40
Brazil			76	77	Honduras	58	58	69	69
Bulgaria	95	94	94	93	Hong Kong	79	73	80	82
Burkina Faso	9	5	14	8	Hungary	70	74	78	82
Burma	59	49	54	49	Iceland	97	92	94	86
Burundi	24	11	19	12	India	63	35	65	41
Cameroon, U. R.	59	41	72	56	Indonesia	55	43	78	65
Canada	87	86	94	94	Iran	67	37	81	55
Cent. Af. Rep.	51	22	55	28	Iraq	68	29	101	78
Chad	28	9	29	10	Ireland	91	93	95	100
Chile	86	89	95	96	Israel	83	83	86	91
China			98	77	Italy	85	77	85	83
Colombia	66	67	81	86	Ivory Coast	47	25	61	36
Comoros	26	12	77	52	Jamaica	82	82	75	79
Costa Rica	76	77	79	81	Japan	93	92	97	98
Cuba	75	76	91	90	Jordan			93	90
Czechoslovakia	73	78	74	82	Kenya	49	33	78	68
Dem. Yemen	59	15	73	29	Korea, Rep.	80	71	97	91
Denmark	89	86	102	101	Kuwait	84	66	87	79
Ecuador	64	62	77	76	Lao P.D.R.	36	21	63	51
Egypt	69	40	77	51	Lebanon	85	68	86	80
El Salvador	61	58	63	63	Lesotho	49	74	58	85

Table 14 *continued*

Country (or area)	1970 M	F	1980 M	F	Country (or area)	1970 M	F	1980 M	F
Liberia	43	20	58	33	Rwanda	47	36	48	43
Luxembourg	82	81	78	79	Saudi Arabia	42	18	59	39
Madagascar	55	46	58	50	Senegal	31	18	36	22
Malawi	30	17	52	36	Sierra Leone	28	17	32	20
Malaysia	66	57	72	69	Singapore	79	74	79	80
Mali	20	10	25	13	Somalia	11	3	31	17
Malta	80	76	92	87	Spain	91	85	96	97
Mauritania	13	4	31	15	Sri Lanka	72	69	74	73
Mauritius	65	59	73	72	Sudan	30	18	42	29
Mexico	70	63	89	86	Suriname	93	92	79	77
Mongolia			93	95	Swaziland	65	61	82	81
Morocco	42	22	59	36	Sweden	90	90	90	94
Mozambique			55	39	Syrian Ar. Rep.	78	43	87	64
Nepal	30	6	64	23	Thailand	61	55	67	62
Netherlands	91	86	98	96	Togo	55	24	98	53
New Zealand	94	92	91	92	Trinidad	82	84	77	80
Nicaragua	54	54	74	80	Tunisia	79	48	75	53
Niger	10	5	18	10	Turkey	80	53	82	60
Nigeria	27	16			Uganda	31	19	38	28
Norway	85	89	98	99	UK	89	88	90	92
Oman			54	27	Untd. Arab. Em.	75	48	84	91
Pakistan	37	13	50	18	U.R. Tanzania	30	19	66	58
Panama	76	75	90	91	Uruguay	85	86	81	83
Papua N. G.	40	24	46	33	USA	99	101	99	99
Paraguay	70	64	69	64	Venezuela	69	70	75	73
Peru	78	66	93	84	Vietnam			84	71
Philippines			91	93	Yemen	14	1	49	7
Poland	88	87	92	92	Yugoslavia	81	73	91	86
Portugal	84	77	89	88	Zaire	67	37	72	47
Qatar	80	71	84	93	Zambia	69	53	73	61
Romania	89	85	94	92	Zimbabwe	52	42	60	52

POLITICS

15. Membership of national legislative bodies

Country (or area)	1970		1980	
	M	F	M	F
Australia	187	4	170	19
Austria	213	23	206	30
Barbados	23	1	26	1
Belgium	368	26	360	34
Bulgaria	322	78	317	83
Burundi			59	6
Byelorussia	271	159	305	130
Canada	360	15	343	39
Chile	185	15	77	3
China	2232	653	2346	632
Costa Rica	55	5	55	4
Cuba	376	105	386	113
Cyprus	35	0	34	1
Czechoslovakia	251	99	251	99
Denmark	149	30	137	42
Dominica	20	1	20	1
Dominican Rep.	103	15	139	8
Ecuador			134	4
Egypt			615	43
El Salvador			50	10
Eq. Guinea			58	2
Finland	154	46	138	62
France			770	38
German Dem. Rep.	332	168	338	162
Germany, F. R.	480	38	469	51
Greece	293	7	286	14
Guyana	44	9	55	16
Honduras			76	6
Hungary	251	101	243	109
Iceland	57	3	51	9
India	523	19	514	28
Indonesia	429	31	418	42
Ireland	197	11	206	20
Israel	112	8	112	8
Italy	928	23	886	66
Ivory Coast	99	11	139	8
Japan	701	25	733	26
Kenya	168	4	169	3
Korea, Rep.	213	8	268	8
Luxembourg	56	3	53	6
Malawi	83	4	96	10
Malaysia	148	6	146	8
Mauritius	67	3	66	4
Mexico			110	54
Mongolia			77	23
Nepal			128	7

Table 15 *continued*

Country (or area)	1970		1980	
	M	F	M	F
Netherlands	202	23	182	43
New Zealand	83	4	84	8
Norway	131	24	115	40
Philippines	166	12	165	7
Poland	365	95	346	114
Portugal	230	20	232	18
Romania	275	66	247	122
Rwanda			61	9
Saint Lucia	18	2	26	2
Samoa	46	1	46	1
Senegal	92	8	107	13
Spain	600	27	571	32
Sri Lanka	161	6	147	7
Sweden	274	75	251	98
Switzerland	229	15	221	25
Turkey	627	7	387	12
UK	1715	75	1762	87
Ukraine SSR			416	234
Uruguay	96	3		
USA	516	19	511	23
USSR	1025	475	1008	492
Venezuela			219	12
Vietnam	358	132	389	108
Yugoslavia	86	13	83	17
Zambia	127	8	131	4
Zimbabwe			122	11